1995

S0-AHX-551

In and out of the ghetto :

3 0301 00094483 1

In and Out of the Ghetto presents the results of recent research on German history, Jewish history, and the history of German Jews. This volume brings together specialists in the fields of history, sociology, religious studies, linguistics, literature, and folklore from the United States, Canada, Great Britain, Germany, and Israel. Contributors are J. Friedrich Battenberg, Thomas A. Brady, Jr., Christoph Daxelmüller, Christopher R. Friedrichs, Carlo Ginzburg, Yacov Guggenheim, Alfred Haverkamp, Deborah Hertz, R. Po-chia Hsia, Gershon David Hundert, Jonathan I. Israel, Stefi Jersch-Wenzel, Robert Jütte, Jacob Katz, Hartmut Lehmann, Richard H. Popkin, Theodore K. Rabb, Rotraud Ries, Miri Rubin, Michael Toch, Otto Ulbricht, Mack Walker, and Paul Wexler.

The essays examine the role of economics, politics, social organization, language, and religion in the relations between Jews and non-Jews in central Europe from the fifteenth through eighteenth centuries. The authors grapple with such relevant issues as cultural identity, representation, toleration, and minority–majority relations. Individually, the essays probe the central questions of Jewish social, economic, and cultural development within the territorial states, secular and clerical, and in both rural and urban environments. Collectively, they focus more attention on the period before the emancipation of the nineteenth century and the destruction of German Jewry in the middle of the twentieth, emphasizing both continuities and discontinuities in the history of Jews in Germany.

PUBLICATIONS OF THE GERMAN HISTORICAL INSTITUTE
WASHINGTON, D.C.

Edited by Detlef Junker,
with the assistance of Daniel S. Mattern

In and Out of the Ghetto

THE GERMAN HISTORICAL INSTITUTE, WASHINGTON, D.C.

The German Historical Institute is a center for advanced study and research whose purpose is to provide a permanent basis for scholarly cooperation between historians from the Federal Republic of Germany and the United States. The Institute conducts, promotes, and supports research into both American and German political, social, economic, and cultural history, into transatlantic migration, especially in the nineteenth and twentieth centuries, and into the history of international relations, with special emphasis on the roles played by the United States and Germany.

Other books in the series

Hartmut Lehmann and James Sheehan, editors, *An Interrupted Past: German-Speaking Refugee Historians in the United States after 1933*

Carol Fink, Axel Frohn, and Jürgen Heideking, editors, *Genoa, Rapallo, and European Reconstruction in 1922*

David Clay Large, editor, *Contending with Hitler: Varieties of German Resistance in the Third Reich*

Larry Eugene Jones and James Retallack, editors, *Elections, Mass Politics, and Social Change in Modern Germany: New Perspectives*

Hartmut Lehmann and Guenther Roth, editors, *Weber's Protestant Ethic: Origins, Evidence, Contexts*

Catherine Epstein, *A Past Renewed: A Catalog of German-Speaking Refugee Historians in the United States after 1933*

Hartmut Lehmann and James Van Horn Melton, editors, *Paths of Continuity: Central European Historiography from the 1930s through the 1950s*

Jeffry M. Diefendorf, Axel Frohn, and Hermann-Josef Rupieper, editors, *American Policy and the Reconstruction of West Germany, 1945–1955*

Henry Geitz, Jürgen Heideking, and Jürgen Herbst, editors, *German Influences on Education in the United States to 1917*

Peter Graf Kielmansegg, Horst Mewes, and Elisabeth Glaser-Schmidt, editors, *Hannah Arendt and Leo Strauss: German Emigrés and American Political Thought after World War II*

In and Out of the Ghetto

JEWISH–GENTILE RELATIONS IN LATE MEDIEVAL AND
EARLY MODERN GERMANY

Edited by

R. PO-CHIA HSIA AND HARTMUT LEHMANN

LIBRARY
College of St. Francis
JOLIET, ILLINOIS

GERMAN HISTORICAL INSTITUTE
Washington, D.C.
and

 **CAMBRIDGE**
UNIVERSITY PRESS

Published by the Press Syndicate of the University of Cambridge
The Pitt Building, Trumpington Street, Cambridge CB2 1RP
40 West 20th Street, New York, NY 10011-4211, USA
10 Stamford Road, Oakleigh, Melbourne 3166, Australia

© German Historical Institute, 1995

First Published 1995

Printed in the United States of America

Library of Congress Cataloging-in-Publication Data

In and Out of the Ghetto : Jewish–gentile relations in late medieval and early modern Germany
/ [edited by] R. Po-chia Hsia, Hartmut Lehmann.

    p.   cm. – (Publications of the German Historical Institute)

Papers presented at a conference held in Los Angeles on May 9-11, 1991.

Includes bibliographical references and index.

ISBN 0-521-47064-1

1. Jews – Germany – History – 1096 – 1800 – Congresses. 2. Germany – Ethnic relations –
Congresses. I. Hsia, R. Po-chia, 1953– . II. Lehmann, Hartmut, 1936– . III. Series.
DS135.G3I5   1995
943′.004924–dc20   94-15421
                                                    CIP

A catalog record for this book is available from the British Library.

ISBN 0-521-47064-1 hardback

943.004924
H 871

Contents

155,682

Editors' Prefaces

Beginning in the 1920s, and with renewed emphasis after 1945, scholars have devoted considerable attention to the history of Jews in Germany since the Enlightenment. After World War II, many historians felt a deep commitment to understand and explain the tragic path that led from emancipation to modern anti-Semitism, and from there to the Holocaust. For a long time, however, much less work was done on the history of Jews in Germany in earlier epochs, particularly the period between the late Middle Ages and the Enlightenment. It was only in the past two decades that several historians set out to explore the various aspects of Jewish life in early modern Germany. Since these historians had never met to discuss the results of their research, it seemed important to bring them together.

From May 9 to 11, 1991, thirty specialists in the fields of history, sociology, religious studies, linguistics, literature, and folklore from the United States, Canada, Great Britain, Israel, and Germany met at the William Andrews Clark Memorial Library of the University of California at Los Angeles to discuss Jewish–Gentile relations in late medieval and early modern Germany. We are very grateful to them for preparing stimulating papers, for engaging in discussions with colleagues from other disciplines and other countries, for arguing their cases so eloquently (including those whose native language is not English but who attempted to master this almost unmasterable idiom). The addresses presented at the conference, some of them substantially revised, have been gathered together to form the present volume.

The conference was jointly sponsored by the Center for Seventeenth and Eighteenth Century Studies, the Committee for Jewish Studies, the Center for Medieval and Renaissance Studies, and the Department of History – all at UCLA, and the German Historical Institute in Washington, D.C. I am especially grateful to John Brewer, from the Center for Seventeenth and Eighteenth Century Studies, and to R. Po-chia Hsia, from the Department of History of New York University for helping me organize the conference, as well as to Peter Reill, from UCLA's Department of History, and to the staff of the William Andrews Clark Memorial Library for having been such generous hosts to all of us. Let me also thank Daniel S. Mattern, from the German Historical Institute, for his help in preparing this volume for publication; Rudolf Vierhaus and H. C. Erik Midelfort, who served as readers; and Frank Smith, from Cambridge University Press, for his most valuable advice and his strong interest in this project.

Readers of this volume will notice that there are two quite different avenues of approach to the history of Jewish–Gentile relations in late medieval and early modern Germany. On the one hand, no one who studies this topic can escape the long, dark shadows of the tragic end of German Jewry in the decade before 1945. Almost as strongly as those who work on modern anti-Semitism and the Holocaust, those who study the history of Jews in Germany in the period before the Enlightenment are compelled to look for the causes of this catastrophe. Considering *la longue durée* of social prejudice and political discrimination, this seems justified and not at all anachronistic. On the other hand, the history of tensions, of resentments, and of intolerance that can be traced back to the Reformation and to the pogroms in the era of the Black Death in the middle of the fourteenth century is only part of the story.

This history of antagonism is intertwined with a story of productive interaction, of mutual achievements, and of successful cooperation between Jews and Christians in many parts of the Holy Roman Empire, especially in the period after 1555. Contacts and mutual influence can be observed in areas such as language, popular culture, medicine, and economics. Of course, it would be wrong to overlook the differences: it was in the very nature of prerevolutionary *ständische Gesellschaft* (society of estates or orders) that different groups in society were endowed with different burdens and responsibilities. But it is within the *ständische Gesellschaft* of premodern, preindustrial Germany that Jews played a significant role. They were included in certain cultural, economic, and social processes, but they were excluded from others. They were discriminated against, but they were not the only ones who had to suffer discrimination in a society that was predicated upon notions of privilege and service, of protection and exclusion. What the authors of this volume have attempted to decipher, therefore, is the most difficult, and at times puzzling, *mixtura* of general factors related to many groups in late medieval and early modern Germany and of special factors related exclusively to those who were periodically, though not always and not everywhere, confined to ghettos as Jews. It is our hope that the contributions in this volume address the main issues of Jewish–Gentile relations in pre-Enlightenment Germany, and we look forward to the discussion that they will evoke.

July 1994   Hartmut Lehmann
Göttingen

The essays brought together in this volume represent papers originally presented at a conference held on May 9–11, 1991, in Los Angeles. Jointly sponsored by the German Historical Institute of Washington, D.C., and the University of California at Los Angeles, the conference, entitled "In and Out of the Ghetto: Jewish–Gentile Relations in Late Medieval and Early Modern Germany," drew scholars from Europe, North America, and Israel who work on early modern German-Jewish history and presented the participants with the opportunity to engage in a unique dialogue.

Ninety years ago, German-Jewish historians launched a project to record the history of all German-speaking Jewish communities in central Europe, from the initial settlement to the Congress of Vienna in 1815. The fate of that academic enterprise, the *Germania Judaica,* reflects the fortunes of the German nation and the Jewish people: the first part of volume 1 (to the year 1238) was completed in 1917, but owing to the dislocations of war and defeat the entire volume did not appear until 1934. Work on volume 2 (1238–1350), disrupted in 1938 by the Nazi regime but renewed in 1955 in Israel, was published only in 1968. Volume 3 (1350–1519) is just now appearing in print. Since 1945, the history of German-speaking Jewry has attracted a much broader research interest than the original group of German-Jewish historians, as scholars from different countries and disciplines have investigated the German-Jewish past, not solely from the perspective of Jewish history but also to gain insights into the central European past through focusing on the tragic relationship between the majority and minority populations.

The tradition of "Wissenschaft des Judentums" (Jewish studies) continues today in Israel, but much of the current research on German-Jewish history has been carried out by Gentiles, including two generations of postwar German historians, whose primary academic training has usually not been in Jewish history. And though Israeli and German historians have collaborated individually and on the *Germania Judaica,* their methodologies, approaches, and insights reflect very different perspectives: in general, the first group stresses the continuity of the Jewish experience, explores Hebrew and Judaic sources, and views German-Jewish history from the inside looking out; the second group emphasizes the contextual links between Jewish and German history, concentrates on Latin and German sources, and approaches the history of German Jews from the outside looking in. The broadening of interest also encourages new research agendas: in addition to reconstructing the legal, institutional, economic, and intellectual history of German Jews, scholars have posed questions of demography, family structure, popular culture, and the dynamics of toleration within the larger context of the history and society of central Europe.

The early modern period (fifteenth through eighteenth centuries) represents a crucial but little-known era in German-Jewish historiography. Before 1933, research focused on Jewish communities in the medieval period and during the Second Empire. The focus on the medieval period reflected both the agenda set by the *Germania Judaica* and the prominence of medieval studies in general; scholars were interested in Jews in the *Kaiserreich* because it was during that time that legal restrictions on Jews were abolished and they were integrated into German civil society. Since World War II, attention has naturally shifted to the study of the Holocaust and the modern roots of anti-Semitism in Germany. Interest in the early modern period, however, revived with the publication of several seminal monographs and source editions during the 1950s, 1960s, and 1970s: Raphael Straus's collection of documents on the activities of Regensburg's Jewish community (completed in 1933 but not published until 1960); Heinrich Schnee's monumental work on Jewish court agents in the age of absolutism; Selma Stern's studies of Josel of Rosheim and on the relationship between Jews and the Prussian state. A steady stream of monographs, dissertations, textbooks, conference volumes, and articles appeared in the 1980s; in 1991, *Aschkenas,* the first postwar journal dedicated to German-Jewish history began publication.

Unlike their predecessors before World War II, scholars of German-Jewish history today are a highly heterogeneous group, reflecting a variety of national, historiographical, and methodological perspectives. Our conference attempted a first dialogue across national and disciplinary boundaries: nineteen scholars – eight Germans, five Israelis, three Americans, two Britons, and one Canadian – presented papers on the history, folklore, sociology, and linguistics of German-speaking Jews from the fourteenth through eighteenth centuries. A secondary aim of our conference was to introduce German-Jewish history to a broader audience, namely, historians of general Jewish history and of early modern Germany. This latter group of historians was invited to comment, discuss, and reflect upon the proceedings, and their comments are included in this volume.

In spite of some criticisms, we have retained the conference title for this volume. We do not suggest that the Jewish experience in the Holy Roman Empire was confined exclusively to the ghetto: far from it. Many of the essays presented here demonstrate both a high degree of mobility among German Jews and frequent interaction with the Christian majority. Nevertheless, the ghetto, or a walled-in Jewish quarter, did characterize the experience of the major urban Jewish communities of central Europe between the Black Death and emancipation. The ghetto evolved not only from the Christian authorities' desire to control but also from the need of the Jews for greater security in the wake of medieval massacres. Both the coercive and the voluntary aspects, as Jacob Katz argues and as Alfred Haverkamp exemplifies with the case of Trier, are central to understanding the ghetto. By modifying the word or symbol of "ghetto" with the phrase "in and out," we hope to indicate the dynamic nature of Jewish–Christian relations during the early modern period, an era characterized by restrictions, discriminations, and repressions but also by cultural, economic, and social exchanges. In claiming the middle ground, we do not pretend to represent here the views of all of our colleagues at the conference, some of whom expressed greater pessimism and doubt whereas others chose to emphasize the positive aspects of the Jewish experience. In publishing this collection, we merely wish to suggest the complexity and fascination behind that historical experience.

In his introductory essay, Jacob Katz presents a provocative thesis on Jewish–Gentile relations in late medieval and early modern Germany. He argues, paradoxically, that in the earlier period the juxtaposition of two distinct ethnic-religious groups resulted in a structure of limited anti-Semitism, whereas in the nineteenth century emancipation and integration brought about a new and more intense anti-Semitism, as the target of earlier antipathies lost definition.

Six groups of essays comprise the remainder of the volume. Part I addresses the legacy of the Middle Ages: Jewish cultural identity and the price of exclusiveness. Alfred Haverkamp offers a detailed reconstruction of medieval urban Jewish quarters, focusing on the community of Trier. Drawing upon folkloristic sources and popular Jewish culture, Christoph Daxelmüller demonstrates the high degree of cultural borrowings and exchanges between the majority and minority cultures. Extending the argument into the early modern period, Otto Ulbricht examines the stereotype of the Jewish criminal by analyzing the historical context of the criminality and punishment of Jews.

Parts II through V cover the entire chronological span of our subject. In Part II, the social and economic structure of early modern German Jewry is analyzed by Michael Toch and Stefi Jersch-Wenzel, using specific examples of a rural Jewish peddler in Hesse and the Jewish professions in Brandenburg-Prussia, respectively. In Part III, chapters by Paul Wexler, Yacov Guggenheim, and Robert Jütte discuss Jewish–Gentile contacts before emancipation by focusing, respectively, on the origin and development of

Yiddish; contact between Jewish and Christian vagrants; and the relationship between Jewish physicians and their Christian clients. In Part IV, chapters by R. Po-chia Hsia and Miri Rubin analyze two popular anti-Semitic
representations of Jews in medieval and early modern Germany: the Jew as
usurer, and the Jew as abuser of the Eucharist, respectively. In Part V, three
chapters compare the patterns of authority and limits of toleration within
the Holy Roman Empire: Rotraud Ries examines the relationship between
German territorial princes and Jews; J. Friedrich Battenberg describes conditions of toleration in ecclesiastical territories; and Christopher R.
Friedrichs discusses Jewish communities in imperial cities. At the end of
each part, a historian – respectively Theodore K. Rabb, Gershon David
Hundert, Deborah Hertz, Carlo Ginzburg, and Thomas A. Brady, Jr. – offers a commentary and suggestions for future research.

Part VI is comprised of reflections on the German-Jewish experience by
scholars in neighboring fields of research: Hartmut Lehmann and Mack
Walker, two distinguished historians of early modern Germany, offer their
perspectives from the larger central European context; Jonathan I. Israel,
noted for his research on Hispano-Dutch and Jewish history, presents a reflection on *la longue durée* of German-Jewish history; and, from the unique
viewpoint of the interstice of Jewish–Christian intellectual history, Richard
H. Popkin suggests interesting contrasts between Dutch and German societies in the early modern period.

Three common themes suggested by the essays in this volume seem particularly promising for future dialogue:

1. With their high degree of mobility, the Jewish lower classes represent
a fascinating but neglected subject of research. Questions of vagrancy, criminality, cultural exchanges, anti-Semitism, personal identity, and conversion
are raised in the chapters by Daxelmüller, Ulbricht, Toch, Wexler, and
Guggenheim.

2. A central point of disagreement concerns the degree of Jewish exclusiveness. What constituted Jewish identity in the Holy Roman Empire?
Was it religion, language, customs, physical appearance, or history that defined identity? Did personal perception play a role? Did the repressive and
defining mechanisms in early modern German society permit a sense of individual freedom?

3. Modern anti-Semitism casts a long shadow on the history of German
Jewry in the early modern period. Although the majority of the essays emphasizes the dynamic and changing nature of Jewish–Gentile relations – and
several demonstrate forcefully that German-Jewish history was by no means
merely a history of persecutions and restrictions – the question of historical

continuity remains. The dilemma is addressed by focusing on the different historical contexts that explain the limits of toleration and persecution; the contributions by Jütte, Hsia, Rubin, Ries, Battenberg, and Friedrichs clearly pursue this line of reasoning.

Readers can discover for themselves many other thematic contrasts and disagreements among the discussions in this volume. Our conference and this collection are initial dialogues. We take heart in the lively, substantial, and sometimes heated debates during three days of intense discourse. We can claim no definitive conclusions but merely a stimulating and enriching exchange of ideas.

For that occasion and for the opportunity to publish the proceedings, I would like to thank the participants; the sponsoring institutions; the manuscript editor, Daniel S. Mattern; the director of the Clark Library, John Brewer, who offered us his splendid facilities; and especially Hartmut Lehmann, who first responded with enthusiasm and support to my ideas for such an encounter on a glorious autumn day in Rheinhausen.

August 1994   R. Po-chia Hsia
New York

Contributors

J. Friedrich Battenberg is professor of history at the Technische Hochschule Darmstadt. He is a specialist in the history of Hesse and is the author of numerous articles and books on Hessian and German history of the late medieval and early modern periods, including *Das Europäische Zeitalter der Juden. Zur Entwicklung einer Minderheitengruppe in der nichtjüdischen Umwelt Europas* (1990). Together with Markus Wenninger, he is currently editor of the journal *Aschkenas. Zeitschrift für Geschichte und Kultur der Juden* (1991–).

Thomas A. Brady, Jr., is professor of history at the University of California at Berkeley. He is the author of several studies on early modern Germany, including *Ruling Class, Regime, and Reformation at Strasbourg, 1520–1550* (1978); *Turning Swiss: Cities and Empire, 1450–1550* (1985); and *Protestant Politics: Jacob Sturm (1489–1553) and the German Reformation* (1993).

Christoph Daxelmüller is professor of ethnology and chair of the Institut für Volkskunde at the Universität Regensburg. He is the author of numerous publications on magic, popular superstition, popular piety, folk literature, and popular culture of the seventeenth and eighteenth centuries. He also specializes in the study of Jewish popular culture and folklore. A handbook on the *Geschichte der jüdischen Ethnologie in Mittel- und Osteuropa, 1898–1938* is in preparation.

Christopher R. Friedrichs is associate professor of history at the University of British Columbia in Vancouver. He is the author of *Urban Society in an Age of War: Nördlingen, 1580–1720* (1979) and numerous articles on the social and political history of German cities in the early modern era.

Carlo Ginzburg is professor of history at the University of California at Los Angeles. He is the author of numerous studies of culture in early modern Europe, including *The Cheese and the Worms: The Cosmos of a Sixteenth-Century Miller* (1980) and *Ecstasies: Deciphering the Witches' Sabbath* (1991).

Yacov Guggenheim is on the Faculty of Humanities of the Institute of Jewish Studies at the Hebrew University of Jerusalem, Israel. He is the editor of the third volume of *Germania Judaica*.

Alfred Haverkamp is professor of medieval history at the Universität Trier. He is the author of a standard history of medieval Germany, *Aufbruch und Gestaltung, Deutsch-*

land 1056–1273 (1984), among numerous other publications. He is chair of the recently founded German Society for Research in the History of the Jews / Gesellschaft zur Erforschung der Geschichte der Juden.

Deborah Hertz is associate professor of history at the State University of New York at Binghamton. She is author of *Jewish High Society in Old Regime Berlin* (1988), which appeared in German translation in 1991. She also edited a volume of Rahel Varnhagen's letters. During 1991–92 she was visiting lecturer at the Harvard Divinity School.

R. Po-chia Hsia is professor of history at New York University. He is the author of several books, including *The German People and the Reformation* (1988); *The Myth of Ritual Murder: Jews and Magic in Reformation Germany* (1988); *Social Discipline in the Reformation: Central Europe, 1550–1750* (1989); and, most recently, *Trent, 1475: Stories of a Ritual Murder Trial* (1992).

Gershon David Hundert is professor of Jewish studies and history at McGill University in Montreal, Quebec. His most recent book is *The Jews in a Polish Private Town* (1992). He is also the author of numerous articles and the editor of *Essential Papers on Hasidism: Origins to Present* (1991).

Jonathan I. Israel is professor of Dutch history and institutions at the University of London, England. His latest books include *Empires and Entrepôts: The Dutch, the Spanish Monarchy, and the Jews, 1585–1713* (1990); *Dutch Primacy in World Trade, 1585–1740* (1989); and *European Jewry in the Age of Mercantilism, 1550–1750* (1985). In 1992 he became a fellow of the British Academy.

Stefi Jersch-Wenzel is professor of history at the Technische Universität Berlin and head of the German-Jewish history section of the Historische Kommission zu Berlin. She is the author of *Juden und "Franzosen" in der Wirtschaft des Raumes Berlin/Brandenburg zur Zeit des Merkantilismus* (1978) and most recently "Die Juden im Zeitalter der Aufklärung," in *Zerbrochene Geschichte* (1991).

Robert Jütte is professor of history at the Universität Stuttgart and director of the Institut für Geschichte der Medizin der Robert-Bosch-Stiftung. His fields of research include the history of early modern Europe and the social history of medicine. His most recent books are *Ärzte, Heiler und Patienten* (1991) and *Die Emigration der deutschsprachigen "Wissenschaft des Judentums"* (1991).

Jacob Katz is professor emeritus of the Hebrew University of Jerusalem. He is the recipient of numerous honors, including Honorary Foreign Member of the American Academy of Arts and Sciences, the Israel Prize for Jewish History (1980), and the B'nai B'rith International Award (1981). He has been visiting professor at Harvard University, UCLA, and Columbia University. He is the author of numerous books on Jewish history, including *From Prejudice to Destruction: Anti-Semitism, 1700–1933* (1980).

Hartmut Lehmann is director of the Max-Planck-Institut für Geschichte in Göttingen. His major publications include *Pietismus und weltliche Ordnung in Württemberg vom 17.–20. Jahrhundert* (1969), *Das Zeitalter des Absolutismus* (1980); *Martin Luther in the*

American Imagination (1988); and, with James J. Sheehan, *An Interrupted Past: German-Speaking Refugee Historians in the United States after 1933* (1991).

Richard H. Popkin is professor of history at the University of California at Los Angeles. He is the author of numerous books, articles, and college textbooks, most recently *Isaac La Peyrère (1596–1676): His Life, Work, and Influence* (1987); *Millenarianism and Messianism in English Literature and Thought, 1650–1800* (1988); and *The Third Force in Seventeenth-Century Thought* (1992). He is coeditor, with David S. Katz and Jonathan I. Israel, of *Sceptics, Millenarians, and Jews* (1990), and with Donald R. Kelley of *The Shapes of Knowledge: From the Renaissance to Enlightenment* (1991).

Theodore K. Rabb is professor of history at Princeton University. He is the author of numerous articles and reviews and has been the editor of the *Journal of Interdisciplinary History* since its founding (1970). Among the books he has written or edited are *The Struggle for Stability in Early Modern Europe* (1975); *The New History: The 1980s and Beyond* (1982); and *Renaissance Lives* (1992).

Rotraud Ries is a historian living in Münster, Germany. She has worked on numerous projects involving the history of Jews in Lower Saxony and the relations between Christians and Jews in the modern period.

Miri Rubin is a fellow of Pembroke College, Oxford, and a university lecturer in medieval history at Oxford University. She is interested in later medieval social and cultural history and has published *Charity and Community in Medieval Cambridge* (1987), *Corpus Christi: The Eucharist in Late Medieval Culture* (1991), as well as numerous articles. With Sarah Kay, she has edited *Framing Medieval Bodies* (1994). She is currently working on a book that explores the birth and development of the host-desecration narrative and reactions to it in late medieval Europe.

Michael Toch is associate professor of medieval history at the Hebrew University of Jerusalem. He has worked both in Jewish history and in the economic and agrarian history of the Middle Ages. He is the author of *Die Nürnberger Mittelschichten im 15. Jahrhundert* (1978) and the editor of the fourteenth-century account books of the Bavarian monastery of Scheyern (forthcoming). He is currently working on a history of medieval German Jewry.

Otto Ulbricht is professor of history at the Universität zu Kiel, Germany. He is the author of *Englische Landwirtschaft in Kurhannover in der zweiten Hälfte des 18. Jahrhunderts* (1980) and *Kindsmord und Aufklärung in Deutschland* (1990). He has published articles on agrarian history and the social history of crime during the Enlightenment. He is currently working on a study of an eighteenth-century beggar and is coediting a collection of essays on the opponents of the witch hunts and on female criminality in early modern Europe.

Mack Walker is professor of history at Johns Hopkins University in Baltimore. He is the author of numerous books and articles on German history during the early modern era. He is best known for his study *German Home Towns: Community, State, and General Estate, 1648–1871* (1971). A new study, *The Salzburg Transaction: Expulsion and Redemption in Eighteenth-Century Germany* was published in 1993.

Paul Wexler is professor of linguistics at Tel-Aviv University. He specializes in Slavic and Jewish linguistics. His most recent publications include *Explorations in Judeo-Slavic Linguistics* (1987), an edited collection *Studies in Yiddish Linguistics* (1990), and "Yiddish – the 15th Slavic Language," *International Journal of the Sociology of Language* (1991).

Reflecting on German-Jewish History

JACOB KATZ

The history of modern German Jewry is of exceptionally great interest to scholarly as well as more general intellectual audiences. This exceptionality is obviously connected with the tragic end of German Jewry in the course of the Holocaust. True, other European Jewish communities suffered no less than the German Jews, some of them even more. The Polish Jewish community, for example, lost a higher percentage of its members during the German occupation than its German counterpart did under the Nazis. One thinks of German Jewry as having been partly saved through emigration. Yet, as I explained on another occasion, the fate of Polish Jewry at the hands of the Germans was unconnected with its previous history.[1] Its misfortune was brought upon it by external forces. Polish Jewry's doom, therefore, did not create an impulse to trace its earlier history. Not so in the case of German Jewry. Although its doom was likewise unforeseen and unpredictable, the experience of the German-Jewish community was part of a continuous evolution that can be traced, stage after stage, phase after phase, starting with the integration of ghetto dwellers into state and society in the wake of emancipation,[2] continuing with the vicissitudes of its integration, and ending with the fateful turn it took in the Nazi era, leading to its destruction as a community.[3]

There is no reason for the historian to be embarrassed by the insight that his or her interest in a certain subject derives from the end result of a historical development. What he or she must avoid, however, is viewing the earlier stages from the perspective of the unforeseen and unforeseeable future. Although interest in a subject may come from the finale, historical understanding has to be gained from its antecedents. I assume that this

---

1 Jacob Katz, "The Unique Fascination of German Jewish History," *Modern Judaism* 8 (1989): 141–55.
2 On emancipation generally, see Jacob Katz, *Out of the Ghetto: The Social Background of Jewish Emancipation, 1770–1870* (Cambridge, Mass., 1973).
3 Jacob Katz, *From Prejudice to Destruction: Anti-Semitism, 1700–1933* (Cambridge, Mass., 1980).

methodological rule guided the editors of this volume to explore the topic
of the history of Jewish–Gentile relations in premodern times, though the
main subject matter is the history of these relations in the modern period.
For it is true that, although many of the vicissitudes of the Jewish position
in modern times can be explained by tracing changing conditions in contemporary society, deeper insights into its nature can be gained only by exploring the residual remains of former times that have been ignored or
discounted in contemporary consciousness.

The very fact that at a certain juncture contemporaries viewed themselves
as having been liberated from the burden of the past is of course characteristic of the situation. Jews and Gentiles alike, in the last decades of the eighteenth and the early decades of the nineteenth century, witnessed the
changing role of religion in the new, enlightened world. Religion's new
role supposedly rendered obsolete the previous relations between the adherents of Judaism and Christianity.

Historians have attempted to trace the precursors of this development.
They have shown that medieval exclusiveness, which was based on a gap
between the dogmas and tenets of the two religions, gradually gave way to
a more tolerant attitude. I do not quarrel with these findings. I myself contributed to them in my *Exclusiveness and Tolerance,* where I show that on the
Jewish side a slow process of amelioration in the judgment of Christians and
Christianity took place.[4] There is, however, a basic difference between a
silent and possibly unconscious change of attitude that views itself as still remaining within the bounds of tradition and one whereby a new approach
presents itself to contemporaries as an outspoken break with that tradition.
In the first case, the change is limited to mental evaluation, without practical consequences. In the second, the new attitude imposes the obligation of
social action.

Transcending by far his rabbinical predecessors, Rabbi Jacob Emden
evolved a theory about Christianity in the 1760s and 1770s that exempted
it from the blemish of polytheism, a blemish derived from the dogma of the
Trinity. Rabbi Emden believed himself to be thinking within the terms of
Jewish tradition. Accordingly, no tangible consequences were to be drawn
from his theory. It did not occur to him that this theory could lead to the
justification of intermarriage between Jews and Christians. Being a strict,
traditional rabbi, Emden of course upheld all the ritual and dietary restrictions that kept Jewish society apart from the Gentile surroundings.[5] One or
two generations later, when the social barriers between Jews and Gentiles

---

4 Jacob Katz, *Exclusiveness and Tolerance: Studies in Jewish–Gentile Relations in Medieval and Modern Times*
   (Oxford, 1961).
5 On Emden, see Katz, *Out of the Ghetto,* 36, 143–5.

broke down, the removal of the blemish of polytheism served as a direct justification for intermarriage. Indeed, it also served as a basis for demands that the Jewish minority merge into the Gentile majority. This development was, of course, accompanied by the rejection of tradition in its entirety, not simply a reinterpretation of a certain part of it.

Similar developments took place on the Christian side. Philanthropic Christians of the seventeenth and eighteenth centuries, like Hugo Grotius, condemned the traditional and still prevalent harsh treatment of Jews by the authorities and by the general public. He pleaded for a benevolent approach to the Jews, in the name of Christian love. It was thought that rather than humiliation, such an attitude would lead to the hoped-for turning of Jews toward Christianity. Thus, these so-called philo-Semites retained the Christian vision of the absorption of the Jews after their conversion.

A real revolutionary shift took place only when, in the wake of rationalism and the Enlightenment, religious differences were either entirely discounted or their significance to a large extent minimized. This paved the way for the inclusion of Jews in the secular state and their formal membership in Gentile society. True, there were people who, even at this stage, did not give up the hope of seeing the Jews ultimately become Christians, but they viewed this process only as one of accommodation, not as a precondition for their acceptance.

The belief that the process of accommodation or assimilation would obliterate the differences between Jew and Gentile, at most leaving two mutually tolerant faiths, was shared by Jews and Gentiles alike. The logic behind this view was the fact that the exclusion of Jews in traditional times derived from their religious nonconformity. When religion as such lost its overriding importance and influence, people could easily assume that the members of the two religious communities would now meet on the common ground of pure humanity. What was overlooked in this reasoning, however, was that Jewish religious nonconformity was only the formal, historical ground for the Christian–Jewish division. Religious nonconformity carried with it other aspects of separateness. Jewish traditional society embraced the elements of a full-fledged civilization that was different from that of the Christian environment. Jews used their own literary language – rabbinical Hebrew – and their own unique vernacular – Yiddish. Jews had their own law, the Talmud, and together with the Hebrew Bible in its original language, they served as a cultural means of socialization, initiating every new generation into the national culture. Indeed, until the last third of the eighteenth century no one doubted that Jews, though living amid European nations, represented a unique species, harking from biblical and postbiblical times.

True, experience taught that individual Jews could, in traditional period, divest themselves of these characteristics by converting. This divestment, of course, was part of the psychological effect of religious conversion; it meant the absolute identification of the convert not only with the tenets of his adopted faith but also with all of the values of the society that he joined upon his conversion. It is not for nothing that theologians define conversion as a new birth, for, if it is genuine, it can have the effect of a mutation of personality.

The assumption that, after secularization, laxity or negligence concerning religion would have the same effect as did conversion in the religious age is a misconception that looms behind the expected result of Jewish acculturation and assimilation. For, contrary to conversion, acculturation and assimilation are slow processes, that need the span of generations to do their final work. It is for this reason that Jews, especially in the first phases of assimilation, remained culturally and mentally Jewish, even if indifferent or outrightly antagonistic to their former religion. They may have been ignorant of the Jewish national language, Hebrew – indeed most of them were – and have seemingly exchanged the Yiddish vernacular of their ancestors for High German, but they still retained some residual linguistic peculiarities. We know of the efforts of Jewish educators to eradicate the traces of Yiddish that popped up inadvertently in the speech and writing of their pupils. This was especially likely to happen in intimate conversation between Jews. Years ago, the correspondence between Heinrich Heine and Giacomo Meyerbeer came to light. Here were two active contributors to contemporary European culture – and they were certainly assimilated. Yet in their personal correspondence they resorted to expressions like *nebich, risches, rosche, reschoim* – indicating their particular Jewish intimacy. That Gershon Bleichröder, Bismarck's banker, used Hebrew letters and, no doubt, Jewish idioms in his personal letters to Rothschild in Frankfurt am Main we know from Fritz Stern's biography.[6]

The common Jewish background created an affinity for reciprocity, even when and where there was a conscious attempt to extricate oneself from the confinement of Jewish exclusiveness. I found a telling example of this when dealing with the history of Jewish attempts to be accepted into Masonic lodges. Since its declared intention was to join equal-minded men irrespective of religious background, Freemasonry seemed to offer an ideal opportunity for a Jew to gain entrance into Gentile society. Socially ambitious Jews did indeed try to avail themselves of this opportunity, and in my book

---

6 Fritz Stern, *Gold and Iron: Bismarck, Bleichröder, and the Building of the German Empire* (1977; New York, 1979), 135.

upon this subject I described their struggle, which I shall return to later.[7] Nonetheless, despite the basic principle of the universal openness of Freemasonry, Jews had difficulty being accepted. This could be partially attributed to the prevailing prejudices against Jews, yet at times I found the Freemasons blaming the Jews for behavior incompatible with the spirit of Freemasonry. Members of the lodge were expected to communicate with each other on an equal footing. Jews, so the complaint ran, tended to cluster together whenever they appeared in the lodge, creating a subgroup, a clique. Similar observations were made in other quarters as well. I do not think this accusation was a figment of their imagination with no basis in fact. Jewish historical experience, as well as Jewish concepts and practices, created a mentality functioning as a factor of cohesion among Jews, and thereby as a barrier between them and non-Jews.

Many other tangible factors supported Jewish separateness: family ties, owing to the tendency to marry among themselves; their concentration in certain fields of economic endeavor; and, of course, their formal or informal membership in the Jewish community and Jewish organizations. Most of these organizations were maintained contrary to the assimilationist ideology, which mandated a complete integration of Jews that would efface all traces of their different social physiognomy. A sometimes silent, but at other times noisy, controversy went on between the two parties as to why this was happening. Jews argued that they were unable to give up their occupational activities as well as their particular social situations because many occupations, as well as Gentile social circles, remained closed to them. Their critics, however, attributed this behavior to Jewish clannishness or to other, even more reprehensible Jewish propensities. Both closed their eyes to the sociological rule demonstrated in our generation by Simon Kuznets, that as long as a religious minority retains its religious conformity, even only in a very limited way, it perforce also functions as a separate entity in economic and social contexts.[8] At any rate, if total assimilation was the goal, it could be expected only over the course of many generations. But both parties on the German scene, the Christians and the Jews, were in a hurry.

Christians, in the age of faith, made every effort to convert the Jews in their midst to Christianity, even though the results of their efforts were disappointing. Nonetheless, they did not give up hope of the ultimate outcome. It was an article of Christian faith that at the end of their days the Jews would give testimony to the truth of Christianity. Being of an irra-

7 Jacob Katz, *Jews and Freemasons in Europe, 1723–1939* (Cambridge, Mass., 1970).
8 Simon Kuznets, "Economic Structure and Life of the Jews," in Louis Finkelstein, ed., *The Jews, Their History, Culture, and Religion*, 3rd ed. (New York, 1960), 1597–1666.

tional nature, this belief withstood the effects of disappointment. Now that the expectation of conversion was replaced by the expectation of assimilation, the article of faith became a rationally observable process, and thus the questions repeatedly asked were: Are the Jews on their way to becoming Germans? Have they succeeded in divesting themselves of their Jewish propensities?

On the Jewish side, there were signs of impatience as well. The Jewish press registered with satisfaction every case of Jewish advancement on the way to social integration, censuring at the same time any rebuff of Jews by whatever political or social agency. Occasionally Jews did not limit themselves to protests but tried to respond with action. It is grotesque, for example, to see them struggle to be accepted as invited members of a dancing club, something that happened in Königsberg in the late 1840s.[9]

The best example of active Jewish endeavors to break down the barriers of society, however, is the struggle for admission to the Masonic lodges. This commenced in the first decade of the nineteenth century, when some socially ambitious Jews of Frankfurt am Main and Berlin tried to enter the local lodges and were refused. In Frankfurt, the Jews succeeded in establishing their own lodge, which in principle was open to members of any religion but in fact (with some exceptions) had mostly Jewish members. Their contemporaries therefore aptly dubbed this the *Judenloge*. In the era of liberalism, more and more of the regular lodges admitted Jews, but not all of them did. Moreover, according to the general rule, members of a lodge who showed their membership card in another lodge had to be permitted to enter. Nonetheless, many other lodges refused even visitation rights to Jews. Those who were refused did not refrain from making public scandals of their rejection.

Still, during the liberal era progress was made in admitting Jews until the outbreak of anti-Semitism of the 1870s, when most of the Masonic lodges excluded Jews or made their remaining impossible, because of the anti-Jewish atmosphere. Some of these former Freemasons thought of establishing B'nai B'rith lodges and appealed to the American leadership of this organization to accept as affiliates their German counterparts.

This episode highlights the basic difference between the American and German situations. American Jews, though equal citizens before the law, kept to themselves, as far as social contact was concerned. Those who aspired to be accepted by non-Jewish fraternities or clubs were an exception in America. Although the term "pluralism" had not yet been coined, the

---

9 *Allgemeine Zeitung des Judenthums*, November 10, 1845, 685–6.

idea of voluntary division of the population according to differing religious, social, or ethnic background served as a guideline for social behavior. In Germany, not only the term was lacking but the concept was absent as well. According to the ideal of liberalism and the concept of the equality of all men, anyone ought to have been eligible for any association. Social units such as lodges, fraternities, clubs, and the many *Vereine* (associations) that were typical of German society, however, were exclusive, not only of Jews but often particularly of them. Knowing this, Jews were embittered, and they had to learn the hard way that voluntary association could not be enforced like formal citizenship. They had to accept the fact that, as descendants of the former pariahs of European society, they still carried the stamp of their forebears.

I am aware of the fact that many colleagues of mine, some of them historians of rank, such as the late Professor Salo Wittmayer Baron, objected to the use of the term "pariah" in the Jewish context, even if it was applied to the characterization of Jews during the ghetto period. Jews were, so the argument runs, not untouchables, nor were they inescapably bound to their original group.[10] They could escape, by conversion. Max Weber, who did apply the term to characterize the Jewish situation in premodern times, was, of course, aware of these qualifications. Nonetheless, he found in the Indian pariahs a model for separated underprivileged groups that performed certain necessary functions for society at large. He therefore accepted the term, ignoring the other features of the Indian pariahs, their untouchability and their absolute confinement to their group. In this limited sense, the term is certainly applicable to the Jews of the ghetto times and before. For Jews were no doubt separate by mutual consent; they were certainly underprivileged and limited to certain economic functions. In my opinion, this application of the term is therefore not wrong, but it does not exhaust the breadth and depth of the situation, especially with regard to the presence of the Jews in a Christian environment, the subject of our concern here.

For the division between the Gentile majority and the Jewish minority was not simply that of two groups belonging to different religions: the religions of the two groups were related to each other in an intimate, and at the same time most entangled, fashion. Christian believers did not simply deny the truth of Judaism; rather they maintained a claim to the allegiance of Jews. As the brethren in flesh of the founder of Christianity, Jews ought to have been the first to accept his message, the core of which was, in effect, the invalidation of Judaism. Christianity espoused an ambivalent atti-

10 See Salo Wittmayer Baron, *A Social and Religious History of the Jews* (New York, 1952), 1:23–4, 297.

tude. On the one hand, Christians tolerated Jews, because of their historical connection with Christianity and the hope of gaining their ultimate ac-
knowledgment. On the other hand, Christians felt entitled to keep the Jews
in their midst in the pariah situation. Jews, aware of the Christian claim to
their conversion potential and knowing about the possible enticement involved, reacted with what psychologists would perhaps define as overcom-
pensation. They maintained an anxious avoidance of contact with any part
of the Christian culture saturated with Christian symbols. Thus, despite
physical proximity and actual intercourse between the two societies, the result was an ever-widening estrangement between them that served as fer-
tile soil for misjudgment and prejudice. This was therefore not simply a
relationship between two ethnic or religious groups who happened to live
together but were basically uninterested in each other. Jews were an ever-
present subject for Christians, not only on the higher theological level but
in the popular imagination as well. The same was true for Jewish interest in
the role of the non-Jewish world, though perhaps not particularly qua
Christians but more generally as the ruling *goyim* (Gentiles). This almost
compulsive preoccupation with each other was, however, not based on mutual observation but on traditional notions and preconceived stereotypes.

As long as the two societies lived in physical proximity but, for all sociological intents and purposes, as two separate societies, these abstract notions about each other did not have much impact upon their practical
relationship. With the exception of periodic outbreaks of violence by the
majority against the minority, the contact between the two societies was
governed by the rules of economic and political exigency. The mental
reservations of the Jews concerning the Gentiles, especially Christians, did
not prevent Jews from seeking the protection of the current incumbents in
power nor from serving non-Jews or anyone willing to pay. The same was
also true for Christians. Despite harboring prejudices against the Jews,
Christian rulers protected the Jews in their midst and availed themselves of
their economic services. The Prussian King Frederick I lent a hand to the
publishing of Eisenmenger's *Das endeckte Judenthum,* a despicable collection
of anti-Jewish accusations presenting itself as a repository of Christian tradition and teaching.[11] At the same time, it was King Frederick's granting of
privileges to the Jews that laid the foundation for the thriving Jewish community in Prussia.

Abstract thinking about each other and their practical attitude toward
each other were somehow kept apart, in medieval times. Paradoxically, the

---

11 Johann Andreas Eisenmenger, *Endecktes Judenthum,* 2 vols. (Königsberg, 1710). On Eisenmenger,
see Katz, *From Prejudice to Destruction,* chap. 1.

abstract and the real elements became combined when the barriers between the two societies were pulled down and their possible merger was conceptualized. Now the validity of the traditional concepts concerning each other became the subject of discussion and examination. The very volume of publicistic literature about Jewish emancipation and possible integration, the repetition of the anti-Jewish arguments by their foes, and refutation of these arguments by their friends are telling testimony to the formidable obstacles the Jews entering the Gentile world had to overcome. Ultimately, emancipation – and, in part, also integration – were realized not through reconciliation and mutual understanding but through discarding differences or suppressing them, under cover of abstract ideologies.

The alleged elimination of religious elements through the process of secularization served as a major instrument in this accommodation. What has been overlooked, however, is the fact that even if secularization is capable of expunging the cognitive elements of religion, it cannot uproot the deep-seated emotional sentiments or the ingrained mental traits conditioned by religious belief. Secularized Jews and Christians were still estranged, though they were not aware of the sources of their disagreement. The very fact of dissension was frustrating and confounding, for, according to prevailing ideology, common membership in state and society ought to have eliminated the traces of differing backgrounds and origins. To resolve the riddle, all kinds of theories were evolved on both sides – among them that of racially conditioned propensities, with all its sinister implications.

Turning to the starting point of our deliberation, we may state that whereas in premodern times Jews and Gentiles confronted each other as members of two different groups, each with a corresponding system of concepts and beliefs, in modern times the boundaries between the two societies were blurred, without adequate cognitive or ideological justification. This discrepancy between reality and its reflection in perception goes a long way toward explaining how Jewish society became a target of criticism and, finally, an object of deadly attack and destruction.

PART I

The Legacy of the Middle Ages: Jewish Cultural Identity and the Price of Exclusiveness

1

The Jewish Quarters in German Towns during the Late Middle Ages

ALFRED HAVERKAMP

Daniel Cohen in Memoriam

In this essay I shall avoid the central theme of this volume, namely "ghetto," and resort instead to the more neutral concept of "Jewish quarter." This concept means no more than a rather large, spatially concentrated Jewish settlement.[1] In this way I wish to avoid a long-standing confusion that is still apparent, even in recent research. This confusion manifests itself, for example, in the *Encyclopaedia Judaica* under the entries "Jewish Quarter" and "Ghetto." The first asserts that the "ghetto did not appear as a permanent institution until its introduction in Venice in 1516." It is, however, conceded that the "idea of the ghetto in its restricted sense resulted from the tendency of Christianity from the fourth and fifth centuries to isolate the Jews and to humiliate them." The further use of the term "ghetto" for "quarters, neighborhoods, and areas throughout the Diaspora, which became places of residence for numerous Jews," is rejected as "erroneous."[2] In the same encyclopedia, however, we find under the heading of "Ghetto," and without any visible critical distance, that "it has come to indicate not only the legally established, coercive ghetto, but also the voluntary gathering of Jews in a secluded quarter, a process known in the Diaspora time as well, before compulsion was exercised." In this wider sense, therefore, "ghetto" means any Jewish settlement "in a secluded quarter."[3]

This study originated as part of a research project entitled "Zur Geschichte der Juden im hohen und späten Mittelalter in der Landschaft zwischen Maas und Rhein und angrenzenden Gebieten (C1)," directed by myself, a section of the Sonderforschungsbereich 235, "Zwischen Rhein und Maas," at the Universität Trier. This essay is essentially a written form of what I presented to the conference in Los Angeles. I am obliged to Franz-Josef Ziwes and Gerd Mentgen for their suggestions, as well as to Friedhelm Burgard, Christoph Cluse, and Daniel S. Mattern of the German Historical Institute.

1 The footnotes in this chapter are confined to the most important information. Quotations from German sources are translated in the text but kept in the original in the notes.
2 Cecil Roth, "Jewish Quarter," in *Encyclopaedia Judaica*, vol. 10 (Jerusalem, 1971), 81–4, 82.
3 Eli Davis, "Ghetto," in *Encyclopaedia Judaica*, vol. 7 (Jerusalem, 1971), 542–3; similarly, see Adolf Kober, in *Jüdisches Lexikon*, vol. 3 (Berlin, 1929), 457–60: "Erst allmählich, seit dem Ende des 13. Jhdts., ist in Deutschland das typische Judenviertel entstanden. Diese Judengassen oder -viertel sind nunmehr zur ausschliesslichen Wohnung der Juden bestimmt und gegen die christliche Umgebung durch Mauern und Tore abgesperrt."

The answers to the questions of when such "quarters" first came into existence in the German lands are as confusing as the various uses of the term "ghetto." According to Israel Abrahams, "compulsory ghettos" existed "in parts of Germany even in the twelfth and thirteenth century," while he confirms "voluntary congregations of Jews in certain parts of the towns" as "very common by the thirteenth century."[4] In his studies on the "yellow badge," the well-known legal historian Guido Kisch distinguishes between "garb and ghetto" as "voluntary" and as "compulsory institutions" in Germany. For him, the "development of the Ghetto" as "compulsory institution" began "at the end of the thirteenth century."[5] On the other hand, according to Helmut Veitshans's 1970 study this kind of compulsory living area for Jews is not supposed to have become common in Germany until the middle of the fourteenth century.[6] Markus Wenninger argues for an even later date. "In Germany," he writes, a "ghetto development in the particular sense, as a strict geographical separation of Jews from the Christian environment, achieved by the creation of walled-in Jewish residential areas outside of which Jews were forbidden to live," was "relatively rare and generally did not occur until the fifteenth century."[7]

---

4 Israel Abrahams, *Jewish Life in the Middle Ages* (London, 1896; reprinted: Cleveland, 1961), 62 note 3: "Though the era of the ghetto proper begins with the sixteenth century, numerous records are extant of the seclusion of Jews in special quarters several centuries earlier."

5 Guido Kisch, "The Yellow Badge in History," first published in *Historia Judaica* 19 (1959), reprinted in Kisch, *Forschungen zur Rechts-, Wirtschafts- und Sozialgeschichte der Juden* (Sigmaringen, 1979), 115–64, 121.

6 Helmut Veitshans, *Die Judensiedlungen der schwäbischen Reichsstädte und der württembergischen Landstädte im Mittelalter* (Stuttgart, 1970), 57; see also Veitshans, *Kartographische Darstellung der Judensiedlungen der schwäbischen Reichsstädte und der württemburgischen Landstädte im Mittelalter* (Stuttgart, 1970).

7 Markus J. Wenninger, *Man bedarf keiner Juden mehr: Ursachen und Hintergründe ihrer Vertreibung aus den deutschen Reichsstädten im 15. Jahrhundert* (Vienna, 1981), 37. According to Yosef Hayim Yerushalmi, "The enforced ghetto is a phenomenon and hallmark of early modern times." See his "Medieval Jewry: From within and from without," in Paul E. Szarmach, ed., *Aspects of Jewish Culture in the Middle Ages* (Albany, N.Y., 1979), 16. Research on this topic has varied greatly; in chronological order: Adolf Kober, *Das Grundbuch des Kölner Judenviertels: Ein Beitrag zur mittelalterlichen Topographie, Rechtsgeschichte und Statistik der Stadt Köln* (Bonn, 1920), 12: "Erst allmählich, seit dem Ende des 13. Jahrhunderts, ist das typische Judenghetto entstanden. . . . Die Unglücksjahre 1348/50 bilden hierbei insofern einen Abschnitt, als nach dieser Zeit die Juden dort Wohnung nehmen müssen, wo man sie ihnen zuweist, und diese vielfach in entlegenen Strassen und befristet." For a similar view, see Ellen Littmann, *Studien zur Wiederaufnahme der Juden durch die deutschen Städte nach dem schwarzen Tode* (Breslau, 1928), 25. Owing to the sources he consulted, Kurt Hönig, "Die Entwicklung der Rechtseinrichtung des Ghettoes im Rahmen des Judenrechts des deutschen Mittelalters," Ph.D. diss., Universität Münster, 1942, gives a more detailed view concerning our question than the author's anti-Semitism would suggest. According to Hönig, the "Zwang seitens des christlich-deutschen Wirtsvolkes" that led to the introduction of the ghetto, dates "frühestens . . . seit der 2. Hälfte des 14. Jahrhunderts"; it was an "unausbleibliche Konsequenz des mittelalterlichen Antisemitismus" and "in seiner Tragweite bisher durchweg bei weitem überschätzt worden" (214ff.). Mainly concentrated on early modern times is Willehad Paul Eckert, "Das Ghetto – Geschichte und Gestalt," *Germania Judaica: Mitteilungsblatt der Kölner Bibliothek zur Geschichte des deutschen Judentums* 5, nos. 2–3 (1966): 1–36. Eckert traces the "inneren [und] äusseren Gründe für die Entstehung des Ghettos" back to the

Let us conclude this brief survey of the literature with the observation that the use of the term "ghetto" as a description of Jewish settlement during the High and late Middle Ages is based on a distinction between "voluntary" and "compulsory" forms. That makes for obvious difficulties – reflected also in the different periodization – in deciding whether the Jews' own and in that sense "voluntary" intentions or externally imposed compulsions were indeed the determining or dominant factor. The distinction becomes even more problematic when the protection of the Jews by Christian authorities and the Jewish need for such protection are considered. In fact, the measures taken by the Christian leaders to protect the Jews from persecution probably always corresponded to the will of the Jews, even when – or still precisely because – their houses and settlements were thereby separated from the Christians'. Thus, Wenninger argues further that the "decisive factors" for the "beginnings of ghetto development in the early fourteenth century" were "without doubt" the "Jewish need for protection" and the desire of the "town authorities for law and order." This admittedly diminishes the fact that the Jews' "need for protection" depended on the degree of their supposed or actual threat from Christians, and such measures as were taken with regard to the Jews cannot, therefore, be evaluated as "fully voluntary," as Wenninger claims.[8]

Consequently, the existential factors for Jewish life in a Christian environment combined the need for protection and the granting of the same. Research that has, until now, usually dichotomized geographical segregation of Jewish settlements into "voluntary" or "compulsory" has proved unsatisfactory, if not misleading. Decisive for the formation of Jewish settlements – apart from religious and cultural requirements – was the Jewish need for protection within the Christian environment. But this depended essentially on the attitudes and behavioral codes of the Christians

High Middle Ages. My own earlier essay, "Die Juden im spätmittelalterlichen Trier," in Georg Droege et al., eds., *Verführung zur Geschichte* (Trier, 1973), 90–130, 125, employs the term ghetto in an unreflected way. Schlomo Spitzer, "Die jüdische Gemeinde im Mittelalter: Institutionen, Kompetenzen und Aufgaben," *Kairos* 21 (1979): 48–59, 58. Spitzer notes that bans on Christians selling in Jewish neighborhoods were not enforced until the end of the sixteenth century, when status differences were beginning to weaken in Europe and authorities tried to halt this process through legislation. For a superficial account, see Andreas Angerstorfer, "Von der Judensiedlung zum Ghetto in der mittelalterlichen Reichsstadt Regensburg," in Manfred Treml and Josef Kirmeier, eds., *Geschichte und Kultur der Juden in Bayern* (Munich, 1988), 161–72. Rather more useful is Benjamin C. I. Ravid, "From Geographical Realia to Historiographical Symbol: The Odyssey of the Word 'Ghetto,' " in David B. Ruderman, ed., *Essential Papers on Jewish Culture in Renaissance and Baroque Italy* (New York, 1992), 373–85. Citing the example of "the Jewish quarter of Frankfurt, established in 1492," Ravid notes that "segregated and enclosed Jewish quarters had existed prior to 1516 in a few places" (381), and he observes that the loose and imprecise use of the term may sometimes "involve a desire . . . to portray the life of the Jews in the Diaspora unfavorably" (384).

8 Wenninger, *Man bedarf keiner Juden mehr*, 38.

toward the Jews. It also depended on the relationship of the Jewish minority to the Christian majority, which was strongly determined by the latter.

Although the rather broad topic indicated so far must serve as our methodological guide, in this essay I shall concentrate on the geographical situation of Jewish quarters in medieval German towns. The major part of the discussion is devoted to an outline, or rather a sketch, of the typology of the towns and other places with Jewish residential areas as well as a typology of these settlements themselves. Following this typology, which must also include the location of Jewish settlements within the towns, I address the question of whether and to what extent we can accept the general opinion that the location of the Jewish domiciles and their geographical position in a town was an "expression of the social, economic, legal, and political position" of the Jews. Veitshans has, for example, formulated this thesis even more sharply.

The closer their [i.e., the Jews'] residential areas lay to the most important streets and squares of a town, the more significant was their situation; the farther away from the main streets and forced to the periphery they were, the less important was their economic and especially their social position.[9]

The difficulties of formulating a typology of the towns and places that included short- or long-term Jewish settlements is immediately apparent in the quantitative findings. In the two centuries from the middle of the twelfth century to the time of the Black Death, the number of Jewish settlements rose from about 50 to somewhat over 1,000. This increase followed in the wake of urbanization, during a period in which the number of towns within the *regnum teutonicum* increased from about 500 to 3,500 – or about sevenfold. But nine-tenths of the 3,500 towns had fewer than 4,000 inhabitants and a walled residential area of at most 30 hectares; some two-thirds of the total had even fewer than 2,000 inhabitants, all the way down to very small towns that were virtually indistinguishable from villages. After the first half of the fourteenth century, the proportion of minor towns and/or towns with stunted growth increased considerably.[10] From the end of the thirteenth century onward, small towns accumulated in western and southern Germany, notably in the central Rhineland, in Swabia, and in Alsace – traditional homelands in which Jews had settled in large numbers through the middle of the fourteenth century.[11]

---

9 Veitshans, *Judensiedlungen*, 58.

10 Alfred Haverkamp, *Medieval Germany, 1056–1273* (Oxford, 1988; reprinted: 1990), 173ff., 294ff., and especially, Heinz Stoob, "Die hochmittelalterliche Städtebildung im Okzident," in Stoob, ed., *Die Stadt: Gestalt und Wandel bis zum industriellen Zeitalter* (Cologne, 1979), 131–56; Stoob, "Stadtformen und städtisches Leben im späten Mittelalter," in *Die Stadt,* 157–95; see also the recent survey by Eberhard Isenmann, *Die deutsche Stadt im Spätmittelalter, 1250–1500* (Stuttgart, 1988), 26ff.

11 On the basis of *Germania Judaica,* vol. 2: *Von 1238 bis zur Mitte des 14. Jahrhunderts,* ed. Zvi Avneri, 2 pts. (Tübingen, 1968), I have endeavored to place this phenomenon in a wider context in the

The findings reveal a preponderance of Jewish settlements in small towns or markets that very often go back to palatinate, castle, and administrative locations. This tendency became even more pronounced after the mid-fourteenth century. This applies particularly to half the total after 1350, that is, those approximately 500 locations where no Jews had been evident before 1350. From the beginning of the expulsions from larger towns at the turn of the fifteenth century, Jewish communities were increasingly concentrated in small towns, where the various territorial rulers maintained tighter control. Moreover, in the course of the fifteenth century the proportion of Jewish settlements in villages also greatly increased.[12]

It would be going too far, typologically, to distinguish between the places of settlement on the basis of their constitutional and economic features. I restrict myself to those approximately 24 towns in which – as the material in *Germania Judaica* reveals – around 150 or more Jews may have lived temporarily between the second half of the fourteenth and the first decades of the sixteenth century.[13] Almost half of the towns – namely, Cologne, Hildesheim, Magdeburg, Mainz, Worms, Bamberg, Würzburg, Augsburg, Regensburg, Basel, and Constance – were originally cathedral towns. Politically and, in part, legally, however, they held the status of "free towns" or "imperial cities," though the bishops generally claimed or enforced rights over the Jews within the towns. The royal boroughs or imperial cities of Frankfurt am Main, Nuremberg, Rothenburg ob der Tauber, Esslingen, Erfurt, and Eger fall into a very similar category.[14] The remaining towns with sometimes extensive Jewish settlements, such as Braunschweig, Landshut, Munich, Vienna, Wiener-Neustadt, Breslau, and Prague, were princely capitals or residential towns. Of these 25 towns, the only ones where the Jews never suffered expulsion until the first decades of the sixteenth century were Frankfurt am Main, Worms, Würzburg, and

---

essay, "Lebensbedingungen der Juden in spätmittelalterlichen Deutschland," in Dirk Blasius and Dan Diner, eds., *Zerbrochene Geschichte: Leben und Selbstverständnis der Juden in Deutschland* (Frankfurt/Main, 1991), 11–31.

12 Haverkamp, "Lebensbedingungen," 20–3, and see my "Die Juden im mittelalterlichen Deutschland," in Staatliches Friedrich-Wilhelm-Gymnasium Trier, ed., *Jahresbericht 1986/87* (Trier, 1988): 233–53; also, see the next note.

13 *Germania Judaica*, vol. 3: *1350–1519*, ed. Arye Maimon, no. 1: *Ortschaftsartikel Aach-Lychen* (Tübingen, 1987). Thanks to the kindness of the late editor, who beginning in the early 1970s has encouraged many younger medievalists to study the history of the Jews in German-speaking regions, I was able to consult a draft of the second number of this volume, which should appear in 1993 (cited here as *Germania Judaica*, vol. 3, no. 2). The project, which will include a third number on territories, is being continued by Mordechai Breuer (Jerusalem).

14 Michael Toch, "Siedlungsstruktur der Juden Mitteleuropas im Wandel vom Mittelalter zur Neuzeit," in Alfred Haverkamp and Franz-Josef Ziwes, eds., *Juden in der christlichen Umwelt während des späten Mittelalters* (Berlin, 1992), 29–39. This study is likewise based on the material from *Germania Judaica*, cited previously.

Prague, though the number of Jews in each of these towns from time to time decreased sharply.

The severe reduction of the Jewish population within these settlements after the mid-fourteenth century – at least within the traditional German homelands and in some cases anticipated by the persecutions of 1336–8 – is also evident from the decline in the number of traceable synagogues. In Alsace, in the first half of the fourteenth century, for example, there is evidence – as my student Gerd Mentgen shows in his doctoral thesis – for 13 or 14 synagogues serving a total of almost 50 urban Jewish settlements, which makes a ratio of about 1 to 3.5. In the second half of the same century, the number of synagogues declined to either 4 or 5 and the number of urban settlements to about 27, so that the ratio becomes about 1 to 6. This relation remained basically unchanged until 1520. Moreover, not until the last decades of the fifteenth century do we see an increase in the number of Jewish cemeteries in Alsace. This development might be related to the dramatic increase in the number of Jewish settlements in villages, eventually even outnumbering those in urban areas.[15]

The Jewish residential areas in small communities and in the many settlements where, especially after 1349, only one or a very few Jewish families lived remained restricted to a few houses or a single Jewish enclave (*Judenhof*). Similar enclaves were occupied by Christians in many towns, and they could be extended with additional structures built in courtyards or in a cul-de-sac.[16] In such a complex, the Jews in Donauwörth – a town with fewer than 20 hectares of walled residential area – lived until 1493 in more than sixteen dwellings near the town hall and corn market.[17]

Perhaps more common than the sources verify, more or less small Jewish settlements or residences also developed in suburbs or in parts of the towns outside the jurisdiction of the municipal authorities that had expelled the Jews. Evidence from the second half of the fifteenth century exists for Hildesheim-Neustadt and Halle-Neuwerk, from the sixteenth century

15 Gerd Mentgen, "Studien zur Geschichte der Juden im mittelalterlichen Elsass," Ph.D. diss., Universität Trier, forthcoming; for an equally sharp analysis concerning the area of the Middle Rhine, see the dissertation of Franz-Josef Ziwes, "Studien zur Geschichte der Juden im mittleren Rheingebiet während des späten Mittelalters," Ph.D. diss., Universität Trier, forthcoming; on the archbishopric of Trier, see Alfred Haverkamp, "Die Juden im Erzstift Trier während des Mittelalters," in Alfred Ebenbauer and Klaus Zatloukal, eds., *Die Juden in ihrer mittelalterlichen Umwelt* (Vienna, 1991), 67–89.

16 See, e.g., the findings of Veitshans, *Kartographische Darstellung*. A *Judenhof* is mentioned in the sources for Schwäbisch-Gmünd, a *Judenhaus* for Lindau (see entries in *Germania Judaica*, vol. 3, no. 2). For another *Judenhof*, in Alsatian Reichenweier (Riquewihr), see Moses Ginsburger, "Der Judenhof in Reichenweier," *Mein Elsassland* 2 (1922): 203.

17 *Germania Judaica*, vol. 3, no. 1, 237, and note 48 to this chapter.

for Goslar, Göttingen-Weende, and Hannover-Neustadt, to give but a few examples.[18]

After the middle of the fourteenth century, larger Jewish communities were to be found in only a very small percentage of all settlements. This is known to have had far-reaching effects on the ability of the Jewish community to exercise its functions. After 1349, considerably fewer Jews than before lived in these relatively few major settlements, the great majority of which had seen pogroms at the time of the Black Death. (Of the Jewish communities in the 24 towns mentioned earlier, only the Jews of Regensburg, Prague, Vienna, Wiener-Neustadt, and Graz were spared.) The situation was probably similar in the vast majority of other towns, where fewer than 150 Jews settled after the middle of the fourteenth century.

I would like to illustrate this by the example of the episcopal city and *civitas libera* of Trier. It can be shown that around 1338 about fifty Jewish families lived in the *vicus iudeorum*, an area near the cathedral immunity and leading away from the marketplace. They used this enclosed section of 0.7 hectares – appointed with at least three gates – so intensively that even today, almost 650 years after the pogrom of 1349, this Jewish quarter still has the greatest density of buildings within the old town (Figure 1.1). The houses were held in hereditary leasehold or had been acquired at high prices in the previous decades. Between the resettlement around 1370 and the expulsion of 1418, no more than twelve to fifteen families lived in the Jewish quarter at any given time, and then only for a short period.[19]

A similar building density, and thus also a constriction similar to the situation in Trier before 1349, was, at a later date, not reached even in Regensburg, one of the three largest Jewish communities after the middle of the fourteenth century. There, shortly before the expulsion of 1519, almost 600 Jews lived in approximately thirty "obviously multi-story Jewish houses," which "in some cases had additional structures to the rear." The

18 For Passau, see note 45 to this chapter; for Hildesheim, see *Germania Judaica*, vol. 3, no. 1, 555–6; mention of Jewish settlement "auf der dompröbstlichen Neustadt bereits vor 1478," i.e., after the expulsion from the Old Town in 1457, "vor dem Goschentor" near the former Jewish cemetery in Rotraud Ries, "Soziale und politische Bedingungen jüdischen Lebens in Niedersachsen im 15. und 16. Jahrhundert," Ph.D. diss., Universität Münster, 1990, 42. A map, albeit somewhat difficult to read, is to be found in Peter Aufgebauer, *Die Geschichte der Juden in der Stadt Hildesheim im Mittelalter und in der frühen Neuzeit* (Hildesheim, 1984), 76. For Halle, see *Germania Judaica*, vol. 3, no. 1, 498–9, and Fritz Backhaus, "Judenfeindschaft und Judenvertreibungen im Mittelalter: Zur Ausweisung der Juden aus dem Mittelelberaum im 15. Jahrhundert," *Jahrbuch für die Geschichte Ost- und Mitteldeutschlands* 36 (1987): 275–332. Neumarkt was the craftsmen settlement near Stift Neuwerk, north of Mortizburg castle, founded by the archbishop of Magdeburg after 1479 on the spot where Jews had been living until 1454–8. For Göttingen-Weende, see *Germania Judaica*, vol. 3, no. 1, 448, and Ries, "Soziale und politische Bedingungen," 174ff., for Hannover-Neustadt, ibid., 142ff.

19 Alfred Haverkamp, "Die Juden im mittelalterlichen Trier," *Kurtrierisches Jahrbuch* 19 (1979): 5–57, 32.

Figure 1.1. The settlement of the Jewish quarter in Trier to ca. 1349. Scale is 1:333⅓. Sequential numbers in circles designated by author. (Based on Delhougne and Lutz, *Modellplan Bebauung 1800;* drawn by Thelen, draft by Haverkamp.)

total area was only 1.2 hectares. After the middle of the fourteenth century, only Jews would have lived inside the Regensburg Jewish quarter, which had been provided, even before 1350, with a surrounding wall and six gates that the Jews themselves opened and closed.[20]

20 *Germania Judaica*, vol. 3, no. 2, under "Regensburg." For the community of Regensburg, see also Raphael Straus, *Die Judengemeinde Regensburg im ausgehenden Mittelalter* (Heidelberg, 1932), and his *Regensburg and Augsburg* (Philadelphia, 1939).

On the other hand, as a result of the pogrom of 1349, considerably more Christians than before lived in Trier's *vicus iudeorum*. It may also be generally assumed that this applied in towns where fewer Jews inhabited the Jewish quarters after the severe pogroms at the close of the thirteenth century and especially during the Black Death.

As a rule, it may also be assumed that the Jews, both before and after the middle of the fourteenth century, lived in a very close-knit manner. It was, of course, by no means always possible, particularly after the pogroms, to reestablish this communality. The few Jews who settled in Salzburg after the pogrom of 1404 and remained there until the final expulsion of 1498 did not live in the centrally situated Jewish row but were spread out over the town.[21] It is necessary to distinguish such instances from those relatively few cases in which several Jewish residences or settlements existed in one town, owing to constitutional factors. The best-known example of this is Magdeburg. Before and after 1350, most Magdeburger Jews lived in a "Jewish village" (*Judendorf*) in the suburb of Sudenburg, which was under the protectorship of the archbishop. In contrast, Jews subject to the town council's jurisdiction lived in the middle of the old town, near the town hall.[22]

One of the decisive questions in the scholarly discussion of the predecessors and early forms of the ghetto was whether the close-knit manner in which the Jews lived led to the creation of a walled or otherwise segregated, solely Jewish settlement. Precisely these criteria, it is well known, were the essence of those decrees which the papal envoy issued at the provincial Synod of Breslau in 1267, thereby tightening the resolutions of the Fourth Lateran Council (1215). Not even in Breslau, however, were these resolutions enforced in the subsequent period.[23] Equally well known is that the Council of Basel, in 1434, forbade cohabitation of Jews and Christians and demanded further that Jews should be forced to live as far away from Christians and churches as possible.[24]

In the few towns in which the Jewish quarters or alleys were separated from Christian areas by means of a wall or other structure, Christians also

---

21 *Germania Judaica,* vol. 3, no. 2, under "Salzburg" and under "Salzwedel." For Esslingen, see *Germania Judaica,* vol. 3, no. 1, 334.

22 For Magdeburg, see Alexander Pinthus, *Die Judensiedlungen der deutschen Städte: Eine stadtbiologische Studie* (Berlin, 1931), 40 ff. Backhaus, under "Judenfeindschaft," 280. *Germania Judaica,* vol. 3, no. 2. For Halle, *Germania Judaica,* vol. 2, 319–22, and ibid., vol. 3, no. 1, 498–507. Backhaus, "Judenfeindschaft," 291ff. For Halberstadt, *Germania Judaica,* vol. 2, 317–19, and ibid., vol. 3, no. 1, 495 note 1.

23 Julius Aronius, *Regesten zur Geschichte der Juden im Fränkischen und Deutschen Reiche bis 1273* (Berlin, 1887–1902; reprinted: Hildesheim, 1970), 301ff., no. 724; *Germania Judaica,* vol. 2, 129.

24 Max Simonsohn, *Die kirchliche Judengesetzgebung im Zeitalter der Reformkonzilien von Konstanz und Basel* (Breslau, 1912), 37–45; for a recent survey, see Johannes Helmrath, *Das Basler Konzil, 1431–1449: Forschungsstand und Probleme* (Cologne, 1987), with a brief passage (336–7) on the decree of September 7, 1434, regarding Jews and neophytes.

lived among the Jews, often as next-door neighbors, until the middle of
the fourteenth century. This applied to Trier as much as to Cologne, Vienna, or Regensburg. Only in Worms is there as yet "no evidence that before, or even after 1349, there were also Christian inhabitants of the Jewish
alley," according to Fritz Reuter.[25] There is no reliable evidence for Vienna
until the period between 1350 and 1421,[26] and for Regensburg and Worms
until somewhat later.[27] But since no pogroms occurred in Regensburg and
Vienna in the middle of the fourteenth century, and the Jewish settlement
in Worms was resurrected in the same location after 1349, one cannot speak
of a movement to segregate the Jews in any of these cases. In contrast, this
meager information is outweighed by a great deal of evidence for the cohabitation of Jews and Christians, for example, in Cologne, Trier, Braunschweig, Hildesheim, Magdeburg, Prague, Wiener-Neustadt, Graz,
Frankfurt am Main (until 1460), Bamberg, Nuremberg, and Rothenburg
ob der Tauber – all of them with larger Jewish settlements.[28]

In the three other cases mentioned, it would also make little sense to
ask whether Jewish residential segregation reflected their wishes or
was imposed upon them. It is worth mentioning, though not a compelling
argument, that one of the German law books, a treatise by lawyer John
Purgolt from 1503–4, contains a regulation that would imply such compulsory measures: "Their houses should be separate from us Christians
and next to one another, and ropes be stretched out across the lanes."[29]
A regulation concerning the distinctive clothing of the Jews followed
this law. It is also certain, however, that the walling in of the Jewish
quarter in Vienna in the 1360s was done at the request of a Jewish resident.[30] Likewise, closing a street by means of ropes and chains was in no
way peculiar to Jewish alleys, as can be supported by evidence from
Nuremberg (1378) and Hildesheim (1411).[31] Therefore, the erection of

25 Fritz Reuter, *Warmaisa: 1000 Jahre Juden in Worms* (Worms, 1984), 90ff., 91; see, however, *Germa-
    nia Judaica,* vol. 2, 922 note 39; also, see note 47 to this chapter.
26 *Germania Judaica,* vol. 3, no. 2, under "Wien."
27 *Germania Judaica,* vol. 3, no. 2, under "Regensburg" and under "Worms."
28 See the entries in *Germania Judaica,* vol. 3. Until 1313, even the chapel of Sankt Moritz in Nurem-
    berg fell within the limits of the Jewish Quarter. See ibid., vol. 2, 602. The situation in Augsburg is
    less certain. See ibid., vol. 3, no. 1, 40 with note 12.
29 "Ir [i.e., the Jews'] huser sullen gesundert sey us den cristen und beyeinander, und seyle uber die
    gassen gezcogenn." Quoted in Guido Kisch, *Jewry-Law in Medieval Germany: Laws and Court Deci-
    sions concerning Jews* (New York, 1949), 116; see also Veitshans, *Judensiedlungen,* 56–7, and note 31
    to this chapter.
30 Ignaz Schwarz, *Das Wiener Ghetto: Seine Häuser und seine Bewohner,* vol. 1: *Das Judenviertel in der in-
    neren Stadt bis zu seiner Aufhebung im Jahre 1421* (Vienna, 1909), 40; *Germania Judaica,* vol. 3, no. 2,
    under "Wien."
31 *Germania Judaica,* vol. 3, no. 2, under "Nürnberg." In 1378, a "chainpole" (*Kettenstock*) was dug in
    "bei den Juden" to protect them against assaults. Aufgebauer, *Die Geschichte der Juden in der Stadt*

ropes within the newer Augsburg Jewish quarter (allegedly 1434) cannot simply be regarded, as has been done, as an anti-Jewish measure,[32] particularly since the same measure could have been undertaken to mark the Jewish *Eruv*.[33]

Even the tendency to limit the number of the Jews, which clearly can be made out in some towns even before the fourteenth century, cannot always be interpreted as solely anti-Jewish. Such intentions or measures must be seen in relation to the "laws of amortization" (*leges de non amortizando*), the means by which citizens in episcopal towns acted against the accumulation of ecclesiastical, and thus in a wider sense lordly, properties.[34] These tendencies also constituted attempts to maintain a legal and financial monopoly and to strengthen authority – a phenomenon that cannot be fully examined here.[35]

I will concentrate instead on the question of where the Jewish quarters and alleys were situated in the towns. One of the many new findings of the *Germania Judaica* is the observation that in the majority of the approximately 500 locations where Jews resettled after 1349, often after an interval of more than a decade, they generally relocated to places they had previously occu-

---

Hildesheim, 14, 29: there is evidence that in 1437 chains were not only fixed to the Jewish alley, where they already appear in 1411 but also to the adjacent Ropemakers' Street. For ropes as instruments of segregation, see John Purgolt. Also, see Hönig, "Entwicklung," 125–6, 227–8.

32 *Germania Judaica*, vol. 3, no. 1, 40, "Die jüngere Judengasse wurde durch gespannte Seile abgesperrt (1434)," with reference to Richard Grünfeld, *Ein Gang durch die Geschichte der Juden in Augsburg* (Augsburg, 1917), 33. In fact, Grünfeld refers to a "moderation" of the clothing regulations decreed four weeks earlier after the Jews had requested "dass sie wenigstens in der Judengasse, 'als weyt ir saile ussgespannen seind,' und beim Gottesdienste ohne Judenzeichen gehen dürfen."

33 See preceding note; in his study, Hönig quotes from the records of the Nuremberg Council of 1484: "Item der Judischhait ist vergönnt, uf eins rats widderruffen ein dratt von dem prunnen eins zu ziehen, darunter sie an iren sabbath nach dem gesetze wasser holen mögen," Hönig, "Entwicklung," 125. Also, see Eckert, "Das Ghetto," 2, and Zvi Kaplan, "Eruv," in *Encyclopaedia Judaica*, vol. 6 (Jerusalem, 1971), 849–50.

34 Franz Irsigler, "Amortisationsgesetze," in *Lexikon des Mittelalters*, vol. 1 (Munich, 1980), 542–3; Bernd Moeller, "Kleriker als Bürger," in *Festschrift für Hermann Heimpel zum 70. Geburtstag am 19. September 1971*, vol. 2 (Göttingen, 1972), 195–224. The regulations decreed by the city council of Cologne in 1341 "dass fortan Juden Immobilien von Christen nur mit einstimmiger Genehmigung des Rates erwerben dürfen" also has to be seen in this context; *Germania Judaica*, vol. 2, 426. Such measures developed from a very early date in the imperial city of Metz, where there were no Jews. On this, see Pierre Mendel, *Les atours de la ville de Metz: Étude sur la législation municipale de Metz au Moyen Age* (Metz, 1932) and the soon-to-be-published study by Margit Müller, "Im Schnittpunkt von Stadt und Land: Die Benediktinerabtei St. Arnulf zu Metz im hohen und späten Mittelalter," Ph.D. diss., Universität Trier, 1991, chap. 3.2.2.2. Of general interest concerning this problem, see Ernst Voltmer, *Reichsstadt und Herrschaft: Zur Geschichte der Stadt Speyer im hohen und späten Mittelalter* (Trier, 1981), 105ff., and Alfred Haverkamp, " 'Zweyungen, Zwist und Missehel' zwischen Erzbischof und Stadtgemeinde in Trier im Jahre 1377," *Kurtrierisches Jahrbuch* 21 (1981): 22–54.

35 See Haverkamp, "Lebensbedingungen," 26ff., and " 'Innerstädtische Auseinandersetzungen' und überlokale Zusammenhänge in deutschen Städten des Spätmittelalters," in Reinhard Elze and Gina Fasoli, eds., *Stadtadel und Bürgertum in den italienischen und deutschen Städten des Spätmittelalters* (Berlin, 1991), 89–126.

pied.[36] Exceptions include Nuremberg, Strasbourg, Würzburg, Rothenburg ob der Tauber, and perhaps Goslar, where no pogrom took place during the middle of the fourteenth century. In Nuremburg, the area where the Jewish quarter had been was used as the town's main market after the Sabbath pogrom of December 5, 1349. The erstwhile synagogue was converted into a church devoted to Saint Mary, which served as a chapel for the town council. Jewish houses were given over to Nuremburg patricians, some of whom had protested strongly to the emperor when in 1344 a Jew bought the house of one of their peers, Heinrich Holzschuher.[37] Without doubt, Jewish aspiration toward this location and these houses was one of the most important motives that induced the new pro-Luxemburger patrician council to plan the extermination of the Jews.[38] The value of the former Jewish quarter increased sharply when the two towns of Saint Sebald and Saint Lorenz, which had until then been topographically separated, were unified at about the same time. Jews who were readmitted after December 1349 were allowed to settle an already partly developed area a few hundred meters farther to the east and yet far enough from Saint Sebald's city wall, which dated from Staufen times.[39]

In Strasbourg, the houses belonging to the Jews who had been murdered in February 1349 had long ago passed into the hands of burghers or been put to other uses, when in 1369 the city readmitted Jews. These Jews probably settled, until their final expulsion only two decades later, on the place of their former cemetery, northeast of the city wall and not far from the former Jewish row.[40] Despite the fact that even more time had elapsed since the pogrom of 1349 and the first settlement of Jews in Würzburg (where a marketplace had been established on the spot of the Jewish quarter), the new

36 Haverkamp, "Lebensbedingungen," 21ff.; Toch, "Siedlungsstruktur."
37 *Germania Judaica,* vol. 2, 602, with note 51; see Wolfgang von Stromer, "Die Metropole im Aufstand gegen König Karl IV. Nürnberg zwischen Wittelsbach und Luxemburg, Juni 1348–September 1349. Mit einer Beilage 'Das hochmittelalterliche Judenviertel Nürnbergs,' eine topographische Rekonstruktion von Karl Kohn," *Mitteilungen des Vereins für Geschichte der Stadt Nürnberg* 65 (1978): 55–90.
38 Alfred Haverkamp, "Die Judenverfolgungen zur Zeit des Schwarzen Todes im Gesellschaftsgefüge deutscher Städte," in Haverkamp, ed., *Zur Geschichte der Juden im Deutschland des späten Mittelalters und der frühen Neuzeit* (Stuttgart, 1981), 27–93; and with only minor variations, František Graus, *Pest – Geissler – Judenmorde: Das 14. Jahrhundert als Krisenzeit* (Göttingen, 1987; 2nd ed., 1988), 155ff., 208–13; also Johannes Heil, "Vorgeschichte und Hintergründe des Frankfurter Pogroms von 1349," *Hessisches Jahrbuch für Landesgeschichte* 41 (1991): 105–51; Amalie Fössel, "Der 'Schwarze Tod' in Franken, 1348–1350," *Mitteilungen des Vereins für die Geschichte der Stadt Nürnberg* 74 (1987): 1–75.
39 Fritz Schnelbögl, "Topographische Entwicklung im 14. und 15. Jahrhundert," in Gerhard Pfeiffer, ed., *Nürnberg – Geschichte einer europäischen Stadt* (Munich, 1971), 88–92.
40 Mentgen, "Studien."

settlement was not far from the old one.[41] In Rothenburg, the area near the marketplace that had served as the Jewish quarter was no longer available to Jews returning to this imperial city about 1370. Instead, Jews were given a newly habitable area only 100 meters away, on the site of the town's first moat and old fortifications, which by the beginning of the thirteenth century had already been replaced by considerably extended walled defenses.[42] At Goslar, the new Jewish quarter, acquired between 1337 and 1368, lay in an even more central position than before.[43]

The relocation of Jewish residential areas carried out later did not always turn out to be disadvantageous for the Jews. Owing to the construction of fortifications in Augsburg between 1376 and 1389, the Wagenhals suburb where Jews had lived until then was demolished, forcing their relocation to an even more central position within the town.[44] In contrast, there is little doubt that the transfer of the Jews of Passau from the Jewish blocks near the market and the banks of the Inn River, where Christians also lived, to the *oppidulum iudeorum* before the episcopal castle, on the right bank of the Ilz River, was related to anti-Jewish measures, or occurred in their wake.[45]

Previous research has justly paid much attention to the events in the prominent trading town of Frankfurt am Main – as much, that is, as contemporaries did. In 1462, the Jews, who had been subjected to repeated intrusions by the Habsburg royal and imperial courts as well as to continuous pressure from the religious establishment of this imperial city, were eventually displaced from their previous settlement near Saint Bartholomew's Church. Against their will, and without regard to Jewish readiness to raise the walls higher between the synagogue and the church where the *rex Romanorum* was elected, the Frankfurt Jews were forced into an area around the *Wollgraben* near the old city wall. On the site of the former Jewish quar-

---

41 *Germania Judaica*, vol. 2, 931; ibid., vol. 3, no. 2, under "Würzburg," and Winfried Schich, *Würzburg im Mittelalter: Studien zum Verhältnis von Topographie und Bevölkerungsstruktur* (Cologne, 1977), 160.

42 Veithans, *Kartographische Darstellung*, 1, 8; Erich Keyser and Heinz Stoob, eds., *Deutsches Städtebuch: Handbuch städtischer Geschichte*, vol. 5: *Bayerisches Städtebuch* (Stuttgart, 1971), 461; *Germania Judaica*, vol. 3, no. 2, under "Rothenburg."

43 *Germania Judaica*, vol. 3, no. 1, 450; see Alfred Haverkamp, "Topografia e relazioni sociali nelle città tedesche del tardo medioevo," in Jean-Claude Maire Vigeur, ed., *D'une ville à l'autre: Structures matérielles et organisation d'espace dans les villes européennes (XIIIe–XIVe siècles)* (Rome, 1989), 25–54; *Germania Judaica*, vol. 3, no. 2, under "Stuttgart"; Veithans, *Judensiedlungen*, 46–7, and *Kartographische Darstellung*, 21.

44 *Germania Judaica*, vol. 3, no. 1, 40.

45 See W. M. Schmid, "Zur Geschichte der Juden in Passau," *Zeitschrift für die Geschichte der Juden in Deutschland* 1 (1929): 119–35; cf. Josef Kirmeier, *Die Juden und andere Randgruppen: Zur Frage der Randständigkeit im mittelalterlichen Landshut* (Landshut, 1988), 113. Kirmeier's statement that "Die Judengasse wurde in der 2. Hälfte des 14. Jahrhunderts häufig zum Ghetto, fernab von den zentralen Handelsplätzen" is in error; *Germania Judaica*, vol. 3, no. 2, under "Passau."

1557682

LIBRARY
College of St. Francis
JOLIET, ILLINOIS

ter, the town council erected houses and communal buildings, thus ending Jewish ownership of land and houses. The Jews made futile attempts to oppose the measure, notably by arguing that they were losing the armed protection of their Christian neighbors. But the council regarded this resettlement as an alternative to expulsion.[46] Jews had, by this time, already been removed from half of those two dozen towns with major Jewish settlements: Strasbourg, in 1390; Vienna, in 1421; Cologne, in 1424; Augsburg, in 1438–40; Graz, in 1438; Munich, in about 1442; Constance, in 1448; Landshut, in about 1450; Breslau, in 1453; Erfurt, in 1453–4; Esslingen, in 1453–65; and Hildesheim, in 1457.

The expulsions continued during subsequent years. Transfers like the one that occurred in Frankfurt am Main, however, can be seen to have taken place only in the small imperial town of Donauwörth in 1493.[47] Probably instigated by a preacher, the town decreed a sharply anti-Jewish *Judenordnung* at about the same time. The eviction of the Jews from their homes into a street regarded as filthy was a move of little more than 100 meters.[48]

Until the first decades of the sixteenth century, towns banished Jews to peripheral, isolated residential areas only rarely, and then mainly in those towns where jurisdiction over the Jews comprised one of the most important holdovers of royal or imperial authority. Compared with expulsion and other anti-Jewish measures, resettlement within the town was of only marginal importance, even taking into account the key role played by Frankfurt am Main. This state of affairs is confirmed by the fact that geographical segregation of Christian minorities – for example, prostitutes, beggars, and representatives of dishonorable trades – did not

---

46 *Germania Judaica*, vol. 3, no. 1, 347; Fritz Backhaus, "Die Einrichtung eines Ghettos für die Frankfurter Juden im Jahre 1462," *Hessisches Jahrbuch für Landesgeschichte* 39 (1989): 59–86.

47 From a quarrel between Count Philipp of Hanau and the town of Friedberg, we have evidence of the community's intent to force the "unter hanauischer Lehnshoheit stehenden Friedberger Juden in eine gesonderte Gasse." This, however, failed, and so did a second attempt in 1497. At the time, the Jews were in fear of being "beslossen gehalten," after the "example" of Frankfurt am Main and Worms. See Uta Löwenstein, ed., *Quellen zur Geschichte der Juden im Hessischen Hauptstaatsarchiv Marburg, 1267–1600*, vol. 3 (Wiesbaden, 1989), 233–4. Thanks to Franz-Josef Ziwes for drawing my attention to this source.

48 *Germania Judaica*, vol. 3, no. 1, 328. The source for this anti-Jewish measure is Johannes Knebel, member of the Cistercian abbey of Kaisheim, in his hometown chronicle. Universität Augsburg, Bibliothek, Cod. III.2.2.18, fol. 199r–v. From the context of this chronicle, the "Ölgasse" need not have been regarded as particularly filthy before the Jews were forced to settle there. On the author (d. 1530), see Maria Zelzer, *Geschichte der Stadt Donauwörth von den Anfängen bis 1618*, 2nd ed. (Donauwörth, 1979), 139ff. On the topography, see Veitshans, *Kartographische Darstellung*, 3–4, 19. The regulations referred to by Knebel, with their extreme restriction of the Jews' freedom of movement, are edited in Raphael Straus, *Urkunden und Aktenstücke zur Geschichte der Juden in Regensburg, 1453–1738* (Munich, 1960), 282–83, no. 807.

go beyond a few preliminary attempts until the first half of the sixteenth century.[49]

These findings also do not support the notion, widely found in research on Jewish quarters, that there was a negative social gradient from a town's center to its periphery. This notion may apply to individual towns, such as Nuremberg, which grew out of small nuclei. By their outstanding economic attractiveness, the towns spawned a kind of receiving camp on the suburban periphery and even marked it off in their taxation systems. But the concept of a social gradient from center to periphery cannot be applied to the numerous small towns, including those places that can hardly be called towns, where the bulk of the Jews settled and dwelled in the German lands during the later Middle Ages. Because of their size, these towns offered no possibility for topographical differentiation.

The supposed gradients, particularly in such small urban settlements, were interrupted by the arrival of local highways that assigned a functionally central role to the outer areas. At least as important within the *regnum teutonicum,* with its diversified structure of lordship, were the conditions of constitutional topography, which, for example, could transform the geographical periphery by the existence of monasteries or other religious institutions, even in the suburbs, into centers of economic importance.

Aspects of historical genesis, together with the constitutional topography, raise doubts about the applicability of modern social categories of "central" versus "peripheral." Eminently more important for the determination of the location of Jewish quarters in German towns was the time at which Jews had obtained permission to settle. That the overwhelming percentage of Jewish settlements in towns of the *regnum teutonicum* were centrally situated is a consequence of the early presence of Jews in the urbanization process of central Europe, where they were welcomed or appeared as indispensable.

The discrimination against the Jews, the persecutions, the pogroms, the expulsions, and – as a hardly effective substitute for the expulsions – the topographical displacement of the Jews were equally complex. Much more important than the relatively few shifts in settlement preceding and following the Black Death were the legal changes that occurred after that time. Among these was the more or less pronounced deterioration in the Jews' proprietary rights, the effect of which was significantly increased by the impoverishment of many Jews, increased tax burdens, arbitrary dispossession,

---

49 Haverkamp, "Topographia e relazioni sociali"; or more directly, Werner Buchholz, "Anfänge der Sozialdisziplinierung im Mittelalter," *Zeitschrift für Historische Forschung* 18 (1991): 129–47. Jews are treated in a questionable combination with "marginal groups" in Bernd-Ulrich Hergemöller, ed., *Randgruppen der spätmittelalterlichen Gesellschaft: Ein Hand- und Studienbuch* (Warendorf, 1990).

and cancellation of debts owed to the Jews. Equally disadvantageous were, on the one hand, temporal restrictions on residence permission and the attempts of other rulers to restrict the Jews' freedom of movement, on the other. These and other conditions increased considerably the geographical mobility of the Jews and their restlessness, while weakening their attachment to place of residence and the wider environment. Consequently, and because so few Jews lived in the majority of settlements, only restricted possibilities of development remained for Jewish community life.[50]

These were further restricted by the now widespread contractual agreements of Christian rulers with individual Jews or heads of families. The Jews thus increasingly found themselves in the crossfire between competing rulers. Among this group, the urban communities – or rather the town councils – tended to extend monopoly rights and exclusive authority, which also, and particularly – even if by no means solely – sought to control the Jews' everyday life. These factors, including the economic and, above all, religious and ecclesiastical processes and developments, which I can only hint at here, altered the Jews' living conditions more fundamentally than the location and arrangement of their housing.[51] Nevertheless, in spite of the general deterioration in the Jews' situation, good personal relations between individual Christians and Jews still existed in the late medieval period.[52]

---

50 Eric Zimmer, *Harmony and Discord: An Analysis of the Decline of Jewish Self-Government in Fifteenth-Century Central Europe* (New York, 1970); Israel Jacob Yuval, *Rabbis and Rabbinate in Germany, 1350–1500* [in Hebrew] (Jerusalem, 1988).
51 Haverkamp, "Lebensbedingungen."
52 See, e.g., Wolfgang von Stromer, "Wassernot und Wasserkünste im Bergbau des Mittelalters und der frühen Neuzeit," in Werner Kroker and Ekkehard Westermann, eds., *Montanwirtschaft Mitteleuropas vom 12. bis 17. Jahrhundert* (Bochum, 1984), 50–72, esp. 52, 56–8, 65–7.

2

Organizational Forms of Jewish Popular Culture since the Middle Ages

CHRISTOPH DAXELMÜLLER

The background and the conditions of postmedieval history in the German territories, as well as of the history of European Jewry generally and of German Jews especially, are known. First, following the expulsion of the Jews from the imperial cities after 1450, rural and small-town Jewish communities arose. Until the end of the Napoleonic wars, only about 7 percent of all German Jews lived in the three largest Jewish communities: those in Hamburg, Breslau, and Frankfurt am Main. The vast majority still lived in villages and small urban centers. To a great extent, this environment (*Lebensraum*) shaped the intellectual and social history of the Jews. Second, violent expulsions were gradually replaced by "peaceful" expulsions. Sovereigns who profited handsomely from Jewish settlers extended the practice of *Schutzjudentum* (protected Jewry). Although the Jews were doomed to transient lives, they were welcomed by the lords of the manor because of innumerable special taxes and tolls. Third, the anti-Judaism of Martin Luther and other religious reformers abetted the growing distinctions between Jews and non-Jews. The common medieval anti-Jewish topoi of the Jew as ritual murderer and host profaner survived the apocalyptic period and were fixed, for example, at Catholic places of pilgrimage. Fourth, because Jews were excluded from nearly all skilled trades, they had to get along as moneylenders, traders, and door-to-door salesmen. Most of them lived at the subsistence level, and only a few advanced socially as *Hoffaktoren* (Jewish court agents).[1]

Fifth, the Thirty Years' War (1618–48) affected both Jews and non-Jews. The Jewish quarter often gave shelter to both Protestants and Catholics, but in many cases it could not protect the Jews themselves against the soldiery. The belligerents' attitudes toward the Jews were ambivalent. Because they

---

1 Compare, e.g., Joseph Isaak, *Unmassgebliche Gedanken über Betteljuden und ihre bessere und zweckmässigere Versorgung menschenfreundlichen Regenten und Vorstehern zur weitern Prüfung vorgelegt* (Nuremberg, 1791).

were needed as financiers, Jews were afforded protection. But a Jewish-German poem, written by Alexander ben Isaak between 1622 and 1627, shows that they suffered just as much as the Christian population:

> Strange things occur in the world:
> One hears little talk about peace,
> Emperor and king support each other.
> They war with the Dutch.
> They are the enemies of the duke of the Palatinate
> And wage great war against the new faith.
> . . . best friends and brothers fight each other.[2]

After the war, the Jews were again at the mercy of the European governments' interest and involvement in the fractured German territories. Yet Jews made important contributions to the rebuilding of a destroyed Germany; baroque culture, after all, is Jewish culture as well.

In search of those structures that determined popular Jewish culture in early modern times, we have to stress the influence of the new *Lebensraum* – villages and small towns – on Jewish identity.[3] At the same time, however, it would not be correct to characterize the period between the end of the fifteenth and the second half of the nineteenth century as an era of *Dorfjudentum* (rural Jewry). A small number of Jews continued to live in cities such as Worms, and rural Jews never lost contact with the cities. In southern Germany, for example, important new Jewish communities grew up in the vicinity of cities such as Nuremberg and Würzburg, from which the Jewish inhabitants had been expelled, and developed into religious and intellectual centers, including Fürth and Schnaittach a few miles away from Nuremberg, Heidingsfeld and Höchberg, now suburbs of Würzburg. Moreover, Jewish merchants attended markets and fairs such as those in Frankfurt and Leipzig.[4] These merchants became intermediaries between

---

2 Original: "es stet selzom im olom: / man hert wenig sagen fun / scholom. / kessar un melech halten zu anander / milchome haben mit den holender, / den falezdukus haben / ssone, / gros milchome haben mit der neien / emune. / . . . die besten vreind un brider / anander sein zu wider." Oxford, Bodleian Library Ms. Opp. 608; cf. Walter Röll, "Man hört wenig sagen vom Frieden. Ein Jüdisches Lehrgedicht aus dem Mayen des 17. Jahrhunderts," *Kurtrierisches Jahrbuch* 16 (1976): 40–2; Chava Turniansky, "Alexander ben Yitzhak's Bilingual Manuscript *Sefer massah u'merivah* (1627)," Ph.D. diss., Hebrew University, Jerusalem, 1973. For the Jewish contribution to the rebuilding of Germany after the Thirty Years' War, see Alfred Schröcker, "Jüdische Finanziers des Fürstbischofs Lothar Franz von Schönborn (1655–1729)," *Jahrbuch für Fränkische Landesforschung* 37 (1977): 125–37.

3 See, e.g., Werner J. Cahnman, "Village and Small-town Jews in Germany: A Typological Study," *Publications of the Leo Baeck Institute, Year Book* 19 (1974): 107–30.

4 See Max Freudenthal, *Die jüdischen Besucher der Leipziger Messen in den Jahren 1675–1764* (Frankfurt/Main, 1928).

urban and rural cultures, furnishing the village population with products for both daily and luxury use.[5] In folkloristic terms, they played the role of "trickster," since they had an intellectual advantage over the peasants and rural craftsmen. Their importance for the rural infrastructure becomes obvious in those regions where they had a monopoly; when Jewish traders were eliminated after 1933, the distribution of goods collapsed.

Isaak Holzer's statement that in the seventeenth century the Jews of Germany were culturally "children of the Middle Ages" is true only up to a point.[6] Like anyone else, Jews also had to accommodate themselves to the quickly changing social and economic conditions. Nevertheless, between the *culture des élites* and the *culture des masses*, we find structural elements that remained constant beyond the threshold of modern times.

Christian theologians' fascination with the Hebrew language, beginning in medieval times, continued. Thus, Elijahu ben Ascher ha-Levi, called Elia Levita Bachur (or Levita, 1469–1549), author of the Jewish-German *Bovo Bukh*, was highly esteemed as a Hebrew grammarian by the humanists.[7] Italian scholars, foremost among them the Florentine Neo-Platonists, especially Pico della Mirandola (1463–94), discovered in cabalistic manuscripts a mystical system that could be used for Christian philosophical, esoteric, and magical speculations.[8] Christian cabalistics (*gabalia*) became an intellectual trend as well as a model of perceiving God and feeling the harmony of the cosmos. Not only Judaizing individuals like Antonia von Württemberg (1613–79) but also scientists with an international reputation like the Jesuit Athanasius Kircher (1601–80) took up the cabalistic *systema sephiroticum* as a way to comprehend God's nature and to explain the *harmonia mundi*.[9]

The reception of cabalistic ideas by Christian philosophers, however, did not result in a dialogue between Christians and Jews. Rather, these ideas turned out to be dangerous in the hands of a semieducated class that reduced

---

5 See Christoph Daxelmüller, "Jüdische Kleider- und Schnittwarenhändler," in Wolfgang Brückner, ed., *Fränkisches Volksleben im 19. Jahrhundert. Wunschbilder und Wirklichkeit. Möbel – Keramik – Textil in Unterfranken, 1814 bis 1914* (Würzburg, 1985), 177–81; Daxelmüller, "Kulturvermittlung und Gütermobilität. Anmerkungen zur Bedeutung des jüdischen Handels für die ländliche und kleinstädtische Kultur," in Nils-Arvid Bringéus et al., eds., *Wandel der Volkskultur in Europa. Festschrift für Günter Wiegelmann zum 60. Geburtstag*, vol. 1 (Münster, 1988), 233–53; Utz Jeggle, *Judendörfer in Württemberg* (Tübingen, 1969).

6 Isaak Holzer, "Aus dem Leben der alten Judengemeinde zu Worms, nach dem *Minhagbuch* des Juspa Schammes," *Zeitschrift für die Geschichte der Juden in Deutschland* 5 (1935): 169–86, esp. 171–2.

7 The *Bovo Bukh* is a translation of the Italian *Historia di Buovo Antone*, which goes back to the English adventure story *Sir Bevis of Southhampton* (twelfth century).

8 Compare, for example, Gerhard Scholem, *Das Buch Bahir. Ein Schriftdenkmal aus der Frühzeit der Kabbala* (Leipzig, 1923; reprint: Darmstadt, 1970).

9 Compare, for example, Reinhard Breymayer and Friedrich Häussermann, eds., *Die Lehrtafel der Prinzessin Antonia. Kritische Ausgabe*, 2 vols. (Berlin, 1977).

the speculative systems of the Jewish mystical literature to ritual magic and intellectual discussion of the essence of God to a series of partly absurd Hebrew names for God, the angels, and the demons. In the sixteenth and seventeenth centuries, the Jew as magician and sorcerer took the place of the medieval Jew as heretic.[10] He roused the suspicions of an illiterate population because he could read books in a strange language, namely, Hebrew. But he still remained an unsafe contemporary. Thus, at the beginning of modern times the negative image of the Jew had not changed, merely the arguments that justified anti-Semitism.

I

An ethnologist speaking about popular Jewish culture is tempted to give an extremely selective view of Jewish life and manners in the past. Accordingly, the Jewish way of life is often reduced to a catalog of popular customs stretching from birth to death, extending from Sabbath to Rosh hashana, covering folk songs, literature, and narratives as well as popular sayings, beliefs, superstitions, and magical practices. But these elements exist more in the minds of the folklorists than in reality. In this essay, I would instead like to use another method to reconstruct the existential conditions, behaviors, and mentalities of the period by looking for the constitutive elements responsible for the tradition and change of popular cultural forms.

First of all, we have to state that neither medieval nor postmedieval Jewish culture was the culture of the ghetto. The Jewish quarter of the cities and small towns or the *Judengasse* of the small villages did not demarcate a limited area of perception but represented an intellectual process of giving external (Christian) ideas and things entering the Jewish home – and necessary for its survival – a Jewish meaning. Jewish culture in the *galut* was above all a culture in contact. It accepted new fashions and behaviors and yet continually struggled with the problem of combining non-Jewish cultural elements with Jewish identity. The most important achievement of Jewish life before the Holocaust was probably the creation of normative rules which made it possible to participate in the European cultural changes that have taken place since the Middle Ages.

---

10 See Joshua Trachtenberg, *The Devil and the Jews: The Medieval Conception of the Jew and Its Relation to Modern Antisemitism* (New Haven, 1943; reprinted: New York, 1966); and *Jewish Magic and Superstition: A Study in Folk Religion* (New York, 1970); Stefan Rohrbacher and Michael Schmidt, *Judenbilder. Kulturgeschichte antijüdischer Mythen und antisemitischer Vorurteile* (Reinbek bei Hamburg, 1991).

I will summarize these structural elements, which helped to organize popular Jewish culture, as follows:

1. Space and *Lebensraum:* meaning, the village and the small town.
2. Time: How could the Jews arrange to live in two time cycles, a biblical near-Eastern one and the Christian one? How could they combine the Jewish and the Christian week, the Jewish and the Christian year, the changing times of sunrise and sunset, important for *erev Shabbath* and the end of *Shabbath*? Probably calendar books and almanacs were, after the Bible, the most popular Jewish reading material.[11]
3. The reading Jew, or: literacy and reading fashions as symbols of Jewish life.
4. The *Tekunoth*, or the fascinated viewing of non-Jewish life forms.
5. The normative function of the *minhag* and the organization of popular piety.

Using these elements, I will demonstrate that "ghetto" is probably the most misleading term we could use to explain Jewish life before the establishment of the Warsaw Ghetto in 1940 by Nazi Germany.

The development of popular Jewish culture since the Middle Ages can be characterized as a strategy for living, as well as one for surviving. Because they were in constant and permanent contact with the outside world, Jews took part in and accepted the ruling cultural norms and values by giving them a Jewish meaning. In all likelihood they had little choice but to engage in this process as a means for preserving their Jewish identity. But these processes of adaptation contained an important creative element as well.[12]

II

In Zolkiew, Galicia, a very popular anecdote was told until the 1930s about Rabbi Zwi Hirsch Chajes (1805–55), a famous scholar and grandfather of

---

11 For the problem of living in two time cycles, see Christoph Daxelmüller, "Jewish Popular Culture in the Research Perspective of European Ethnology," *Ethnologia Europaea* 16 (1986): 97–116; and "Die Zeit des Alltags. Jüdische Lebensformen in fränkischen Landgemeinden," *Archäologie und Geschichte*, Schriften des Fränkische-Schweiz-Museums, no. 3 (1990): 67–83.
12 Thus Theodor H. Gaster refuses to use the term "Jewish folklore": "much of it [Jewish folklore] is due to direct borrowings from other peoples and can therefore not be described as distinctive. The material thus embraced is by no means homogeneous, for the peoples in question never constituted a single ethnic unit nor possessed a single common culture . . . just as a great deal of what passes to-day for Jewish folklore really represents direct borrowings from the Gentile peoples among whom the Jews happen to have been dispersed"; Theodor H. Gaster, "Semitic Folklore," in Maria Leach, ed., *Dictionary of Folklore, Mythology and Legend*, vol. 2 (New York, 1950), 981–9, 981–2.

Zwi Perez Chajes (1876–1927), later the chief rabbi of Vienna. One day
Rabbi Chajes was deeply grieved when he came to the synagogue. The
people asked him why he was sorrowful. "Goethe is dead," he answered.
The whole *Kehilla* (community) became sad, and some pious people considered reciting the kaddish for "Reb Goethe."[13] The *Vintz Hanss Lied*, a
Jewish-German ballad describing the pogrom of August 22, 1614, in Frankfurt am Main, had to be sung to the *niggun* (melody) of *Pavia is die shlakht*.[14]

    As these anecdotes highlight, the most constitutive element in organiz-
ing popular Jewish culture was probably reading. Most of the popular reading matter was of non-Jewish origin with non-Jewish content. No other
subject can better represent the structure of Jewish folk culture than the capacity of reading and contemporary literary fashions to fascinate Jewish audiences. Learning to read was an integral part of Jewish socialization and
education and, at the same time, a precondition of *Bar Mitzvah*. *Seder Pessach* demanded the reading of the Haggadah. Reading and studying was an
ideal of Jewish life. And according to Moses b. Maimon, all Jews are obligated to study the Torah.[15] In the *Sefer hayashar* it is written,

it is essential that not even one day should occur on which he does not read the
words of the Torah or the words of our Sages, of blessed memory. For concerning
the words of the Torah, it is said [Joshua 1:8]: "This book of the Torah shall not
depart out of thy mouth, but thou shalt meditate therein day and night."[16]

A *Minhagim-Bukh*, printed in Frankfurt in 5522 (1762), contains the following instruction for reading on the Sabbath:

After the Saturday meal, you should study, and those who cannot study [i.e., read
religious Hebrew texts] should read in godly [pious] books in German, because Saturday complains before the Lord that all things have their companion and Saturday
has none. So the Lord says [: the people of] Israel should be your companion, by
studying the Torah with you on the day of rest.[17]

The importance of reading – and the overall literacy of Jewish culture – becomes even more clear when compared to the illiteracy of non-Jews. The

13 Salcia Landmann, *Erinnerungen an Galizien* (Munich, 1983), 33–4.
14 The ballad is reprinted in Johann Jakob Schudt, *Jüdischer Merckwürdigkeiten Vorstellende Was sich
    Curieuses und denckwürdiges in den neuern Zeiten bey einigen Jahrhunderten mit denen in alle IV. Theile
    der Welt, sonderlich durch Teutschland, zerstreuten Juden zugetragen. III. Theil. In sich haltend Einige Doc-
    umenta Und Schrifften, Deren in vorhergehenden beyden Theilen Meldung geschehen* (Frankfurt/Main and
    Leipzig, 1714), 9–36.
15 Moses b. Maimon, *Sefer ha-Madda', Hilekhot Talmud Torah*, ed. Jacob Cohen et al. (Jerusalem, 1964),
    chap. 1.
16 *Sefer hayashar*, chap. 13; *Sefer hayashar: The Book of the Righteous*, ed. Seymour J. Cohen (New York,
    1973), 212–13.
17 See Max Grünbaum, *Jüdischdeutsche Chrestomathie. Zugleich ein Beitrag zur Kunde der hebräischen Lite-
    ratur* (Leipzig, 1882; reprinted: Hildesheim, 1969), 340.

Christian trading partner's fear of fraud surely originated in the fact that Jews were literate and that they used strange Hebrew characters for both Hebrew and Jewish-German texts, which helped to create the image of the Jew as magician and sorcerer.

But one cannot suppose complete bilingualism in the Jewish lower classes. Only the elite had a good knowledge of Hebrew, whereas the majority's reading and understanding of Hebrew was largely limited to prayers. In the Middle Ages, for example, sermons were first delivered in the vernacular language and only afterward translated into Hebrew. This situation explains the boom in Jewish-German translations and editions after the invention of the printing press. Popular literature of the late sixteenth, seventeenth, and eighteenth centuries was incorrectly termed *Weiberliteratur* (literature for women). Moreover, the Jewish-German dialect was referred to as *waiber taitsch*; the translation of the Torah was called *waiber chumesh*. That Jewish women were excluded from training in Hebrew and therefore read Jewish-German and vernacular literature explains in part the use of such terms. But the most popular Jewish-German book, the *Ein schön maesse buch*, printed in Basel in 1602, was written for men as well as women (*liben manen 'un' vrauen*). Moreover, Jewish-German editions were consumed by all classes. Considering Jewish pauperism and the conditions of everyday life, only a few privileged men had the time to acquire knowledge sufficient to read Hebrew publications.

The Jewish reading public did not, however, content itself exclusively with Jewish religious reading material. It was also enthusiastic about love and adventure stories, those with honest knights and beautiful princesses.[18] The popular author Glückel von Hameln (1645–1724), for instance, quoted the Talmud and other sources in her autobiography.[19] This fact testifies to Jewish fascination with non-Jewish cultures. To be up to date, Jews also learned many foreign languages, among them French.[20] Other sources also refer to Jewish enthusiasm for learning other languages. For example, Hirsch Kaidenower's *Kab hajashar*, printed in 1705 at Frankfurt am Main,

---

18 For example, see Christoph Daxelmüller, "Jüdischer Geschicht-Roman / von dem grossen König Arturo in Engelland / und dem tapffern Helden Wieduwilt (Ein schin ma'asse fun kinig artiss hof). Herausgegeben von Johann Christoph Wagenseil (1633–1705). Königsberg 1699," in Theodor Brüggemann and Otto Brunken, eds., *Handbuch zur Kinder- und Jugendliteratur. Von 1570 bis 1750* (Stuttgart, 1991), 942–61.

19 See Alfred Feilchenfeld, ed., *Denkwürdigkeiten der Glückel von Hameln* (Berlin, 1920), 306–17.

20 "Mein Vater hat von ihr [the first wife of Glückel's father] keine Kinder gehabt. Sie hatte aber aus ihrer früheren Ehe eine einzige Tochter, die an Schünheit und Tugend nicht ihresgleichen hatte. Französisch konnte sie wie Wasser, was meinem sel. Vater auch einmal zu nutze gekommen ist." Ibid., 21–2.

laments the bad habit that children learned French, Italian, and other languages before they could say a single prayer in Hebrew.

Since the beginning of early modern times, the most popular literature among the Jews was non-Jewish. But here we face a peculiar contradiction: the Jews, who were not permitted to wear weapons and whose ethics did not know the he-man heroism of late medieval epic poetry and the *Volksbuch*, loved chivalric romances. And, since the twelfth century, Jewish theologians in both France and Germany debated whether or not Jews should be allowed to read illustrated war stories in the vernacular on the Sabbath.[21] In the Jewish quarters many epics were sung to the melody of the *Hildebrandslied*. In 1279, the legend of King Arthur was translated into Hebrew, and, starting in the sixteenth century, a lot of Arthurian motifs were introduced into Jewish-German folk literature. In the early fifteenth century a Jew copied, sometimes defectively, the *Iwein* manuscript "a." A Jewish-German version of the *Sigenot* was printed in Cracow in 1597. From Worms came Eisik Wallich's hand-written song collection (Oxford, Bodleiana), which includes the younger *Hildebrandslied, Ein schin ma'asse fun kinig artiss hof*, better known under the title *Widuwilt*. This work has been handed down in three sixteenth-century manuscripts and was published for the first time in 1683 in Amsterdam.[22]

Nearly all German *Volksbücher* were translated into Jewish-German, including *Till Eulenspiegel*,[23] the *Schildbürger*,[24] and the *Sigenot*.[25] Jewish-German versions of the "Seven Sages" (*Die sieben weisen Meister*) were published in Amsterdam (1663), Berlin (1707), and Offenbach (1717).[26] Furthermore, the *Historie von dem Kaiser Octaviano* (Homburg, 1730),[27] the *Historie von Ritter Siegmund und Magdalena* (e.g., Prague [after 1704]; Offenbach, 1714), *Florio und Bianceffora* (e.g., Offenbach, 1714), the *Fortunatus* (Frankfurt/Main, 1699), and the *Schöne Magelone* (Offenbach, 1714) were also translated into the Jewish-German dialect. A final example is Elijahu ben Ascher ha-Levi's *Bovo Bukh*, published in many editions into the nineteenth century.

The Jewish translators and editors of this popular literature had a difficult time eliminating the much too Christian and non-Jewish character of these

---

21 Rabbenu Jehuda; in *Tosafot*, tract. Sabbat F. 116; cf. Josef Karo, *Schulchan Aruch*, vol. 1, chap. 307, 16; von Moritz Steinschneider, "Über die Volkslitteratur der Juden," *Archiv für Litteraturgeschichte* 2 (1872): 1–21, 11.
22 Stadtbibliothek Hamburg, Codex 288 (289); Codex 327 (255); Cambridge, Trinity College Library.
23 Manuscript, Staatsbibliothek München, Cod. hebr. monac. 100, fols. 134–91; late sixteenth century.
24 Printed editions were published, for example, in 1727 in Amsterdam, in 1777 in Offenbach, and in 1798 in Fürth.
25 Cracow in 1597.
26 Manuscript, Staatsbibliothek München, Cod. hebr. monac. 100, fols. 90–132.
27 Ibid., fols. 1–66.

epics. In the *ma'esse der kaiserin mit zwai' sünen*, for example, the bride does not convert to Christianity but to Judaism,[28] and the Roman prince saddles his horse "ê er tallis/un thefillin benscht" (before the morning prayer).[29] Although these versions sometimes tried to give the story or at least some passages a Jewish sense, Jewish annotations were mostly limited to the preface or the epilogue. The last two lines of the *Widuwilt* story, for example, contain a short prayer for the arrival of the Messiah: "das 'uns got m[a]schi[a]ch send" (that God send us a messiah).[30] Although the morality of such Christian reading matter was originally non-Jewish, it was acceptable to the Jewish reader.

Understandably, the reading of these books, especially on the Sabbath and during the festivals, was a thorn in the sides of religious authorities. Characteristic of Jewish participation in the common culture, as well as for the special life situation of the Jews and its resultant creativity, was that it tried to replace Christian heroes with brave Jewish fighters. A fifteenth-century author called Mosche Esrim Wearba found his Jewish hero in the person of *melekh* David and, using the literary techniques of Christian epic literature, wrote the *Schemuelbuch*.[31] Although essentially a Jewish *Volksbuch*, this collection could not diminish the popularity of other, non-Jewish editions. The literate Jew continued to dream of the adventures of King Arthur and his fellows, of princesses robbed by ferocious dragons, and of hidden treasures; he lived in a world full of monsters and demons, heroes and witches.

Whereas the Jews absorbed the contents of popular, non-Jewish literature, and whereas the Jewish quarter was open to all new ideas, pleasures, as well as to intellectual and material fashions, the Christian quarter continued to remain closed to Jewish influences. In Jewish private libraries we find the chivalric romances, but the common Christian reader was not interested in Jewish popular literature, such as the *Brantshpigl* or the *Ma'asse Bukh*. The only exception was the small circle of academically trained theologians or philologists who used these stories in their anti-Jewish arguments.[32]

---

28 Ibid., fol. 49v.   29 Ibid., fol. 16v.

30 Johann Christoph Wagenseil, *Belehrung der Jüdisch-Teutschen Red- und Schreibart* (Königsberg, 1699), 292.

31 Felix Falk, *Das Schemuelbuch des Mosche Esrim Wearba. Ein biblisches Epos aus dem 15. Jahrhundert*, 2 vols., ed. L. Fuks (Assens, 1961).

32 For example, Christoph Helvicus (Helwig) (1581–1617) translated the stories of the *Ma'asseh Bukh* as *Jüdische Historien oder Thalmudische Rabbinische wunderbarliche Legenden so von den Jüden als warhafftige vnd heylige Geschicht an ihren Sabbathen vnd Feyertagen gelesen werden*, pts. I–II (Giessen, 1611–12; 2nd ed.: Giessen, 1617); see Christoph Daxelmüller, "Die Entdeckung der jüdischen Erzählliteratur. Rezeption und Bewertung populärer jüdischer Erzählstoffe in der Gesellschaft des 17. and 18. Jahrhunderts," *Rheinisches Jahrbuch für Volkskunde* 26 (1985–6): 7–36.

III

In her memoirs, Glückel von Hameln praised the piety of the Jewish community in Metz because nobody had worn a wig in the shul (synagogue): "When I first came here, Metz was a very beautiful, pious community and the elders were all venerable people, who were an adornment of the meeting hall. At that time there was no one present in the meeting hall who wore a wig."[33] The Jews never lived in the hermetic space of the ghetto but were exposed to the intellectual attractions of the world around them. Early modern times witnessed rapid changes in social and cultural conditions. The discovery of a new continent, America, enlarged the known world and altered the outlook on life. New cultural assets came to Europe, and luxuries like coffee or tobacco gradually became everyday objects for all social classes. In a time when smoking was not considered harmful to one's health, the smoking of a pipe was not only an individual enjoyment but also a social ritual and a gesture. The tobacco pipe became part of the *habitus*, like a wig or one's jewelry. But what is the use of a pipe when it may not be lighted on the Sabbath?

No other source reflects the mentality, identity, and fascination in cultural developments and fashions better than the *Tekunoth* – the instructions of Jewish communities concerning luxury goods. These instructions were modeled on contemporary non-Jewish *Kleiderordnungen* (sumptuary laws) and referred, above all, to quickly changing clothes fashions. They tried to control the kind of fashions worn and prevent people from buying textiles considered too expensive. We do not know the extent to which these ideas were followed, but in this context the question is of less importance, because the *Tekunoth* nevertheless reflect the ongoing confrontation of the Jews with external cultural influences – with new habits and customs – that fascinated them. Last but not least, the *Tekunoth* also highlight the problem of whether and to what extent this new cultural behavior contradicted Jewish religious traditions.

Thus, the *Tekunoth* of Hamburg, Altona, and Wandsbek – the *Dreigemeinden* of Hamburg – which were enacted in 1715, treated, among other things, the use of tobacco. It prohibited taking snuff or smoking in the synagogue: "The use of snuff or Brazilian tobacco is prohibited in the synagogue under penalty of 2 taler."[34] But on smoking at home a compromise was made: people could smoke or chew tobacco after having said grace.[35] An

---

33 *Denkwürdigkeiten der Glückel von Hameln*, 292.
34 "Schnupftabak oder brasilianischer Tabak ist bei 2 Tlrn. Strafe in der Synagoge verboten." Max Grunwald, "Luxusverbot der Dreigemeinden (Hamburg-Altona-Wandsbek) aus dem Jahre 1715," *Jahrbuch für jüdische Volkskunde* (1923): 227–34, 231, §41.
35 "Bei einem Festmahl 'kein Tabak zu schmecken' vor dem Tischgebet, bei 1 Tlr. Strafe." Ibid., 231, §42.

identical regulation can be found in the *Tekunoth* of the Fürth community (1728), which are handed down only in the translation of Andreas Würfel:

At all ritual meals, it is prohibited to smoke tobacco / not only in the room where the meals are taken / but also in any other room, until after the food had been blessed / the penalty is 4 Rthlr. [Reichsthaler] for he who committed the offense and the same amount for he who failed to prevent this transgression during the meal.[36]

Snuff taking in the synagogue was strictly forbidden in Fürth. This prohibition indicates that the Jews already had begun to use tobacco during the service or that the community was suspecting they one day might.

The use of snuff tobacco or Brazilian cigars is prohibited – in old, new, or other synagogues – penalty of 4 Rthlr. to be paid out in charitable contributions.[37]

It is easy to understand why the *Tekunoth* tried to limit or to prohibit the purchase of costly imported goods. One wished that the members of a community, who not only had to pay for the subsistence of the rabbi, the teacher, and other community officials but also for the support of the synagogue, would not live beyond their means. Moreover, it was hoped that their financial assets would remain within the community. Accordingly, the consumption of expensive imported goods, such as coffee and tea, was substantially limited in Fürth.[38] In addition, other non-Jewish customs and "bad" habits were spreading. Fireworks, for example, were an important if costly part of the staging of baroque festivals. Why not add pyrotechnics to Jewish festivals as well? When it was tried, the result was a religious ban. In 1726 the *Tekunoth* of the *Dreigemeinden* of Hamburg reiterated a prohibition from 1698 banning fireworks in the synagogue at *Simchat Thorah*. The book of regulations stated that it was forbidden

under penalty of 10 Rthlr., on certain holidays no one is allowed to shoot gunpowder or launch rockets in the synagogue, as well as abstain from hitting and throwing, punishable by a fine of 4 Rthlr.; therefore, everyone in the community is obligated to warn his children and servants that they should obey this order.[39]

---

36 *Das Tekunos Büchlein der Fürther Juden. d. i. Der Aeltesten und Vorstehere der Jüdischen Gemeinde daselbst, ertheilte Instructiones, Wie sich ihre Bürgere bey ihren freywilligen und gebottenen Mahlzeiten, Gürtelgeben, Hochzeitmahlen, Schenkwein, Brautgeschenken, Kleydung und andern Vorfallenheiten verhalten sollen,* in Andreas Würfel, *Historische Nachricht von der Judengemeinde in der Hofmark Fürth unterhalb Nürnberg, Der II. Theil* (Frankfurt/Main and Prague, 1754), 107–70, 142–4, §26.

37 Ibid., 154, §12.

38 "Desgleichen darf man keinen Thee und Coffe geben / so wohl über der Mahlzeit, als nach der Mahlzeit. Und dieses darf nicht geschehen von dem Herrn der Mahlzeit / als auch mit List von anderen / bey 6 Rthl. Straf ins Almosen." Ibid., 144, §27.

39 [Max Grunwald], "IV. Trachten und Sitten. Aus den Gemeindeverordnungen der Dreigemeinden Hamburg-Altona-Wandsbek vom Jahre 1726," *Mitteilungen der Gesellschaft für Jüdische Volkskunde* 2, fasc. 1 (1899): 29–33, 29, §28.

The Jews were not only exposed to the ways non-Jews celebrated their festivities, but they also partly assimilated alien customs and rituals. It was thus permitted to visit theatrical comedies on Purim. The presentation of sometimes gross but always amusing farces, the *Purimshpils* (Purim plays), and processions were a traditional part of the holiday that Christian theologians called "Jewish carnival," or *bacchanalia Judaeorum*.[40] Nevertheless such amusements were limited to Purim and Hanukkah and strictly forbidden on the Sabbath and other holidays. While frequenting public houses, theaters, skittle alleys, or fencing rooms was a popular leisure-time activity for non-Jews on Saturday and Sunday, Jewish communities prohibited this kind of diversion on the Sabbath. In 1726, the Hamburg *Tekunoth* prohibited "both sexes from walking to public houses or inns, or from visiting bowling alleys, fencing schools, or comedies on the Sabbath and holidays. Women should under no circumstances attend the opera."[41] Fascinated by the cultural temptations of their environment, the Jews tried to escape the ghetto where they lived. In their wish to be up to date, the Jews were particularly drawn to the sensual, that is, to the sensations of the body and the reigning ideal of beauty. The pious Glückel von Hameln, as we have noted, approvingly observed that in Metz the Jews avoided wearing wigs in the synagogue. But other Jewish communities, for example the one in Fürth, stopped fighting the new fashions, and it was only forbidden to wear powdered wigs in the shul.[42] Indeed, the *Tekunoth* of Hamburg permitted in 1726 the wearing of wigs but strictly prohibited the wearing of fake curls on the Sabbath and holidays. It also prohibited having one's hair done.[43] On this point, it seems, fashion was inconsistent with religious rules.

Sometimes such attention to dress was punished with bad jokes. Johann Wilhelm Friedrich Santerre, a hairdresser in Ansbach, used to dress the Sabbath wigs on top of a smoking cookstove. When a Jew put on such a "prepared" wig, his or her *ponem* (face) became covered with soot.[44] When women tried to conceal warts with artificial beauty marks, the 1715 Hamburg *Tekunoth* prohibited their application: "The application of artificial beauty marks is prohibited for women and girls. It is only allowed

---

40 See Christoph Daxelmüller, "Ester und die Ministerkrisen. Wandlungen des Esterstoffes in jüdisch-deutschen und jiddischen Purimspielen," in Franz Link, ed., *Paradeigmata. Literarische Typologie des Alten Testaments*. pt. 1: *Von den Anfängen bis zum 19. Jahrhundert* (Berlin, 1989), 431–63.
41 Grunwald, "IV. Trachten und Sitten," 30, §34.
42 "Wer eine Peruque trägt / und genöthiget ist / damit in die Schule zu gehen / darf sie nicht pudern lassen." *Tekunos Büchlein*, 150, §7.
43 Grunwald, "IV. Trachten und Sitten," 32, §186.
44 See Siegfried Haenle, *Geschichte der Juden im ehemaligen Fürstenthum Ansbach. Mit Urkunden und Regesten* (Ansbach, 1867), 131, quoting the autobiography of Johann Wilhelm Friedrich Santerre of 1808.

on the temples."[45] The *Tekunoth* of Fürth gave a similar instruction: "Short pinafores and artificial beauty marks, aside from those placed on the temples for health reasons, are prohibited. It is also forbidden to learn how to dance."[46]

Care of the face and of the hair played an important role in women's everyday life. The fashions of the day were not created in the Jewish quarter but came from France, and they fascinated both Jewish and non-Jewish women alike. Well-to-do Jewish families set great store by their representational appearance in public life. Thus, Glückel von Hameln mentions the custom of hiring wedding carriages and the increasing popularity among the Jews of taking coaches. But the Hamburg *Tekunoth* of 1715 allowed riding to the synagogue in carriages only when it rained.[47] Moreover, only the bride and up to three bridesmaids had permission to come to the wedding ceremony by coach.[48] On this point, Fürth's *Tekunoth* were more liberal: "The bride or groom may be conveyed but only in one coach pulled by one horse under penalty of 4 imperial talers in alms."[49]

Whereas such behavior was acceptable and demonstrated the cultural openness of the Jewish quarter, fascination with contemporary fashion, however, met with disapproval. Engravings of the seventeenth and eighteenth centuries offer only stereotypes of Jews, showing details of the Jewish costume, such as the round beret (*Schabbesdeckel*), the wheel-shaped collar, and the knee-length wrap. But literary sources contradict this stereotypical image, documenting instead a wide variety of fashions and types of clothing. As in other areas, the Jews followed the example set by the majority and desired to dress in the latest fashionable attire. An analysis of the *Tekunoth* indicates that Jewish communities attempted, albeit in vain, to resist novelties in contemporary dress. The sumptuary orders of Hamburg stated in 1715 that new fashions should not be introduced ("Es ist keine neue Mode aufzubringen").[50] But in 1726 the administration of the *Dreigemeinden* appeared resigned:

Were one to witness that men, married women, and even unmarried women began, step by step, to introduce new fashions not written down in this book, as it is impossible to forewarn of all trends, then one would have to regulate this in due time and punish the wrongdoers.[51]

45 "Pflästerchen ins Gesicht 'zu legen' ist verboten für Frauen und Mädchen. Nur auf die Schläfe ist es erlaubt." Grunwald, "Luxusverbot," 228, §15.
46 *Tekunos Büchlein*, 158, §26.   47 Grunwald, "Luxusverbot," 229, §24.   48 Ibid., 230, §32.
49 "Man darf Bräutigam oder Braut entgegen gehen aber nur mit einer Gutsche und einem Pferd / bey Strafe 4 Rthlr. ins Allmosen." *Tekunos Büchlein*, 144, §28.
50 Grunwald, "Luxusverbot," 229, §23.   51 Grunwald, "IV. Trachten und Sitten," 32, §187.

It is striking that Jewish luxury instructions focused on fashion trends and tried to influence individual behavior in this regard. But they fail to mention a central problem: the prohibition of using textiles containing threads of both linen and wool. The Jews of early modern times depended upon textiles not produced according to the Jewish rules; they had to buy and use the cloth available to them. They traded in new and used clothes and textiles, but only in the early eighteenth century did they begin to employ non-Jewish weavers under their own management.

But clothes are composed of several materials, such as hides, metal threads, and other applied objects. As a consequence, such clothing often possessed a considerable weight. People wondered whether wearing such heavy clothing constituted work and therefore contradicted the Sabbath rules. In Fürth, for example, a new cape became popular among Jewish women, following the example set by the non-Jewish women of Nuremberg. Opinions of the observant members of the community were divided: Was this cape too heavy for the Sabbath? To answer this question, they dressed a doll with the textile and sent it to a rabbi in Poland. His decision was clear: the cape should not be worn on the Sabbath.[52]

IV

Most of the Jewish-German *minhagim* books of the seventeenth and early eighteenth centuries are illustrated with woodcuts. In the chapters on Purim, the fool symbolizes this Jewish festival.[53] He is wearing all the fool's attributes, including the characteristic cap known from medieval iconography. But the image of the fool that appears, for example, in frescoes in churches is a Christian symbol of human imprudence, vice, and rebellion against God.[54] The fool is an element of Christian, not Jewish, ethics. Why did this figure become a symbol of Purim?

One answer may be that as early as the seventeenth century Christian moralizing connected with the fool had fallen off. His function in popular customs at carnival time had been reduced to that of a jester, the *Hanswurst,* who was a popular figure in the *Purimshpils* and in Purim processions until the twentieth century. Deprived of his original meaning, the fool became acceptable for Jews both as mummery and as a symbol.

---

52 *Tekunos Büchlein,* 156, commentary by Andreas Würfel.
53 E.g., *Minhagim* (Amsterdam, 1707), fol. 56r.
54 See Werner Mezger, *Narrenidee und Fastnachtsbrauch. Studien zum Fortleben des Mittelalters in der europäischen Festkultur* (Constance, 1991).

It is surprising that the figure of the *Hanswurst* appears in a popular literary genre, the purpose of which was to provide moral instruction. *Minhagim* books guided readers by evaluating which of the new behaviors, rituals, and customs corresponded with traditional Jewish identity. Probably the literature of the *minhagim*, which among other things prescribed the customs of a community (*minhag ha-makom*), is the best example of both the intercultural situation and the reality of permanent political, cultural, and ritual changes. The climax of popular (Jewish-German) *minhagim* books in the seventeenth and early eighteenth centuries was tied to the return migration of eastern European Jews to central and western Europe as well as to the inner mobility of the *Schutzjuden*. One factor that significantly influenced the development of Jewish life after the Thirty Years' War was the migration and settlement of eastern European Jews in German towns and rural communities, as a result of the Bogdan Chmelniecki pogroms (1648–57).[55] According to contemporary sources, about one hundred thousand Jews were killed. Glückel von Hameln, for example, reported on refugees from Vilnius who came to Hamburg:

At that time it so happened that the Jews of Vilnius had to emigrate to Poland. Many of them came also to Hamburg and brought infectious diseases with them. There were no Jewish hospitals, or other facilities, in which one could house sick people. We therefore had probably ten sick people on our floor, for which my deceased father cared: some of them got well, others died.[56]

In his study, Hermann Pollack describes the consequences of the immigration in the period after 1648.

When the Jews of the Ukraine and Poland fled to Germany during the Cossack massacres, the cultural heritage that they brought with them influenced Jewish social life wherever they settled. The scholars, rabbis, and writers who came from eastern Europe made a cultural impact on German Jewry at a time when communal life was being revived. As a result, east European lore spread in Germany and became part of the popular beliefs and customs of Jewish daily life.[57]

Some customs brought by immigrants or by expelled *Schutzjuden* looked strange to the resident Jews. Therefore, a *minhag* decision (or *responsum*) became necessary as to whether or not new rituals accorded with traditional Jewish practice. The *minhag ha-makom* is the sum of such decisions regulating the customs of holidays and everyday life and the result of continually changing living conditions and the influence of the environment. But the

55 See, e.g., Friedrich Battenberg, *Das europäische Zeitalter der Juden. Zur Entwicklung einer Minderheit in der nichtjüdischen Umwelt Europas*, vol. 2 (Darmstadt, 1990), 34–6.
56 *Denkwürdigkeiten der Glückel von Hameln*, 30–1.
57 Herman Pollack, *Jewish Folkways in Germanic Lands, 1648–1806* (Cambridge, Mass., 1971), xvi.

minhag represents not only "custom" but also the comingling of past and present, of tradition and change. *Minhag* is "the vehicle by which the Jew demonstrated his devotion to God in a manner wholly spontaneous and embracing something of his own personality."[58] The *Sefer ha-Mat'amim*, quoting *Homot Yesharim*, defined the *minhag* as "the Jew's love of the *mitzvot* by embellishing them with additional observances [*hiddur mitzvah*]."[59]

Following the Talmud, the *minhag* repeals the *halacha* (minhag m'vutal halakha), and the custom becomes an expression of popular piety:

I'm not saying that piety culminates or exhausts itself in custom, but that it is extremely important is beyond doubt. In the course of time books of customs developed, which recorded and handed down the specific customs of a certain community or region. This especial devotion to the *Minhag* generally and to the *minhag ha-makom* in particular remains in effect until this day. There are always people everywhere who jealously guard rituals and who have an overvalued esteem for them – overvalued compared with other areas in which they were somewhat less highly valued.[60]

As Jeschajahu Awiad-Wolfsberg states, the power of the *minhag* increased in the rural environment, that is, in the *Lebensraum* of the Jews from the late Middle Ages until the period of emancipation.

Under rural conditions, its importance grows. In its originality, naivete, childlikeness, and cheerfulness – or in genuine mourning – it corresponds in its nature to the simple and narrow environment in which one does not reflect much. By contrast, the big-city Jew, who practiced the *Minhag* exactly, appears at times unnatural, his behavior is at times artificial and at times not without coquettishness. This rich modern milieu and life-style stands oddly in contrast to the world of the *Minhag* – which is in style more remote from modern civilization than the halacha. Thus small-town Jewry has in fact remained the actual carrier, the true and cheerful preserver of tradition, as far as it also felt the power of the irrational in itself. The rustic nature of these people corresponded to the nature of traditional custom.[61]

Custom as visualizing act and as concretizing play supports individual piety beyond the strict rules of halacha. It embraces all elements that govern the festivals as well as everyday life. Therefore, Pollack divides the *minhagim* into three general classifications: "ritual *minhagim*, such as those associated with birth, marriage, and burial; dietary *minhagim*, related to foods and table usage; and extralegal *minhagim,* practices relied upon to overpower demons or evil forces."[62] In any case, the *minhagim* books, which, even to-

---

58 Abraham Chill, *The Minhagim: The Customs and Ceremonies of Judaism, Their Origins and Rationale* (New York, 1979), xix.
59 Ibid., xx.
60 Jeschajahu Awiad-Wolfsberg, "Minhag und Halacha," *Leo Baeck Institute Bulletin,* no. 1 (1957): 27–30, 28.
61 Ibid., 29. 62 Pollack, *Jewish Folkways in Germanic Lands,* xiv.

day, are probably the most exact source for popular religious practice, contributed – as normative literature – to the organization of popular Jewish culture and to the demarcation between Jewish and non-Jewish elements.

Let us take Purim as an example. The source for the custom of making noise whenever the name "Haman" is mentioned is the biblical verse "For I will utterly blot out the remembrance of Amalek from under the Heavens" (Exodus 17:14). Flat stones or wooden paddles upon which the word "Haman" was inscribed were used. By pounding them together, the letters would be erased in a short time.[63] The Amsterdam *minhagim* of 1707 related this custom as follows:

One has the *minhag* so that young people can knock Haman. It comes from the *minhag* that they have had in earlier days. They have written [the name] "Haman" on a stone. And they smash the stone on another stone when the name of Haman begins in the *megillah*.[64]

Another similarly noisy custom was the public burning of Haman's effigy. On Purim in Israel in 1991, during the Persian Gulf War, effigies of Saddam Hussein were burned; Hussein (at least for the time being) was the last Haman in the history of the Jewish people, and his name also begins with the letter *H*. The hanging or burning of the wicked Haman in effigy is attested as early as the fifth century. Kalonymos ben Kalonymos, for example, who lived in Provence during the latter part of the thirteenth century, informs us that in his day it was customary to commemorate the fall of Haman by riding through the streets holding fir branches and by blowing trumpets around a puppet of Haman, which was first raised aloft and subsequently burned.[65]

The custom of hanging Haman is based on the Book of Esther in the Bible. Thus, this biblical story became the basis for a popular comedy, which was imitated above all by Jewish children. Pollack interprets the burning of Haman's effigy as a magical act and compares it with the Christian custom of Midsummer Eve bonfire. Custom held that fire eradicates sins and destroys demons: "It was also the practice on Purim to leap over fire with the effigy of Haman or dance around the fire before burning the effigy. Evidently by the eleventh century the ceremony of dancing around a fire to destroy the 'evil spirit' had become part of the Purim celebration."[66]

---

63 See, e.g., Chill, *Minhagim*, 263.

64 Original: "Man hat den minhag das di' jung'n Haman klopf'n. D's kumt her fun dem minhag das si' habn frier'n gihat. Hab'n 'in 'ein shtein geschrib'n Haman. Un' hab'n den zelkhen shtein 'oif 'ein 'ander'n shtein gishlag'n wen m'n Haman ginent hat 'in der megillah." *Minhagim* (Amsterdam, 1707), fol. 57r.

65 Theodor Herzl Gaster, *Purim and Hanukkah in Custom and Tradition: Feast of Lots, Feast of Lights* (New York, 1950), 66–7.

66 Pollack, *Jewish Folkways in Germanic Lands*, 177.

Like the election of a Purim king, usually a young boy (in medieval monasteries and cathedral schools the analogous figure during carnival was the *Kinderbischof*), the custom of burning an effigy is not an original Jewish rite but belongs to the ritual of the *executio in effigie*, which originated with magical beliefs and practices. The *bacchanalia Judaeorum* accepted many elements from the non-Jewish way of celebrating carnival.

The importance of the literature of the *minhagim* as a normative factor becomes evident if one looks at the Jewish social and intellectual situation. Jewish life was a "life in conflict" and a "culture in contact," meaning that acculturation was a combination and a result of curiosity, fascination, and techniques of survival. The *minhagim* decisions had to consider carefully, to regulate, and to define the Jewish sense of new behaviors. The normative power of the *minhag ha-makom* was identical with the organization of Jewish popular culture.

V

The *charoset*, a very tasty sweet and one of the dishes of *Seder Pessach*, has a brown color that symbolizes clay as part of the Jewish bondage in Egypt. The traditional ingredients – sweet red wine, dates, and figs – give it this characteristic dark consistency. But where could German Jews buy imported fruits before Passover, and who was able to buy these expensive things? In central Europe, poor Jews found a way out by using grated apples instead of costly dates and figs, which produced the same results.

To restate the general thesis with which I began this essay: in Germany, as well as in other European countries, no ghetto existed before the Warsaw Ghetto of 1940. The term "ghetto" implies an enclave that is totally closed off from people and ideas. But why, for example, do the medieval synagogues of Worms, Regensburg, or Miltenberg resemble churches in their architecture? Why is the meaning of piety as an individual and emotional act in Jehuda ben Samuel he-Chassid of Regensburg's (1140–1217) *Sefer Chassidim* (written between 1190 and 1215) similar to that of Saint Francis of Assisi? And why are some stories of the *Sefer Chassidim* identical with those of Caesarius of Heisterbach (ca. 1180–ca. 1240) in his *Dialogus Miraculorum*?[67] Furthermore, how could the Jews of Prague, in April 24, 1741, on the occasion of the birth of the archduke of Austria, who later be-

---

67 See Joseph Dan, "Rabbi Juda the Pious and Caesarius von Heisterbach: Common Motifs in Their Stories," in Joseph Heinemann and Dov Noy, eds., *Studies in Aggadah and Folk-Literature* (Jerusalem, 1971), 18–27.

came Emperor Joseph I, organize a *trionfo* wherein they appeared as heralds dressed in the Spanish fashion of the fifteenth and sixteenth centuries, as an engaged couple in rococo costumes, and as classical gods, demigods, and heroes? And why did they reenact a folkloristic country wedding at the end of this lengthy procession?[68]

Louis Saladin, probably a non-Jewish musician, composed his *Canticum Hebraicum* about 1670 on the occasion of a *Brith Mila* for a Jewish family in Avignon or Carpentras. The works of Salomone de Rossi Ebreo (ca. 1565–1628) combine the late Renaissance mold with a forward-looking baroque style. The language of the music is identical with the contemporary style, while the language of the texts is Hebrew and its meaning Jewish.

We may neither depict the Jewish ghetto in history as closed and dark, nor may we reduce Jewish popular culture only to the fixed rules and instructions of the religious traditions that mark life's passage between birth and death: Rosh hashana, Purim, kashruth, and daily praying. Popular culture connects Torah, Talmud, and the Christian romances of chivalry, the tallith, and the latest craze. A Jewish house is signified by the mezuzah, not by its architecture. The degree of individual observance determines to a large extent which of the two cultures in contact predominates.

The characteristics of Jewish folkways in early modern Germany do not consist solely of the repertoire of traditional religious rituals and beliefs that meant to condemn the Jews subsequently to ghetto life. In fact, the ghetto is both the result of social discrimination and of the Christian's indifferent attitude toward Jewish culture as well as a fiction of historiography and of the *Wissenschaft des Judentums* (Jewish studies), which, in the period of assimilation, began to search for Jewish identity and a lost cultural heritage.[69]

Tekunoth and *minhagim* may reflect the existential condition and the intellectual and religious creativity of the Jews in their struggle to survive as human beings within a hostile environment. Jewish popular culture can thus be characterized as "tradition in motion" and as a strategy to make the objects "Jewish" and to give them a Jewish meaning. A household appliance bought from the non-Jewish potter, and therefore "unclean," had to be cleaned by cooking or washing in running water; the cavalier of the romance did not pray – he *benscht*.

---

68 "Ein jüdischer Festzug in Prag vor 146 Jahren," *Jeschurun. Wochenschrift zur Förderung jüdischen Geistes und jüdischen Lebens in Haus, Gemeinde und Schule* 20, n.s.5, no. 18 (1887): 281–2; see Christoph Daxelmüller, "Volkskultur und nationales Bewusstsein. Jüdische Volkskunde und ihr Einfluss auf die Gesellschaft der Jahrhundertwende," *Jahrbuch für Volkskunde* 12 (1989): 133–46, 136–7.

69 Battenberg, *Das europäische Zeitalter der Juden*, 22–3.

Tradition is not a mummy but an animate being that forces pragmatic creativity, as a Talmudic story relates:

A lord gave a sack of grain and a bundle of wool each to two of his friends as good-bye gifts.

The first friend had his grain ground immediately in order to make dough out of the flour and eventually bread. He also had his wool spun and woven into a table-cloth. The other friend, in contrast, left untouched the gifts that he had received. Upon the lord's return, he called upon his friends to account for the gifts. The one invited him to his table and showed him the tablecloth, made of the wool, and gave him some bread, baked from the grain that he had been given. The other friend had nothing to offer but grain and wool. The lord loudly praised the wisdom of the first friend and scolded the second.[70]

The Jews had to come to terms with their fascination with the outside world. A later example of the struggle between inside and outside, between tradition and intellectual pleasure – which continues to exist – demonstrates how it was done. The day before Yom Kippur in 1836, Heinrich Graetz (1817–91) ran away from his family's home in order to escape the ritual of *Kappores-Schwingen*. His father forced him to return by threatening to burn the son's books.[71] Graetz's decision to save his library started him down the path that led to his becoming one of the most important Jewish historians, as well as the teacher of Max (Meïr) Grunwald (1871–1953), the father of Jewish folklore studies.

70 Julius Dessauer, *Spruch-Lexikon des Talmud und Midrasch. Der Urtext, wortgetreu übersetzt, erläutert und verglichen mit den Lehr- und Kern-Sprüchen aus alter und neuer Zeit* (Budapest, 1876), 206, under "Tradition."
71 Markus Brann, "Aus H. Graetzens Lehr- und Wanderjahren," *Monatsschrift für Geschichte und Wissenschaft des Judentums* 62, n.s. 26 (1918): 231–65, 253–7.

3

Criminality and Punishment of the Jews in the Early Modern Period

OTTO ULBRICHT

At first sight it might seem out of place to make the criminality and punishment of Jews in the early modern period the subject of an essay. That is to say, it may be unseemly to study the crimes of the victims of persecution and expulsions, of repression and discrimination, and, it might be added, of robberies and theft. Nevertheless, if it can be demonstrated that the topic enhances our understanding of Jewish–Gentile relations, then no doubt such a study is important and appropriate. The importance of the investigation of Jewish criminality can be shown by looking at the various stereotypes of the Jew. Before 1650, accusations of ritual murder, desecration of the host, and poisoning of wells were commonplace. Whereas this stereotyping was intimately connected with the role of the Christian religion in society, the traditional reproaches of usury and fraud, though not without religious underpinnings, originated basically in the world of business and commerce. The old reproach of usury and fraud continued to be leveled at Jews after 1650, but in the seventeenth century accusations like ritual murder began to be regarded with skepticism and were replaced by another, real crime.

By 1700, Jews were viewed as thieves and robbers, an image that survived well into the nineteenth century.[1] Writers no longer distinguished between *Gauner* and *Spitzbuben* (crooks and scoundrels) and Jews. In 1710, for example, Paul Jacob Marperger spoke indistinctly of "all kinds of deceitful Jewish and scoundrelly vermin,"[2] and in 1729 a newspaper report from Düsseldorf maintained that Jews were involved in practically all thefts in the region.[3] In the 1730s the image of Jud Süss, the unfortunate Stuttgart court Jew, was fashioned along the lines of the Jewish "bandit," as a recent study

---

1 Barbara Gerber, *Jud Süss. Aufstieg und Fall im frühen 18. Jahrhundert* (Hamburg, 1990), 60, 63.
2 "Allerhand betrügerisches Juden- und Spitzbuben-Geschmeiss": Paul Jacob Marperger, *Beschreibung der Messen und Jahr-Märckte* (Leipzig, 1710; reprinted: Frankfurt/Main, 1968), 62.
3 Eberhard Buchner, *Religion und Kirche. Kulturhistorisch interessante Dokumente aus alten Zeitungen* (Munich, 1925), 288.

has pointed out.[4] The stereotype became even more widely accepted during the following decades.[5] In 1773, one author wrote that the Jews had made stealing and robbing their profession.[6] Small wonder that Jewish criminality was hotly debated when the struggle for emancipation began in the same decade. In his famous treatise on the civic improvement of the Jews, Dohm admitted that Jews committed more offenses than Christians.[7] In a review of that book, Professor Michaelis of Göttingen tried to quantify the Jewish share. Half the members of all robber bands, he maintained, were Jewish. Since they comprised one twenty-fifth of the population of Germany, it followed, so Michaelis concluded, that Jewish criminalia was twenty-five times higher than Christian criminality.[8] For many readers this must have confirmed their view that Jews were criminals and that criminals were Jews.

From these contemporary remarks it is obvious that Jewish crime played an important part in Jewish–Gentile relations, be it as an argument in an ideological battle or as a social phenomenon. But it also affected relations within the Jewish community, for crimes committed by its members placed the Jewish minority in a precarious position vis-à-vis the larger society.

The subject of the criminality and punishment of the Jews is far from a mainstream research topic, and attention paid to it has been extremely uneven. On the one hand, Jewish crime receives no attention whatsoever in general histories of the Jews in Germany. Even authors like Elbogen and Sterling, who are aware of its existence, do not devote a single paragraph to it, reflecting past historiography's devotion to the history of politics and ideas.[9] On the other hand, Jewish crime and its punishment loom large in some recent studies by social historians, all of them relying to some degree on Glanz's pioneering study of the Jewish lower classes.[10] These investigations, however, concentrate on only one particular aspect of Jewish crimi-

---

4 Gerber *Jud Süss,* 58–63.
5 See Paul Nicol Einert, *Entdeckter Jüdischer Baldober, Oder Sachsen-Coburgische Acta Criminalia Wider eine Jüdische Diebs- und Rauber-Bande* (Coburg, 1737); J. J. Bierbrauer, *Beschreibung Derer Berüchtigten Jüdischen Diebes-, Mörder- und Rauber-Banden* (Cassel, 1758); also Ernst Schubert, *Arme Leute, Bettler und Gauner im Franken des 18. Jahrhunderts* (Neustadt/Aisch, 1983), 171.
6 *Aktenmässige Nachricht von der 1773 in der Nacht von 29. bis 30. Mai in Lemgo verübten dreyfachen grausamen Mordthat* (Lemgo, 1773), preface.
7 Christian Wilhelm Dohm, *Über die bürgerliche Verbesserung der Juden* (Berlin and Stettin, 1781; reprinted: Hildesheim, 1981), 34.
8 Dohm, *Über die bürgerliche Verbesserung der Juden,* pt. 2 (Berlin and Stettin, 1783), 34. On the importance of this review, see Robert Liberles, "From *Toleration* to *Verbesserung:* German and English Debates on the Jews in the Eighteenth Century," *Central European History* 22 (1989): 13.
9 Ismar Elbogen and Eleonore Sterling, *Die Geschichte der Juden in Deutschland* (Frankfurt/Main, 1966), 106; Wanda Kampmann, *Deutsche und Juden* (Frankfurt/Main, 1979).
10 Rudolf Glanz, *Geschichte des niederen jüdischen Volkes in Deutschland* (New York, 1968).

nality, namely, Jewish "banditry." The study of Jewish gangs of thieves and robbers reflects, however faintly, a very old tendency that identified banditry as a Jewish and gypsy phenomenon.[11] Carsten Küther's book on robbers and swindlers is one such investigation; Uwe Danker's study of banditry around 1700 is another.[12] The large number of local and regional studies do not fill in the gaps. As a rule, they ignore this aspect of Jewish life in the early modern period. When they investigate Jewish society, which some of them do at great length, their definition of society is nevertheless traditional.

To date, a systematic investigation of crime in Jewish communities and of Jewish crime as such is lacking, as is the study of offenses originating in the business world, such as false bankruptcy, fraud, or perjury.[13] This essay cannot redress the situation entirely, but it can at least outline the main features of Jewish criminality and of the punishment of the Jews. It will become clear that the Jewish bandit is as important a figure in Jewish–Gentile relations as the court Jew. I therefore describe at some length the Jewish robber bands of the eighteenth century and demonstrate that special punishment of Jews for theft disappeared in the early modern period. Moreover, I discuss the role that the Jewish community played in the life of the bands, raising the question of Jewish solidarity, and, finally, examine the treatment of Jews in criminal courts.

I

Before looking at the different categories of crime, it may be useful to ask whether there is any truth in the statements made by Dohm and Michaelis. As is usually the case, reliable statistics are available only from the first half of the nineteenth century onward. A rough estimate of the crime rate can, however, be made for the Jews of Frankfurt am Main at the end of the seventeenth century. It shows that the rate was a little higher for the Jews in the crowded ghetto than for the Christians (about 1:90 for the Jews and

---

11 Friedrich Christian Benedikt Avé-Lallemant, *Das deutsche Gaunertum in seiner sozialpolitischen, literarischen und linguistischen Ausbildung zu seinem heutigen Bestande*, pt. 1 (Lübeck, 1858; reprinted: Wiesbaden, n.d.), 21.

12 Carsten Küther, *Räuber und Gauner in Deutschland* (Göttingen, 1976); Uwe Danker, *Räuberbanden im Alten Reich um 1700* (Frankfurt/Main, 1988). The Nazis, of course, did not fail to exploit this aspect of Jewish criminality; see Johann von Leers, *Judentum und Gaunertum. Eine Wesens- und Lebensgemeinschaft* (Berlin, [1940]), 36–52, for the period covered here.

13 With the exception of Georg Faust, *Sozial- und wirtschaftsgeschichtliche Beiträge zur Judenfrage in Deutschland vor der Emanzipation unter besonderer Berücksichtigung der Verhältnisse in der ehemaligen Grafschaft Solms-Rödelheim* (Giessen, 1937).

about 1:140 for the Christians).[14] In the duchy of Westphalia, 254 Christians and 12 Jews were put on trial between 1805 and 1818, of whom 192 Christians and 4 Jews were actually tried. This amounts to 1 criminal per 720 inhabitants for the Christians and 1 per 455 for the Jews.[15] This statistic is somewhat distorted because it only considers those Jews born in the duchy. Another statistic, this one for Baden, shows that although Jews made up 1.66 percent of the population between 1829 and 1844, 1.75 percent of the accused and 1.20 percent of the tried defendants were Jews.[16] This suggests a decline, but it must be mentioned that neither Westphalia nor Baden had a high percentage of Jews. Furthermore, under the *Kaiserreich* the Jewish crime rate was considerably lower than the Christian one.[17] So it seems possible that the Jewish crime rate was indeed somewhat higher in the early modern period, perhaps as a result of more rigid social control and a higher level of reporting. But it certainly decreased in the century of emancipation, until it compared favorably to the Christian rate.

Jewish crime shares some of the main features of Christian crime, but it also shows some peculiarities. We can distinguish three broad categories of offenses: crimes against persons, crimes against property, and crimes against the state and/or the church.

Because their incidence is generally low, crimes against persons and against the state require no lengthy discussion. In fact, crimes against persons may have been lower for Jews than for Christians. Cases of manslaughter are rare;[18] equally rare are cases of the murder of fellow robbers who had betrayed their friends.[19] The records contain, moreover, a few cases of infanticide,[20] reflecting the miserable lot of an increasing number of Jewish maidservants in the eighteenth century and the shame of single motherhood.[21] Thus, it seems that Andreas Osiander in the sixteenth century and Moses Mendelssohn in the eighteenth were right when they

---

14 For figures on the judicial punishment of Christians and Jews, 1562–1696, see Richard van Dül-men, *Theater des Schreckens,* 2nd ed. (Munich, 1988), 190–1; *Hessisches Städtebuch* (Stuttgart, 1957), 131, 147. Total population (including Jews): in 1685, 21,000; in 1700, 23,000. In 1694, there were 415 Jewish households; in 1703, some 2,364 Jews lived in 436 households. In Hameln's special jail (*Stockhaus*), 7% of the inmates were Jews, a disproportionately high number. Thomas Krause, *Die Strafrechtspflege im Kurfürstentum und Königreich Hannover. Vom Ende des 17. Jahrhunderts bis zum ersten Drittel des 19. Jahrhunderts* (Aalen, 1991), 223.

15 Jacob Toury, *Der Eintritt der Juden ins deutsche Bürgertum* (Tel Aviv, 1973), 166–7.

16 Reinhard Rürup, "Die Judenemanzipation in Baden," *Zeitschrift für die Geschichte des Oberrheins* 114 (1966): 284.

17 Franz von Liszt, "Das Problem der Kriminalität der Juden," in Reinhard Frank, ed., *Festschrift der Juristischen Fakultät in Giessen zum Universitäts-Jubiläum* (Giessen, 1907), 371–418.

18 Faust, *Sozial- und wirtschaftsgeschichtliche Beiträge zur Judenfrage,* 71.

19 Danker, *Räuberbanden,* 304.

20 Otto Ulbricht, *Kindsmord und Aufklärung in Deutschland* (Munich, 1990), 29.

21 Glanz, *Geschichte,* 157.

stated that, except among professional thieves, murder was not a typically Jewish crime.[22]

Jews were more often the victims of assault than assailants who inflicted bodily harm on others, including their own fellow Jews. Assaults by Jews were nonetheless significant; they made up the second largest category of Jewish crimes.[23] Among Christian crimes, assaults also ranked second. A number of these crimes were committed on the Sabbath or in the synagogue, indicative of tensions within the Jewish community. For example, in 1793 in the electorate of Mainz a Jew who had been banned by his community was beaten while at prayer.[24]

Serious sexual offenses were also very rare, another characteristic trait of Jewish criminality. In some places in late medieval Germany, sexual intercourse between Jews and Christians was a crime punishable by death; it was still forbidden in the early modern period, but the death penalty had been replaced by forced exile. Examples of banishment can be found into the mid-seventeenth century.[25]

Although anti-Semites advanced the opposite view, crimes against the state, too, were rare. When Dohm pointed out that the Amsterdam Jews had not been found guilty of such a crime for over two hundred years, he was not far off the mark.[26] Data for two villages near Frankfurt tell of six offenses against the Jewish or Christian authorities for a period of 148 years, for one village, and of one such offense for the period of 1713 through 1770 for the other.[27] The one exception, however, is that of counterfeiting, which was regarded as a typically Jewish crime.[28] Indeed, it can be found

22 "How can anyone suspect the Jews of such unnatural and cruel crimes [ritual murder] when one does not even hear of them committing murders?" R. Po-chia Hsia, *The Myth of Ritual Murder: Jews and Magic in Reformation Germany* (New Haven, Conn., 1988), 138, summarizing Osiander's arguments; Horst Steinmetz, ed., *Lessing – Ein unpoetischer Dichter* (Frankfurt/Main, 1969), 52: letter by Mendelssohn to Salomon Gumperz, 1754.

23 Faust, *Sozial- und wirtschaftsgeschichtliche Beiträge zur Judenfrage,* 71–2.

24 Berhard Post, *Judentoleranz und Judenemanzipation in Kurmainz, 1774–1813* (Wiesbaden, 1985), 322–4.

25 Karl-Ernst Meinhardt, "Das peinliche Strafrecht der freien Reichsstadt Frankfurt/Main im Spiegel der Strafpraxis des 16. und 17. Jahrhunderts," Ph.D. diss., Universität Frankfurt, 1957, 208–9; 241. Sometimes a fine was the preferred punishment. See, e.g., R. Froning, ed., *Frankfurter Chroniken und annalistische Aufzeichnungen* (Frankfurt/Main, 1884), 300.

26 Dohm, *Bürgerliche Verbesserung,* 95.

27 Faust, *Sozial- und wirtschaftsgeschichtliche Beiträge zur Judenfrage,* 72; the first village consisted of 52 households of protected Jews in 1763; the other had between 12 and 19 Jewish households in the eighteenth century. For misdemeanors see, e.g., Günter Hans, "Juden im Busbecker Tal," in Günter Hans, ed., *Buseck. Seine Dörfer und Burgen* (1986), 49–50.

28 Dohm, *Bürgerliche Verbesserung,* 96; individual cases can easily be spotted; for example, cf. Christian Becker, ed., "Peter Müllers, hiesigen Bürgers und Mahlers, handschriftliche Chronik aus den Jahren 1573 bis Juny 1633," *Archiv für Frankfurts Geschichte und Kunst* 2 (1862): 62; Jürgen Ackermann, "Die Juden in und um Birstein im 17. und 18. Jahrhundert," *Zeitschrift des Vereins für hessische Landeskunde* 93 (1988): 109; Toury, *Der Eintritt der Juden,* 167; another trial of a Jew for counterfeiting (1703–5) can be found in the Landesarchiv Schleswig, sec. 7, no. 3067.

on almost any list of Jewish crimes. As money changers, Jews were both victims of Christian forgers and themselves offenders.[29]

Crimes against Christianity and the Christian church are well documented. Burglaries of Christian churches always received considerable attention, but they did not necessarily constitute a crime against Christianity as such. Even more attention was paid to a "special" sort of crime that happened under particular circumstances. Defendants found guilty and sentenced to death were usually given spiritual support by a priest. In the case of the Jews, this could be a rabbi.[30] But this was rarely done, because the early modern period was not characterized by religious tolerance. Jews were usually given over to Christian pastors who wanted to use this unique opportunity for conversion, fulfilling the long-cherished dream of the conversion of the Jews, at least in individual cases. Thus, before each execution of a Jew a battle of religions ensued. Generally, condemned Jews were willing to give up their faith only if their life was spared, and that the authorities were not prepared to grant. So they died affirming their faith.[31]

Since Christian vicars often found it hard to bear defeat, they aggressively continued their missionary work on the scaffold. This was the moment when the spectacular acts of blasphemy, reported in contemporary works, occurred. As an act of defiance and revenge, some of the Jews resorted to cursing the Christian religion in front of huge crowds of spectators. The most famous case is that of Jonas Meyer, a member of a band that had stolen one of Germany's greatest treasures, the golden altar of Lüneberg, in 1696. While being hoisted up, he cried: "I have lived as a Jew, and I shall die a Jew. Cursed be anyone in whose heart there is a fiber that believes in Jesus Christ."[32] Such blasphemous offenses were punished severely; in the case of Jonas Meyer the punishment was executed on the corpse.[33]

For Christians and Jews alike, the bulk of crime, at least since the early modern period, has always consisted of crimes against property. Contemporary literature gives quite a range of Jewish crimes against property, but here it may suffice to distinguish three kinds: *Beutelschneiderei* (literally, "purse cutting"), house burglary, and theft by robber bands.[34] *Beutelschnei-*

---

29 Meinhardt, *Das peinliche Strafrecht,* 195–7.

30 This was indeed sometimes done, e.g., in Hanau in 1615; see Johann Jacob Schudt, *Jüdische Merkwürdigkeiten,* vol. 1 (Frankfurt/Main, 1717): 391.

31 As a Jew in Kiel did in 1725, who said he wanted to stay true to the faith of his ancestors. Uwe Danker, "Acten-mässiger Bericht von einer zu Kiel im Umschlag 1725 ertappten Diebes-Rotte," *Demokratische Geschichte* 4 (1989): 41.

32 Hosmann, *Juden-Hertz,* 19.

33 For another example, see Radbruch, *Geschichte,* 145.

34 The preliminary report to Bierbrauer's *Beschreibung* lists ten different groups. By the early nineteenth century, the number had risen to nineteen; see C. T. P. Schwencken, *Notizen über die berüchtigsten jüdischen Gauner und Spitzbuben* (Marburg and Cassel, 1820), 16–22; also Toury, *Der Eintritt der Juden,* 169–71.

derei, the early modern equivalent of pickpocketing, was mainly committed at markets and fairs. The number of Jewish purse cutters was considered to be very large.[35] Poor Jews sometimes sent their children to these *Kissler,* as they were called, to be trained as *Beutelschneider.* The master thief had to feed and clothe them, and they had to give him their booty in return.[36] For the English reader, images of Fagin in *Oliver Twist* come to mind.

Stealing from houses was an offense probably most often committed by individual vagrant Jews who made good use of opportunities that presented themselves. Called *Kuttenschieber,* they slipped into a house or an inn during the daytime, when they found the doors open, and stole what they could grab, for example, a silver spoon.[37] Subgroups either made use of religious feelings by pretending a desire to convert to Christianity to enter the houses of vicars and priests or used master-keys.[38] By far the largest number of thieves belonged to these two groups.

In the eyes of contemporaries, however, it was burglary and theft by bands that typified Jewish criminality, from the late seventeenth century onward.[39] The number of Jews in Christian robber bands and in all-Jewish bands was a shock to the German public, which was fascinated by them out of all proportion. Books on the subject were published for over a century, from 1735 to 1841. One famous all-Jewish band was that of the Long Hoyum, which robbed the Coburg gold-and-silver-lace factory in 1732. Another was the well-known Great Dutch band from the late eighteenth century, which consisted mainly of Jews and was led by an old Jew.[40] The Jewish bands receive the highest praise from all historians writing on the subject. In his 1988 study of three early eighteenth-century robber bands, one of them Jewish, Uwe Danker describes one as old-fashioned because it

---

35 Toury, *Der Eintritt der Juden,* 170, according to a source from 1823.
36 *Acten mässige Designation Derer Von einer Diebischen Juden-Bande verübten Kirchen-Raubereyen und gewaltsamen mörderischen Einbrüche, Samt Angefügter Beschreibung Derer meisten Jüdischen Ertz-Diebe,* 3rd ed. (Coburg, n.d.), suppl.; Einert, *Entdeckter Jüdischer Baldober,* 545.
37 See "Steck-Brief" for the Jew Samuel Jacob and another one, arrested in Osnabrück for the theft of two silver spoons, in *Wöchentliche Osnabrückische Anzeigen* (1767), 331–2, or the "Steckbrief" for the Jew Levin Abraham (or "Levin Hirsch" or "Hartog"), ibid. (1772), 267–70.
38 Peter Aufgebauer, *Die Geschichte der Juden in der Stadt Hildesheim im Hochmittelalter und in der frühen Neuzeit* (Hildesheim, 1984), 87–8.
39 Practically nothing is known about any precursors of these bands. It is interesting, however, that the only member of a large band in the Wetterau who was caught and tried in 1666 was a Jew. Meinhardt, *Das peinliche Strafrecht,* 228. In Wilhelm Treue's *Eine Frau, drei Männer und eine Kunstfigur. Barocke Lebensläufe* (Munich, 1992), Samuel Herz Löw Oppenheim spends three (fictional?) years, in the 1660s, with a band that included Jews. See 60–4.
40 Hermann Bettenhäuser, "Räuber- und Gaunerbanden in Hessen," *Zeitschrift des Vereins für hessische Geschichte und Landeskunde* 75–6 (1964–5): 324–6; Norbert Finzsch, "Räuber und Gendarme im Rheinland: Das Bandenwesen in den vier rheinischen Departments und während der Zeit der französischen Verwaltung (1794–1814)," *Francia* 15 (1987): 452–3. On a successful Jewish band in London that had connections with Holland, see Frank McLynn, *Crime and Punishment in Eighteenth-Century England* (London, 1989), 43–4.

used brute force, another as craftsmanlike, and the Jewish band as highly professional.[41] Carsten Küther characterizes the Jewish thieves as innovators, as the driving force behind change.[42] Ernst Schubert counts the members of the Coburg band among "the greatest figures in the history of crime in Germany," because most of them, in contrast with the glorified robber heroes, were never caught.[43] Yet another study describes the Jewish bandits as avant-garde criminals.[44]

The question arises, What was it that made the Jewish bands so efficient, so professional? The answer to this question is twofold: First, it had to do with the way they went about their business; and second, their close contacts with other parts of Jewish society yielded certain advantages. This second aspect leads to the causes and conditions of Jewish banditry.

The operative mode was characterized by careful planning and thorough organization.[45] First of all, as much information as possible was collected about the house to be robbed and the objects to be stolen. Second, a cost-benefit calculation was made, and, since the Jews considered their potential booty merchandise for sale, sometimes the project was dropped if the potential profit appeared too small. They waited patiently for the right moment to arrive, which sometimes was a very long time. Directions to the house to be burglarized were obtained from cooperating beggar Jews, who also often served as lookouts. Hostels were booked in advance to provide band members with places to stay. The members of a band planning a burglary traveled separately to a secret meeting place, met precisely on time, committed the burglary while a lookout was at his post, generally avoided violence (this ideal was temporarily abandoned at the end of the eighteenth century), and pretended to belong to a different religious or social group. After the burglary they rode for hours through the night, to put as much distance as possible between them and the scene of the crime, which was located far from their places of residence. As a rule bandits did not commit offenses in the villages in which they lived; they hoped to avoid attracting attention and wished to keep the peace with the local authorities. Thus, Jewish bandits were modern in choosing all of Germany as

---

41 Danker, *Räuberbanden*, 237.
42 Küther, *Räuber und Gauner*, 41. Küther bases his verdict on the view that the form of organization described next came into existence at the very end of the eighteenth century.
43 Schubert, *Arme Leute*, 175.
44 Barbara Suthoff, "Gaunertum als Träger plebejischer Kultur," *Kriminalsoziologische Bibliografie* 41 (1983): 62–4.
45 For this paragraph, *Designation*; Glanz, *Geschichte*, 102–4, 112–14; Schubert, *Arme Leute*, 176; Danker, *Räuberbanden*, 234–6.

their "place of work" but traditional in selecting their place of residence, as will become clear shortly.[46]

The structure of the bands differed from what popular (and academic) imagination supposed. There were no stable bands, and there was no established hierarchy with a recognized leader. Bands were flexible associations. For most thefts, the composition and the number of participants changed, as did the leadership.[47] This remained true for most of the eighteenth century and continued on into the next. The only exception was the Great Dutch band. The booty was either split according to one's role in the breakin – on the basis of its monetary value – or each participant was given an equal share, sometimes with the exception of the ferret. The latter was often the case in the small number of thefts where violence was involved.[48]

Why did Jewish bands achieve this high level of perfection earlier than other kinds of bands? Glanz's rather general answer, that Jewish criminality mirrored Jewish life, may be put into more concrete terms.[49] A high degree of mobility, rationality, and nonviolence can be found in the world of both the law-abiding and the criminal Jew. It might be argued, however, that some of these qualities belonged solely to the Jewish elite, yet their world and that of the bandits were not necessarily all that far apart. The bandit Alexander Saladin, who was executed in Celle in 1699, had previously been in the service of Oppenheimer in Vienna. Another thief was in fact the servant of a Düsseldorf court Jew, and yet another servant, reputed to be an arch-thief, worked in the household of a court Jew.[50]

Jewish bands had a specific social profile. Their members were older than their Christian counterparts,[51] and, in adherence to Jewish traditions, most of them were married.[52] Of a sample that Danker analyzed, 88 percent were married and 71 percent had fathered children.[53] In this they differed distinctly from Christian bandits. Jewish members of bands of thieves abided by the norms and customs of their religion and their society. They observed the Sabbath, the eating habits, and the traditional way of dressing, though sometimes a compromise had to be found to escape detection. When in 1778 the famous German penal-law reformer Hommel said, in an attack on

---

46 [Carl Philipp Theodor Schwencken], *Aktenmässige Nachrichten von dem Gauner- und Vagabonden-Gesindel* (Cassel, 1822), VIII.

47 The average size of a unit was five to six persons; the more serious a crime, the higher the number of participants.

48 Danker, *Räuberbanden*, 283–90.   49 Glanz, *Geschichte*, 112.

50 Hosmann, *Juden-Hertz*, 357; Einert, *Entdeckter Jüdischer Baldober*, 553. Unprotected Jews were often taken in as servants by privileged Jews.

51 Danker, *Räuberbanden*, 248.   52 Glanz, *Geschichte*, 109, 115.

53 Danker, *Räuberbanden*, 267.

formal religion, that even a simple-minded, evil Jew, who would otherwise steal and kill whenever the opportunity presented itself, would not think of stealing on the Sabbath, even if you put a hat full of money in front of him, he was absolutely right.[54] Quite typically, a Jewish criminal was at prayer in the synagogue when his persecutors arrived.[55] That band members adhered strictly to the laws and customs of German Jews was also reflected in the all-male character of Jewish banditry. This fact mirrored the seclusion of Jewish women in their own society. Moreover, up to one-third of the many German women in the lists of criminals consisted of the companions of thieves working in bands.[56]

Hardly anything can be said about the social origins of Jewish criminals, because for the authorities the description "a Jew" was generally sufficient. Some of them, it can be shown, came from families with a criminal past.[57] As places of birth or last residence, Frankfurt, other parts of Hesse, the Netherlands in the west, and Bohemia and Poland in the east were frequently given.

Turning to the second point, namely, the connections of the organized thieves with the rest of Jewish society, it makes sense first to look at the larger society. Jonathan Israel writes: "From court Jew to pedlar, those divergent groupings penetrated and depended on each other economically, as well as in religion and commercial life. It would be idle to deny," he continues, "that there was exploitation as well as collaboration and interdependence, but such exploitation existed on all levels and operated in all ways."[58]

Jewish robbers are not mentioned in Israel's sober analysis, but there can be no doubt that they should be included. For their well-planned burglaries, the Jewish thieves depended on ferrets, fences, private charity, and community poor relief. In terms of social support, they depended on respectable members of Jewish society as well as on the integrated lower classes and on the marginal Jews. It was the particular close-knit quality of the minority group, as well as the special functions it fulfilled for the majority, that made this interconnectedness more efficient than what their Christian competitors had at their disposal and that turned the minority status into an advantage. Yet some of those who helped the criminals were also, at least partly, dependent on the Jewish thieves. Thus, there was real interdependence.

54 Karl Ferdinand Hommel, *Des Herrn Marquis von Beccaria unsterbliches Werk von Verbrechen und Strafen*, ed. John Lekschas (Berlin, 1966), 9.
55 Danker, "Actenmässiger Bericht," 38.   56 Glanz, *Geschichte*, 185–6.
57 Ibid., 192–6.
58 Jonathan Israel, *European Jewry in the Age of Mercantilism, 1550–1750* (Oxford, 1985), 171–2.

Contemporary literature distinguished three kinds of ferrets.[59] First, the respectable ferret, who not only knew where to make substantial booty but was also the brains behind a particular burglary. Second, the Jewish peddler, who supplied necessary information and guided the band on that particular night. And third, the ferret whose collaboration was restricted to a tip.[60] Respectability obviously did not coincide with financial security; otherwise it is difficult to understand why a respectable member of society should have endangered his reputation for a double share of the booty. But perhaps the risk of being discovered was very low because ferrets from the upper classes took great care to keep their names secret. Fortunately for historians, at least one of them was not careful enough and was arrested, put on trial, and executed. Thus, the Meiningen court Jew Mendel Carbe, who was the ferret for the spectacular robbery of the Coburg gold-and-silver-lace factory in 1732, has become the classic example of the respectable ferret.

The fences are another group that profited from burglary and theft. Their contribution to the efficiency of Jewish crime is often stressed. Because Jews were permitted to engage only in trades with low esteem, such as pawnbroking, dealing in secondhand clothes, and hawking, contact with thieves was almost unavoidable. As a result of this and their poor economic circumstances, Jews came to dominate the trade in stolen goods. Accordingly, when the authorities really set their minds to recovering stolen property, they turned first to the Jews. After the treasures of Frankfurt had been taken from the city hall in 1635, for example, the authorities appealed to the Jews of the town to turn in all valuables they had received from a certain suspect, which proved to be a successful measure.[61] Like some of the ferrets, some of the fences also belonged to both worlds: they were shady recipients of stolen goods at night and respectable dealers during the day. At the beginning of the eighteenth century, a prominent Jew in the Jewish community in Halle, in fact one of its cofounders, became the general fence for all of central Saxony.[62] As was to be expected, fences exploited the thieves, who complained bitterly about the little money they received for their valuable booty.[63]

Beadles in hostels and well-to-do heads of households supported Jewish bandits by following the customs of their faith and the prescriptions of the Talmud. According to the latter, poor Jewish travelers had to be offered a

---

59 Bierbrauer, *Vorbericht.*   60 On bourgeois fences, see Glanz, *Geschichte,* 116–17.
61 Richard van Dülmen, *Theater des Schreckens,* 2nd ed. (Frankfurt/Main, 1988), 17–18; Danker, *Räuberbanden,* 350.
62 His name was Assur Marx. Glanz, *Geschichte,* 98; for his role in Halle, see Guido Kisch, *Rechts- und Sozialgeschichte der Juden in Halle, 1686–1730* (Berlin, 1970), 27–31.
63 Danker, *Räuberbanden,* 316–17.

bed for the night, a meal, and a little help to continue their trip. In small communities, this was done by individuals; the larger ones had established their own hostels, the *Judenschlafstätten,* which were run by beadles.

Since it was part of their religious duty, respectable individuals willingly took in bandits. But observing the rules of their faith may have been a perfect camouflage for the host, though it is often hard to tell what it was. After two separate burglaries, a group of thieves spent the night each time at the house of Stolberg's court Jew, Touffies.[64] It is not possible to determine whether he knew he was harboring criminals or merely pretended not to know.

There cannot be any doubt, however, that the beadles knew with whom they were dealing.[65] Nor can there be any doubt that some members of the Jewish lower classes felt that they were discriminated against and not paid enough to make a decent living, and thus collaborated with thieves. In a list of thirty-one places where criminal Jews stayed, published in 1735, the *Judenschlafstätten* are named five times.[66] Clearly, these hostels were resthouses for criminals on the way to a burglary, as well as venues where the booty was divided up or stashed. For their help, the beadles received a small share. Through these close contacts with criminals, the children of beadles sometimes turned into well-trained robbers and thieves.

In addition to such interdependence, I would like to advance a somewhat provocative hypothesis: Seen objectively, at the beginning of the eighteenth century these thieves were actually working for the state. Due to the enormous toll taken by wars, epidemics, bad harvests, and the demands of absolutist ambitions, many German territories were desperate for money in the form of precious metals. This was especially true in the first thirty years of the century. They naturally turned to the court Jews, who, eager to please, assured them of great amounts of silver, which in reality they could not obtain. In 1723, the Gumpertz brothers, for example, promised Prussia's "Soldier King," Friedrich Wilhelm I, 300,000 talers worth of silver within eighteen months.[67] Even with good international business connections, such a large amount was impossible to come by. Not only was the price of silver extremely high at this time, but many countries had also banned its export. The Gumpertz brothers soon found themselves in dire straits.

At the same time, Jewish (and other) thieves were systematically stealing silver from churches and private homes. The extraordinary number of

64 Einert, *Entdeckter Jüdischer Baldober,* 552, 554.
65 For this paragraph, see Glanz, *Geschichte,* 149–53.
66 Einert, *Entdeckter Jüdischer Baldober,* 551–3.
67 Selma Stern, *Der preussische Staat und die Juden,* vol. 2, pt. 1 (Tübingen, 1962), 119–21.

church thefts can be explained partly by the existence of silver objects in the churches. Often silver made up the largest part of booty from church thefts. Even if that had not been the case, the robbers could still be certain of one or two items of silver and take the precious materials and the coins in the poorbox. If one looks at all thefts committed by three early eighteenth-century bands, thefts of silver make up one-third of them.[68] The bandits knew that the silver trade was in the hands of Jews and that the precious metal was in high demand by fences, of whom some dealt in silver.[69] True, some of the silver may have stayed with the thieves' families; some of it may have been taken to distant fairs. But it seems very likely that a considerable part was sold to court Jews like the Gumpertz brothers, who, in their desperation to fulfill their contract, turned to local dealers in silver, albeit without ultimate success.

As described here, Jewish banditry needs to be interpreted more closely. Can it be viewed as social banditry?[70] Did the bandits in some way right the wrongs the Jews experienced at the hands of Christians, or were they just simply criminals, representing a Jewish professional class? A discussion of three points – the relations between the bandits and the rest of German Jewry, the choice of victims, and the matter of whether their deeds were justified – may shed some light on this question.

In the historical literature, the relations of Jewish society to the bandits are frequently addressed. Jewish solidarity is often regarded as a decisive factor behind the kind of collaboration just described. Ernst Schubert, for example, argues that since Christian authorities were hostile to all Jews, any Jew would rather support a criminal fellow Jew than a Christian. According to such an interpretation, no clear boundaries existed, therefore, between "straight" and criminal Jews.[71] In the words of another author, together the Jews formed an antisociety.[72] This means that for him one of the essential criteria of social banditry, namely, receiving help and support from the group to which they originally belonged, is established. Unknowingly, Schubert shares the view of some early eighteenth-century sources, where exactly the same argument is advanced. According to these sources, Jews were either thieves or ferrets; in short, all were criminals.[73]

68 Danker, *Räuberbanden*, 224.
69 And suppliers for the state mint, such as "Salomon Michel, Casselischer Silber-Livrant zu Abterode in Hessen, . . . welcher mit den Dieben in sehr vertraulicher Bekanntschaft gelebet, und das meiste aus Kirchen und sonsten geraubte Silber wissentlich erkaufft und eingeschmelzet hat." *Designation*, no. 70; also Einert, *Entdeckter Jüdischer Baldober*, 536.
70 Eric Hobsbawm, *Bandits* (Harmondsworth, 1972).
71 Schubert, *Arme Leute*, 176–7; also Faust, *Sozial- und wirtschaftsgeschichtliche Beiträge zur Judenfrage*, 75.
72 Küther, *Räuber und Gauner*, 26, 101.
73 *Designation*, suppls. 2 and 16.

This pattern of implicating all Jews is very old and can also be found, for example, in the accusations of ritual murder. In his classic study of the Jewish lower classes, Glanz, however, holds the opposite view.[74] Over and over, he gives instances of Jews informing on the thieves. For him, respectable and criminal Jews lived in two different worlds; he argues that solidarity with criminals would have endangered the whole Jewish community and thus was shunned.

It seems to me that Glanz is closer to the truth, though a slight qualification seems necessary. In principle, a minority can react in the ways mentioned: members either report a crime to authorities or enter into a collaboration. Since the second alternative involved considerable risk, it was chosen only under special circumstances. The first was chosen when Jewish authorities learned about activities of lower-class Jews that were undoubtedly felonious. Glanz supplies sufficient examples of this attitude to challenge Schubert's view of group solidarity, and Danker shows that members of the Jewish elite interfered resolutely when they learned about the contacts of acquaintances or subordinates with criminals.[75] During the fair in Frankfurt, for example, the rabbis admonished local Jews on the first morning of the fair not to put up Jewish thieves or to buy anything from them.[76] This attitude of Jewish leaders was typical. It was different, however, when members of the elite came under suspicion and the accusations left considerable room for interpretation. In such cases, the suspect was often given the community's full support, because his downfall, in contrast to the execution of a criminal, would have been detrimental to the whole elite and, therefore, to the whole Jewish community. In this way, many a respectable fence escaped criminal punishment.[77]

The characteristics of the victims also seem to point to the existence of a social dimension to Jewish banditry. Jewish bandits stole almost exclusively from Christians. No breakins into houses of court Jews, or representatives of the Jewish community, or synagogues (in contrast to the many burglarized churches) were reported. This situation implies a double moral standard. But such an argument is hardly convincing. The risk of detection when stealing from fellow Jews was extremely high, for rumors spread fast in the small and close-knit Jewish community. Moreover, there simply were many more rich Christians compared to the tiny number of rich Jews.

A third argument favoring the presence of a social dimension to Jewish banditry is its ideological justification. Crimes against Christians, so it runs,

---

74 Glanz, _Geschichte_, 40, 42, 97, 171.   75 Danker, _Räuberbanden_, 304–5.
76 Johann Jacob Schudt, _Jüdische Merkwürdigkeiten_, vol. 2 (Frankfurt/Main, 1717), 212.
77 Ibid., 121–5.

are no sin, because all goods in the world originally belonged to the seed of Abraham and are, therefore, unlawfully owned by Christians.[78] This argument, too, is a tricky one. First of all, the bandits themselves did not justify their crimes in this way; rather, it was Christian persecutors who used this argument to explain why Jews stole almost exclusively from Christians. Second, Judaism condemns crimes against property as vehemently as Christianity; the Ten Commandments are fundamentals of both religions. So one has to conclude that in spite of some peculiarities, Jewish banditry was basically the work of criminals – as Hobsbawm stated many years ago – who profited from the minority status of the group from which they came.[79]

But what causes and conditions explain the rise in thefts by Jewish bands during the early modern period? Three structural factors, which contributed to the difficult economic situation of the Jews, need to be mentioned: first, the legal and economic restrictions under which the Jews were forced to live; second, the large number of Jews that settled in the countryside in the early modern period; and third, the growth of the Jewish population after 1700. Finally, we need to look at the political situation at the beginning of the eighteenth century.

Scholars frequently comment upon the legal and economic restrictions imposed on Jews. Usually only a small number of Jews was permitted to stay in a given territory. This meant that many Jews had no right to remain where they lived and were expelled when their existence became known. Although the wholesale expulsion of a territory's Jewry had become rather rare after 1648, it had not completely disappeared, as the expulsion of the Viennese Jews in 1670 shows. In addition to individuals driven from their homes, persecution forced even more people onto the road, as the example of the violent attacks on Polish Jews after 1648 documents. Expelled individuals, parts of expelled groups, and the victims of persecution increased the vagrant population, at least temporarily. Some people may well have stayed on the road for good and in the course of time turned to criminal activity.[80] Furthermore, some of the trades open to Jews were, almost by definition, criminality-prone: pawnbroking, hawking (which often was a mere camouflage occupation), and dealing in old cloth. Considering the financial exploitation (in the form of taxes) that Jews experienced day in and day out, doing business with criminals was practically unavoidable. The context, therefore, created the right atmosphere for crime to flourish.

The settlement of large numbers of Jews in rural areas after the expulsions of the late fifteenth and sixteenth centuries deserves more attention. The

---

78 *Designation,* suppl. 16; Bierbrauer, *Beschreibung,* preliminary report.
79 Hobsbawm, *Bandits,* 39–40.
80 Gustav Radbruch and Heinrich Gwinner, *Geschichte des Verbrechens* (Stuttgart, 1951), 140.

focus of study is too often on urban Jews. Although Jews could be found in almost any rural area, they were crowded "like swarms of bees," as Schudt wrote in 1717, in areas like Hesse and Franconia.[81] But here even fewer opportunities for them to earn a living existed: Jews were excluded from the few trades allowed in rural areas and were forbidden to acquire real estate, which kept them out of agriculture. What remained were moneylending to poor peasants, peddling, and cattle dealing. Settling in the country thus meant a deterioration in the economic situation for most Jews. The difficulty in making ends meet must have induced some to consider a criminal career.

The political organization of the Holy Roman Empire determined the rural areas where great numbers of Jews settled.[82] Crowding occurred in the minuscule territories belonging to the imperial knights, who deliberately tried to attract Jews in order to populate their ministates.[83] The security they enjoyed in these territories may be regarded as a faint reflection of the special status they used to have under the emperor, before the rise of the territorial states. That is why I mentioned earlier that Jewish thieves were "traditional" in their choice of a place of residence: They lived in the least modern parts of Germany. It seems more to the point, however, to view this security as a result of the economic and political weakness of these territories, their lack of efficient administration, and their poor finances. The poorly paid officials in these territories deliberately disregarded the criminal past of their subjects because the state profited in two ways from their stay: first, they made the bandits pay for it, even if their stay was only temporary, and, second, their subjects were spared by these bandits.[84] These were the conditions under which the robber villages came into existence. For instance, the small village of Fauerbach in the duchy of Solms-Rödelheim, had an extremely low rate of thefts but a high number of Jews carrying letters of protection. These individuals had been accused of felonies in other distant places.

The growth of the Jewish population in the eighteenth century,[85] which began in the last third of the preceding century[86] and included an influx of Jews from eastern Europe, led to widespread impoverishment and social

81 Schudt, *Jüdische Merkwürdigkeiten,* 1:394.
82 On changes in the political structure of early modern Europe and banditry, see Bruce Lenman and Geoffrey Parker, "The State, the Community and Criminal Law in Early Modern Europe," in V. A. C. Gatrell, Bruce Lenman, and Geoffrey Parker, eds., *Crime and the Law: The Social History of Crime in Western Europe since 1500* (London, 1980), 40–1.
83 Schubert, *Arme Leute,* 151, 154; J. Friedrich Battenberg, "Des Kaisers Kammerknechte. Gedanken zur rechtlich-sozialen Situation der Juden in Spätmittelalter und früher Neuzeit," *Historische Zeitschrift* 245 (1987): 592–3.
84 Ackermann, "Die Juden in Birstein," 109–10.   85 Schubert, *Arme Leute,* 154–5.
86 Israel, *European Jewry,* 169–70.

polarization. The Jewish lower classes became larger and with them the number of beggar Jews. In the last quarter of the eighteenth century, the lower classes made up 66 to 75 percent of the Jewish population.[87] Not surprisingly, the Jewish system of poor relief was overwhelmed and consequently broke down. While the poor relief officer could not help and sent the vagrants on to the next community, the rich were neither willing nor any longer able to cope with increased Jewish poverty.[88] The same developments can be observed on the Christian side. The result was strong competition among the lower classes and marginal groups for available resources – a major factor in the growth of bands.[89] There can be no doubt that this development considerably enlarged the recruitment base of the Jewish criminals. Those Jews already living the criminal life were confirmed in the view that it was best to train their children in this trade.[90]

To these long-term, structural conditions has to be added another factor: the political situation in the first two decades of the eighteenth century. Not only did the War of the Spanish Succession and the Great Northern War force the governments to focus on these crucial issues, but they also deprived them of their main instrument for combatting banditry – the troops that were often employed in raids against bandits. Thus, at the beginning of the century the political situation was favorable to the rise of banditry. (It was also favorable at the century's end, I might add.) It seems that these conditions and factors offer a better explanation of the rise of Jewish banditry than to link its origin in a very general way with the rise of commerce and the persecution of beggars, which, according to one author, triggered a guerrilla war against property that in turn gave rise to bands of thieves.[91]

II

In the Middle Ages, Jews in Germany were under the penal jurisdiction of the emperor, because they were his *Kammerknechte*.[92] Although they retained this status, most Jews also fell under the jurisdiction of the territorial

---

87 Toury, *Der Eintritt der Juden*, 145.   88 Glanz, *Geschichte*, 130–3.
89 Heinz Reif, "Vagierende Unterschichten, Vagabunden und Bandenkriminalität im Ancien Régime," *Beiträge zur historischen Sozialkunde* 11 (1981): 37.
90 Küther, *Räuber und Gauner*, 79.
91 Helmut Reinicke, *Gaunerwirtschaft. Die erstaunlichen Abenteuer hebräischer Spitzbuben in Deutschland* (Berlin, 1983), 130–1.
92 Historically, a *Kammerknecht* was a Jew who enjoyed the emperor's protection in return for paying a tax. Battenberg, "Des Kaisers Kammerknechte"; Rotraud Ries, "Juden. Zwischen Schutz und Verteidigung," in Bernd-Ulrich Hergemöller, ed., *Randgruppen der spätmittelalterlichen Gesellschaft* (Warendorf, 1990), 231–41. In some areas the Jews had retained their own jurisdiction over the less violent crimes.

princes, whose territories were slowly gaining sovereignty. This meant that
Jews were tried before ordinary (Christian) courts, sometimes before special committees. With respect to criminal jurisdiction, therefore, the Jews
did not form "a republic apart"[93] but were part of the "republic" around
them. Although in matters of ritual and, sometimes, in civil litigation among
themselves they enjoyed their own jurisdiction, Jews could not try their
own criminals. Such a state of affairs filled authors like the well-known Wagenseil, who admonished the princes to maintain criminal jurisdiction over
the Jews, with great satisfaction.[94] It is here that the political function of penal jurisdiction becomes obvious. The ruler not only could control the
Jews; he could also try to curb the power of city councils and estates that
claimed jurisdiction over them. What has been said applies equally well to
secular or to ecclesiastical states, such as the archbishopric of Cologne,
which, like the other states, set up, in the early modern *Judenordnungen,*
courts responsible for Jews.[95]

When we turn to imperial penal law and to the views of famous jurists,
we find that in the punishment of offenses no distinction was made between
Jews and Christians. The criminal code of Emperor Charles V, introduced
in 1532, did not establish different penalties for the adherents of different
religions. In fact, the word "Jew" does not even appear in the code. Most
jurists of the sixteenth and seventeenth centuries shared this view, and they
opposed special punishments for Jews.[96] The imperial code, however, left
local and regional traditions intact, and it allowed territorial princes to issue
their own laws. It is on this level that we find special punishments, for example, for theft committed by Jews. For a major theft, Christians were punished by hanging and so were Jews. But local tradition in some areas ordered
a special kind of hanging for the Jews: they were hung by their feet, with
live dogs at their side, strung up in the same way.[97]

Since we must distinguish between the penal code and the practice of
criminal justice, we need to ask whether this penalty was ever actually

---

93 Israel, *European Jewry,* 202.
94 Johann Christopher Wagenseil, "Christliche Ankündigung an alle Hohe Regenten und
   Obrigkeiten / Welche Juden unter / ihrer Bottmässigkeit haben / wegen des Eingrifs / Welchen
   die Juden in Ihre Hoheiten / Regalien / und Jurisdiction zu thun / sich unterstehen," in *Hofnung
   der Erlösung Israels* (Nuremberg and Altdorf, 1707), 275.
95 Hedwig Heider, "Die Rechtsgeschichte des deutschen Judentums bis zu Ausgang des Absolutismus
   und die Judenordnungen in den rheinischen Territorialstaaten," J. D. diss., Universität Bielefeld,
   n.d. (1973?), 101–2.
96 Wilhelm Güde, *Die rechtliche Stellung der Juden in den Schriften deutscher Juristen des 16. und 17. Jahrhunderts* (Sigmaringen, 1981), 59–60.
97 Guido Kisch, "The 'Jewish Execution' in Medieval Germany and the Reception of Roman Law,"
   L'Europa e il diritto romano. Studi in memoria Paul Koschaker, vol. 2 (Milan, 1954), 63–93; Glanz,
   Geschichte, 42–4; Dülmen, *Theater,* 137; Güde, *Die rechtliche Stellung,* 56–8.

applied. For the fifteenth century, when this punishment began to be regarded as one suited for Jews, the answer is yes; however, examples are few
and far between for the sixteenth century.[98] But by then the number of Jews
in Germany was very small, owing to the expulsions that began in the late
fifteenth century. That this penalty for theft disappeared probably reflects
the civilizing process, since a number of atrocious punishments fell into disuse at the same time.[99] The way the penalty was applied in Frankfurt am
Main in 1615 confirms this view. The Jewish thief was hung by his feet, but
dogs were no longer used. Moreover, the thief was taken down after some
time and then strangled.[100] In most of the seventeenth century, this punishment was meted out only when an additional or a particularly atrocious
crime had been committed. For example, when a baptized Jew, who, together with two other Jews, had been sentenced to death in Vienna in 1642,
returned to the faith of his ancestors on the way to the scaffold, thus becoming a heretic, his punishment was changed to include this brutal form
of hanging.[101] In 1693, Doepler criticized this form of punishment as not
only brutal and harsh but also as contradicting Christian principles.[102] In the
eighteenth century, the practice was abandoned completely, a view corroborated by an enlightened reformer who stated, in 1785, that it had been
completely forgotten by the time he was writing.[103]

But this penalty should be seen in broader perspective. Early modern
criminal justice was not based on the principle of equality: women were not
punished in the same way as men, and servants not in the same way as their
masters. There was nothing special in meting out different punishments.
The discrimination arises from its particular form. The way Jews were
hanged, for example, made death much more brutal because it was drawn
out, and the use of dogs made it more cruel and degrading at the same time.

Another special law regarding Jews and theft, on the books in Prussia
until 1801, also deserves mention. It stated that if a theft had been committed, and if it had been established that the suspect was a Jew who had
eluded capture, then the Jewry as a whole was liable. For example, when
a royal stamp (*Stempel*) disappeared in East Prussia in 1704 and the thief,
believed to be a Jew, was not caught, the Jewry was made to pay 600

98 Hans von Hentig, *Die Strafe*, vol. 1: *Frühformen und kulturgeschichtliche Zusammenhänge* (Berlin, 1954), 252–3; Hosmann, *Juden-Hertz*, 338–53; Glanz, *Geschichte*, 42–4, 47.
99 Dülmen, *Theater*, 121.   100 Schudt, *Jüdische Merkwürdigkeiten*, 1:391.
101 Hosmann, *Juden-Hertz*, 369–70; Kisch, "Jewish Execution," 90–1. As a penalty for murder and robbery, Hosmann, *Juden-Hertz*, 299–300. The sentence was eventually changed.
102 Jacob Doepler, *Theatrum poenarum, supplicorum et executionum criminalium oder Schau-Platz Derer Leibes und Lebens-Strafen* (Sondershausen, 1693), 1085 (chap. 40, vi).
103 Christian Gottlieb Gmelin, *Abhandlung von den besonderen Rechten der Juden in peinlichen Sachen* (Tübingen, 1785), 77–8.

taler.[104] As in other areas, the Jews were seen as a corporate body, not as individuals.

The most interesting question concerning the courts is whether or not Jews received fair treatment in them. Owing to the current state of research, no definitive answer can be given. A look at the procedure, however, might give us an idea of how Jews were treated.

Court procedure involved two stages, which may have influenced the outcome of trials against Jews.[105] The first of these stages was torture, in Germany, as in other states of early modern Europe, a generally approved means of extracting a confession from the defendant, which was needed to convict. Torture, so it seems, was particularly dangerous for Jewish defendants because of the general prejudice against Jews. They were said to be extremely stubborn, obdurate, and full of hatred for Christians. This gave them the strength, it was argued, to withstand torture.[106] A certain judge maintained that Jews could enjoy a pipe of tobacco while great pain was being inflicted on them.[107] The courts also believed that Jewish and other criminals prepared themselves for torture by voluntarily undergoing it as part of their training as criminals.[108] Investigators were clearly worried by the number of criminals who managed to keep their secrets under torture. In such cases, the accused individual was nonetheless expelled from the town, sometimes with a whipping.

For these reasons, jurists demanded that torture be used with less restraint against Jews.[109] In 1735, for example, a Jew was arrested in Fulda and tortured, because the authorities thought he was a well-known robber. All degrees of torture were applied in vain. He had to be set free, only to be arrested again after a short while and subjected to seven days of torture, yet no confession could be obtained.[110] For the authorities this confirmed their prejudice; that he might be innocent did not cross their minds. Lists printed in 1758, telling of the fate of Jewish criminals, show that two died undergoing torture, which only confirms the fact that, even in the eighteenth century, torture was indeed used unscrupulously against Jews.[111]

Second, a trial could end with the obligation of the defendant to swear an oath to God stating that he had not committed the crime he was accused of (*Reinigungseid,* or *iuramentum purgationis*). Such an oath was equated

---

104 Stern, *Der preussische Staat,* vol. 1, pt. 1, 85.
105 I am leaving aside here the much-discussed question of the Jewish oath, since the criminals were in court as defendants, not as witnesses.
106 Glanz, *Geschichte,* 123.   107 Einert, *Entdeckter Jüdischer Baldober,* 509.
108 Bierbrauer, *Beschreibung, Vorbericht;* Küther, *Räuber und Gauner,* 79.
109 Gmelin, *Abhandlung,* 108.   110 Einert, *Entdeckter Jüdischer Baldober,* 509.
111 Bierbrauer, *Beschreibung.*

with spiritual torture and considered to be very effective in the early modern period, when religious tensions were high. Yet Jews, it was argued, could not swear such an oath, since nothing but perjury was to be expected of them.[112] It probably does not make a great difference, however, that Jews were barred from this way out. The number of trials ending in this verdict was never large, and the practice rapidly disappeared during the eighteenth century.

With regard to sentences, no systematic research has been done to date, let alone a systematic comparison. This has not kept different authors from stating their views with great force. Radbruch is convinced that Jewish criminals were not given fair treatment in court: "The Jews were always punished more severely," he states, "and the death penalty for them was designed in the most cruel and degrading way possible."[113] By way of explaining the disparity between punishments, he points to the function of penal law in the early modern period: to fight sin and the devil. But neither this reason nor Radbruch's examples carry much weight. The atrocious mutilations he stresses were the result of blasphemous offenses on the scaffold; had a Christian insulted his religion in the same way, a similar punishment would have been meted out. As to the argument based on the functioning of penal law, it can be countered by pointing out that most jurists of the sixteenth and seventeenth centuries thought that Jews should not receive any extra punishment on account of their religion.[114] Another author maintains that when Jews stole from churches, a particularly egregious offense, they were always punished more severely.[115] This statement, however, is not based on actual data and disregards the many different kinds of church theft. For example, a distinction has to be made based on the object (sacred or not). In contrast to Radbruch, Glanz is of the opinion that no distinction was made in court between lower-class or marginal Jews and Christians.[116] Moreover, in her study of the relations between the Prussian state and the Jews, Selma Stern mentions that in civil courts Jews were treated fairly.[117] This conclusion is interesting when one considers the constant attacks that were made on the way the Jews conducted their business affairs.

It must be pointed out that early modern penal justice was organized around the offense; the felony committed, not the defendant, was at the

---

112 Gmelin, *Abhandlung*, 105.   113 Radbruch, *Geschichte*, 144–5.
114 Güde, *Die rechtliche Stellung*, 56–8.
115 Danker, *Räuberbanden*, 351; Peter Robertz, *Die Strafrechtspflege am Haupt- und Kriminalgericht zu Jülich von der Karolina bis zur Aufklärung (1540–1744)* (1943; reprinted: Jülich, 1987), 65, gives a late seventeenth-century example. In this case the Jews were condemned to death by hanging.
116 Glanz, *Geschichte*, 30.   117 Stern, *Der preussische Staat*, vol. 2, pt. 1, 34.

center of investigation. As a guideline for future research, it seems reasonable to suggest that the sentences given convicted Jews did not differ from those given Christians. This seems to be a sounder approach than trying to confirm the prevailing opposite view. In future explorations of this subject, historians should contrast the sixteenth and seventeenth centuries, when religious intolerance played such a preeminent role, with the enlightened eighteenth century. But historians must also bear in mind that local traditions, the use of torture, and particular events may have led to more convictions and different forms of punishment. Crimes where religion was involved should be treated separately. In addition, a distinction should be made between secular and ecclesiastical courts.

It was during the Enlightenment that Jewish crime was first regarded as the classic example of criminality caused and conditioned by social circumstances.[118] Aided in no small measure by other developments, emancipation was, in due time, to prove this view correct.[119] After 1830, Jewish banditry began to disappear, and after the middle of the century nothing more was heard of it. When full legal emancipation was finally reached in Imperial Germany in 1871, the Jewish crime rate was considerably lower than the Christian one.[120]

---

118 Besides Dohm, see the statement by an official from Nassau written in 1785, printed in Toury, *Der Eintritt der Juden,* 34.
119 Raphael Straus, *Die Juden in Wirtschaft und Gesellschaft* (Frankfurt/Main, 1964), 82.
120 Liszt, "Das Problem der Kriminalität der Juden," 371–2.

4

Jews and Gentiles in the Holy Roman Empire – A Comment

THEODORE K. RABB

To be required to make the initial comment on the subject of this volume is to be struck by the elusive and kaleidoscopic quality of its theme – an impression that Chapters 1 through 3 only reinforce. For a start, whether the geographic focus of study is called (anachronistically) "Germany" or (more accurately) the "Holy Roman Empire," it is vague at best. The territory covered by the empire did have formal boundaries in late medieval and early modern times, but it included more than Germans, some of whom – to add to the confusion – lived beyond those boundaries. At no time, moreover, was the empire organized into a coherent political structure or centered on a single capital city like London, Paris, or Madrid.

And yet the very disarray may have been the reason that it seemed to offer so interesting a home for Jews. The elusiveness of central authority and the variety of political systems created a landscape that was marked by precisely the cracks and fissures that allowed outsiders to flourish. It therefore seemed almost the agenda of early modern German Jews, particularly after the expulsions of the late Middle Ages, to find places for themselves in the interstices of this fragmented society. To a far greater extent than was true of the relatively stable Jewish communities of Italy, Poland, the Netherlands, and (later) England, they had to thrive in the marginal activities that were available in so localized a polity, with its multiple and contrasting regimes. It was entirely appropriate, therefore, that here, unlike elsewhere in Europe, they often lived in rural areas, in scattered and tiny settlements, and only rarely formed large and visible groupings such as the one in Frankfurt am Main, that echoed the ghettos of Italy. The varied character of their communities has encouraged, in turn, a kaleidoscope of research – studies that seem to lack common threads precisely because they have such disparate subject matter.

Since it is the task of a commentator to find unifying themes amid the complexities, it might be appropriate to begin with the consistencies that

71

do emerge from the different responses of the Jews to the diverse conditions they faced in the empire. Given that they had to seek out the openings into which pariahs like themselves might fit, it was only natural for them to undertake high-risk ventures. That they should have been associated in early modern times with such hazardous trades as those in jewelry and fur, and that they should have created their own unique pattern of nonviolent banditry, as Ulbricht has so elegantly shown (Chapter 3), might almost have been expected. These were, after all, classic "between-the-cracks" activities. The dangers were sufficiently great to deter all but the intrepid, and those few who were willing to brave the peril had to learn to keep a low profile and to rely on friends and contacts in many places. Transporting highly valuable goods in a lawless age was no less a skill than burglary and required the same assets – a daring yet inconspicuous disposition and a multitude of safe havens. The widely scattered Jews of Germany were at an advantage on both counts, and thus the particular practices that often set them apart can, in some circumstances, be seen as the reward, not the price, of the exclusiveness that was forced on them. Segregation and dispersal could encourage the very qualities that promoted success in high-risk enterprises.

To some extent, of course, this basic relationship with the Gentile world was common to all the Jews of Europe. But the evidence suggests that it took a more extreme form in the empire, creating a broader spectrum of experiences and types of community – from the two households Glückel knew in Hameln or the rural village settlements to the familiar ghettos of Worms and Frankfurt am Main, or the cities from which Jews were completely excluded, like Cologne. It was the very diversity that opened up the fissures, and it seems to have operated even within individual cities, where the porous ghettos Haverkamp so cogently describes (Chapter 1) encouraged constant adaptation. The Jews' ceaseless movement took them not only from one city to another but also from neighborhood to neighborhood within the same walls. Given the small size of most urban areas, a new home may have been only a ten-minute walk from the old, but the process of dislocation would itself have reinforced the sense of marginality. And this again proves to be a unifying theme, despite the variety of the individual cases and the highly specialized research they require.

Yet the permeability of the divide between Gentile and Jew, which Daxelmüller also makes unmistakable in the world of popular culture (Chapter 2), did not remove the reality of the separation. Even if there were links and influences, the Germans, no less than the Italians, lived in cultural – even if not always physical – ghettos. For the discrimination and the disabilities were always worse than they were for other outsider groups. Whether at the higher levels of theologians like Luther or in the *bürgerlich* outlook of such works as Jost Amman and Hans Sachs's *Ständebuch,* the Jew represented the antithesis of Christian virtues. Even beggars and lepers could be saved; the Jew, by contrast, was a perpetual reminder of the incompleteness of Jesus' work and subject always to the most stringent legal and social restraints. The result was that for all the evidence of interaction and the frequent absence of formal ghetto walls, Jewry in the empire had to remain essentially a self-contained culture and society. The closest kinship was with coreligionists, however distant, rather than with Gentile neighbors.

The very need for resilience, however, not only promoted high skills in marginal activities but also created a rich cultural life. If the extraordinary variety of the communities makes it difficult to characterize German Jews, or even to find a common motif in their relations with Gentiles – which could range from alternating periods of accommodation and persecution to mutual indifference – that is not to say that their widely different histories were merely local reflections of the need for convenient ways to camouflage their presence. On occasion, their contributions could become essential to the vitality of the societies in which they lived. One has but to think of Prague in the age of Rudolf II – non-German, yet imperial – and consider how different a place it would have been without such prominent figures as Meisel and Rabbi Loeb, in order to appreciate how much Jews could add to the vigor of economic and intellectual life. Long before the rise of the court Jew, and in settings far less hospitable than those of Spain before 1492 or Holland after 1600, some communities were capable of putting their mark on their times, even while elsewhere their brethren were keeping low profiles.

What all of these considerations suggest is a set of questions that need to be answered before either the general character or the distinctiveness of German Jewry can be defined, let alone explained, and before the main elements of Jewish–Gentile relations can in turn be portrayed with some degree of subtlety and nuance.

The first has to do with the nature of the Jewish communities themselves. Were they so disparate as to be unconnectable, or did they share common features that went beyond those traits that are usually apparent throughout western Jewry – religious and charitable practices, high levels of literacy, early age at marriage? Were there additional regularities in their societies (elements of popular culture, perhaps, patterns of banditry, or informality of segregation) that mark them as German, or at least as products of the fragmented empire? In other words, was there something both identifiable and distinct about these communities that set them apart from their Italian or Polish equivalents?

Second, and more complicated, is the question of influence in the other direction. Is there a pattern, peculiar to these territories, in the way that Jews affected the wider society? Banditry, after all, is virtually universal, but the cabala became famous throughout Europe. And even the particular forms of exploitation that one associates with the German princes – the special taxes, the use of the *Hofjude* – are not easily defined as peculiar to the empire. It may be that the identification with such dangerous pursuits as the jewelry trade or the predilection for travel, international contacts, and early forms of capitalism that is so notable in the career of Glückel will be a means of giving a distinct character to the impact of these communities on the empire at large.

In any such effort, the problem will be to find a balance between excessive and insufficient claims. On the one hand, the local study, though vivid, becomes exemplary all too quickly and does not feed the comparative focus that alone sustains broader understanding. Scholars tend to enjoy such weighings of alternatives because diverse societies that elude attempts to see them as coherent wholes open up endless possibilities for research. But each probe makes the subject more comprehensible, and thus the chapters in Part I, even on topics as different as those treated by Ulbricht, Haverkamp, and Daxelmüller, suggest common patterns in the experience of the Jews in the late medieval and early modern Holy Roman Empire.

PART II

The Social and Economic Structure of German Jewry from the Fifteenth through the Eighteenth Centuries

5

Aspects of Stratification of Early Modern German Jewry: Population History and Village Jews

MICHAEL TOCH

The basic contours of the social stratification of early modern Ashkenazic Jewry were outlined some twenty years ago. In 1971, Jacob Katz wrote:

From all aspects traditional Jewish society appears as an open society. But this openness does not imply equal opportunity for each person to achieve a certain position. There was considerable distance between the top and the bottom in all the scales of stratification. Wealth and poverty, learning and ignorance, key ruling positions and lack of all political power, lineal distinction and complete absence of all family ties – all of these were found side by side in their extremes. [1]

Another researcher, Jonathan Israel, is in accord with Katz when he describes early modern European Jewry as a "uniquely mobile, shifting society."[2] The purpose of this essay is to complement this insight, centered as it is on the culturally and economically dominant Jewish classes, through observations on population history.

The first of these observations touches on the pace, phases, and direction of settlement history. We already know the outcome of this development: on the one hand, an urban Jewry comprising the great communities of Prague, Frankfurt, Hamburg-Altona, Vienna, and Berlin, to name only the most famous; on the other hand, by the early nineteenth century, German Jews made up varying percentages of the population of German villages and small towns, reaching 90 percent in some areas, according to one estimate.[3] During the nineteenth and early twentieth centuries, German Jewry was once again transformed, this time into a highly urbanized community, surely a precondition for the prominent cultural and economic role that it subsequently played.

---

1 Jacob Katz, *Tradition and Crisis* (New York, 1971), 205.
2 Jonathan I. Israel, *European Jewry in the Age of Mercantilism, 1550–1750* (Oxford, 1989), 206.
3 W. J. Cahnmann, "Village and Small-town Jews in Germany. A Typological Study," *Leo Baeck Institute, Year Book* 19 (1974): 107–30.

Yet we know little of the beginnings and dynamics of the process by which Jews became the inhabitants of rural areas in earlier centuries. We know even less of the texture and quality of this rural life. For one thing, we still lack a complete census of the Jewish communities reestablished in Germany following the late medieval expulsions. Except for Frankfurt am Main, Mainz, and a few other cities usually cited, were no other medieval urban communities of Jews left? How many Jews migrated to eastern Europe or to Italy, and how many settled in small towns and villages? To what extent was settlement continuous? Or do we have to imagine German Jewry emigrating in at least two waves, at the close of the Middle Ages and then again during the Thirty Years' War, only to immigrate back again afterward?[4] Not until the completion of the fourth volume of *Germania Judaica,* the handbook of early modern Jewish communities in the Old Reich, can we hope for the aggregate evidence necessary to answer these questions in full.

Nevertheless, I have tried to assemble some material on Jewish communities in Germany in order to gain a preliminary indication of the timetable and regional structure of their reestablishment in the early modern period. The starting point for this investigation is volume 3 of *Germania Judaica,* in which more than one thousand medieval communities are covered.[5] By 1580, most of these had disappeared. Their waning, that is, the breakup of the medieval pattern, is depicted in Figure 5.1.[6]

A measure of continuity, however, exists in the approximately one-tenth of the total number of communities that managed to survive into the modern age. For all the medieval communities – the ones that persisted and the ones that were destroyed and later reestablished – I have charted the pace of reconstitution in the early modern centuries, again using the material collected in volume 3 of *Germania Judaica* (Figure 5.2).[7] The left side of the

---

4 Moses A. Shulvass, *From East to West: The Westward Migration of Jews from eastern Europe during the Seventeenth and Eighteenth Centuries* (Detroit, 1971).
5 Arye Maimon, ed., *Germania Judaica,* vol. 3 (Tübingen, 1987), no. 1. I would like to thank the editors for letting me use the still-unpublished manuscript of their material (communities lettered M through Z). For an overview of developments in late medieval population history, see my "Siedlungsgeschichte der Juden Mitteleuropas im Wandel vom Mittelalter zur Neuzeit," in *Zeitschrift für historische Forschung, Juden in der christlichen Umwelt während des späten Mittelalters,* ed. A. Haverkamp and F.-J. Ziwes, suppl. 13 (1992): 29–39. It is expected that the forthcoming third volume of *Germania Judaica* will have much more refined map and statistical material.
6 Source: *Germania Judaica,* vol. 3; Toch, "Siedlungsgeschichte."
7 Source: *Germania Judaica,* vol. 3, augmented by L. Davidsohn, *Beiträge zur Sozial- und Wirtschaftsgeschichte der Berliner Juden vor der Emanzipation* (Berlin, 1920); L. Müller, *Aus fünf Jahrhunderten. Beiträge zur Geschichte der jüdischen Gemeinden im Riess* (Augsburg, 1899); Paul Sauer, *Die jüdischen Gemeinden in Württemberg und Hohenzollern* (Stuttgart, 1966); Bernhard Brilling, *Die jüdischen Gemeinden Mittelschlesiens. Entstehung und Geschichte* (Stuttgart, 1972); Paul Arnsberg, *Die Jüdischen Gemeinden in Hessen,* 2 vols. (Frankfurt/Main, 1971).

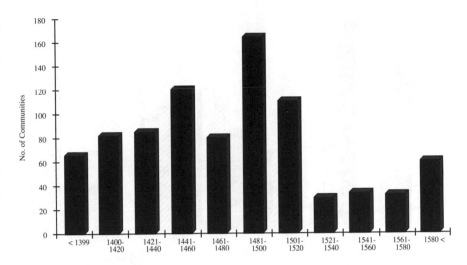

Figure 5.1. Last references to medieval communities, 1350–1700.

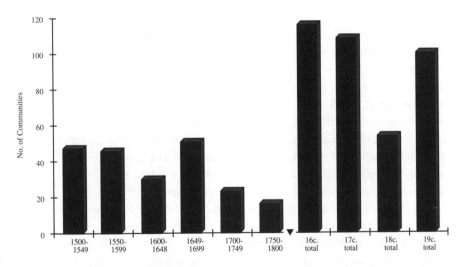

Figure 5.2. Rebuilding medieval communities, 1500–1900.

graph shows that the pace of reestablishment, measured by half centuries, was fairly even. Things are more distinct, however, if we look at the right side of the graph, which shows the totals by century, including the nineteenth century. Thus, the main periods of reconstitution were the early sixteenth through the late seventeenth centuries, with a clear lull in the eighteenth century and a new peak in the nineteenth century. But this is

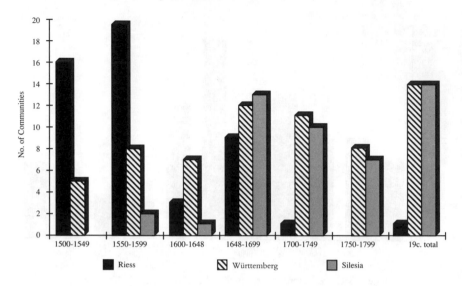

Figure 5.3. Phases of settlement: Riess, Württemberg, Middle Silesia.

only part of a larger pattern, since these communities had already been in existence during the Middle Ages.

There is as yet no way to determine all the places where Jewish life came into being only during early modern times. Using regional studies we can, however, chart the development in some parts of Germany (Figure 5.3). In the Riess area of Swabia in central southern Germany (black column), Jewish settlement took place mainly during the sixteenth century and then again after the Thirty Years' War.[8] The cross-hatched column shows Württemberg in the southwest, where growth was more even, rising to a definite peak in the nineteenth century. [9] In contrast, central Silesia in the east, the shaded column, indicates a different trend.[10] Jewish life here was allowed to develop only after the Thirty Years' War, and then in the wake of emancipation. These are but three regional examples, each one with its own pace. Rather than a single pattern applicable to the whole of Germany, one instead finds significant regional differences, dependent on the divergent political developments in the individual German states. In some places Jewish resettlement appears as a direct continuation of the late medieval phase; in others it reflects a much more modern pattern. On this point, at least, it

8 Source: Müller, *Aus fünf Jahrhunderten.*   9 Source: Sauer, *Württemberg und Hohenzollern.*
10 Source: Brilling, *Mittelschlesien.*

seems worthwhile to wait for the aggregate material promised by volume 4 of *Germania Judaica*.[11]

Other important questions, nevertheless, await our scrutiny. To what extent is the well-known contrast between a medieval pattern of urban communities and an early modern one of rural and small-town Jewish settlements – apart from the few great centers mentioned previously – verifiable? According to some scholars, German Jews settled in the countryside during the fifteenth and early sixteenth centuries, with a shift back to the cities following the Thirty Years' War.[12] Others see two distinct phases during which urban Jews became residents of rural areas: during the sixteenth and early seventeenth centuries, as a result of the medieval expulsions; and then again during the first half of the eighteenth century, but now tied to economic decline and pauperization.[13] Is this medieval–early modern dichotomy a reality? As before, we are on safer ground looking first at the late medieval picture.

The size of Jewish communities is one significant indicator. For roughly half of the thousand or so communities in late medieval Germany, we have some indication of their population. I have assembled data on indicators of size in diagram form (see Figure 5.4).[14] Already in late medieval times, there can be no doubt that the prevailing pattern consisted of minuscule and small Jewish communities. This finding would be even more decisive if we had information on the other five hundred communities. Such a result, however, does not mean that Jewish life, especially cultural life, was not shaped to a great extent in the larger settlements, with their scholars, academies, and communal institutions. But the typical pattern of a handful of Jewish

---

11 Here I beg to differ from the general argument put forward by Jonathan I. Israel in his *European Jewry* and in his "Central European Jewry during the Thirty Years' War, 1618–48," *Central European History* 16 (1983): 3–30. See also his contribution to this volume (Chapter 19). Basically, there are two different points of departure and differences of emphasis. Israel argues inward from the European centers of change and modernization, mainly the Netherlands and Prussia, towards the slowly changing regions of inner Germany. I argue the other way round, from the slowly moving parts of southern and central Germany, viewing the much more progressive northwestern and northeastern perimeter as important in its own right but little connected to the areas and structures with which this essay is concerned. As stated in my essay, the great Jewish communities that were the foci of modernization are not treated, and their role is left untouched by my argument. The emphasis is rather on a social, economic, and spatial structure that lived a very different life of its own. Clearly, these divergent views address two different yet related aspects of the Jewish experience that will have to be reconciled at a later stage of research.

12 S. W. Baron, *A Social and Religious History of the Jews*, vol. 14 (New York, 1969), 293.

13 Israel, *European Jewry*, 74, 239–40, 249–50.

14 Source for Figure 5.4 and discussion: Toch, "Siedlungsgeschichte"; systematic information on community sizes in Bohemia is absent from volume 3 of *Germania Judaica*; see instead the map and table in Maria Tischler, "Böhmische Judengemeinden, 1348–1519," *Die Juden in den böhmischen Ländern* (Munich, 1983), 39, 55–6.

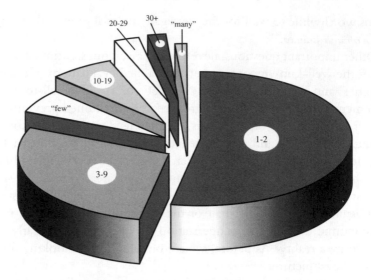

Figure 5.4. Community size by family.

families living in a community, though often transient, was already in place in medieval times. Whatever their sizes, it is true that the vast majority of Jewish communities (over 70 percent) were located in towns. But we have to accept that these towns also included a great number of small places dependent on agriculture and petty trade.[15] Another 11 percent can be found in townships and markets, with 15 percent in villages proper. Almost all of the villages lay in a southern belt stretching from Alsace in the west, across Baden, Württemberg, Swabia, the Palatinate, and Hesse, to Franconia and Bohemia in the east. These late medieval settlements were to become the loci of early modern and nineteenth-century village Jewry, to which only Moravia and Bavaria would be added subsequently.

What was the population of this rural Jewry? Before the nineteenth century, nothing in the way of comprehensive demographic information is available. But one fairly well-documented regional example may be indicative of the broader pattern.[16] In 1550, the authorities in the Palatinate counted 148 licensed Jewish families, living in 88 different places. Only one of the latter, Heidelberg, could be called a town by any reasonable standard. The remainder resided in villages and townships. By 1722, when the next head count was taken, the number of licensed families had more than dou-

---

15 Hektor Ammann, "Wie gross war die mittelalterliche Stadt?," in Carl Haase, ed., *Die Stadt des Mittelalters*, vol. 1 (Darmstadt, 1978), 415–22.
16 Leopold Löwenstein, *Geschichte der Juden in der Kurpfalz* (Frankfurt/Main, 1895), 43–8, 179–84, 296–309.

bled, to 349. Yet there was only a slight increase in the number of places of residence. Of these, three-quarters exhibited no continuity with medieval times; they were settled by Jews only after the mid-sixteenth century, and mostly later. Not only were there gaps of settlement between the Middle Ages and the early modern period, but we also have to reckon with similar breaks within the early modern centuries. In other words, until emancipation and the developments of the nineteenth century, Jewish settlement in any one place was an extremely transient and fragile matter.

With a growing population and only a marginal increase in the number of places of residence where Jews were permitted to live, the communities of the eighteenth century were consequently larger than their predecessors of the sixteenth century. By 1743, these demographic trends were even more in evidence. Now the population was three and one-half times that of the sixteenth century and over twice as large as that of 1722. To accommodate this increase, authorities opened merely an additional 25 places to Jewish residence. It is therefore not surprising that the mean ratio of families to place of dwelling rose from 1.7 in 1550 to 3.3 in 1722 and nearly 4.0 in 1743.[17] As Figure 5.5 shows, however, no real break in the fundamentally dispersed pattern of settlement occurred. It also shows the distribution of community size, measured by the number of families, for the census years 1550, 1722, and 1743. Small communities clearly predominated, but less so as time went by. According to these data, there were no communities with ten or more families in the sixteenth century. Such communities show up in the censuses beginning only in the eighteenth century, and then only in a few towns. But compared to the general pattern of the late Middle Ages (righthand column, data from *Germania Judaica,* vol. 3), did such a great difference exist? Despite numerous discontinuities in the actual settlement of the Jews, the basic pattern of small numbers and a high degree of dispersion, most of it now in rural places, remained consistent over long periods of

---

17 A point raised at the conference concerning Jewish population numbers needs to be stressed: a small community encompassing only a few licensed families did not necessarily indicate a small Jewish population in that locality. Jewish families tended to be considerably larger than non-Jewish ones, in part because licensed heads of households had to accommodate grown-up and married children not yet permitted to set up their own independent households. Family size therefore reflected a response to the official settlement policy rather than of demography proper. Also, licensed Jewish households belonged to the propertied strata of society and possessed the needs and the means to employ large numbers of male and female servants and tutors. Similar to the general state of affairs in pre-industrial Europe, but even more pronounced in this case, the servant population typically did not show up in the census returns. A community made up of a single or a few families thus had no difficulty mustering the ten males needed for communal prayer. For a case study on the problem, see M. Toch, "Die soziale und demographische Struktur der jüdischen Gemeinde Nürnbergs im Jahre 1489," in J. Schneider, ed., *Wirtschaftskräfte und Wirtschaftswege. Festschrift für H. Kellenbenz,* vol. 1 (Stuttgart, 1978), 387–410.

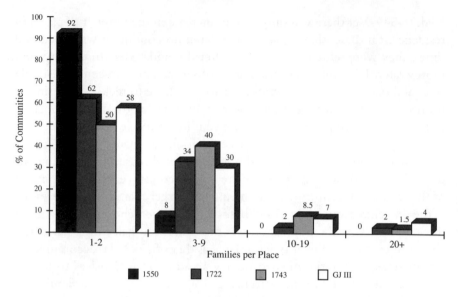

Figure 5.5. Palatinate (1550, 1722, 1743) and Germany in the late Middle Ages.

time. Such a deeply entrenched pattern must have had profound consequences for the economic life of the Jews, as well as for their social space and social organization.

The economic profile of this *Landjudenschaft* had many contours, ranging from traditional credit operations to itinerant peddling and the more modern pattern of fixed village shops, as well as to the better-known horse and cattle trade. This was not just some outlandish appendix to the economic activities of urban Jews. For in the critical areas of supplying foodstuffs and horses for the army, the competitive edge of those at the very top, the court Jews, wholly depended upon their ability to activate regional and local networks manned by village Jews.[18] At the opposite end of licit economic pursuits, the notorious criminal edge of early modern Jewry was rooted in this rural milieu as well. Witness a scene in the story of *Simplicius Simplicissimus,* the epic wanderer of the Thirty Years' War. The hero and his robber friend are resting from their exploits in a rural inn, waiting to sell stolen horses to two Jews summoned to the spot by the innkeepers.[19] The Jews turn out to be highly competent and well

18 This point is particularly stressed in a recent addition to the literature on court Jews: M. Graetz, "Jewish Economic Activity between War and Peace: The Rise and Fall of Jewish Army Suppliers" (in Hebrew), *Zion* 56 (1991): 255–73.
19 Hans Jakob Christoph von Grimmelshausen, *Der abenteuerliche Simplicius Simplicissimus* (Frankfurt/Main, 1968), chap. 23.

versed in the political geography of the war. But in the same chapter we also find the portrait of another Jew, ambushed on the road, tied to a tree and left to die in the cold, and finally robbed of the coins hidden in his mouth.

Local documentation from sixteenth-century Hesse allows us to view these Jewish horse dealers in their natural setting.[20] In 1519, a Jew of the village of Aula sold his house, a garden, two fields, a meadow, and a hedge. He had rendered taxes in cash and in kind to the Abbey of Hersfeld for this property: one goose, two cocks, one hen, as well as messenger services.[21] Slightly later a village priest leased to the Jew Isaack a garden and a meadow, on condition that he should water and manure the meadow as the neighbors did.[22] In 1499, the Jews of the small town of Münzenberg leased a meadow in order to fatten their cattle.[23] In 1575, a Jew of Witzenhausen was sued for letting his herd graze on the village meadow.[24] In 1586, the Jews of Windeck complained to the authorities concerning the lord's hay. At the time, they were forced to pay for the hay rather than make it themselves, as they used to in the past. On this matter the local official dryly commented that one should rather have them pay, "since the Jews are very unskilled [*ungeschickt*] in such matters."[25]

Only in such an environment do the satire and homilies from the seventeenth century make sense. A satirical Yiddish poem of around 1675, entitled "Di Beschreibung von Aschkenas und Polack," puts it this way:

> wann man hebt Schma Israel an
> schreit er sein Eysickl an
> wann ich dir's schenk
> warum hast du den gaul nit getrenkt?[26]

> (in the synagogue they can't keep their mouths shut;
> one talks of his colt, the other of his horse;
> they shout at each other;
> "Why didn't you water the horse?")

A moralistic poem of the same time, the *Shire' Jehuda* by Jehuda Leb of Selichov, makes the same association between idle business talk in the synagogue and the raising of horses, oxen, cows, and sheep:

20 Uta Löwenstein, *Quellen zur Geschichte der Juden im Hessischen Staatsarchiv Marburg,* 3 vols. (Marburg, 1989).
21 Ibid., vol. 1, no. 832.   22 Ibid., no. 870.   23 Ibid., no. 21.   24 Ibid., vol. 2, no. 2301.
25 Ibid., no. 1914.
26 M. Weinreich, "Two Yiddish Satirical Songs about Jews" (in Yiddish), *Yvo, Philological Writings,* vol. 3 (Vilnius, 1929), 544.

und wert geret vil debhorim betelim

. . . .

vun masso umattan un sechorou
vun behemoth sus schour uforoh
ouch vun schaf lemmer boeck und zigen.[27]

(and they talk much idle words;

. . . .

on business deals and merchandise;
about cattle horse oxen and cow;
also about sheep lamb ram and goats.)

There is nothing new about such dire ranting on the laxity of religious observance and the feeling of superiority flaunted by scholars over the unlettered. But it seems significant that in this period such homilies were situated in the village and that the Jewish boors were equated with cattle-raising country bumpkins. Jewish people felt the strain of this stereotype and the associated prejudice. Witness the anonymous seventeenth-century autobiography of a thoroughly frustrated Bohemian Jew who blamed his own inability to progress in religious studies on his inept father, who confined his son to the village.[28] It was not the distance to the centers of learning that kept him ignorant, for such distances were insignificant, but rather his family's poverty.

Living alone, or almost alone, as a Jew among Gentiles might mean a rural lifestyle and cultural disadvantage, but it did not isolate one in an inaccessible corner. This brings us to the last point: village Jews and their social arrangements. Given the dispersed nature of Jewish settlement, such social arrangements were at the same time also spatial networks. A rare document from late sixteenth-century Hesse illustrates this aspect well. It tells of the travels of a solitary Jew during one summer month in 1571 (see map, Figure 5.6). I have drawn up a synopsis of the deposition this man gave after his arrest for the attempted evasion of a road toll.[29]

In late May, 1571, Manus of Steinhaus, a native of a village near Fulda, was married in Frankfurt am Main (*1*) to the daughter of another villager. On Sunday, June 3, he left Frankfurt with his wife for the town of Friedberg (*2*), where the couple spent the night. The next day they traveled to the village of Gleiberg (*3*), where they stayed with members of the bride's

---

27 Jehuda Leb Selichover, *Shire' Jehudah* (Amsterdam, 1697), quoted in M. Grunwald, *Hamburgs deutsche Juden bis zur Auflösung der Dreigemeinden 1811* (Hamburg, 1904), 218–22.
28 Alexander Marx, "A Seventeenth-Century Autobiography: A Picture of Jewish Life in Bohemia and Moravia," *Jewish Quarterly Review* 8 (1917–18): 268–304, 278–9, 282–3.
29 Löwenstein, *Quellen,* vol. 2, no. 2092, 173–5. In my text, numbers mark each place on Manus's itinerary.

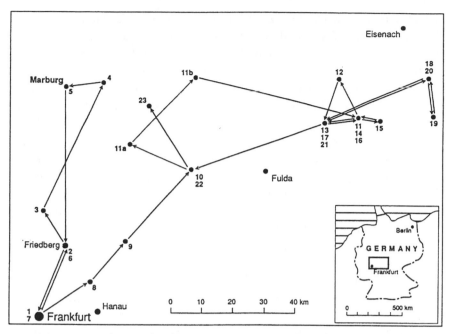

Figure 5.6. The travels of Manus. Hesse, 1571. (Data from Löwenstein, *Quellen*, vol. 2, no. 2092, 173–5.)

family. The next stretch on Tuesday, June 5, was a strenuous one and took them to Kirchhain (*4*), a small town with a few Jews, including some family. Once in Kirchhain, Manus left his wife with a brother and looked into the possibility of settling down. The following day, Wednesday, June 6, he was in Marburg (*5*) to claim payment for some loans for which he had pawns in his possession. Via Friedberg (*6*), where he spent the night with a man called Salomon, he then made his way back to Frankfurt (*7*). His purpose was to see his aunt and her Jewish innkeeper and to receive part of his wife's dowry, totaling a meager 100 gulden. When he left Frankfurt again, on Friday, June 8, he carried about 40 gulden and a diamond-studded gold ring with him. By evening he had made it to the small town of Windecken (*8*), the place of the hay-making Jews. Here he spent the Sabbath with a Jew called "der alte Marckey." Sunday, June 10, saw him and a young Jewish companion on the road to Ortenberg (*9*). After a short stopover with one of the two Jews in that place ("the one who is not deaf"), he was back on the road again. Then a night's sleep, possibly by the roadside, and another $8\frac{1}{2}$ miles to the village of Steinheim (*10*), where he stayed until the morning of Wednesday, June 13. There follows a detour to Gemünden (*11a*) and

Maulbach (*11b*), where he claimed payment on more outstanding loans belonging to some foster children. Probably on Thursday, June 14, Manus
reached the village of Mansbach (*11*) and remained there with a Jew called
Isaac for the Sabbath rest. On Sunday, June 17, he was back on the road
again, this time to Vacha (*12*) in order to visit the market. He had meant to
buy cloth, but people would not accept his coins, and he had to spend the
night there in the company of another Jewish wayfarer. The next day, Monday, June 18, he was in the village of Geisa (*13*), where he tried in vain to
claim several outstanding debts. He then returned to Mansbach (*14*). By
now Manus appeared exhausted, since he remained in Mansbach with his
host Isaac for a full week, from Monday to Sunday. On Sunday, June 24, it
was market time again, in Rossdorf (*15*) for a change, but here, too, no one
wanted to touch his coins. After what must have been a frustrating day, he
went back to his base in Mansbach (*16*), accompanied by two Jews. On the
next day, Monday, June 25, he walked back to Geisa (*17*), where he finally
was paid by the wife of his Jewish debtor, who was shortly to incriminate
him on charges of handling counterfeit money. His companion, another
young Jew, called "Charius," was at this point with other Jews of the village, so Manus had no witness to the transaction. With this escort, and on
the same Monday, Manus walked all the way to the village of Brotterode
(*18*), where the two spent the night. After another unsuccessful attempt, on
Tuesday, June 26, to unload his coin in the town of Schmalkalden (*19*), he
returned to Brotterode (*20*). The following day, Wednesday, June 27, still
with Charius at his side, Manus again went to Geisa (*21*) and stayed there
over the Sabbath. Sunday, July 1, brought him back to the village of Steinheim (*22*), where he rested until the morning of Tuesday, July 3. Later that
day Manus was arrested near Kirtorf (*23*). He had spent thirty-one days on
the road and walked about 400 miles. We know nothing more of his fate.

But perhaps we are able to imagine the determination and sheer physical
stamina required by such a life, with all its fears, frustrations, loneliness, and
rare, small joys. We might also imagine the circumstances that forced a hard-
working and probably not too scrupulous young man, just married, toward
an uncertain fate. It is tempting to sense in our Manus an incarnation of
some of the more pertinent features of early modern Jewish existence in
Germany: the lowly origins and bare subsistence, the individualistic drive,
the mixture of traditional economic pursuits such as moneylending and a
more modern one such as trade. In the background was the physical layout
of villages, with one or two Jewish families, stables with neighing beasts, and
wet meadows to be crossed on the way. Add to our picture the relatives and

hosts that were spread thinly over great regions and the structures of rural and small-town Jewry with their solidarities and strains. These structures, fragile and vulnerable as they were to sudden upheavals, pointed back a long way to the Middle Ages. Yet at the same time they formed the background and backbone, and indeed provided the driving force behind an astonishing process of modernization, in a larger society tragically ill equipped to cope with rapid change.[30]

30 Another point raised and debated at the conference was the supposed openness of Jewish culture to outside influences. This point attains a different dimension when viewed from the rural perspective put forward in my essay. In a rural environment, the segregation of the Jews by Christian society was reinforced, rather than mitigated, by virtue of the general cultural background which, more than the urban environment, tended to reiterate traditional prejudices and stereotypes. This apartness was reinforced by the cultural outlook of *Landjuden* (rural Jews), which tended to emphasize the family and its rituals, mainly those of the Jewish holidays, on account of their own ritualistic rather than spiritual interpretation of Judaism. In such a system there was little room for the all-embracing values developed by the Jewish enlightenment and nineteenth-century Reform Judaism. For a personal view of some of these issues, see Hermann Schwab, *Jewish Rural Communities in Germany* (London, 1956).

6

Jewish Economic Activity in Early Modern Times

STEFI JERSCH-WENZEL

I originally planned to contribute an essay to this volume on the occupational structure of Jews in Germany from the fifteenth to the eighteenth centuries. It may be more stimulating, however, to focus on Jewish economic activity generally. Whereas the occupational structure of the Jews in this period changed relatively little, their economic activity during the era of absolutism took on, at least in part, completely new dimensions. Examples include the multifarious tasks that were transferred to the court Jews (*Hoffaktoren*) and the early capitalist manufacturers who experimented with previously unknown forms of production.

Furthermore, the assertion that the great majority of Jews supported themselves by means of moneylending and commodity trading, through pawnbroking or as intermediaries, does not reflect the variety of their presence in economic life. From the legal regulations governing Jewish residence or settlement, we know which trades the Jews were allowed to take part in and which trades were barred to them. We know about their exclusion from craft guilds and from corporately organized trade; we also know about their confinement to a small number of trade activities. But we need to know much more about how actual economic activity was carried out in everyday life. I shall first attempt to explore this question using petitions filed by Christian complainants who desired to combat the competition that they saw coming from the Jews.

The best period for examining Jewish economic activity in the early modern era is the second half of the seventeenth century, before mercantilist economic principles had thoroughly taken hold. For the most part, the economic principles of the sixteenth and early seventeenth centuries still held sway. In the pages that follow, I outline the changes that Jewish economic activity underwent from the mid–seventeenth century through the middle of the eighteenth century, concentrating primarily on Brandenburg-

91

Prussia.[1] Although Jewish life in Brandenburg-Prussia was not typical of Jewish life in general, especially when compared to life in the small German territories, it was here that a great transition took place during these centuries. The number of Jews permitted to settle, as well as official policy toward them, changed considerably. There was also a transition in Jewish self–identity at this time. It remains to be asked whether and how this development was reflected in the economic sphere.

Contemporary petitions and complaints recorded the reactions of the resident population to the settlement of a group of people whose economic behavior seemed alien to them and who were viewed as a threat, even before it was possible for Jews to expand their economic activity. The records also provide indications of Jewish attempts to secure a place in the Brandenburg economy. One must take into account, however, that the authors of such petitions and remonstrations desired to produce a powerful effect; therefore, the degree of actual or feared damage must be evaluated within the context of the authors' likely intent.

In the "Petition of the Estates to the Great Elector," from November or December 1672, the Jews are described as being "more harmful than useful to the state."[2] They are even said to cause "a complete ruination of trade and the maintenance of the state." The main accusation of the estates is directed against the different way the Jews practiced trade. Jews not only found themselves faced with occupational confinements, exclusion from corporations and guilds, as well as the increasing uncertainty of changing economic times, but they were then also blamed for exploiting this situation. It was feared that in the future they would have access to unrestricted trade "in all goods and commodities equally, also much more than is permitted the residents," since they are "not bound by any guild regulations or constitutions, deal in wool, cloth, silk, canvas, shoes, clothing and all other goods without any difference," whereas the "citizens and residents . . . live according to the regulations and constitutions of the guild" and must "be satisfied with certain trades and livelihoods." The resident merchants feel that "apart from that, trade is being diverted from the local lands" and that the Jews "are completely taking away the little that is left over." This attitude, which centers on the "idea of livelihood," offers insight into why people felt threatened and why their fears manifested themselves in ideas of

---

1 For details, see Stefi Jersch-Wenzel, *Juden und "Franzosen" in der Wirtschaft des Raumes Berlin/Brandenburg zur Zeit des Merkantilismus* (Berlin, 1978), 45–69 and 95–103.
2 "Eingabe der Landstände an den Grossen Kurfürsten," reprinted in Selma Stern, *Der preussische Staat und die Juden* (Tübingen, 1962), pt. 1, sec. 2, 28–31.

otherness and in stereotypical accusations against Jews.[3] The complaint that Jews "wander in the villages and in the cities, peddle and force their way on the people," reflected the defensive attitude of the small merchant, who was bound to the corporation and awaited customers in his shop in accordance with the traditional statutes of his trade. The standard assessment that the cheaper goods sold by Jews represented a deception of the buyer as to quality conformed to the second part of the sentence: that the Jews "sell their goods, which are for the most part old and dilapidated, at a cheaper price, and thereby attract and allure the buyer, a man from the countryside, in effect, however, cheating him."

Two issues especially aroused the indignation of the resident population: cheap prices, and the sales method of going to the customer and directly offering him the goods. These ideas were unfamiliar in early modern times, but by the middle of the nineteenth century, at the latest, both had become part of standard business practice. Cheaper prices increased turnover, balanced out possible losses, and created needs, through direct or indirect solicitation, and expanded markets.

Although a further accusation was grounded in religious differences, namely, the "activity of buying and selling on the Holy Sunday, the offering of goods in the villages and in the inns," the accusation of usury against the Jews was based on a centuries-old prejudice. There were undoubtedly cases of charging excessive interest – in 1677 some Jews apparently were demanding 54 percent – yet it must be taken into account that, in the wake of earlier ecclesiastical prohibitions on the collection of interest by Christians, the Jews were allowed to extract higher interest rates. The actual consequences of this were demands for a new expulsion of the Jews. But the elector rejected the petitions of the estates outright, "as we are still of the consistent opinion that the Jews with their trade are not harmful to us or the land but that they, on the contrary, appear advantageous."[4]

Similar petitions were sent in these years by "all the guilds in Berlin and Cologne" and the "merchants and tradesmen of the new city of Brandenburg" – both in August of 1673 – as well as by "all merchants, clothiers, and other craftsmen" from Frankfurt an der Oder and all the merchants, bakers, shoemakers, and cloth makers from the city of Rathenow.[5] Such petitioners, however, including later ones, more often than not received a negative

---

3 On the term *Idee der Nahrung,* cf. Werner Sombart, *Der moderne Kapitalismus,* 2nd ed., vol. 1 (Munich, 1911), 195.
4 Stern, *Der preussische Staat,* 31.
5 Stern, *Der preussische Staat,* 33–6; A. B. König, *Annalen der Juden in den preussischen Staaten* (Berlin, 1790), 99–100.

reply, and sometimes none at all. Thus, an extraordinarily detailed writ from 1688, sent by "all of Frankfurt an der Oder's most humble and most obedient merchants and tradesmen," went unanswered.[6] In this writ, which in its detailed theological-historical introduction aimed to prove the eternal "unalterable depravity" of the Jews, the causes for the "ruination and destruction of all commerce (and trade) by the Jews" were outlined in sixteen points. Besides a number of accusations that were similar to those voiced in the aforementioned petition by the estates, some twenty years after the initial settlement of the Jews in the territory the number of complaints mounted regarding peddling, trading with old clothes or stolen goods, and the ever-present assumption that it was the intent of Jews to cheat the customer.

Accusations of deceit (as in the money trade of the usurer mentioned earlier), or theft, or receiving stolen goods resulted in the complaints listed in the numerous indictments. In the electoral declarations as well, they were repeatedly assumed to have validity against which a prohibition had to be issued. The reason for this may be found in the moneylending and pawnbroking trades, which were almost exclusively Jewish occupations, and the trade in forfeited pledges connected to them. In addition to these pledges – clothing, furniture, and jewelry – there were often older goods, bought during peddling and secondhand dealings. Only in such an assortment could thieves hope to fence stolen goods without being immediately discovered. There were at least twenty-five such shops in Berlin alone at the turn of the eighteenth century, underscoring the notion that the Jews, "in contemporary opinion . . . were connected . . . inseparably with dirty and dishonest dealings."[7] In most of these shops and stalls, small-time Jewish traders also dealt in so-called *Kramwaren* (sundries). The Jewish sundries trade prompted a yearlong flood of complaints by the shopkeepers' guild, which finally, following numerous prohibitions, brought about instead an electoral sanction permitting this activity.[8] One passage in this electoral act stated that "in some places where Jews have been admitted they have been allowed to engage in trade. This has not caused any damage to trade, as the examples of Holland and other places have demonstrated." This statement sheds light on the economic orientation of the Brandenburg-Prussian princes toward the Dutch model and illustrates, as do many similar state-

---

6 "Unterthänigste gehorsambste sämmtliche Kauff- und Handelsleuthe in Franckfurth an der Oder," reprinted in König, *Annalen,* 106–17.
7 Hugo Rachel, "Die Juden im Berliner Wirtschaftsleben zur Zeit des Merkantilismus," *Zeitschrift für die Geschichte der Juden in Deutschland* 2 (1930): 175–96, 177.
8 Stern, *Der preussische Staat,* 189–90, 216, 239; see also Rachel, "Die Juden im Berliner Wirtschaftsleben," 178–80.

ments, the readiness of the government to use the Jews against other subjects, if necessary.

It is undisputed that the focal point of Jewish economic activity at the
end of the seventeenth century lay in trade, especially in those areas, built
up mostly by the Jews, on the margins of corporately protected trade. These
included not only moneylending, pawnbroking, peddling, and secondhand
trades but also the trading of *Kramwaren* and products from fairs. Beyond
these broad categories, Jews were represented in other occupations, but
these were for the most part singular cases. Some individuals, for example,
were needed to provide the necessary services for the practice of Judaism.
In addition to a rabbi and a cantor, almost every larger community had several teachers or schoolmasters, scribes, ceremonial masters, *Schulklöpper*
(shammosim), and butchers. There were also physicians, dentists, and bar-
bers, as well as printers of Hebrew books.[9]

Jews were also found in occupations not subject to guild controls, which
had been practiced by Jews for centuries: seal engraving, gem cutting, and
krätzwaschen (metal extracting). One exception was that of a brewer and distiller, who resided in Berlin around 1690. The record also periodically mentions Jewish goldsmiths and silk embroiderers. Jewish tailors, it appears,
often attempted to settle, sometimes unregistered, in the cities. Frankfurt
am Main recorded three of them in 1688; in 1700 a registered Jewish tailor
was also found in Berlin.[10] The exceptionally broad expansion of the tailor
trade among the Polish Jews and the competition among them caused many
to attempt to earn their living in nearby Brandenburg. Together with the
"bunglers," the non-Jewish tailors who worked outside the guilds, these
migrants formed a reservoir of craftsmen for Jewish traders, who paid them
to remodel old clothing and sew new clothing, which, according to law,
was work reserved for members of the guilds.

With the exception of the few attempts to enter other spheres of economic activity, one may assume that, in terms of occupation, the designation "Jew" was identical with that of "trader" in the period around 1700.
This fact constituted the basis for the limited and yet continuous electoral
protection offered the Jews in the first decades after their (re-)settlement.
State policy toward the Jews, however, was determined by expectations of
commercial or, more precisely, financial reward in return. One hoped that
the Jews would just as strongly invigorate the Frankfurt fairs as they had
those in Breslau and, especially, Leipzig. Similarly, the Jews on both sides

9 Stern, *Der preussische Staat,* 529–30; Ludwig Geiger, *Geschichte der Juden in Berlin* (Berlin, 1871), 1:
   25–6, 2:10.
10 Stern, *Der preussische Staat,* 527, 529.

of the nearby border with Poland had provided the greater bulk of trade with that country since the fifteenth and sixteenth centuries. This was owing largely to the fact that the "legal and customs insecurity" in Poland made other merchants in the Mark content to deal within the border towns.[11]

Jews also attempted to earn their livelihoods in smaller localities, such as the small city of Biesenthal (*Kreis* Oberbarnim), which had approximately 480 residents in 1624 and 1,227 in 1730. It remains unclear why this town, whose main branches of industry, even in 1800, were still agriculture and livestock farming and which "lay distanced from all postal routes," had a relatively large Jewish settlement – the fifth largest in the Mark Brandenburg.[12] In 1688, only 2 registered Jews were mentioned, but in 1692 there were a total of 62 people: 16 men, 15 women, 29 children, and 4 servants – thus, a community with a solid social base.[13] One possible explanation may be found in the following two statements. Livestock farming in Biesenthal and its surroundings, as well as in the entire district, was "very considerable and important. The majority were engaged mainly in sheep breeding." In a report from September of 1693, the court treasurer complained that in

the jurisdiction and small city of Biesenthal, 10 Jewish families are in residence . . . which, along with their servants and assistants . . . in Strausberg, Landsberg, Biesenthal, and surrounding areas, were secretly and openly engaged in trade. They bought up sheepskins by the hundreds and large amounts of wool; they provided the cities of Strausberg, where over 100 linen makers live, and Neustadt-Eberswalde, where 20 linen makers live, with wool, so much so that in this year alone they provided Strausberg with 1,000 talers and Neustadt with over 200 talers worth of wool.[14]

In a region equally wealthy in wool and in linen makers, it can be assumed that Jews settled in order to become suppliers in the putting-out system, a position otherwise barred to them. In that way they could be sure that the quality and price of manufactured goods would not be dependent upon the products of the native merchants.

The second small town in which a significant number of Jews had settled was the noble *Mediatstädtchen* Buckow, 5 miles south of Berlin.[15] The sources mention 6 registered and 3 unregistered Jews, which leads us to assume that approximately 50 Jews lived in this villagelike settlement.[16]

---

11 Stern, *Der preussische Staat*, pt. 1, sec. 2, 51–2; Gustav Schmoller, *Die Mark Brandenburg, ihre Grenzen, Ströme und Nachbarn bis zum Jahre 1740* (Leipzig, 1898), 14.
12 Cf. F. W. A. Bratring, *Statistisch-topographische Beschreibung der gesamten Mark Brandenburg*, 3 vols. (Berlin, 1804–9; reprinted: Berlin, 1968), 762–4.
13 König, *Annalen*, 105, 119, 127.   14 Stern, *Der preussische Staat*, pt. 1, sec. 2, 184–5.
15 Bratring, *Statistisch-topographische Beschreibung*, 819–20.   16 König, *Annalen*, 127.

Buckow offered little economic attraction. The possibilities were restricted to the distribution of raw products made from hops and tobacco cultivation and to the four or five fairs and cattle markets that took place annually. It is possible, however, as was often the case in the eastern provinces, that Buckow's *Mediatstadtcharakter* provided a protection, willingly accepted, that was granted to the Jews as the almost exclusive possessors of trade connections, which were necessary for this small "residence."

As previously mentioned, the greatest number of Jews settled in the easternmost region of Mark Brandenburg, the Neumark, which borders directly on Frankfurt an der Oder. In 1690, there were 116 Jewish families in this region; in 1700, the Neumark registered 232 such families, including 165 women, 308 children, and 12 domestic servants.[17] They were spread out in small towns and villages. From these locations they attempted to acquire products needed for trade with the eastern Prussian provinces as well as Poland and Russia. As early as the 1650s, individual Jews made use of this opportunity, as the petitions of a number of cities in the Neumark document.[18]

The largest Jewish community in the Neumark in 1700 was in Landsberg an der Warthe. Geographically, Landsberg was favorably situated on the route from Berlin to East Prussia and connected by various waterways to northern Germany as well as to the provinces of East and West Prussia.[19] Besides general agriculture, livestock farming, the brewery, and the distillery, the main source of the city's income was the production of and trade in wool. Three of the four annual fairs – the shopkeepers', livestock, and horse fairs – simultaneously served the wool trade. At each of the fairs, a considerable amount of wool from the surrounding area was sold. As early as 1690, 21 Jewish families had settled here, comprising 5 percent of the city's population.[20] Indicative of the consolidation of the Jewish community is the fact that in July 1692 they secured permission to employ their own rabbi, "who was to settle the small arguments among them according to their laws and ceremonies" and thus gained a certain degree of independence from the rabbi responsible for the entire Mark Brandenburg.[21]

As is reflected in two complaints, the Jews apparently played an important role in the economic life of the city, in the wool trade, in the sheepskin trade, as well as in the cutting of garments. This prompted local merchants to protest the government's interest in Jewish activity, which appeared to be especially strong in the area of wool trade and production.[22]

---

17 Ibid., 118, 128.   18 Stern, *Der preussische Staat*, 3–5.
19 Bratring, *Statistisch-topographische Beschreibung.*   20 König, *Annalen,* 118.
21 Stern, *Der preussische Staat*, 24–5, 181.   22 Ibid., 25–6, 184–5.

On the whole, the economic activity of the Jews in Brandenburg-Prussia in the seventeenth century corresponded to that in other German territories. There were, of course, specific regional differences, such as the preponderance of rural Jewry in the west and southwest, or the Jewish tenant farmers and operators of breweries and distilleries in the east, where court Jewry also became established. The great mass of Jews, however, earned their livelihoods in the ways described here. One may wish to see in the Jews' wholesale activities – their purchase of wool and hides from producers and their further distribution – an early form of the capitalist means of production. But this, too, proceeded in the traditional way.

Finally, let us cast a glance at the situation around 1750. The Jews continued to be prohibited from engaging in the bourgeois trades, that is, in trade that was organized by guilds. Nonetheless, those who "had received, or wished to receive special concessions in order to establish certain types of factories, or to distribute to a number of Christian manufacturers, were to be protected the same as before."[23]

As had previously been the case, the Jews were dependent upon trade, though they could engage in it only to the extent that they did not thereby harm Christian merchants. The bulk of the goods in which the Jews were permitted to trade were thus products from local factories. Jewish activity was particularly concentrated in the textile factories and textile distribution. Jews, moreover, traded in luxury items whose acquisition was often impossible without connections abroad (jewels, precious foreign fabrics, tea, coffee, chocolate, snuff and tobacco, tallow, wax, and honey), as well as in the money and exchange trades, pawnbroking, and the broker's business.[24]

The occupational data recorded in 1749 in a list of Jews living in Berlin corresponded to these regulations as well. According to the list, 321 Jewish families – engaged in 455 livelihoods – resided in the city. Rather than providing accurate data on occupations, the list yields a profile of Jewish participation in the Berlin economy more generally. [25] The reason why many individuals listed multiple occupations was perhaps that competition within the limited number of accessible occupations, not only inside the Jewish community but also outside of it, was too great. Trade with only one product or from one occupation would not have yielded an income large enough to support a family and to pay the considerable taxes. Furthermore, this type of economic activity provided greater protection against fluctuat-

---

23 "Revidirtes General-Privilegium und Reglement, vor die Judenschaft im Königreich Preussen" (1750), printed in Ludwig von Rönne and Heinrich Simon, *Die früheren und gegenwärtigen Verhältnisse der Juden in den sämmtlichen Landestheilen des Preussischen Staates* (Breslau, 1843), §11, pp. 252–3.
24 Ibid., §14, 16–18, pp. 253–5.
25 Jacob Jacobson, *Jüdische Trauungen in Berlin, 1723–1759* (Berlin, 1938), 93–115.

ing trends, problems in turnover, sudden stoppages in the procurement of goods from abroad, or other dangers to which someone outside a guild or corporately organized trade was exposed.

Of the 455 occupations recorded in the list of Jews, 353 (77.6 percent) were related to trade: 119 to wholesale trade, 223 to trade in open shops, three to broker's business, and 8 to the *Kramwaren* trade. The largest group within the wholesalers was made up of 49 money dealers, bankers, money-lenders, money exchangers, and coin distributors. They were followed by 42 pawnbrokers, who in a larger sense belonged to the group of other wholesale traders. The third largest group of wholesalers was represented by the traders in goods on consignment, fair traders, retail traders, and wine traders. The surprisingly low number of brokers may be explained by the fact that many arrangements, later reserved for sworn brokers, were made in connection with other business transactions and that those arrangements were not yet regarded as constituting an independent occupation.

Of the 223 traders with open shops, 96 sold products from the textile and clothing branches named in the regulations, above all household linen, silk, goods, cotton, and canvas products. Another 40 traders dealt in luxury items, such as jewels, watches, fancy goods, tobacco, and East Indian goods. A third, comprehensive group was formed by the 74 clothing traders, who dealt in both new and old clothing. The cooperation of Jewish traders and non-Jewish tailors, that is, the "bunglers," who did not belong to guilds and who produced made-to-order clothing of standard sizes, which were then sold by the Jews, marked the emergence of increasing Jewish activity in the *Oberbekleidungskonfektion* (manufacture of ready-to-wear outer garments) in the nineteenth century.

In accordance with legal regulations, declarations about professional activities seldom appeared. Consequently, we have information only on ritual cake bakers, meat grinders, and butchers, on typesetters and printers in Hebrew printing houses, on traditional gem cutters and seal engravers, and on licensed jewelers, gold and silver cutters, and gold and silver embroiders. In addition to these twenty-five declarations, there were three on seamstresses and one on pencil producers. The remaining eleven declarations from the professional sector designated manufacturers, who, in any case, were exempted from the legal restrictions.[26] Furthermore, they became manufacturers not on the basis of artisanal training but mostly on the basis of a successful trading occupation. Their main activity also involved purchasing and distribution. As was the case with the traders, their emphasis

---

26 Rönne and Simon, *Die früheren und gegenwärtigen Verhältnisse*, §11, p. 253.

was on production, which was strongly promoted by the state, namely, the textile and clothing industries (two silk, one velvet, one embroidery, one ribbon, four of finished products); besides these, two hair sieve manufacturers are mentioned. Altogether, the declarations from the professional sector constituted less than 9 percent.

In the service sector, thirty of the forty-three occupational declarations must be classified as "Jewish public employees." These community employees were paid by the community and, in a very few cases, were allowed to marry and have a family. In every case, these individuals were "extraordinary" *Schutzjuden* (protected Jews), a status limited only to the employee's own lifetime. It is, therefore, not surprising that of the fifty-four employee posts permitted to the Berlin Jewish community, only thirty-nine were occupied. All others successfully circumvented prohibitions against trade and business and performed their services for the community by means of additional income, so that their positions seemed unoccupied to the state inspectors. They thereby relieved the community treasury for a certain time, while simultaneously creating the possibility of refuge for Jews otherwise not tolerated by the city.

Thus, if one takes as a starting point the legal opportunities to earn a living, then, for the most part, the Jews were left with a limited share of the trade with money and goods. Within this narrow sector of the economy arose such a state of competition that the Jews had to become keenly inventive in order to survive. This competition was made all the more intense by regulations such as the reoccurring prohibition against peddling, which forbade Jews from "peddling in cities other than during the yearly fairs, entering inns or other houses with or without goods, offering or recommending their goods." It ordered them further "to follow the behavior of the Christian merchants generally and only to leave their houses and shops with goods when there was demand."[27] An actual abandonment of this first form of advertisement of one's own products would have placed the Jews in a considerably disadvantageous position vis-à-vis Christian competitors who were socially much more secure. Further damaging to the status of their credit was the fact that their accounting ledgers had no evidential force in the courts. Although starting in 1750 a *Pfandbuch* (register of obligations) in German had to be kept, the regulations for this *Pfandbuch* were so discriminatory and the rules for the *Wechselausstellung* (issuance of a bill) by Jewish money traders contained such degrading ceremonies that the Jews protested vehemently against this special treatment, which made them appear untrustworthy in the eyes of the German business world.[28]

27 Ibid., §19, p. 255.   28 Ibid., §26, p. 258.

Even though the Prussian royal capital cannot be viewed as representative of smaller cities, a tendency emerged in Berlin, which, from that point on, gathered strength. The creation of a rising Jewish middle class, which later formed an essential component of the early industrial bourgeoisie, was one of the most significant developments of the period. Whereas the court Jews' function came to an end with the downfall of the system they had helped stabilize, the wholesalers, brokers, bankers, and early entrepreneurs were now coming into their own. For a number of decades these groups were socially mobile before such mobility became the norm for the entire society. This development reached its full extent only in the nineteenth century.

7

Comparative Perspectives on Economy and Society: The Jews of the Polish Commonwealth – A Comment

GERSHON DAVID HUNDERT

With these remarks I hope to provide a frame of reference for the comparison of some economic and social aspects of Jewish life in German lands with the situation of the more numerous Jewish community in the Polish Commonwealth. By the end of the seventeenth century, Polish-Lithuanian Jews probably numbered between 300,000 and 350,000; in German lands at the same time there were certainly no more than 60,000 Jews.[1] Any list of the outstanding cultural figures of the period would show that most spent their lives in the Polish-Lithuanian Commonwealth. The remainder, with only a very few exceptions, were at least educated there. The single most important center of Jewish cultural activity west of Poland was Prague. But the outstanding figures in the Bohemian capital also had strong connections with Poland.[2]

The distinctiveness of Polish-Lithuanian Jewry when compared with German Jewry was considerable. In the Polish Commonwealth, about 6 percent of the total population and almost half of the urban population was Jewish. The number of Jews living in rural areas increased during the eighteenth century but probably never exceeded one-third of the total Jewish population. The Jewish villagers tended to be widely dispersed, averaging one family per village, and to be found in the central and especially the eastern regions. In the villages, as is well known, the most common occupations were related to the production and sale of alcoholic beverages.

In general, the economic activities of Polish Jews were characterized by heterogeneity and fluidity. If, in a typical town, about one-quarter of the economically active Jews was involved in commerce, one-quarter was artisans, and one-quarter was involved in the manufacture and sale of alcoholic

1 For the literature on the history of Jews in Poland-Lithuania in this period, see Gershon David Hundert and Gershon Bacon, *The Jews in Poland and Russia: Bibliographical Essays* (Bloomington, Ind., 1984), and Gershon David Hundert, "Polish Jewish History," *Modern Judaism* 10 (1990): 259–70.
2 Most recently, see the encyclopedic taxonomy of Jewish cultural activity in this period by Jacob El-baum, *Petihut vehistagerut* (Jerusalem, 1990).

beverages, there was considerable movement by individuals among these fields of endeavor. An artisan might market his goods, merchants often resorted to artisanry, a distiller might also be a merchant, and so forth.[3] In a word, occupational specialization was foreign to this society.

Commerce, as carried on by Polish Jews, was characterized by small quantities and rapid turnover. Generally speaking, the greatest merchants of early modern Poland were neither Polish nor Jewish but German and Italian. Some of the complaints against Jewish traders in Brandenburg-Prussia, described by Jersch-Wenzel in Chapter 6, had their analogue in Poland as well. For example, the practice of meeting the peasants' carts outside the city walls and buying up the best produce and livestock was referred to repeatedly throughout the early modern period.

City merchants objected and repeatedly forbade the Jews "to get ahead of the Christians" in this way, demanding that the Jews trade only in the *rynek* [marketplace]. This practice and the apparently ineffectual response of the towns provides one key to understanding the ability of . . . Jews to compete successfully with the Christian merchants. The latter were inhibited by the archaic and restrictive customs of the urban marketplace.[4]

Despite the colorful and vociferous complaints of bourgeois authors in the first half of the seventeenth century, most notably those of the Cracow professor Sebastian Miczynski, which suggest that Jews were a prevalent element in the commerce of the period, recent research has shown that Jewish merchants were indeed far from predominant.[5] Still, it has been estimated that as early as 1700 about two-thirds of the Polish trade with Silesia was in Jewish hands.[6] It was during the eighteenth century that Jews came to play a decisive role in the trade of a significant number of the regions of Poland-Lithuania. In private towns, Jews were frequently virtually the only commercial element in the population. Polish toll records for the

---

3 See Gershon David Hundert, "The Role of the Jews in Commerce in Early Modern Poland-Lithuania," *Journal of European Economic History* 16 (1987): 245–75; M. J. Rosman, *The Lords' Jews: Magnate–Jewish Relations in the Polish-Lithuanian Commonwealth during the Eighteenth Century* (Cambridge, Mass., 1990), 48–51.
4 Hundert, "Role of the Jews in Commerce," 260–1.
5 Zenon Guldon and Karol Krzystanek, "Żydzi z miast województwa sandomierskiego na rynku krakowskim w I polowie XVII wieku," manuscript of a paper delivered at the International Conference on the History and Culture of Polish Jews, Jerusalem, February 1988; Honorata Obuchowska-Pysiowa, *Udzial Krakowa w handlu zagranicznym Rzeczypospolitej w pierwszych latach XVII w* (Wrocław, 1981); Daniel Tollet, "La littérrature antisémite polonaise, de 1588 à 1668. Auteurs et éditions," *Revue française d'histoire du livre* 14 (1977): 73–105.
6 Marian Wolanski, *Związki handlowe Śląska z Rzeczapospolitą w XVII wieku* (Wroclaw, 1961), 301.

1760s and the well-known figures for the Leipzig fairs show the remarkable numerical prominence of Jews among Polish merchants.[7] A list of fifteen "Merchants from Little Poland Returning from the Frankfurt Fair," recorded at a toll station in western Poland in 1765, included only Jews.[8]

One of the important questions awaiting systematic investigation is the precise nature of trade ties and economic relations between Polish-Jewish merchants and the *Hofjuden*.[9] Although Jews were often integral to the management of the huge private holdings of Polish aristocrats, there was no true Polish analogy to what Jersch-Wenzel has termed elsewhere an *importiertes "Ersatzbürgertum."*[10] In short, there were no Polish *Hofjuden*. One of the most striking differences between the Polish and German situations has to do precisely with the general absence of a state-managed economic policy in Poland. Jews were part of economies, of minieconomic systems administered by aristocrats, but they were not integrated into state-managed economic enterprises. Indeed, it must be said that this alliance of interests between Polish aristocrats and Jews was the critical element in the latter's economic freedom of activity. The weakness of urban guilds was more symptomatic than causal in this regard.[11]

The nature of social links between German and Polish Jews also warrants study. It can certainly be maintained that not only were German lands culturally peripheral to Poland-Lithuania but that there evolved significant differences between the self-identification of German and Polish Jews; each would feel him- or herself foreign in the territories of the other.[12] Con-

7 See the more than two hundred records of toll stations for the years 1764 through 1767 in Warsaw, Archiwum Glowne Akt Dawnych [AGAD], AK III; Max Freudenthal, *Leipziger Messgäste. Die jüdischen Besucher der Leipziger Messen in den Jahren 1675 bis 1764* (Frankfurt/Main, 1928); Richard Markgraf, *Zur Geschichte der Juden auf den Messen in Leipzig von 1664–1839* (Bischofswerda, 1894); Gershon David Hundert, *The Jews in a Polish Private Town* (Baltimore, 1992).
8 "Rewizja kupców małopolskich z jarmarku frankfortskiego reminiscere," AGAD, AK III/ 1604/5. The merchants were from the following towns: Brody, Janów (2), Konska Wola, Konskie, Kozienice, Kurów, Miedzyborz, Przysucha (2), Radom, Satanów, Witków, Zasław, Żółkiew.
9 See Max Grunwald, *Samuel Oppenheimer und sein Kreis. Ein Kapitel aus der Finanzgeschichte Österreichs* (Vienna, 1913).
10 Stefi Jersch-Wenzel, *Juden und "Franzosen" in der Wirtschaft des Raumes Berlin-Brandenburg zur Zeit des Merkantilismus* (Berlin, 1978). See the comments of Artur Eisenbach in his *Emancipation of the Jews in Poland, 1780–1870,* trans. J. Dorosz (Oxford, 1991), 50.
11 Compare Jonathan I. Israel, *European Jewry in the Age of Mercantilism, 1550–1750* (Oxford, 1985), 165–6, 182.
12 See Chone Shmeruk, "Young Men from Germany in the Yeshivot of Poland" (in Hebrew), in *Yitzhak F. Baer Jubilee Volume,* ed. S. W. Baron et al. (Jerusalem, 1960), 304–17; also see other sources cited in Gershon David Hundert, "An Advantage to Peculiarity? The Case of the Polish Commonwealth," *Association of Jewish Studies Review* 6 (1981): 27–8, and the material assembled by M. Rosman, "Dimyo shel beit Yisra'el be-Folin ke-merkaz torah aharei gezerot tah-tat," *Zion* 51 (1986): 435–48.

temporary observers in Poland also perceived these differences. An article appeared in a Warsaw newspaper to mark the fifth anniversary of the death of Moses Mendelssohn. Written by its Berlin correspondent, the report mentioned some of the leading lights of the Berlin Jewry, including Hartwig Wessely and Isaac Euchel. It offered an analysis of the "moral and political" situation of Jews in Prussia and concluded with the following comment:

Accustomed to seeing our Itsiks and Moshkes sitting in the inns and getting the people drunk, it is amazing for us [to behold] people of the same nation and faith who, in other lands, are so useful and enlightened.[13]

13 *Gazeta narodowa i obca,* no. 37 (1791), cited in Emanuel Ringelblum, "Żydzi w świetle prasy war-szawskiej wieku XVIIIgo," *Miesięcznik Żydowski* 2 (1932): 42–3.

PART III

Jewish–Gentile Contacts and Relations in the Pre-Emancipation Period

8

Languages in Contact: The Case of Rotwelsch and the Two "Yiddishes"

PAUL WEXLER

I

When discussion turns to the initial settlement of the Jews in the German lands, one thinks of French and Italian Jewish migrants to the Rhineland and, more marginally, to Bavaria in the ninth and tenth centuries. When discussion turns to their linguistic profile, it is invariably Yiddish, allegedly a variant of High German, that comes to mind. These two claims have been at the heart of German-Jewish historiography and Germanic linguistics for some time. And yet both of them, I believe, are essentially erroneous.

Speaking heterogeneous Romance and non-Romance languages, Jews settled in different parts of the German lands, where they developed two indigenous languages: (1) in the extreme southwest, imported Judeo-French was supplanted by a judaized form of High German (which I will call "Ashkenazic German," following the native-language epithet *aške-nazes*) and, ultimately, by Yiddish; (2) elsewhere, Balkan Jews, presumably speaking Balkan Romance, Slavic, and/or Greek, became speakers of Judeo-Sorbian, which subsequently developed into Yiddish. Contrary to common opinion, the latter is a West Slavic language with an unusually large German vocabulary and is genetically unrelated to High German. An evaluation of the historical contacts between the two Jewish languages – or "Yiddishes" – and *Rotwelsch* first requires a reassessment of the time and place of the genesis of Ashkenazic German and Yiddish, their component makeups, and their genetic classifications.[1]

---

1 See the discussion of *Rotwelsch* in Section V of this chapter. For a definition of the term, see the attempt by Yacov Guggenheim in his essay "Meeting on the Road: Encounters between German Jews and Christians on the Margins of Society," Chapter 9 of this volume. The phonetic symbols *č* and *š* used here in Yiddish words are equivalent to German *tsch* and *sch*, respectively.

II

The traditional scholarly view is that Yiddish comes from German stock. The first systematic exposition of the genesis of Yiddish was given by Matthias Mieses (1885–1945). He posited the venue of the birth of Yiddish in the eastern central German lands, on an exclusively Italian substratum. From here, Yiddish subsequently fanned out to the west (the Rhineland, Switzerland, and Alsace), the south (northern Italy), and the east (Poland).[2]

The second major exposition of the genesis of Yiddish can be credited to Max Weinreich, a leading historian of the Yiddish language (1894–1969). In his opinion, the first German Jews spoke judaized variants of French and Italian.[3] Weinreich was the first to present a well-documented exposition of the theory of a combined Franco-Italian substratum, which has since been accepted by most scholars.[4] In the German lands, the Jews abandoned Romance and adopted – or, more precisely, adapted – the local German speech.[5] The latter combined with a small Romance substratum to form a unique speech that was exclusive to the Jews and that by the 1600s was called "Yiddish." This uniquely judaized German amalgam was enriched from the very outset by a mainly colloquial Hebrew-Aramaic component, in part inherited via French and Italian from Judeo-Latin and Judeo-Greek (the last two Jewish languages in direct contact with colloquial Palestinian Hebrew and Aramaic), and in part newly lifted from liturgical texts by Yiddish speakers. As Jews migrated from the Rhineland to the central and southeastern German lands, the Germanic component of Yiddish became exclusively High German. In the twelfth century, the Jews established contact with Slavic languages. Although the Slavic contribution to the total spoken Yiddish lexicon probably never exceeded 10 percent, Slavic – along with Hebrew – was held responsible for the dramatic reshaping of Yiddish phonology, semantics, and syntax that produced such a marked gap between those dialects of Yiddish spoken in the Slavic lands and all of the Ger-

---

2 Matthias Mieses, *Die jiddische Sprache* (Berlin, 1924), 106.
3 Mieses did not speak of a specifically judaized Italian.
4 For brief mention of the Franco-Italian origin hypothesis, see Ismar Elbogen, "Deutschland," in Marcus Brann et al., eds., *Germania Judaica*, vol. 1 (Breslau, 1934), xvii–xlviii, xviii.
5 *Gešixte fun der jidišer šprax*, vols. 1–4 (New York, 1973); partial English translation (Chicago, 1980). Judeo-French could have become extinct in the southwestern German lands by the mid-fifteenth century, after the Jews were definitively expelled from the kingdom of France and Franche-Comté in 1394. There is no evidence that German Jews spoke Judeo-Italian, though exposure was assured when Ashkenazic Jews migrated to northern Italy between the fourteenth and sixteenth centuries. Italian Jews have developed their own dialects of Italian, but there is disagreement over the age of these dialects; the linguistic behavior of the Jews in France remains a subject of debate. For details, see Paul Wexler, *Judeo-Romance Linguistics: A Bibliography (Latin, Italo-, Gallo-, Ibero- and Rhaeto-Romance except Castilian)* (New York, 1989), preface.

man dialects from which Yiddish was allegedly derived. The geographic separation in the Slavic lands between metropolitan German and Yiddish was also said to have contributed to the maintenance in Yiddish of German archaisms and deviations from German norms.

Although Mieses's southeastern German homeland for Yiddish was at first eclipsed by the southwestern German venue (with its two-pronged Romance substratum), few linguists today would deny the correctness of his theory. There are several reasons for this. First, there are few features of southwestern German dialect in any dialect of Yiddish.[6] Second, Western Yiddish is relatively monolithic, compared with the extreme heterogeneity of the co-territorial western German dialect landscape, which hints at a late arrival of Yiddish in the area.[7] Third, the small, unique Romance component of Yiddish, which has attained for the most part a pan-Yiddish status, can be shown to be of northern Italian, Friulan, or Balkan Romance extraction.[8] These elements, together with a small corpus of unique Grecisms in Yiddish, suggest that the major path of Jewish migration from the Mediterranean to northern Europe was through the Balkans, Bohemia, and Hungary, rather than through France.

Fourth, Yiddish has only a very minor French component – primarily in its southwestern German, Swiss, Alsatian, and Dutch dialects; conversely, all other nonnative components (e.g., unique non-French Romance, Greek, West Slavic), surface throughout Yiddish dialects – a fact which points to the (south) eastern German lands as the conduit.[9] And fifth, the possibility of deriving many Slavisms in Western and Eastern Yiddish from Sorbian strongly supports the view that Yiddish was conceived in the orig-

---

6　See Jechiel Bin-Nun, *Jiddisch und die deutschen Mundarten (unter besonderer Berücksichtigung des ostgalizischen Jiddisch)* (Tübingen, 1973); Alice Faber and Robert D. King, "Yiddish and the Settlement History of Ashkenazic Jewry," *Mankind Quarterly* 24 (1984): 393–425; R. D. King, "Proto Yiddish Morphology," in Dovid Katz, ed., *Origins of the Yiddish Language* (Oxford, 1987), 73–81; and James W. Marchand, "Proto Yiddish and the Glosses: Can we reconstruct Proto Yiddish?" in Katz, ed., *Origins of the Yiddish Language*, 83–94.

7　Western Yiddish broadly comprises the dialects spoken in Bohemia, Moravia, western Hungary, and Holland; Eastern Yiddish is spoken in Poland, the Ukraine, Belorussia, Rumania, and the Baltic lands (except for Courland, where historically a mixture of Western and Belorussian / Baltic Yiddish were spoken).

8　By "unique" I mean romanisms not found in coterritorial German or Slavic. See details in my *Balkan Substratum of Yiddish: A Reassessment of the Unique Romance and Greek Components* (Wiesbaden, 1992). I believe that many Italian and Friulian elements were acquired by "pre-Yiddish" in the Balkans. For example, pan-Yiddish *benčn* ("bless") has close formal links with southern Italian *benedicere* (~ standard Italian *benedire*), but the geographical distance poses a problem; French *bénir* is a late-learned borrowing from Latin and thus an unlikely etymon. Both *bene-* and *dicere* are found in Balkan languages (e.g., Albanian *bekoj*, Croatian *dîčiti [se]*, Hungarian *dicser*, "to praise"), and all the Balkan languages have translations of the Romance (Latin) expression, e.g., Bulgarian *blagoslavjam*, Rumanian *binecuvînta*.

9　See Paul Wexler, *Three Heirs to a Judeo-Latin Legacy: Judeo-Ibero-Romance, Yiddish and Rotwelsch* (Wiesbaden, 1988), chap. 2.

inally bilingual Germano-Slavic lands rather than in the monolingual German lands.

III

A fresh view posits that Yiddish comes from Slavic stock. Although I follow Mieses in claiming that the lands between the Danube River in Bavaria and the Saale and Elbe rivers in Saxony provide a far more plausible homeland for Yiddish than the Rhine Valley, I would insist on two innovations: (a) Yiddish is not a "form of German," and (b) the southwestern and southeastern German lands were independently settled by two different groups of Jews, though possibly simultaneously. The two groups shared, inter alia, some kind of Romance background, but they developed diverse linguistic profiles in their new homelands.

Let us begin by looking at the language of the latter group, those Jews who settled the mixed (south)eastern Germano-Slavic lands. A close inspection of the total Slavic component in Yiddish, in its distributive, etymological, and geographic parameters, leads me to conclude that the Jews who resided – since at least the ninth to tenth centuries – in the bilingual Germano-Slavic lands east of the *Limes sorabicus*[10] were originally speakers of Sorbian.[11] Judeo-Sorbian underwent "re-lexification" to German, at various times and in various locales, by at least the ninth to tenth centuries but at the latest by the early thirteenth century. The product of such a "partial language shift" was the grafting of High German vocabulary (reaching about 75 percent, in most contemporary eastern European dialects of Yiddish and even higher in Western Yiddish) onto a Judeo-Sorbian syntax and phonology.[12] On the basis of its syntax and phonology, and despite its "German

10 The *Limes sorabicus*, the border wall constructed by Charlemagne in 805, separated the Slavic-controlled areas to the east from the Holy Roman Empire to the west. The *Limes* passed through Bardowiek, Magdeburg, Erfurt, Hallstadt, Forchheim, Brennburg, Regensburg, and Lorch; Theodor Frings, *Nemeckaja dialektografija*, ed. Viktor Maksimovič Žirmunskij (Moscow, 1955), 150–205, map no. 61. The Catalonian Jewish traveler Ibrāhīm ibn Ja'qūb visited Jewish settlements in the present-day Sachsen-Anhalt during a visit about 965; see Tadeusz Kowalski, *Relacja Ibrāhīma ibn Ja'kūba z podróży do krajów słowiańskich w przekazie al-Bekrīego* (Cracow, 1946).

11 Until approximately the thirteenth through fourteenth centuries, Sorbian speakers inhabited the eastern half of the present-day German lands in various strengths; today, Sorbs number some seventy thousand bilinguals in the Nieder- and Oberlausitz. Slavic died out in many areas only in the early fifteenth century (e.g., in Brandenburg, northeastern Bavaria, Rügen) and was still spoken in the Lüneburg area as late as the eighteenth century. There are no records of Judeo-Sorbian, but traces of the language can be found in medieval Hebrew documents. Most of these traces have traditionally been described as "Czech." See Roman Jakobson, "Řeč a písemnictví českých židů v době přemyslovské," *Kulturní sborník ROK* (New York, 1957), 1–12; and in non-Jewish languages (e.g., German and Slavic). On judaized variants of Slavic, see my *Explorations in Judeo-Slavic Linguistics* (Leiden, 1987). Some Yiddish romanisms with Balkan Slavic traits suggest that the Jews knew Slavic prior to their arrival in the Germano-Slavic lands.

look," Yiddish remains a West Slavic language; its genetic classification hardly changes because of its lexical reorientation.[13] In the mid-thirteenth century, Judeo-Sorbian/Yiddish, was transported for the first time to Poland and, by the late fourteenth century, to Belorussia.

My proposal is supported by a variety of evidence included in the following seven points.[14] First, the small West Slavic component in Western Yiddish dialects cannot be attributed to Eastern Yiddish immigrants to western Europe in the mid-seventeenth century, as has been widely proposed, since the corpus is nearly uniform throughout Western Yiddish. These words can be smoothly derived from Sorbian. A few examples are Alsatian Y *bā*, EY *babe, bobe,* "grandmother" (~ So *baba*), EY *blince,* "pancake" (see also Silesian G *Plins[en]*) (~ So *blinc*), OWY, EY *bok,* "non-Jewish God" (this component surfaces in G *Bockshorn* now understood as "goat's horn" but originally a replacement for the tabu *Gotteszorn,* "the anger of God") (~ So *bóh,* "God"), WY (Regensburg, fifteenth century), EY *dunaj,* "Danube" (~ So *Dunaj*), Y *jojx,* "broth" (versus G *Jauche,* "sewer water") (~ So *juška*), WY *kawleč,* EY *kojleč,* "festive bread" (Thuringian G *kalatsche,* "baked goods") (~ So *kołač*).[15]

Second, Yiddish possesses an inordinately large Hebrew component that finds no parallel in any other Jewish language. In addition, Hebrew exercises dominance over other components – including the majority German lexicon – that takes the form of formal and/or orthographic hebraization of non-Hebrew components, as well as their outright replacement by Hebrew loans. For example, the *i* of Y *nitl,* "Christmas," of Romance stock (see It *Natale, nedal,* Dalmatian *nadal,* etc.), is widely explained by association with He *nitlah,* "hung," a derogatory reference to the crucifixion of Jesus

---

12 On the "exchange" of a lexicon, or "re-lexification," see Sarah Grey Thomason and Terrence Kaufman, *Language Contact, Creolization and Genetic Linguistics* (Berkeley and Los Angeles, 1988).

13 It is hard to imagine another language spoken in the heart of Europe and as well known as Yiddish whose genetic affiliation has been so variously and imprecisely defined by linguists; see the plethora of terms applied to Yiddish, e.g., *jüdisch-(mittelhoch) deutsch, Judendeutsch, jüdisch gefärbtes Deutsch, hebräisch-mittelhochdeutsch, Hebrew-German* and *Germano-Judaic,* etc., cited by Werner Weinberg, "Die Bezeichnung Jüdischdeutsch: Eine Neubewertung" *Zeitschrift für deutsche Philologie,* suppl. 100 (1981): 253–90; see also Jerold C. Frakes, *The Politics of Interpretation: Alterity and Ideology in Old Yiddish Studies* (Albany, 1989), and Gabriele L. Strauch, "Methodologies and Ideologies: The Historical relationship of German Studies to Yiddish," in Paul Wexler, ed., *Studies in Yiddish Linguistics* (Tübingen, 1990), 83–100.

14 Abbreviations: E = eastern, Fr = French, G = German, He = Hebrew, It = Italian, O = Old, Pol = Polish, Rtw = Rotwelsch, So = upper Sorbian, W = western, Y = Yiddish.

15 In Wexler, *Explorations,* chap. 6, I compiled a brief list of sorbianisms in Yiddish; much new evidence is given in Wexler, *Yiddish – The Fifteenth Slavic Language: A Study in Partial Language Shift from Judeo-Sorbian to German* (Berlin, 1991), chap. 3 sec. 23. For Rotwelsch reflexes of the last slavism (1753ff.) from a German dialect or from Yiddish, see Siegmund A. Wolf, *Wörterbuch des Rotwelschen* (Mannheim, 1956), no. 2430.

Christ.[16] The use of hebraisms might have been a means of repelling the tide of germanization that threatened the German Slavs with complete language shift to German, a development presumably unattractive to the Jews, since germanization was tantamount to Christianization. The success of the Jews and some of the Sorbs in withstanding germanization may have been a function of German settlement (for example, it was relatively sparse in the Lausitz area) and the close ties between the Jews (and some Sorbs) with their less threatened Bohemian compatriots.

Third, Yiddish tends to use hebraisms (and occasionally unique romanisms) where Sorbian uses germanisms. An example is Y *lej(en)en*, "read" < Romance (compare North It *lejere*) versus So (archaic) *lazować* < G dialectal *//lazen//*.[17] The overlapping distribution of borrowed lexicon – not found with any other Slavic language – suggests that Jews and Sorbs must have once been coterritorial, with each group responding to the pressures of germanization in its own way.

Fourth, a number of slavisms in Polish Yiddish, which are clearly not of Polish origin, have often been derived from Belorussian and Ukrainian, even though they were widely known in Yiddish in areas far from the two East Slavic languages. Diffusion from Eastern Yiddish dialects is an unattractive hypothesis, but there are no linguistic obstacles to regarding the bulk of the "east slavisms" in Polish Yiddish as sorbianisms. For example, Y *mučn*, "to torment," looks like Ukrainian *mučyty* or Belorussian *mučyc'*, but its presence in western Poland makes So *mučić* a more attractive etymon; Pol *męczyć* must be excluded as an etymon on formal grounds.[18]

Fifth, the re-lexification of Judeo-Sorbian to German vocabulary took place before the first eastward migrations of the German Jews; but Eastern Yiddish dialects nevertheless differ in their Judeo-Sorbian "profile." The contemporary Belorussian-Baltic Yiddish dialects (except for Courland Yiddish), in place since the thirteenth to fourteenth centuries, retain more Judeo-Sorbian phonological and grammatical features than Polish Yiddish, which continues the relatively more germanized Judeo-Sorbian/Yiddish brought from Germany in the 1600s.[19]

---

16 The first example of the reshaping is FrHe *njtl* with *t* < He *nitlah* (instead of expected *njtl*) in a fourteenth-century document from Vesoul, Franche-Comté. See Isidore Loeb, "Deux livres de commerce du commencement du XIVe siècle," *Revue des etudes Juives* 8 (1884): 163–96, 193. Yiddish has no examples with a vowel other than /i/. For Rotwelsch examples meaning "gallows" (179ff.), see Wolf, *Wörterbuch*, no. 3845.

17 On Rotwelsch forms of *lejenen* (since the eighteenth century), see Wolf, *Wörterbuch*, no. 3196.

18 For many more examples, see Wexler, *Yiddish*.

19 The Yiddish that remained in Germany underwent a particularly extreme germanization, involving the incorporation of many German syntactic and phonological features, thus facilitating the replacement of Yiddish by High German in the late eighteenth century.

Sixth, there is evidence that the Jews themselves were uncertain of the relationship of their language to coterritorial German and Slavic. A non-committal language name, *jidiš* ("Jewish") has been in use since the sixteenth century. The language has been receptive in the last century to any Hebrew elements but relatively closed to modern German and Slavic. There is an ambivalent attitude to German and Slavic components. For example, old Slavic morphemes are replaced by synonymous German morphemes, for example, the verbal infix *-eve-* > *-ir-*, but *-eve-* appears in Yiddish neologisms and in new loans from Slavic.

Finally, the term *aškenaz*, now associated with Germany and the historically Yiddish-speaking communities, was originally associated with the Slavic lands.[20]

IV

The next issues of importance are the origins of Ashkenazic German, the language of the Jews in the southwestern German lands. Weinreich saw Yiddish as the sole Jewish language to take root in the German lands, ultimately carried eastward into the monolingual Slavic lands. I believe that the Jews in the southwestern German lands were originally not involved in the development of Judeo-Sorbian/Yiddish, though the fates of the two speech territories were to become intertwined.[21] Originally, French Jews settled these areas, between the tenth century and their expulsion from France in 1394. These Jews became speakers of either Yiddish, when the latter spread from the east into the Rhineland, Alsace, and western Switzerland, or of a mildly judaized (that is, gallicized) Ashkenazic German, based on the immediately coterritorial German dialects. In any case, Yiddish eventually supplanted Ashkenazic German.

Ashkenazic German, with written records dating from the fourteenth and fifteenth centuries (in the form of native texts as well as French and Hebrew works in early German *Rotwelsch*), shows signs of neither extreme component fusion nor of a Slavic component; its small, unique French component, still marginally found in some Western Yiddish dialects, is entirely unknown in Eastern Yiddish, except for a few personal names. In the contacts that developed between the two Jewish communities, Sorbian Jews influenced Ashkenazic German speakers linguistically, though the latter assumed the upper hand in shaping the common religious culture of the German Jews.

20 Wexler, *Explorations*, 160.
21 I use the term "Yiddish" to denote re-lexified Judeo-Sorbian.

V

The history of *Rotwelsch* mirrors Jewish linguistic history in the German lands. Beginning with Avé-Lallemant in 1858–62, the *Rotwelsch* testimony has been studied repeatedly, but it could not be properly evaluated as long as Jewish linguistic behavior in the German lands was perceived as monolithic. An examination of the *Rotwelsch* of the fourteenth through the late seventeenth centuries contributes to the reconstruction of the linguistic profile and settlement history of the German Jews, by providing chronologically and geographically ordered evidence of Judeo-French and its heir, Ashkenazic German, and of Judeo-Sorbian/Yiddish (the predecessors of which – that is, Balkan Slavic, Romance, and Greek[?] – are unattested in the German lands).

Wolf's dictionary of *Rotwelsch* terms, covering the fourteenth century to the present, contains a significant Hebrew component, attributed to Yiddish.[22] The preponderance of Hebrew is to be expected, since most German terms in Yiddish would be easily understood and thus unsuitable for Yiddish and German secret lexicons. Yiddish could only contribute obsolete or German dialectal words to *Rotwelsch* – for example, Rtw *Jauche*, "soup" (1814) – with German form and Yiddish meaning.[23] This means that *Rotwelsch* uses Yiddish to reactivate discarded or regional German elements.

Because of his blind assumption that all Jewish terms had to be of direct (Germanic) Yiddish origin, many of Wolf's etyma are unconvincing. He accepted the traditional argument that regarded *Rotwelsch* hebraisms, which deviated from Yiddish pronunciation norms, as distortions introduced by Christian speakers[24] or as learned borrowings from classical Hebrew made by Christians.[25] Given several Hebrew etyma, some scholars reconstructed according to the Hebrew corpus in Yiddish.[26] Scholars have tended to ignore the evidence that earlier *Rotwelsch* preserves hebraisms unknown in these forms or meanings in Yiddish, for example, Rtw *Schöchervetser*, "innkeeper," *Lehem*, "bread" (1510) are unknown in Yiddish;[27] contemporary Bavarian *Rotwelsch* (found in the villages of Schillingsfürst and

22 For an elucidation of many early *Rotwelsch* roots, see Robert Jütte, *Abbild und soziale Wirklichkeit des Bettler- und Gaunertums zu Beginn der Neuzeit* (Cologne, 1988).
23 See Wolf, *Wörterbuch*, no. 2337.
24 A. F. Thiele, *Die jüdischen Gauner in Deutschland, ihre Taktik, ihre Eigenthümlichkeit und ihre Sprache*, vol. 1 (1840; Berlin, 1843), 199.
25 Matthias Mieses, *Die Entstehungsursache der jüdischen Dialekten* (Vienna, 1915), 25.
26 Friedrich C. B. Avé-Lallemant, *Das deutsche Gaunertum in seiner social-politischen, literarischen und linguistischen Ausbildung zu seinem heutigen Bestande*, vols. 1–4 (Leipzig, 1858–62), 3:148, 156.
27 See Wolf, *Wörterbuch*, nos. 3170 and 4832.

Schopfloch) contains examples found in the earliest lists, for example, Rtw *dift* (ca. 1490), *difftel* (1510), "church," differ formally from Y *tifle* < He *ti-flah*, "foolishness."[28]

The percentage of hebraisms in *Rotwelsch* rises dramatically after the mid-seventeenth century. For example, whereas the *Liber vagatorum* (1510 and later editions) had approximately 21 percent hebraisms, the contemporary Westphalian *Schlausmen* jargon – the regional name for this variant of *Rotwelsch* – has upward of 50 percent.[29] The size of the Hebrew component is reminiscent of "Hebrew-component dominance" that was most characteristic of Judeo-Sorbian/Eastern Yiddish. Were Yiddish the sole or major purveyor of hebraisms to early *Rotwelsch*, we would expect to find more hebraisms in the latter. Even the regional names for *Rotwelsch* are mainly of Hebrew origin, beginning with the early eighteenth century. On the basis of the changing form of the Jewish component in *Rotwelsch*, I assume that the shift from Judeo-French / Ashkenazic German to Yiddish was completed by the late seventeenth century. The relative paucity of hebraisms in early *Rotwelsch* might also indicate the relative absence of Hebrew-component dominance typical of Western Yiddish. The formal changes in the hebraisms that *Rotwelsch* has retained over the centuries attest to the growing importance of the Yiddish purveyor as well. For example, compare Rtw *kielam*, "city" (1510), with Rtw *kihlo* (1840), "(Jewish) community."[30] The first form may be from He *gahal*, "(Jewish) community" + He *-im* (a plural suffix widely used in Yiddish) versus Y *kōl*, *kūl*, "community, public" (no plural); the latter is from related He *gehilah*, "(Jewish) community" – the source of Y *kile*. Moreover, the absence of *Rotwelsch* hebraisms in Yiddish does not necessarily rule out Yiddish speakers as the purveyors; hebraisms not used in Yiddish would have been appropriate for crypto-Yiddish.

Rotwelsch provides a clue to French-speaking Jewish settlement in the German lands. A tentative Judeo-French origin can be postulated for *Rotwelsch* hebraisms displaying: (a) phonological, morphological, and/or semantic features associated with Judeo-French hebraisms, (b) French morphological machinery that (c) has surface cognates in Judeo-French (but not in German Yiddish), or that (d) differ in form and/or meaning from the Western Yiddish surface cognates; (e) a few French elements in early *Rotwelsch*, which may be of immediate Judeo-French origin. Possible ex-

28 Ibid., no. 5828.
29 See Robert Jütte, *Sprachsoziologische und lexikologische Untersuchungen zu einer Sondersprache. Die Sensenhändler im Hochsauerland und die Reste ihrer Geheimsprache* (Wiesbaden, 1978), and Jütte, *Abbild*.
30 See Thiele, *Jüdischen Gauner* (1843), and Wexler, *Three Heirs*, 145.

amples of Judeo-French and gallicized Hebrew words are Rtw *dormen*, "sleep" < Fr *dormir*, unknown in the Yiddish spoken east of the Rhineland and in western Switzerland; in *Rotwelsch*, it surfaces as far east as Vienna;[31] Rtw *barl(er)en*, "speak" (1510) (< OFr *parlier*), also unknown in Yiddish.[32] A particularly revealing index of Judeo-French impact is the elimination of the Hebrew letter *ḥet* / *ḥ* / in *Rotwelsch* hebraisms. *Ḥet*, like *xaf*, has the value of /x/, in most European Jewish languages, including (Slavic) Yiddish. Whereas the French Jews pronounced the letter *xaf* as /x/, *ḥet* lacked phonetic value;[33] Yiddish has no examples of *ḥet* as zero except for a few personal names, for example, EY *icik*, male < He *jiḥaq*, *sime*, female < He *śimḥah* (but note EY *simxe*, "male," from the same source).

Early *Rotwelsch* lists provide an example of a hebraism without the historical *ḥ*, which is not generally used in Yiddish dialects – He *leḥem* "bread" > Rtw *lem*, etc. The geography of this hebraism without *ḥet* in *Rotwelsch* is very revealing: Basel, from the fifteenth century up to 1733; Constance, 1791; Württemberg, eighteenth through twentieth centuries; Berne, 1900; Luxembourg, 1937.[34]

The occasional appearance of this hebraism in areas east and north of the southwestern German lands is relatively recent and is probably the result of internal *Rotwelsch* diffusion. Intervocalic /x/ would have become either /x/ or /ç/ in *Rotwelsch*; hence, the word must have come directly from Judeo-French (or Ashkenazic German). East of the southwestern German lands, old *Rotwelsch* occasionally had the form with /x/: for example, Zurich *lechem* (ca. 1490).[35] Also see the Bavarian Y *lechem* in the writings of the Jewish apostate Pfefferkorn (1509).[36] This example suggests that *Rotwelsch* was simultaneously receptive both to Judeo-French/Ashkenazic German and Yiddish enrichment.

31 See Wolf, *Wörterbuch*, no. 1064, and Wexler, *Three Heirs*, 123, 148.
32 The first form is found in G. Edlibach about 1490, the second in the *Liber vagatorum*, 1510ff. (Both are cited in Wolf, *Wörterbuch*, no. 320.) Note that earliest *Rotwelsch* lacks -*ier*-, typical of French verbs in German (e.g., G *parlieren* sixteenth century, Rtw *barlaren* 1652). Yiddish unique romanisms never appear with -*ir*-, e.g., *benčn*, "bless," *lej(en)en*, "read" – versus *marinirn* "marinate," received through German.
33 *Ḥet*, as "zero," in Germany was noted by Rabbi Iserlin (b. Regensburg, 1390; d. Wiener-Neustadt, 1460) and by the hebraist Stefan Bodeker (1384–1459), bishop of Brandenburg. See Karl Habersaat, "Materialien zur Geschichte der jiddischen Grammatik," *Orbis* 11 (1962): 352–68, 352, and Bernhard Walde, *Christliche Hebraisten Deutschlands am Ausgang des Mittelalters* (Münster, 1916), respectively, and Wexler, *Three Heirs*, 97ff.
34 For references, as well as other examples, see Wexler, *Three Heirs*, 99–100, 103–5. Might the occasional *Rotwelsch* spelling with *h* reflect compensatory lengthening in the preceding vowel for the missing *ḥet*? (See Wolf, *Wörterbuch*, no. 3170.)
35 Edlibach, ca. 1490; see Wolf, *Wörterbuch*.
36 Johannes Pfefferkorn, *Ich bin ein Buchlinn* (Augsburg, 1509).

In the cultivation of doublet forms of a Hebrew root, *Rotwelsch* differs sharply from the Jewish languages. Another example, besides Rtw *le(che)m*, is He *qahal*, "(Jewish) community" > Rtw *kielam* ~ *gallen*, "town" (1510). Doublets could both come through a Judeo-French carrier, for example, Rtw *klapot* (Basel, 1411–63) versus *claffot* (Strasbourg, 1510), "clothing."[37] He *-ot* plural is an unlikely source of Rtw *-ot*, since this ending would have yielded *-o(t)s* and *-os/ -es* in the Judeo-French and Yiddish pronunciations of Hebrew, respectively. Furthermore, it is suspicious that a plural morpheme would appear with a singular noun. A more felicitous source is He *qlaf*, "parchment, peel, bark" + OFr *-ot* (diminutive) (1510). Similarly, Rtw *bsaffot*, "letter" (1510) < He *ktav*, "writing, inscription" (*k* > *b* is unexpected) + OFr *-ot*.

It is curious that both the outright French loans and the gallicized hebraisms tend to disappear from *Rotwelsch* listings after the mid-seventeenth century – presumably after the extinction of Judeo-French.[38] Of course, Judeo-French terms could have survived in *Rotwelsch* long after the obsolescence of Judeo-French.

Non-Germanic elements from Yiddish other than Hebrew are relatively rare in *Rotwelsch*. An example is Y *šabaš*, "portion of thieves' loot" (1851) < Iranian.[39] The nearly total absence of slavisms in *Rotwelsch* is significant, for example, *nebç*, "unfortunate" (1822),[40] and *Jauche*, "soup" < (Judeo-) Sorbian (?)/Yiddish. Since the iranianism and the slavisms are not attested before the mid-eighteenth century, they cannot be direct borrowings from Judeo-Sorbian prior to its re-lexification to German.

In the mid-eighteenth century, the Jews in the German lands began to exchange their unique linguistic patrimony for Christian speech, though

37 The respective sources are *Die Basler Betrügnisse der Gyler* (fifteenth century) and the *Liber vagatorum* (1510 and later editions). See Wolf, *Wörterbuch*.

38 *Bsaffot* disappears after the *Liber vagatorum* (1547). Wolf, *Wörterbuch*, no. 422, derives the term from unattested "Y"He *bezefes*, "in pitch." *Claffot* is attested up to 1547–and then once in F. L. A. von Grolman, *Wörterbuch der in Teutschland üblichen Spitzbuben-Sprachen* (Giessen, 1822); see also Wolf, *Wörterbuch*, no. 2736. Other forms, e.g., *klaft, kluft*, are contemporary *Rotwelsch*. PolY slang *kliftling*, "garment," in Wiktor Ludwikowski and Henryk Walczak, *Żargon mowy przestępców* (Warsaw, 1922), 37, may be a *Rotwelsch* borrowing (see section V of this chapter).

39 Rudolf Fröhlich, *Die gefährlichen Klassen Wiens. Darstellung ihres Entstehens, ihrer Verbindungen, ihrer Taktik, ihrer Sitten und Gewohnheiten und ihrer Sprache* (Vienna, 1851). Wolf, *Wörterbuch*, no. 4886, confuses the term with Y *šibeš*, "error" < Hebrew. For a detailed discussion of the iranianism in Yiddish ("tip given musicians by guests dancing at a wedding" – the original Iranian meaning) and in German, Dutch, Hungarian, Belorussian, Ukrainian, Russian, and Turkic (in various, unoriginal meanings), see my "Two Comments on Yiddish Contacts with Indo-Iranian Languages," in Wexler, ed., *Studies in Yiddish Linguistics*, 127–41. The practice, though not the term, is known to various Slavic groups and to Germans in the former Slavic (Polabian) area of Lüneburg. For details, see my new book *Ashkenazic Jews: A Slavo-Turkic People in Search of a Jewish Identity* (Columbus, Ohio, 1993).

40 The term is found in von Grolman, *Wörterbuch*.

not always that of the immediately coterritorial populace. Now it is obsolescent German Yiddish and its successor – a new, transitional Ashkenazic German – that become receptive to sporadic *Rotwelsch* hebraisms: for example, Y *šaxern*, "haggle" < G *schachern* < He *saxar*, "trade," versus genuine GY *saxren* (eighteenth century).[41] The ungrammaticality of initial *s-* in German resulted in the replacement of He *s-* by *sch-*; *s-* is grammatical in Yiddish (as in all Slavic languages) in non-German elements.[42]

To evaluate the reciprocal impact of *Rotwelsch* and Yiddish, we first need to map the geography of the hebraisms in the two speech forms, preferably period by period. A major problem attending this research is that *Rotwelsch* is the basis of slang vocabulary in Dutch, Hungarian, Slavic, and even Baltic and Scandinavian languages; hence, Yiddish could have acquired *Rotwelsch* hebraisms outside the German lands. The marked differences in the Hebrew components of *Rotwelsch* and German Yiddish suggest that the former are not always derivable from the immediately coterritorial Western Yiddish dialects,[43] and that rural German Jews and Christians may have preserved different *Rotwelsch* lexicons. A cautious use of *Rotwelsch* data may even enable us to reconstruct the chronology and geography of the Hebrew corpus of early Yiddish.

The presence of an unmistakably varied Jewish component in *Rotwelsch* contrasts with the absence of any significant Jewish contribution in French slang (perhaps the Jews were expelled prior to the development of the earliest lists), and with a minor direct Jewish contribution to Dutch, Hungarian, and Slavic slang. In the latter, much of the Hebrew component has its immediate origins in imported *Rotwelsch*. The differential impact of *Rotwelsch* and Jewish languages on European slang lexicons calls out for immediate study.

VI

In conclusion, it is appropriate to consider why no students of Yiddish have considered the possibility that Yiddish might be of Slavic origin and why few have chosen to locate Yiddish genesis in the (south)eastern German lands.[44]

41 Paul Wexler, "Ashkenazic German (1750–1895)," *International Journal of the Sociology of Language* 30 (1981): 119–30.
42 For a discussion of this root in German, Dutch, Hungarian, Estonian, Norwegian, and Slavic languages, see my "Hebräische und aramäische Elemente in den slavischen Sprachen: Wege, Chronologien und Diffusionsgebiete," *Zeitschrift für slavische Philologie* 43 (1983): 229–79. See also Y slang *kliftling* in footnote 38 to this chapter.
43 Wexler, *Three Heirs*, 145.
44 See Bin-Nun, *Jiddisch*, Frakes, *Politics*, and Strauch, "Methodologies." Many eighteenth-century German Christian scholars believed that Yiddish could not be related to German because of the large number of deviations from German norms; they had the right observation but the wrong cause (see also Frakes, *Politics*, 7–20).

First, the overwhelming majority of Yiddish vocabulary is of German stock. The Slavic contribution, primarily in the phonotactics, semantics, and syntax, is less visible to the speaker or casual observer. Moreover, where a Slavic impact was obvious, its source was never suspected to be Sorbian – a language whose existence was unknown to many yiddishists and historians of the German Jews.

Second, until the early nineteenth century, the Yiddish literary language was based on Western Yiddish norms, which were much closer to standard German than were the Eastern Yiddish dialects. That the literary norms of a Western Yiddish minority could be attractive to masses of Eastern Yiddish speakers attests to the immense popularity of things "western" among the eastern European Jews.

Third, despite significant research in the late nineteenth century, before World War II our knowledge of Judeo-Slavic linguistics and Slavic settlement history in the German lands was fragmentary.[45]

Fourth, Germanists paid attention to the development of German dialects in eastern European lands but tended to overlook the origin and chronology of their Slavic component.[46]

Fifth, until recently, the phenomenon of language shift has been poorly understood by linguists and yiddishists.

Sixth, with the exception of Birnbaum[47] and M. Weinreich, yiddishists have exhibited little interest in comparative Jewish linguistics, which might have aroused doubts about a Germanic affiliation of Yiddish.[48]

Seventh, dialect geography is a major tool in identifying the partial shift from Judeo-Sorbian to German as well as in delineating the original territories of Judeo-French/Ashkenazic German and Judeo-Sorbian/Yiddish, yet only in the last two to three decades have comprehensive linguistic atlases become available for Yiddish, Sorbian, Polish, Ukrainian, and Belorussian.[49]

And finally, historians of the Jews have long been convinced that the course of Jewish settlement in the German lands after the eleventh century

45 Wexler, *Explorations*, provides a comprehensive bibliography of Judeo-Slavic linguistics; on Slavic settlement history in the German lands, see Joachim Herrmann, ed., *Die Slawen in Deutschland* (Berlin, 1985).
46 Uriel Weinreich, "Yiddish and Colonial German in Eastern Europe: The Differential Impact of Slavic," *American Contributions to the Fourth International Congress of Slavists* (The Hague, 1958), 369–421, 370.
47 Salomon A. Birnbaum, *Yiddish: A Survey and a Grammar* (Toronto, 1979).
48 See Paul Wexler, "Jewish Interlinguistics: Facts and Conceptual Framework," *Language* 57 (1981): 99–149.
49 See especially Helmut Fasske et al., eds., *Sorbischer Sprachatlas* (Bautzen/Budyšin, 1965–), Günther Bellmann, *Slavoteutonica* (Berlin, 1971), plotting the geography of slavisms in German, and Marvin I. Herzog, ed., "Language and Culture Atlas of Ashkenazic Jewry," unpublished maps and files housed at the Department of Linguistics, Columbia University. The first volume has been published (Tübingen, 1992).

proceeded from west to east. This view was based on several considerations. The earliest documentation and material remains of the Jews were found in the southwestern German lands. The *Drang nach Osten* of the Germans offered a model for eastward Jewish migration.[50] And it was believed (erroneously) that Old Yiddish had a rich French component.[51]

The hypothesis that Yiddish began as a judaized dialect of Sorbian necessitates a break with the traditional conception of the genesis of the Yiddish language almost in its entirety and invites historians to rethink their hypotheses. The only part of the traditional view of Yiddish history that strikes me as correct is that some Western Yiddish dialects (my "Ashkenazic German") were created in the absence of a Slavic substratum, when French-speaking and possibly some Italian-speaking Jews shifted completely to German in the Rhineland.[52]

My thesis offers new challenges to a number of disciplines. Yiddishists will need to rewrite significant parts of Yiddish linguistic history. For example, they will have to place the genesis of Eastern and some of the Western Yiddish dialects in the ninth through thirteenth centuries – possibly several centuries later than the traditional periodization of the genesis of (Germanic) Yiddish in the ninth and tenth centuries. I also reject Weinreich's model of Yiddish gradually "moving" away from German.[53] In my view, Yiddish was created when German moved progressively eastward, engulfing Judeo-Sorbian. This suggests that the mobility of the Jewish population in Germany may have been exaggerated. Yiddishists will also have to desist from mechanically viewing the Eastern Yiddish dialects as heirs to Western Yiddish linguistic events, since the two dialect masses partly had different origins and historical developments. Furthermore, linguists will have to reclassify the members of the Germanic and Slavic language families, but in the process they will gain a whole new laboratory in which to study the mechanics of partial language shift.

Germanists will no doubt be dismayed at the "loss" of a branch on the Germanic family tree, especially at a time when they are finding Yiddish attractive as a source of information for the history of German. Nevertheless, Yiddish would retain much of its traditional attraction to germanists for the period after the language shift, when Yiddish and German moved largely in

---

50 On the allegedly tandem migration of Jews and Germans, see Haim Tykocinski, "Österreich," in *Germania Judaica*, vol. 1 (Breslau, 1934), 256–65, 258.

51 See Weinreich, *Gešixte*. For rejection of this view, see Wexler, *Balkan Substratum*.

52 Scholars have often pointed to the migration of the Kalonimos family of rabbis from Lucca to Mainz about the year 1000. (Some scholars suggest the eighth century.) There are, however, no Yiddish italianisms which reflect early dialectal features of Luccan Italian. See details in Wexler, *Balkan Substratum*.

53 Weinreich, *Gešixte*, 1:43.

tandem; it would gain new significance as a Slavic language that acquired an unprecedented massive German component.

Slavists will be surprised to encounter a new member in the Slavic family of languages.[54] Current research has set the Jewish–Slavic contact in the ninth century in Bohemia and in the twelfth century in Poland. The new theory of the genesis of Yiddish sketched here expands the chronology and geography of Jewish–Slavic contacts to the German lands in the ninth to tenth centuries and possibly to the Balkans in the sixth to seventh centuries.

Until now, I was inclined to believe that most Jewish languages were created in a process of total language shift dating from the period of colloquial Hebrew and Judeo-Aramaic.[55] This assumed, for example, that Hebrew was supplanted by Aramaic, Aramaic in turn by Greek, Greek by Latin, and so forth. Only a few lexical elements were carried over from one language to its successor; these, together with ubiquitous (usually written) Hebrew and Judeo-Aramaic elements and an idiosyncratic selection of non-Jewish language material, contributed to the judaization of the latter. Students of comparative Jewish linguistics should now consider to what extent partial language shift may be a factor in the history of other Jewish languages.

Neither the migration routes and chronology of Jewish settlements in northern Europe nor the facts of Yiddish support the "western Eurocentric" bias inherent in the Romance theory of a German-Jewish origin. Historians must now address the possibility that some (most?) northern European Jews came from the Balkans (and the east?), partly in the wake of the *Drang nach Westen* of Slavs, Avars, Magyars, and others, which gathered momentum in the sixth century.[56] The anti-Slavic bias of the early twentieth century, which so impeded objective research into the eastern roots of the German Jews, has abated considerably. Today no one would endorse the remarks of Eppenstein in 1919: "In holding onto the intellectual activity that they brought from Germany and onto the German language, the Polish-Lithuanian Jewry created for itself, until quite recently, a lasting protective barrier against Slavic non-culture."[57]

Since the late Middle Ages, the Slavic lands have harbored the majority of the world's Jews (80 percent in Poland alone, in 1772). It is difficult to see how the tiny Jewish population in the monolingual German lands, sub-

---

54 On the judaization of Slavic languages, see Wexler, *Explorations*, chap. 2.

55 Wexler, "Jewish Interlinguistics," 121–2.

56 Jewish graves have recently been discovered in an Avar cemetery of the eighth century in northern Serbia at Čelarevo, northwest of Novi Sad. See Radovan Bunardžić, *Izložba menore iz Čelareva* (Belgrade, 1980).

57 Simon Eppenstein, "Zur Frühgeschichte der Juden in Deutschland, besonders in literarischer und kultureller Hinsicht," *Monatsschrift für die Geschichte und Wissenschaft des Judentums* 63 (1919): 165–86, 186.

ject to repeated expulsions and persecutions, could have generated such an enormous progeny in the east – especially since no evidence exists of large-scale Jewish migrations into the Slavic lands. This paradox prompted Koestler to posit the largely Turkic Khazars as the major component in the ethnogenesis of the Ashkenazic Jews.[58] I am skeptical of a significant Khazar connection, but the linguistic evidence is compatible with the hypothesis that an originally small Balkan Jewish population in the German lands was swelled when many western Slavs became judaizers/Jews prior to Christianization of the area in the ninth through twelfth centuries. As with the Khazars, who became Jews to avoid political entanglements with their Byzantine and Arab neighbors, Judaism would have been attractive to the Sorbs as a religion with no political attachments, in contrast to Christianity, which was often accompanied by the threat of germanization and German political control.

The Judeo-Sorbian origin of Yiddish also necessitates a reevaluation of possibly reciprocal Jewish-Slavic influences in religion and culture. Historians may also want to explore whether Jews were ever the carriers of Slavic and eastern German linguistic and cultural elements to the western German lands. German Jews should now be viewed as an outgrowth of an earlier Slavic Jewry. Substratal relics in *Rotwelsch* and the Jewish languages have enabled linguists to formulate innovative hypotheses about Jewish settlement in the German lands; it is up to historians to evaluate the implications. This is the exciting joint challenge for our two disciplines.

58 Arthur Koestler, *The Thirteenth Tribe: The Khazar Empire and Its Heritage* (London, 1976). Faber and King, in "Yiddish," suggest that the original Jewish population in the eastern German lands prior to the eastward migrations was substantially larger than hitherto supposed.

9

Meeting on the Road: Encounters between German Jews and Christians on the Margins of Society

YACOV GUGGENHEIM

In many ways the years of the Black Death, from 1348 to 1351, greatly affected the Jews of central Europe.[1] First and foremost was the demographic impact. Not only did Jews suffer directly from the plague, like everyone else – by common estimate between one-quarter and one-third of the population of central Europe perished – but Jews were also widely blamed for the plague and subsequently persecuted, burned at the stake, and expelled from towns. As a result, by the second half of the fourteenth century only approximately seven thousand Jewish families, that is, between 25,000 and 30,000 Jewish individuals, were left in the realm of the Holy Roman Empire. The demographic figures remained stable until the beginning of the sixteenth century, when, for economic reasons, the natural surplus of the Jewish population emigrated to the south and to the east.[2]

Second, the legal status of the Jews was decisively weakened in the course of the fourteenth century. This development was apparently hastened and intensified in the aftermath of the persecutions. As a rule, Jews were not

---

1 This essay forms part of a larger study on the lower stratum of German-Jewish society in the late Middle Ages. It is based on materials collected in preparation for the historical-geographical dictionary *Germania Judaica*, volume 3 for the period 1350 through 1519, under the general editorship of my late teacher and friend Arye Maimon: (number 1, articles A–L, edited by Maimon and Y. Guggenheim [Tübigen, 1987]; number 2, articles M–Z [in press]; number 3, regional articles, introduction, indices and maps [in preparation]). I presented some results in lectures in Vienna, Trier, and Bonn in 1988, others in Jerusalem in 1989. Also, see my "Social Stratification of Central European Jewry at the End of the Middle Ages: The Poor" (in Hebrew), in *Proceedings of the Tenth World Congress of Jewish Studies*, division B, vol. 1 (Jerusalem, 1990), 130–6. I benefited greatly from comments by colleagues and friends, and most of all from Israel Yuval, with whom I have had the privilege of discussing issues of medieval Jewish history for over ten years. My thanks go also to Michael Glatzer, who helped me with language and style.
2 For Jewish demography in central Europe after the Black Death, see the tables in my "Jewish Banking in the Economy of the Holy Roman Empire in the First Half of the Fifteenth Century" (in Hebrew), in *Proceedings of the Ninth World Congress of Jewish Studies*, division B, vol. 1 (Jerusalem, 1986), 123, 125–6, note 29; Michael Toch, "Siedlungsstruktur der Juden Mitteleuropas im Wandel vom Mittelalter zur Neuzeit," in Alfred Haverkamp and Franz-Josef Ziwes, eds., *Juden in der christlichen Umwelt während des späten Mittelalters. Zeitschrift für historische Forschung*, suppl. 13 (Berlin, 1992), 29–40; and my chapter on demography in *Germania Judaica*, vol. 3, no. 3 (forthcoming).

readmitted to the towns collectively but only individually; moreover, Jews were permitted back in the towns for only a given period of time, forcing every family to renew its conditions of residence every few years. The authorities also continually revised the conditions of that privilege.[3] Consequently, two classes of Jews came into being. The first class consisted of privileged Jews, namely, those who possessed a charter defining their rights and obligations. These were wealthier individuals who could afford to pay taxes and who had the economic power to prevail upon the authorities their conditions of residence. The second class was made up of either poorer Jews or Jews who, for reasons of age or profession, were of less interest to Christian authorities. This latter group did not possess privileges but was tolerated in the cities and territories on account of their richer brothers. Less privileged Jews performed services to both individuals and the community, were economically disadvantaged, and were juridically dependent on their privileged coreligionists.[4] In case of persecution or expulsion, which most commonly took the form of nonrenewal of residential rights, they were the first people affected and had to bear the greatest hardship.

Besides the demographic catastrophe and the significant diminution of their legal status, at the end of the Middle Ages central European Jews suffered serious economic setbacks as well, which uprooted many households and caused a radical decrease in their wealth. One result of this development is particularly important: the relative percentage of the underprivileged class in Jewish society rose, during the fifteenth century, from 25 to over 50 percent, as evidenced by censuses in Erfurt and Nuremberg in the years 1389 and 1489, respectively.[5] This doubly dependent group became increasingly vulnerable, and a growing number of individuals did not have a fixed residence, a secure roof over their heads, or a regular source of in-

3 E. Littmann, "Studien zur Wiederaufnahme der Juden nach dem Schwarzen Tod," *Monatsschrift für Geschichte und Wissenschaft des Judentums* 72 (1928): 589–98; J. F. Battenberg, "Zur Rechtsstellung der Juden am Mittelrhein in Spätmittelalter und früher Neuzeit," *Zeitschrift für historische Forschung* 6 (1979): 156–62; Battenberg, "Des Kaisers Kammerknechte; Gedanken zur rechtlich-sozialen Situation der Juden in Spätmittelalter und früher Neuzeit," *Historische Zeitschrift* 245 (1987): 572–4; *Germania Judaica*, vol. 3. See the instructive analysis of an exemplary case which shows that the worsening of the legal status of the Jews was not a direct result of their persecution and which has gone almost unnoticed, H. Fischer, "Die Judenprivilegien der Goslarer Rates im 14. Jahrhundert," *Zeitschrift der Savignystiftung für Rechtsgeschichte, Germanistische Abteilung* 56 (1936): 89–149.

4 This double disability is demonstrated most accurately by the imperial decree to the city of Judenburg, of April 10, 1467, to expel all Jews "so nicht hewslich . . . [in Judenburg] sitzen und uns nicht jerlichen zinnsen" (who are not permanent residents of Judenburg and do not pay the annual tax); *Germania Judaica*, vol. 3, 595 note 13. But as early as 1383, Jung Fifli, a Jew from Zurich, took pains to discredit the testimony of other Jews before the city council by pointing out that they did not pay taxes in Zurich nor were they citizens ("haushablich gesessen") anywhere else; Susanna Burghartz, "Das Zürcher Ratsgericht als Sanktionierungs- und Konfliktregelungsinstanz: Untersuchungen zur Kriminalitäts- und Mentalitätsgeschichte einer städtischen Gesellschaft Ende des 14. Jh.," Ph.D. diss., Universität Basel, 1987, 349 note 78.

5 See my "Social Stratification," 130 and note 2.

come. The last-named group – never more than a few hundred at any given time – was known by a special name in Germanic lands from the Rhine to Bohemia and from the North Sea to the Alps. From the late fourteenth until well into the sixteenth century, they were called *Schalantjuden* – in Hebrew documents of the time, *archei u-farchei* – and they were known to be unprotected by law and extremely poor. In fact, their impoverishment necessitated support from Jewish charities.[6]

At the end of the fifteenth and the beginning of the sixteenth century, the rabbi of Padua, Juda Minz, reported a controversy that arose in the community of Treviso. The *archei u-farchei* who came to the community were given *petakim*, or slips, assigning them to hospitality at the homes of members of the Jewish community. As a rule the *parnass*, the responsible head of the community, handed out these slips by lot. There were members of the community who would have liked to force the poor guests to choose their lots themselves, in order to humiliate them and discourage them from coming back. But Rabbi Minz vigorously opposed this alternative method of allotment.[7]

In 1530, Antonius Margaritha, the famous apostate and son of the rabbi of Regensburg and Poznan, whose uncle was rabbi in Prague, described the feelings of the poor in that Bohemian city.[8] These sentiments corroborated Juda Minz's testimony:

6 Ibid., 131–2. The German term is used, as far as I can see, only until the beginning of the sixteenth century. The Hebrew term, however, continues to be used and later on designates the topological heirs of the *Schalantjuden*, the *Betteljuden* of the seventeenth and eighteenth centuries. See, e.g., Ḥaim Yair Bacharach (1638–1702), responsa no. 106, in *Ḥavat Yair* (Lemberg, 1896; reprinted: Jerusalem, 1987), 142. On itinerant Jewish beggars and the earliest communal hospitals in thirteenth-century Germany, see I. J. Yuval, "Hospices and Their Guests in Jewish Medieval Germany" (in Hebrew), in *Proceedings of the Tenth World Congress of Jewish Studies*, division B, vol. 1, 125–9.

7 Juda Minz, responsa no. 7, in Meir Katzenelnbogen, *Responsa* (Cracow, 1882). For biographical data on the author, see *Encyclopaedia Judaica* (Jerusalem, 1971), vol. 12, cols. 69–70, and *Germania Judaica*, vol. 3, article "Worms," §13b, no. 15.

8 For the biographies of the rabbis Samuel Margoles, Antonius's father, Jakob Margoles, his grandfather, and Isaak Margoles, his uncle, see *Germania Judaica*, vol. 3, articles "Nürnberg," §13b, no. 18; "Prag," §13b, no. 33, and "Regensburg," §13b, no. 78. Antonius was born between the years 1492 and 1498 and baptized in 1522 (ibid., article "Regensburg," note 483). Starting in 1526 he works as a Hebrew teacher in Augsburg (Stadtarchiv Augsburg, Baumeisterbuch 1526, fol. 81r; I owe this important biographical detail to the courtesy of Hava Frankel-Goldschmidt, Jerusalem). Two booklets of his, which have hitherto partially eluded the bibliographers, are to be found in the Hofbibliothek in Vienna, namely, *Ain kurtzer Bericht und anzeigung wo die Christlich Ceremonien vom Balmesel in bayden Testamenten gegründet sei. Auch etlich erdichte falsche Comment und Fabln, So die blinden yetz vermainten halsssterrige Juden von irem zukünftitgen erdichten Moschiach, das ist Christus und von seinem Esel schreiben und liegen. Durch Anthonium Margaritham, der Hebraischen heyligen zungen, bey der Löblichen altn Universitet zu wienn in Osterreich etc. Ordinarium Lectorem* (1541), 8 pages, and *Annthony Margarithe etc. kurtze ausslegung uber das wort Halleluia* (no date), 7 pages. The first one of these booklets must have been known to Ernst Ferdinand Hess, author of *Juden-Geissel* (1598), and possibly to Dieter Schwab, author of *Jüdischer Deckmantel des Mosaischen Gesetzes* (Paderborn, 1615), cited by J. J. Schudt, *Jüdische Merckwürdigkeiten*, vol. 2 (Frankfurt and Leipzig, 1714; reprinted: Berlin, 1922), 43 (1070), as well as to Christian Wolf, *Bibliotheca hebraea*, vol. 1 (Hamburg and Leipzig, 1715), 203. For Antonius's biography and mentality, see H. Frankel-Goldschmidt, "On the Periphery of Jewish Society: Jewish Converts to Christianity in Germany during the Reformation" (in

Where, however, many Jews live together, as in Prague and similar places, their poor have to suffer a lot; on Fridays and on the eve of holidays they need to go into the houses [to beg], on holidays they beg for bread and for leftovers in front of the houses. They have the custom not to sing, as do our students, when they beg in front of the houses, neither do they demand [alms] for God's sake, as do our beggars, but they shout, "schnap!" Some of them wait until a maid or a servant enters or leaves the house and then they ask them for something and not to be forgotten, etc.[9]

Another category of Jewish beggars, the *kabzon*, who wandered the roads did not have the means to marry off their daughters. Their fate was portrayed vividly by Margaritha. They received a letter of beggary, a *kibbutz*, from a rabbi testifying to their need and poverty and bearing evidence of their piety and worthy descent. With this *kibbutz*, the *kabzon* wandered throughout Germany to wherever Jews dwelled. In large communities, such as Frankfurt am Main or Worms, the beggar handed over this letter to the rabbi or the sexton, who passed it on to the *Parnosen*, the *Rosch Hakahöl*, or the *Gaboim*. These officials in turn granted permission to beg before the door of the synagogue or, accompanied by two local Jews, to collect alms by going from door to door. Many wandered with a letter of beggary in Italy (*Welschland*), Bohemia, Moravia, Poland, and Russia (that is, the Ukraine). But mostly they wandered in Hungary, because, according to Margaritha, Hungary was a land of rich Jews. Many Jewish beggars, mostly old people, wandered for 400 or 500 miles at a time and, upon returning home, had scarcely 10 or 15 guilders more in their pockets than they had set out with.[10]

Victor von Carben (ca. 1430–1515),[11] another Jewish apostate, who published his *Judenbüchlein* in 1508/1509, in reaction, presumably, to Pfeffer-

Hebrew), in M. Ben-Sasson, R. Bonfil, and J. R. Hacker, eds., *Culture and Society in Medieval Jewry* (Jerusalem, 1989), 626–7, 638, 640–2, 646–7, 651.

9 *Der gantz Jüdisch glaub mit sampt ainer grüntlichen und warhafften anzaygunge, aller Satzungen, Ceremonien, Gebeten, Haymliche und offentliche Gebrauch, deren sich dye Juden halten, durch das gantz Jar, Mit schönen und gegründten Argumenten wyder iren Glauben. Durch Anthonium Margaritham, Hebrayschen Leser der löblichen Statt Augspurg, beschriben und an tag gegeben MDXXX*, fol. K3r: "Wo aber vil Juden beyainander seindt als zuo Prag unnd dergleichen müssen yre armen gar vil leiden, müssen am freytag und all feyrabend in die heuser geen bettlen an Feyertagen vor den heusern umb brot und was kost uberbliben sey, haben den prauch, wenn sy also vor den heusern betlen, singen sy nit wie unsere Schuoler, hayschen auch nit umb gotswillen wie unsere betler, sondern schreyen schnap. Ettlich warten biss ein magd oder knecht auss end ein geet, bitten sy das man ins etwas mittail und sein nit vergess etc."

10 Ibid., fol. K2r–v. See as well Josef Mieses, *Die älteste gedruckte deutsche Übersetzung des jüdischen Gebetbuches a.d. Jahre 1530 und ihr Autor Anthonius Margaritha* (Vienna, 1916), 53–5. Russia ("Rewssen") is the author's addition in the second edition (Leipzig, 1531), fol. L1v. On begging with letters of recommendation in Germany in the thirteenth century, see Yuval, "Hospices and Their Guests," 126.

11 Victor von Carben was born around 1427 and, according to his own testimony, acted as a rabbi. He converted in the 1470s, possibly in Frankfurt am Main, studied to be a priest, and took orders. In

korn's *Judenspiegel*,[12] mentioned the *Schalantjuden* in a slightly different context. The custom of *Cappores*, that is, of a Jew swinging a white cock or hen
over his own head on the day before New Year's or before Yom Kippur,
was intended to transfer his sins to the animal. Whereas rich Jews would
not, according to Carben, eat this animal loaded with sins, the *Schalantjuden*, who were hungry and therefore less scrupulous, found it a worthwhile
tidbit.[13] At the end of the fifteenth century, the Nuremberg playwright
Hans Foltz also viewed the *Schalantjuden* with contempt, and in his plays he
presented a *Schalantjud* whenever he wanted to ridicule Jewish views and
opinions.[14]

The authorities in townships and territories were also interested in getting rid of nonprivileged Jews, along with other worthless elements that
served no economic purpose. Cases of expulsion on this basis were common. On March 27, 1492, together with the Vitztum of lower Bavaria, the
town of Regensburg decided "in time of need to expel the useless people;
likewise the Jews, who do not make a living on their own, and the super-
fluous clerics."[15] Sharing the same or similar lots, this expelled population,
Christian as well as Jewish, met on the road.

In the files of the case of a Jew accused of ritual murder in the upper
Rhineland from 1504, one finds a rare document of an encounter of a *Schalantjud* with his Christian counterpart. One of the Christian reprobates, a
simpleton, who was arrested and tortured, confessed among other things

1480, he held a disputation with Jewish notables in Bonn (at the Cologne bishop's residence in Pop-
pelsdorf; see *Germania Judaica*, vol. 3, 136, 359) and toward the end of his life he lived as an eccle-
siastic in Cologne, where he died on February 2, 1515. See Frankel-Goldschmidt, "Periphery,"
625–6, 635–8, 642–5, 648, 651–2. His *Judenbüchlein*, published in 1509/1510 in German and in Latin
translation (*Opus aureum ac novum* [Cologne, 1509]; I have not seen the German first edition and
used the second edition from 1550, see note 13), was directed to the same public as Johann Pfefferkorn's *Judenspiegel*.

12 This is strongly suggested by the dates of publication of these two books. Pfefferkorn's *Judenspiegel*
was a great success. This is born out by the fact that in eighteen months it was printed three times
in German and four times in Latin; see Hans-Martin Kirn, *Das Bild vom Juden im Deutschland des
frühen 16. Jahrhunderts, dargestellt an den Schriften Johannes Pfefferkorns* (Tübingen, 1989), 201. Pfefferkorn, in contrast to Victor von Carben, had only a very rudimentary Jewish education, though
before his conversion he probably served as a *shochet*, a slaughterer according to rabbinic law; see
Reuchlin's testimony as to this and that Pfefferkorn was unable to read the "Mordechai," a compi-
lation of rabbinic law from the late thirteenth century, in Reuchlin, *Ain clare verstentnus in tütsch uff
doctor Johannsen Reuchlins ratschlag von den iuden büchern vormals auch zu latin im Augenspiegel ussgangen*
(n.d. [1511/1512]), fols. 39v, 40v.
13 Victor von Carben, *Judenbüchlein* (n.p., 1550), chap. 15, fol. C4r. In the Latin translation (see note
11), fol. B5r, the term used is *pauperes*.
14 Communication by Edith Wenzel, Aachen; see her *"Do worden die Juden alle geschant." Rolle und
Funktion der Juden in spätmittelalterlichen Spielen* (Munich, 1992).
15 "In der not die unnützen leut aus der Stat zu tun. desgliechs die Juden, die ir aigen narung nit haben,
und der geistlichen ubrig leut"; see Raphael Straus, ed., *Urkunden und Aktenstücke zur Geschichte der
Juden in Regensburg, 1453–1738*. Quellen und Erörterungen zur bayerischen Geschichte, n.s., vol. 18,
no. 607 (Munich, 1960). Compare the imperial edict to Judenburg, cited in note 4 to this chapter.

that a year before, when walking with some Jews through the countryside, they addressed him in the following manner: "Dear Michel, you are a poor fellow; if you need something, if only you know about children, young ones or old ones, hide them and inform us; for doing so we will make you into a rich man." He answered: "You are dogs, that's your real name, I won't tell you anything." And they answered: "If anybody calls us dogs, we feel as if somebody were calling us 'Sir.'"[16] Since no names are attached and therefore it had no forensic ramifications, this episode bears the mark of truth in that it reflects the mockery with which the Jewish companions of the reprobate taunted him. Moreover, it suggests a familiarity that becomes possible wherever social and religious restrictions set by custom and religious tradition have slackened.

Not only poor Jews belonged to this class of *Landfahrer* (vagrant) with a Jewish background. Mathias Wiedmann von Kemnat (ca. 1430–75/76), Count Palatine Frederick's chaplain in Heidelberg, wrote the following in his chronicle from the year 1466: "There is another harmful species in Christendom . . . namely the doctors, in Latin *emperici* or *garri medici*. They wander the lands, and mostly they are baptized Jews, they show large sealed documents and claim to come from heathen lands and tell about medicine. But they have never learned or read Apollo nor Esculapius nor Avicenna nor Gallienus. The doctor takes on six or eight servants, mostly baptized Jews, or scholars and clerics who are too ashamed to beg, and these promise their master to keep his secret. He sends them ahead to the bigger towns" and, to make a long story short, deceives the public by using the information his spies provide him to learn about the illnesses and the problems of his patients.[17] A similar group of deceiving doctors, mostly baptized Jews, was documented in Prague in 1490.[18] The sources also tell of proselytes who, for economic reasons, allowed themselves to be baptized repeatedly so that they could collect again and again the *obulus* that the authorities put at the disposal of newly baptized Jews. In line with immediate opportunities and instantaneous benefits, these individuals sometimes posed as Jews and at other times as Christians.[19]

Johannes Reuchlin (1455–1522) was the first to juxtapose *Schalantjuden* and apostates. In his expert evaluation of Pfefferkorn's accusations against the

16 Quoted in F. Pfaff, "Die Kindermorde zu Benzhausen und Waldkirch im Breisgau," *Alemannia* 27 (1900): 287–8.
17 "Matthias Widmann von Kemnat, Chronik Friedrichs I.," *Quellen zur bayerischen und deutschen Geschichte*, vol. 2 (Munich, 1862), 111–12.
18 See *Germania Judaica*, vol. 3, article "Prag," §12.
19 See, for instance, Straus, *Urkunden und Aktenstücke*, no. 149, 211 (see note 15 to this chapter); Rudolf Glanz, *Geschichte des niederen jüdischen Volkes in Deutschland. Eine Studie über historisches Gaunertum, Bettelwesen und Vagantentum* (New York, 1968), 50, 66–7, 69–74, and my "Stratification."

Talmud and other Jewish books, Reuchlin wrote, in his *Ratschlag, ob man den Juden alle ihre Bücher nemmen, abthun und verbrennen soll*: "I am not speaking of the *schalachs büben*, the ones that come to us for reasons of envy, hatred, fear of punishment, poverty, vengeance, ambition, love of worldly pleasures, mean simplicity, and the like . . . and whenever life on our side does not meet their expectations they go to Turkey and become Jews again."[20] Here Reuchlin plays on the words *Schalantjuden* and *Schlecht Buben* (common rascals). Moreover, it is also well attested that Jewish apostates who sought to return to the faith of their fathers went to Turkish lands to reconvert.[21]

These subgroups of the *fahrendes Volk*, the few hundred *Schalantjuden* and the unscrupulous apostates, provided the wandering vagabonds with the Hebrew words that passed into the vocabulary of the *Rotwelsch* language. The Jewish *esprit de groupe*, which had its roots in shared religion, culture, and lore, as well as in shared values and persecution, generated in the German lands, in the fourteenth and the fifteenth centuries, an additional feature, a shared language.[22] It is a curious fact that synchronically with the emergence of a Jewish sociolect, some of its specific features, not only technical words, passed into the language of the beggars and the scum.[23] Use of *Lehem* for "bread," *Johan* for "wine," *bos* for "house," and *sone* for "whore" should not astonish us; the use of *acheln* for "eating" and *alchen* for "going," a Hebrew root and a German conjugation, is a noteworthy phenomenon;

20 "Von denen, die aus neid, hass, forcht der straff, armut, rach, eergeitigkait, liebe der welt, schlechter infeltigkait, und andern dergleichen ursachen zu uns kommen . . . und wan es inen uff diser seitten nit nach irem willen gat, so lauffen sie hin in die türckei und werden wider iuden; von denselben schalachs [!] büben will ich hie nit geredt haben," see Johannes Reuchlin, *Augenspiegel*, quoted in L. Geiger, *Johann Reuchlin* (Leipzig, 1871), 242 note 4.

21 A famous example, Moses Zaret, rabbi in Ulm, is mentioned by Reuchlin; see *Germania Judaica*, vol. 3, article "Ulm," §13b, no. 19. Other converts went to the Ukraine to reconvert; see Victor von Carben, *Judenbüchlein*, chap. 26, fols. F1–2, and Frankel-Goldschmidt, "Periphery," 640; also see note 13 to this chapter.

22 The various stages in the emergence of the Yiddish language are controversial. To this date, however, there are no unequivocal remains of a distinctly Jewish language in the German lands before 1350. For a recent summary of the evidence with a different interpretation from my own, see Erika Timm, *Graphische und phonische Struktur des Westjiddischen* (Tübingen, 1987), 357–86, and "Zur Frage der Echtheit von Raschis jiddischen Glossen," *Beiträge zur Geschichte der deutschen Sprache und Literatur* 107 (1985): 45–81. See *Germania Judaica*, vol. 3, no. 3, chapter on Yiddish language and literature, as well as the next note.

23 In 1385, the Jews of Zurich spoke "Latin" (they "letinetten mit einander"), i.e., they spoke a language that was incomprehensible to the Christian population. See Burghartz, *Das Zürcher Ratsgericht*, 370 note 175, and footnote 4 to this chapter. It is probable that this expression refers to the Hebrew vocabulary in Jewish talk, which, not unlike its Latin counterpart of the learned clergy, was not understood by the common folk. But just as the Latin words used by the clergy do not make us speak of "clergyish," the Jews' language was probably not yet "Yiddish." Seventy years later, however, a Christian plaintiff from Magdeburg thought he could recognize a thief as a Jew, since "he had a long face with a long nose and he talked like a Jew"; see Guido Kisch, *The Jews in Medieval Germany: A Study of Their Legal and Social Status* (Chicago, 1949; reprinted: New York, 1970), 545 note 156. This is, to my knowledge, the first external evidence of a specific language (or dialect) of the Jews in the German lands. I plan to discuss the emergence of a language specific to the Jews of Germanic linguistic background in detail elsewhere.

the expression *sonebos* for "bordello," inverting the construct form under German influence – in Hebrew it would be *bejs sones* – catches our eye.[24] This quick, immediate exchange took place at the periphery of society: on the road, where the Jewish and the Christian homeless met. A comparison of the conditions in which they lived is therefore appropriate.

The basic situation of the Christian *Landfahrer* and the *Schalantjude* differed considerably. Indeed, both were outcasts, both existed on the borderline of hunger, both lacked a constant and secure roof over their heads, both lived off alms, *Zedaka*, and irregular chance-work, and some of them managed to enrich their income by working as hawkers, engaging in petty thievery, and picking pockets. The rural community, where everybody knew everybody else, was closed to both groups. The more neutral, impersonal atmosphere of the towns, moreover, became more and more hostile to "foreigners," that is, to people who did not belong to any of the corporations, to the large body of servants of all kinds, and to the resident needy, which together formed, for better or worse, the social fabric of the community. The Christian vagabond was, therefore, not only pushed to the fringes of contemporary society but, maligned and despised, also left entirely outside of organized human life. Consequently, many vagabonds turned to crime.[25] His Jewish counterpart, however, although his legal status was no better and although he lived on the edge of starvation as well, was not entirely disenfranchised. As long as they did not convert, destitute Jews retained an organized reference group, namely, their fellow Jews, to which they still belonged and which took responsibility for them. Not all their fellow Jews were hospitable "Mah nisei Orh im."[26] But the Jewish ethos de-

---

24 Martin Luther already recognized the Hebrew origin of many *Rotwelsch* words and inferred their Jewish origin. See his introduction to the 1527 edition of the *Liber vagatorum*, quoted by Christoph Sachsse and Florian Tennstedt, *Geschichte der Armenfürsorge in Deutschland vom Spätmittelalter bis zum ersten Weltkrieg* (Stuttgart, 1980), 52, and by R. J. Zwi Werblowsky, "Jüdisch-deutsche Symbiose? Bemerkungen zum Kokem-Loschen und Rotwelsch," in K. E. Grötzinger, ed., *Judentum im deutschen Sprachraum* (Frankfurt/Main, 1991), 90. Werblowsky's interesting and stimulating but at times contradictory theses (ibid. 89–100) require careful examination. The examples that I have given in the text, and many more, are linguistically analyzed by Robert Jütte, *Abbild und soziale Wirklichkeit des Bettler- und Gaunertums zu Beginn der Neuzeit. Beihefte zum Archiv für Kulturgeschichte*, no. 27 (Cologne, 1988), 180–219.

25 The recent literature on marginal groups in late medieval society in general and in Germany in particular is enormous. See, for example, F. Graus, "Randgruppen der städtischen Gesellschaft in Spätmittelalter," *Zeitschrift für historische Forschung* 8 (1981): 385–437; Heiner Boehncke and Rolf Johannsmeier, *Das Buch der Vaganten: Spieler, Huren, Leutbetrüger* (Cologne, 1987); and relevant articles in Richard J. Evans, ed., *The German Underworld: Deviants and Outcasts in German History* (London, 1988).

26 See, for instance, the privilege of Eger Jews from 1435: "Auch haben wir [the city of Eger] In [the privileged Jews] die macht geben umb die schalanp Juden, die do pflegen zu wandern durch die landt, die da ungewerlich weren der Stat oder In, das sy dy mugen straffen und vorweisen aus der Stat; bedorffen sy unser darczu so sullen wir In darczu behulfflich sein, und was dieselben Juden dawider

manded that they help all their poor brethren; this ethos was generally observed, both individually and communally, toward destitute residents as well as outsiders. There was no sizable Jewish community without a *hekdesh*, a hospital, where not only passing strangers and the local needy were lodged and fed but *Schalantjuden* found shelter as well, much to the annoyance of the Christian authorities, who tried to drive them away.[27]

A second reason for the virtual absence of characteristic criminal behavior by the *Schalantjuden* lies in their peculiar situation on the margins of Jewish society.[28] Criminal activity on their part would cause their extradition to the Christian authorities, who could be expected to show a more lenient attitude toward a new convert than toward a Jew, thus providing a stimulus for conversion. Both Jews and Christians, however, regarded these and other "converts for material reasons" with contempt. They were suspected of criminal behavior even when that was not the immediate cause of their conversion. This distrust was not always without foundation, as born out by contemporary forensic documents.[29] Moreover there is some psychological probability to the defection, that is, the apostasy of Jewish criminals, whose social and, above all, family ties with their fellow Jews had weakened, owing to their vagabondage. Stepping over one norm of organized society made it easier to disregard others; embracing one set of rules of a marginal group facilitated the adoption of others, honored by the same people, who became the new reference group. It is therefore highly probable that Jewish society exported some of the criminal elements on its fringe to the larger class of Christian vagrants.[30]

The impact of the "meeting on the fringe of society" was, however, not confined exclusively to issues of language and crime. An additional aspect is the intellectual effect of this encounter. At the highest intellectual level in

---

setzten oder rechten, das sol In un behulfflich sein und den Juden ongeverde" (likewise we, the city of Eger, have given them, the two privileged Jews, authority over the *schalanp Juden*, who wander through the country and constitute a nuisance for the city and for them, so that they may punish them and expel them from the city. If they need our help to do so, we will grant it, and whatever claims these wandering Jews should adduce shall be of no help to them and of no consequence to our privileged Jews); in G. Bondy and F. Dworsky, eds., *Geschichte der Juden in Böhmen, Mähren und Schlesien von 906–1620* (Prague, 1906), 110, no. 226. Compare *Germania Judaica*, vol. 3, 277 note 65, and my "Stratification," 131–2, 134.

27 See note 3 to this chapter and my "Stratification," 130–1.

28 The *Schalantjuden* committed crimes, just like other segments of Jewish and Christian society, but their criminal behavior, when it occurred, did not differ in character from that of their settled contemporaries.

29 See the preceding discussion as well as notes 17 through 20 to this chapter.

30 It is an open question whether geographic exportation of criminals also happened. Glanz, *Geschichte des niederen jüdischen Volkes*, 281, cites the confessions of a predominantly Jewish gang arrested in Posnan in 1502. There is no indication, however, that these thieves had migrated to Poland from Germany. At the time of their arrest all of them were residents of Prussia and the Polish provinces of Posnan and Masovia.

the Germanic lands, we cannot find any mutual influence between Jews and Christians at the close of the Middle Ages. We would be looking in vain for a reflection among Christian contemporary intellectuals of the achievements in Maimonidian philosophy and cabalistic thought of the "Prague Circle" – Avigdor Kara, Lipman Mühlhausen, and Menachem Agler – in the second decade of the fifteenth century, or of the two Maimonidian controversies in the second half of the fifteenth and in the sixteenth century. Likewise, for example, there is no trace in contemporary Jewish speculation of the perennial dispute in late medieval universities between *via antiqua* and *via moderna*.[31] But intellectual contact nevertheless took place on another level. Gershom Scholem has dismissed the work known in English as *The Book of the Sacred Magic of Abra-Melin the Mage, As delivered by Abraham the Jew unto his son Lamech A.D. 1458* as a sixteenth-century forgery. The book is extant in a number of German manuscripts from the seventeenth and eighteenth centuries, in an eighteenth-century French translation, and, partly, in a Hebrew manuscript from the seventeenth or the eighteenth century. After a lengthy introduction that provides us with very interesting biographical data, the author presents a manual of basic initiation and the workings of practical magic. Scholem's reason for denouncing the book as a forgery was the peculiar definition of cabala and magic as mystical theory and its practical application, which he had found for the first time in Pico della Mirandola's theses. A meticulous analysis of the introduction makes it quiet clear, however, that the author, his eccentricity and self-glorification notwithstanding, essentially tells the truth about himself. He was born in Worms in 1359, where he received his basic education from his father. After his father's death in 1379, he studied magic and related lore in Mainz with Rabbi Moses, probably Jacob Molin's father, then traveled for advanced studies to Strasbourg, Prague, Linz, Greece, Constantinople, Egypt, Eretz Israel, and the Arabian desert. On his way back from the east he visited Venice, northern Italy, and Paris. After his return to Worms in 1404, he lived in Germany, probably in his native town. When he wrote his book in the 1450s, he was over ninety years old. He wrote it using either the German or Yiddish language yet employed Hebrew characters, and he possibly translated it himself into Hebrew. It is therefore plausible that he did not

---

31 For Avigdor Kara, Lipman Mühlhausen, and Menachem Agler, see *Germania Judaica*, vol. 3, article "Prag," §13b, nos. 9, 41, 60. For *via antiqua* and *via moderna*, see Elisabeth Gössmann, *Antiqui und Moderni im Mittelalter* (Munich, 1974), 109–16; M. H. Shank, *"Unless You Believe, You Shall Not Understand": Logic, University and Society in Late Medieval Vienna* (Princeton, N.J., 1988). He postulates philosophical and theological contacts between Heinrich von Langenstein (1323–97) and Vienna Jews, but these were very unlikely; see I. J. Yuval, "Juden, Hussiten, Deutsche," in *Juden in der christlichen Umwelt*, 65–6 note 25.

depend on Pico della Mirandola, but vice versa; Pico must have known this book or another similar work before formulating his theses on the relationship between magic and cabala.[32] Most interesting is Abraham ben Samuel's concept of religions: not only is he ready and eager to learn from whoever could teach him any part of the truth, but he is an outstanding representative of the concept of tolerance.[33] He stated the theory that every man should adhere to his inherited religion and that nobody can reach the highest level of truth outside of the religion of his forefathers. In his own words, when he explained why the apostate Joseph of Paris, whom he met on his journey, could not achieve full knowledge of the truth, he says:

I found also at Paris a wise man called Joseph, who, having denied the Christian [in the original text: the Jewish] faith, had made himself a Jew [in the original text: a Christian]. This man truly practiced Magic in the same manner as Abramelin, but he was very far from arriving at perfection therein; because God, Who is just, never granteth the perfect, veritable and fundamental treasure unto those who deny Him; notwithstanding that in the rest of their life they might be the most holy and perfect men in the world.[34]

This was the opinion of Abraham ben Samuel of Worms, a cabalist and magician, who lived on the fringe of contemporary Jewish society not simply because of his deep and unusual interest in magical theory and his ex-

---

32. *Abraham von Worms. Das Buch der Praktiken der göttlichen Magie*, ed. Jürg von Ins (Munich, 1988); I. J. Yuval, "Magie und Kabbala unter den Juden im Deutschland des ausgehenden Mittelalters," in *Judentum im deutschen Sprachraum*, 180–1.

33 In response to this essay, Amos Funkenstein rightly pointed out that religious tolerance was, as a topos, not unknown in the High and late Middle Ages. The parable of the three rings in Boccaccio's *Decameron* (first day, third story) is probably the most famous expression of this; see M. Penna, *La parabola dei tre anelli e la toleranza nel medio evo* (Turin, 1953). For a similar contemporary Jewish appreciation of Christianity and Islam, not without a polemical sting and with a hint about the final conversion of the Hussites to Jewish beliefs, see Yuval, "Juden, Hussiten, Deutsche," 64–5. But the topos was by no means a very common one, and it is quite significant that the only German Jew in late medieval times who consequentially opposed conversion lived on the fringes of Jewish society.

34 *The book of the Sacred Magic of Abra-Melin the Mage, As delivered by Abraham the Jew unto his son Lamech A.D. 1458, Translated from the French translation and edited by S. L. MacGregor-Mathers* (London, 1898), 18. In the Hebrew and the German versions, Joseph was a Jew who converted to Christianity and therefore could not receive the Truth. The translator into French (or his source), and hence the English version, abridged the text and turned this "scandalous" idea inside out, making Joseph a Christian convert to Judaism. The German reads as follows: "Dann obwohl nachmals Josef von Paris auch auf den rechten Weg dieser Kunst kommen, so hat doch Gott als ein gerechter Richter ihm als einem Verräter seines göttlichen Gesetzes und seiner Zeremonien die vollkommene Gnad nit verliehen, dann das ist einmal gewiss: ein geborener Heid, Christ, Jud und ein jeder Ungläubiger kann vollkommener Meister in dieser Kunst [i.e., der Magie] werden, aber ein abtrünniger Jud und Apostata, der einmal des Herrn Gesetz verlassen und mit andern fremden Gottesdiensten gehurt, der kann nimmermehr zu dieser Vollkommenheit gereichen und gelangen." See Abraham von Worms, *Buch der wahren Praktik in der uralten göttlichen Magie und in erstaunlichen Dingen, wie sie durch die heilige Kabbala und durch Elohym mitgeteilt worden* (Cologne, 1725), 15. The date and place of publication are pseudoepigraphic. I use the edition from the Scholem collection in the Jewish National and University Library, Jerusalem, from the end of the nineteenth century. Jürg von Ins has falsified the original meaning while modernizing the language; see 84–5 note 31.

traordinary activity in magical practice. His marginality was born out as well by some of his nonnormative behavior, to which he only alluded in his autobiographical account.[35] His theory on the obligation to adhere to the faith of his ancestors was possible – both theologically and emotionally – only by virtue of the fact that Abraham moved in a society in which traditional values had lost some of their impact. In Germany in the late Middle Ages – and beyond – such an atmosphere existed only on the road. It is significant that Abraham's theory was not taken up by Pico. Similar ideas will be expressed again in the eighteenth century under different auspices and in altered circumstances under the impact of the Enlightenment. Even then they will be unacceptable to the greater part of majoritarian society.[36]

35 In Jürg von Ins, Abraham hints at sexual and hallucinatory experiences with a Christian woman in Linz under the influence of a toxic ointment; see 88–9 note 31.

36 See especially Jacob Katz, *Exclusiveness and Tolerance* (Oxford, 1961), chaps. 14–15; Katz, *Out of the Ghetto* (1973; reprinted: New York, 1978), chaps. 4–6.

10

Contacts at the Bedside: Jewish Physicians and Their Christian Patients

ROBERT JÜTTE

When Jews still lived in a closed Jewish quarter and had to seek the protection of the holders of political power, every encounter between Jews and Gentiles had its well-defined aim. According to Jacob Katz, the "transaction of business, the teaching of Jew by Gentile or vice versa, the treatment by doctors of a patient from the other community, are the recurrent patterns of social encounters between Jews and Gentiles."[1] Although historians have dealt extensively with the medieval Jewish moneylender and the early modern court Jew, they have seldom taken into account the relationship between Jews and non-Jews that was not governed primarily by the immediate purpose of commerce. The few (mostly Jewish) scholars who have taken an interest in the history of Jewish medicine write about great Jewish physicians, their medical works, and their achievements. But historians have left out the most important aspect, namely, that the medical practice of the rank-and-file Jewish physician brought him into close contact with Gentiles of varying social status.[2] The picture of the Jew waiting at home for the Gentile to bring him his urine is

---

1 Jacob Katz, *Out of the Ghetto: The Social Background of Jewish Emancipation* (Cambridge, Mass., 1973), 42.
2 See, e.g., Eljakim Carmoly, *Histoire des médecins juifs anciens et modernes* (Brussels, 1844); Mordechai Horovitz, *Geschichte der jüdischen Ärzte in Frankfurt* (Frankfurt/Main, 1886); Richard Landau, *Geschichte der jüdischen Ärzte* (Berlin, 1895); Louis Lewin, "Jüdische Ärzte in Grosspolen," *Jahrbuch der Jüdisch-Literarischen Gesellschaft* 9 (1912): 367–420; Moritz Steinschneider, "Jüdische Ärzte," *Zeitschrift für hebräische Bibliographie* 17 (1914): 63–96, 121–67 and 18 (1914): 25–57; Isaak Münz, *Die jüdischen Ärzte im Mittelalter* (Frankfurt/Main, 1922); Adolf Kober, "Rheinische Judendoktoren, vornehmlich des siebzehnten und achtzehnten Jahrhunderts," in *Festschrift zum fünfundsiebzigjährigen Bestehen des jüdisch-theologischen Seminars in Breslau* (Breslau, 1929), 2:173–236; Felix Aaron Theilhaber, "Jüdische Mediziner," in Georg Herlitz and Bruno Kirschner, eds., *Jüdisches Lexikon* (Berlin, 1930), cols. 25–42; S. Felsenthal, "Jüdische Ärzte in Alt-Mannheim," *Sudhoffs Archiv* 23 (1930): 184–96; Samuel Krauss, *Geschichte der jüdischen Ärzte vom frühesten Mittelalter bis zur Gleichberechtigung* (Vienna, 1930); Guido Kisch, *Die Prager Universität und die Juden, 1348–1848. Mit Beiträgen zur Geschichte des Medizinstudiums* (Ostrów, 1935; reprinted: Amsterdam, 1969); Harry Friedenwald, *The Jews and Medicine: Essays,* 3 vols. (New York, 1944), and *Jewish Illuminaries in Medical History* (Baltimore, 1946); Jacob Marcus, *Communal Sick-Care in the German Ghetto* (Cincinnati, 1947); Jehoshua

certainly a realistic one.[3] But the details of this picture are blurred, because of the lack of sources.

This type of contact reflects only one aspect of the social intercourse between Jewish physicians and Christian patients. In this period many Jewish doctors, not only the very famous ones, also had to call at the house of the Gentile to examine the patient and to give medical advice.[4] When the patient lived at a considerable distance from the Jewish quarter or the Jewish doctor's home outside the ghetto, if indeed such a privilege was granted by the authorities, the Jew was obliged to stay overnight in the house of a Gentile and/or even to eat a meal there.[5] Such a situation was not an everyday occurrence, but it was not entirely out of the ordinary either.

O. Leibowitz, "Jews in Medicine (Historical Survey)" (in Hebrew), *Yavneh Almanac* 3 (1949): 184–200; "Historical Aspects of the Persecution of Jewish Physicians (in the late Middle Ages)" (in Hebrew), *Dapim refuyim* 12 (1953): 75–9; "Town Physicians in Jewish Social History," in *International Symposium on Society, Medicine and Law. Jerusalem, March 1972* (Amsterdam, 1973), 117–24; "Remarks on the Historiography of Jewish Physicians" (in Hebrew), *Koroth* 6 (1974): 643–6; Jacob Shatzky, "On Jewish Medical Students of Padua," *Journal of the History of Medicine and Allied Sciences* 5 (1950): 444–7; Moses Alter Spira, "Meilensteine zur Geschichte der jüdischen Ärzte in Deutschland," in Joseph Schumacher, ed., *Melemata. Festschrift für Werner Leibbrand zum 70. Geburtstag* (Mannheim, 1968), 149–58; Peter Assion, "Jacob von Landshut. Zur Geschichte der jüdischen Ärzte in Deutschland," *Sudhoffs Archiv* 53 (1969): 270–91; Heinrich Schipperges, "Zur Sonderstellung der jüdischen Ärzte im spätmittelalterlichen Spanien," *Sudhoffs Archiv* 57 (1973): 208–11; Samuel Kottek, "An Oath Taken by Jewish Community Physicians at Frankfort on Main, 1656" (in Hebrew), *Koroth* 7 (1979), 650–6; S. Hindle Hes, *Jewish Physicians in the Netherlands, 1600–1940* (Assen, 1980); Shai Sholovitz, "The Image and Status of the Jewish Physician: A Reflection from Jewish Sources," *Koroth* 8 (1984): 463–6; Volker Zimmermann, "Jüdische Ärzte und ihre Beiträge zur Heilkunde des Spätmittelalters," *Koroth* 8 (1985): 245–54; V. Zimmermann, "Jüdische Ärzte und ihre Leistungen in der Medizin des Mittelalters," *Würzburger medizinhistorische Mitteilungen* 8, (1990): 201–5; and most recently, Manfred Komorowski, *Bio-bibliographisches Verzeichnis jüdischer Doktoren im 17. und 18. Jahrhundert* (Munich, 1991). A still valuable survey on Jewish medical historiography is Yehoshua O. Leibowitz, "A Century of Jewish Medical Historiography (1844–1944)" (in Hebrew), in *Davar Yearbook 1946* (Tel Aviv, 1947), 341–55.

3 Ludwig von Hörnigk, *Medicaster Apella oder Juden-Artzt* (Strasbourg, 1631), 168; Hörnigk's book reports that Jewish physicians had helpers who stood before the entrance to the Jewish ghetto, inviting passers-by to bring their urine to a Jewish physician. In Frankfurt am Main, Jewish doctors, like their Christian colleagues, were allowed to put up a urinal outside their home, indicating that the person living in this house was entitled to practice medicine; see Kisch, *Prager Universität*, 82 note 97. Some patients sent messengers to the ghetto, along with the urine of the person looking for medical help. For a detailed description of such a visit, see the cases in Historisches Archiv der Stadt Köln (hereafter cited as HAStK), Verfassung und Verwaltung, G 249, fol. 110r.

4 See the detailed description by Hörnigk of such a visit in his *Juden Artzt,* 150. Jewish doctors living in Deutz and Mühlheim and getting a permit to treat a particular patient in Cologne often used the opportunity to offer medical help to neighbors and relatives of their clients. This extension of medical practice was, of course, forbidden. See, e.g., HAStK, Ratsprotokolle 114, fol. 128r (May 16, 1667), and Ratsprotokolle 160, fol. 260r–v (September 12, 1659). For Cologne, see also Carl Brisch, *Geschichte der Juden in Cöln und Umgebung aus ältester Zeit bis auf die Gegenwart* (Mühlheim, 1879–82), 2:116–17, and Paul Gerhard Aring, "Das Verhältnis zwischen Christen und Juden im Rechtsrheinischen nach dem Dreissigjährigen Krieg," in Jutta Bohnke-Kollwitz, ed., *Köln und das rheinische Judentum. Festschrift Germania Judaica, 1959–1984* (Cologne, 1984), 75–84.

5 The Jewish physician Dr. Salomon Bing, for example, was granted the privilege of living outside the Frankfurt ghetto; see Horovitz, *Ärzte in Frankfurt*, 27.

The implication of this historical pattern is twofold. First, economic and theological intercourse alone did not shape the difficult and complex relationship between Jews and Gentiles before the emancipation period. Second, the example of the Jewish physician who was also popular among Christians from all walks of life permits us to understand more clearly another aspect of Jewish–Gentile relations. Consulting a Jewish doctor or doing business with a Jew were situations that differed from one another in the degree of intimacy involved. Between the Jewish physician and his client a mutual attachment might have developed. Although relations between the two individuals typically remained superficial, they might have helped to pave the long way to an "institutionalized neutrality" (Jacob Katz) outside the ghetto walls and, finally, to Jewish emancipation.

I

Between the sixteenth and the eighteenth century, relations between Jewish physicians and Christian patients did not differ very much from that prevalent during the Middle Ages. The main difference is that the earlier relationship – for example, between court physician and prominent patient, or between physician in ordinary (*Leibarzt*) and wealthy patient – was superseded by a relationship of greater complexity. The social background of the patients also seems to have changed, as even the lower classes began to flock to the offices of Jewish doctors. This new clientele is of special interest to us, because it brought Jews into close and frequent contact with non-Jews in such a way as to afford opportunity for economically and morally dubious practices as well.

One of the dilemmas in the relationship between Jewish doctors and Christian patients was that it was never free of forces operating from the outside. Among the many external influences that seriously disrupted the medical practice of Jewish physicians beyond the ghetto walls were the various prohibitions issued by lay and ecclesiastical authorities.[6] The earliest record of this type of prohibition, which, as we shall see, found frequent expression in the ecclesiastical laws of the Middle Ages and the Reformation period, is in the writings of one of the early church fathers. Saint John Chrysostom of Constantinople, who lived in the second half of the fourth century, protested vigorously against seeking the help of Jewish physicians and advised Christians that it was better to die. In A.D. 692, the Council of

---

6 The following survey is mainly based on Krauss, *Ärzte,* and Friedenwald, *Medicine.* For the attitude of the medieval clergy to Jewish doctors, see Ludwig Kotelmann, *Gesundheitspflege im Mittelalter. Kulturgeschichtliche Studien nach Predigten des 13., 14. und 15. Jahrhunderts* (Hamburg, 1890), 193–5.

Constantinople forbade all Christians to call upon Jewish physicians. Similar prohibitions against Jewish physicians were repeated by many subsequent councils and finally became part of the papal law (*Decretals*) in the eleventh and twelfth centuries. In 1215, the Fourth Lateran Ecumenical Council not only enacted laws ordering Jews and Muslims to wear badges of special form but also admonished physicians to urge their patients to call for a priest at the beginning of their treatment, an injunction suggesting that Christians should entrust their lives exclusively to Christian doctors. The regional Council of Trier in 1227 ruled against "taking any medicine from Jews," and the Councils of Paris (1225) and Vienna (1267) reaffirmed the law against employing a Jewish physician.[7] This anti-Jewish stance of the church did not change during the later Middle Ages, though things looked quite different in real life. Upon finding out that the previous decrees against the medical practice of Jews among Christians were generally disregarded, Pope Gregory XIII (1572–85), for example, thought it necessary to issue a new papal bull that threatened to punish, for illegal medical practice, not only Jewish physicians but their Christian patients as well.[8]

On this subject, the thoughts of Protestant reformers did not differ much from the teachings of the Catholic Church. Luther, for example, said in one of his table talks that the "Jews who pretend to be physicians take the life and the fortune of those Christians who take their medicine."[9] In the seventeenth century, the theological faculties of the universities of Strasbourg (1642), Wittenberg (1643), and Rostock (1700) declared that Protestants should not employ the services of Jewish physicians because the latter were ignorant, resorted to magic, and were required by Talmudic law to kill their Christian patients.[10] Finally, in 1657 the clergy of Schwäbisch-Hall in southwestern Germany put forth a widely used argument against the medical practice of Jews in their city: "It would be better to die with Christ than to be cured by the devil with the help of a Jewish doctor."[11]

In spite of the many prohibitions against physicians issued by the Catholic and the Protestant churches, it is interesting to learn that in fact many churchmen themselves consulted Jewish physicians, either by openly defying the official decrees or by exempting their private physician from such restrictions. Popes, bishops, monks, priests, deacons, and nuns all sought the aid of Jewish physicians by choice. That this phenomenon was widespread is shown by the furious sermons delivered by fanatical theologians and by

7 Quoted by Friedenwald, *Medicine,* 2:559.

8 An English translation of this document is provided by Friedenwald, *Medicine,* 2:585ff.

9 Quoted by Johann Jacob Schudt, *Jüdische Merckwürdigkeiten* (Frankfurt/Main, 1714–17; reprinted: Berlin, 1922), pt. 2, 393.

10 Marcus, *Sick-Care,* 20–1, Carmoly, *Histoire,* 208–15.   11 Quoted by Krauss, *Ärzte,* 56.

the slanderous tracts published by Christian doctors.[12] This corpus of anti-Semitic literature testifies to the popularity of Jewish physicians in Christian communities.

Although Jew baiters such as Schudt[13] and Ludwig von Hörnigk[14] quoted from a number of ecclesiastical texts containing injunctions against the medical practice of Jewish physicians, both authors scarcely referred to similar prohibitions issued by secular authorities. The first known reference to Jewish physicians in imperial law is found in the legislation adopted by the Imperial Diet of Augsburg in 1530.[15] This legislation did not, however, follow word for word the decrees of church councils and papal bulls that prohibited the medical practice of Jewish doctors. In addition, the majority of communal governments accepted the fact that their citizens sought medical aid from Jewish physicians, though some of these communities had at one time or another expelled the entire Jewish community.[16] German cities that still had a large Jewish community at the beginning of the early modern period were particularly lenient toward the practice of medicine by Jews beyond the ghetto walls. Urban magistrates passed certain by-laws, however, that enabled degreed Christian physicians to supervise the medical care offered by their Jewish colleagues by, for example, making certain that the latter met the standard requirements and qualifications.[17]

Nevertheless, for brief periods officials in some German cities forbade Jewish physicians or surgeons to offer medical aid to Christian patients. In Prague, for example, the imperial governor issued an ordinance in 1641 that prohibited Jewish physicians from visiting or curing Christian patients. Violators were to be expelled from Bohemian territory.[18] That the threat was real is proved by another Prague document, dated October 22, 1644, which mentions the imprisonment of a Jewish physician who had refused to leave the country after he had been caught treating Christian patients in contravention of the 1641 decree.[19] In other imperial cities the spirit of older, medieval canon law persisted, allowing Jews to practice medicine in the

---

12 For the negative depiction of the Jewish physician in late medieval and early modern popular literature, see Krauss, *Ärzte,* 56ff. For a summary of the most important diatribes against Jewish physicians written by Christian doctors, see Krauss, *Ärzte,* 106ff.
13 Schudt, *Merckwürdigkeiten,* pt. 2, 382ff.
14 Hörnigk, *Juden Artzt,* 362ff.   15 Ibid., 334.
16 For a recent survey of the expulsion of Jews from German towns in the late medieval period, see Alfred Haverkamp, "Die Judenverfolgungen zur Zeit des Schwarzen Todes im Gesellschaftsgefüge deutscher Städte," in Alfred Haverkamp, ed., *Zur Geschichte der Juden im Deutschland des späten Mittelalters* (Stuttgart, 1981), 27–93.
17 See the many examples from Rhenish territories given by Kober, "Judendoktoren," 177ff.
18 See Kisch, *Prager Universität,* 143, doc. no. 16.   19 Ibid., 144, doc. no. 17.

Jewish quarter but forbidding them to treat Christian patients except by special permission.[20]

II

A wealth of published information on Jewish medicine is available to those who have the courage to venture into non-German literature as well as into the numerous editions of Hebrew sources. Most of the work, however, deals only with the Jewish aspect of this subject. We may get lists of names and perhaps even a short biography. In rare cases we learn a little detail about the fate of a particular, usually well-known, Jewish physician, for example, Abraham ben Hananiah Yagel (1553–ca. 1623).[21] We might also learn about Jewish physicians' struggles with the church and with the secular authorities. And if we are lucky we can reconstruct their academic background and here and there catch a glimpse of their medical practices. In short, we know a little bit about Jewish physicians living in pre-emancipation Europe but almost nothing about the patients who sought their advice. Before we turn our attention to the terra incognita of Jewish medical practice, we should take a brief look at those Jews to whom Christian patients entrusted their lives. For practical reasons, our inquiry will be confined to Germany.

It is well known that the practice of medicine was widespread among German Jews from the Middle Ages to the Enlightenment. Hundreds of Jewish physicians have been recorded for this period, and the list is manifestly incomplete.[22] Since by law Jews were generally not permitted to attend university, the ordinary channels of medical instruction were closed to them. The happy few admitted to the University of Padua, which was almost the only medieval university opening its lecture halls to Jewish medical students, were the exception.[23] The first graduation of a Jewish doctor in Padua was recorded in 1409.[24] German universities, in contrast, did not accept Jewish medical students until the early eighteenth century. According to Guido Kisch, Moses Salomon Gumpertz from Prague was, in 1721,

---

20 For example, see the policy of the town council in Mannheim, described in detail by Felsenthal, "Jüdische Ärzte in Alt-Mannheim," 188ff. For other examples, see Kober, "Judendoktoren," 180ff.
21 For his biography, see David B. Ruderman, *Kabbalah, Magic and Science: The Cultural Universe of a Sixteenth-Century Jewish Physician* (Cambridge, Mass., 1988).
22 See Steinschneider, "Jüdische Ärzte." The biobibliographies by Hes, *Physicians,* and Komorowski, *Verzeichnis,* contain many new names of Jewish physicians.
23 See, for instance, Shatzky, "Students," 444–7.
24 See Cecil Roth, "The Qualification of Jewish Physicians in the Middle Ages," *Speculum* 28 (1953): 835.

the first Jew to receive an M.D. from a German university.[25] In most cases, however, we cannot take university training into account when medieval and early modern sources refer to a Jewish "doctor." According to some sources, many of the Jewish physicians licensed by German town councils had at least some kind of formal instruction. Typically, the aspiring physician was apprenticed to a qualified Jewish medical practitioner for the purpose of learning the art of healing. Similar to the training of Christian barber-surgeons, the training of Jewish physicians was done by an experienced healer, who was, as often as not, the apprentice's father. Evidence from Frankfurt am Main and towns along the Rhine suggests that a Jewish physician frequently inherited, as it were, the medical practice from a close relative such as a father or an uncle.[26]

Having acquired his medical training, a Jewish physician was ready to practice, but normally he could not do so without receiving further authorization from the government. It became customary for Jewish physicians, at least from the sixteenth century onward, to receive formal sanction before they could begin to practice among Christians. Jewish physicians who had not been duly examined and licensed were considered quacks and were likely to be expelled or otherwise punished. In Frankfurt am Main, municipal laws relating to Jewish medical practice provided that Jewish doctors first had to be examined by a committee consisting of town physicians as well as aldermen and then found expert in their art.[27] They were also exhorted not to come too close to the Christian apothecary while he was preparing medicine according to the Jewish doctor's prescription.[28]

Jewish physicians who went in for a formal examination and asked for special authorization could not be sure that they would be accepted or even tolerated by their Christian colleagues who had acquired their medical knowledge at the university. Due to the often cut-throat nature of the late medieval and early modern medical marketplace, slander against a Jewish competitor was a common practice. Christian physicians claimed that their Jewish colleagues did not know enough Latin and therefore made silly or even dangerous mistakes when writing down a prescription.[29] They also claimed that most Jewish physicians pretended to be medical doctors but had no doctorate from Padua or any other university. As we have said before, the ordinary Jewish physician had

25 See Kisch, *Prager Universität,* 21–2.
26 See, e.g., the many individual careers mentioned by Kober, "Judendoktoren."
27 See Horovitz, *Ärzte in Frankfurt,* 9ff.
28 See Hermann Schelenz, *Geschichte der Pharmazie* (Berlin, 1904), 505.
29 See the examples given by Hörnigk, *Juden Artzt,* and Schudt, *Merckwürdigkeiten.*

no academic degree yet was often known as "doctor" in the Jewish as well as the Christian community.[30] Even the medical fringe among Jewish healers, also known as "empirics," did not mind being called "doctor." Levi Nathan, who called himself a *Judendoktor,* replied to the question posed by his interrogators as to why he had signed his prescriptions using a false title: "He says he did not pretend to be a person with a doctorate, a real doctor, or even a barber-surgeon, rather he says he relies on his skills."[31] And he added that as far as uroscopy, or urine diagnosis, is concerned he knew his profession better than any doctor in the world.

This self-confident answer throws light on the problems of healers who had acquired their knowledge outside the university system. We should not forget that many of the Jewish healers whom one encounters in medieval and early modern records learned their craft empirically, that is, from practice upon their patients, and had neither studied elementary textbooks nor received formal training by an experienced or a senior Jewish physician.[32] It seems, however, that the lack of formal training and academic titles did not damage or decrease their reputation among Christians seeking cures for their various ailments. On the contrary, Christian patients looked for something other than a doctoral degree – in a language they did not understand – when they turned to a Jewish physician. And it is quite revealing that most Jewish physicians did not imitate the ostentatious dress of Christian doctors of medicine. They continued to wear their traditional attire, which was often the laughingstock of Christian colleagues because of its conservative style and alleged shabbiness.[33] But the clothes worn by Jewish physicians departed in one respect from the regulations regarding dress for the Jewish community: prominent Jewish physi-

30 For the meaning of "doctor:" in medieval medicine, see Vern L. Bullough, "The Term 'Doctor,' " *Journal of the History of Medicine and Allied Sciences* 18 (1963): 284–7. See also Conrad Brunner, *Über Medizin und Krankenpflege im Mittelalter in schweizerischen Landen* (Zurich, 1922), 78.

31 "Er gebe sich nicht aus vor ein gedoctorirter, auch nit vor ein ganzen doctor, auch vor keinen barbirer, sonderen auf seine kunst." HAStK, Verfassung und Verwaltung, G 264, fol. 226v, quoted in its entirety by Kober, "Judendoktoren," 222.

32 For the typical career and medical knowledge of a Jewish physician, see Assion, "Jakob von Landshut."

33 See the accusations by Hörnigk, *Juden Artzt,* 209. For a portrait of a seventeenth-century Jewish physician, see N. Allan, "Illustrations from the Wellcome Institute Library: A Jewish Physician in the Seventeenth Century," *Medical History* 28 (1984), 324–8. That Jewish physicians and surgeons were well dressed is shown by an engraving that depicts the procession of Jews on the birth of the Archduke Joseph (April 24, 1741); in Alfred Rubens, *A History of Jewish Costume* (London, 1967), 134, and Kisch, *Prager Universität,* 16–17. For an earlier procession (1716), see the latter, opposite 16. For the representation of the Jews in the visual arts of the early modern period, see Rainer Wohlfeil, "Die Juden in der zeitgenössischen bildlichen Darstellung," paper given at the conference on "Reuchlin und die Juden" (Pforzheim, June 23–6, 1991).

cians, at least, were exempted from wearing the obligatory Jewish badge when leaving the ghetto.[34]

Sources for sketching a fairly comprehensive picture of the career of a sixteenth- or seventeenth-century Jewish physician or for reconstructing the experiences of the patients of such a Jewish healer are scarce. Unlike some of their Christian colleagues and contemporaries, Jewish physicians living in pre-emancipation Germany did not leave medical casebooks. Brief accounts of Christian patients treated by Jewish doctors may be found in a scattered profusion of records, papers, and books, but no great concentration awaits the fortunate historian. Even in the most abundant records, namely, in the surviving town council records of Cologne, traces of Christian patients and of their Jewish doctors are buried among other matters discussed at council meetings.[35] I have used the minutes of these sessions for the following analysis of the typical non-Jewish clientele of Jewish physicians. Moreover, I have analyzed more than 300 safe-conduct applications for Jewish physicians living on the other side of the Rhine, either in Deutz or Mühlheim, whose help was requested between 1647 and 1667 by patients residing in Cologne.

The traditional view of medical historians and Jewish scholars has been that Jewish physicians offered their medical expertise either to the prominent and rich in the Christian community or to those who for one reason or another – lack of money or ignorance, for example – could not afford proper treatment by a Christian doctor. These scholars refer to the medieval period as the age of the esteemed Jewish physician in ordinary and to the early modern period as the age of the Jewish quack, who was still denied academic training and therefore could not easily gain access to patients of the upper classes. But the evidence does not corroborate this black-and-white picture. Jewish physicians catering to the Christian community in Cologne drew their patients from the entire range of the social hierarchy. Few were very rich; few were very poor. Among their patients was the badly paid schoolmaster of Saint Columba School, as well as the local commander of the wealthy and powerful Teutonic Order. Although Jewish physicians were renowned in patrician circles and in the higher clergy, it appears that the bulk of their patients were humble tradesmen and artisans.

34 See the many examples given by Felix Singermann, "Die Kennzeichnung der Juden im Mittelalter. Ein Beitrag zur Sozialgeschichte des Judentums," Ph.D. diss., Universität Freiburg, 1915, 25; Ulysse Robert, "Le signes d'infamie au moyen âge," *Mémoires de la Société Nationale des Antiquairs de la France,* 5th ser., 9 (1988): 57–172, and Rubens, *Costume,* 121.

35 Some German scholars have already referred to this mine of information on Jewish physicians, but so far no one has undertaken a more thorough study of this source. See, e.g., Brisch, *Cöln;* Kober, "Judendoktoren"; and Ernst Ludwig Ehrlich, "Die rheinischen Judendoktoren," in *Monumenta Judaica. 2000 Jahre Geschichte und Kultur der Juden am Rhein* (Cologne, 1964), 264–9.

Table 10.1. *Applications for safe-conduct for Jewish physicians in Cologne, 1647–1667*

Gender	Petitioner		Person in need of medical help	
	No.	%	No.	%
Male	266	85.8	128	41.3
Female	42	13.6	134	43.2
Not known	2	0.6	48	15.5[a]

[a]Includes 9.7% children whose sex is not known.
Source: Historisches Archiv der Stadt Köln, Ratsprotokolle, 1647–67.

Table 10.2. *Relation between petitioner and person requiring help*

	No.	%
For oneself	121	39.0
For a family member	149	48.1
For a distant relative	13	4.2
For a friend	2	0.6
For other people	25	8.1

Source: Historisches Archiv der Stadt Köln, Ratsprotokolle, 1647–67.

Christian patients chose healers not only according to their pocketbooks but also according to their symptoms and their opinions about the merits and risks of various types of treatment and practitioners available in a society not yet fully "medicalized." Moreover, it is incorrect to assume that women, in particular, were driven to seek medical help from Jewish doctors. Status or charisma did not affect the sex ratio of the large group of Christian patients consulting a Jewish healer in seventeenth-century Cologne. Of the 262 patients whose gender is known, in my sample of 310, 128 were male and 134 were female (Tables 10.1 and 10.2). The fact that more men (266) than women (42) applied for the safe-conduct of a Jewish doctor (which of course does not mean that they themselves were the persons in need of medical treatment) can be explained by the patriarchal customs and values of an age that limited women's ability to speak for themselves in public. Almost one-tenth of the patients were children, whose sex usually was not revealed. This rate is low, if one compares it to the statistical findings which show that at least 25 percent of the German population at that time consisted of children under the age of fifteen. The rate is rather high, however, if one bears in mind the assumption of some social historians that in premodern societies parents were accustomed to seeing infants and toddlers sicken and die and therefore must have regarded their children's illnesses not simply as an affliction but also as an expression of the divine will.[36]

An analysis of a much smaller sample, consisting of 26 patient histories recorded in Dr. Ludwig von Hörnigk's diatribe against Jewish physicians living in seventeenth-century Frankfurt am Main, largely supports these findings.[37] As evidence, Hörnigk's reports are biased and certainly manipulated, but they are not bogus concerning the kinds of persons involved. The cases reported by Hörnigk, who relied on firsthand information, indicate that out of the 26 patients, 17 were men and 7 were women. Among the patients treated by Jewish doctors were some distinguished individuals, prominent in the imperial city of Frankfurt. One of them was a well-known officer by the name of Captain Hainhoffer. The other patients, however, were predominantly members of the middle or lower classes (57 percent artisans and shopkeepers) who found the money to pay for the costly services offered by Jewish physicians. To many, these health care providers seemed the most appropriate of the variety of healers available to deal with their problems and ailments.

Patients' expectations concerning the cure offered by a Jewish physician have been discussed at great length in anti-Jewish pamphlets and tracts published since the later Middle Ages. The reflections on this subject by Hörnigk provide an outstanding example of this phenomenon, not only because he was a renowned physician in Frankfurt but also because he was a prolific writer known for his disdain of his unlearned competitors. I have already referred to his diatribe against Jewish medical practitioners. But Hörnigk is more commonly remembered as the author of a work on medical practice in which he classifies Jewish physicians among wise women, crystal gazers, hermits, bankrupts, jugglers, urine prophets, heifer veterinarians, hobos, ratcatchers, devil exorcisers, and gypsies.[38]

36 See, for example, Arthur E. Imhof, "Säuglingssterblichkeit im europäischen Kontext, 17.–20. Jahrhundert. Überlegungen zu einem Buch von Anders Brändström," *Demographic Data Base, Newsletter* 2 (1984): 1–64, and Robert Jütte, "Kinder in der (wund-) ärztlichen Praxis der frühen Neuzeit," paper given at the International Symposium on the History of Medicine, Copenhagen, June 13–15, 1991.

37 Hörnigk, *Juden Artzt,* esp. 220.

38 Ludwig Hörnigk, *Politia Medica* (Frankfurt/Main, 1638), title page. For a similar ranking, see the statement by the sixteenth-century Swiss town physician Dr. Christoph Clauser, quoted in G. A. Wehrli, *Der Züricher Stadtarzt Dr. Christoph Clauser und seine Stellung zur Reformation der Heilkunde im XVI. Jahrhundert* (Zurich, 1924), 99.

Despite his open contempt for Jewish doctors, whom he considered quacks, Hörnigk discusses the reasons why so many of his potential clients sought medical help from them. By listing all the justifications he heard from patients, which he of course refutes, he at least gives us an idea why these healers were indeed so popular in the face of unceasing anti-Jewish feelings among the population.[39] The reasons he gives, which are a clue to the mentality of seventeenth-century German townspeople and peasants, can be classified into several groups.

Some justifications have a common economic base. For example, Jews were supposed to provide good value, that is, treatment, for one's money, because their fellow believers were reliable businessmen and because the entire Jewish community was held accountable before the law for transgressions or the dishonesty of individual Jews. They were also said to charge less than their Christian counterparts. Moreover, their prescriptions were often written in German and could easily be recycled, thus saving patients money in the future. Many Jewish physicians also continued the unlawful habit of preparing and administering the drugs themselves, which, in the eyes of the general public, must have somehow had a positive effect on the cost of medicine.

Another set of reasons stated by patients, according to Hörnigk, is characterized by their common therapeutic denominator. Unlike his Christian colleague, a Jewish physician was free – or at least felt free – to offer all the medical services that a client might require: diagnosis, prescription, preparation and administering of drugs, and even minor surgery. Further explorations of patients' expectations suggest that whereas patients today more often seek relief of symptoms, our ancestors needed to learn the cause of an illness and expected an instant prognosis in order to feel satisfied and reassured. It can be speculated that in part these expectations were not fulfilled by Christian doctors, who, from the late sixteenth and early seventeenth century onward, discarded or discredited the traditional method of uroscopy for not being "scientific" and reliable enough.[40]

Whatever the reason for this change in medical diagnosis, Hörnigk's report and those of other seventeenth-century authors illustrate that it was not only the common folk but also the elite who were still concerned with causation and expected a clear and intelligible diagnosis. The fact that so many Christian patients turned to Jewish physicians, despite the strong admonitions of church authorities and medical experts not to risk their lives and

---

39 See Hörnigk, *Juden Artzt*, 216ff.
40 See, for example, Walter Wüthrich, *Die Harnschau und ihr Verschwinden* (Zurich, 1967). For the history of this diagnostic tool, see Friedrich von Zglinicki, *Die Uroskopie in der bildenden Kunst* (Darmstadt, 1982), and Ortrun Riha and Wiltrud Fischer, "Harndiagnostik bei Isaak Judaeus, Gilles des Corbeil und Ortolf von Baierland," *Sudhoffs Archiv* 72 (1988): 212–24.

souls, indicates that the failure to receive a clear diagnostic statement and a reassuring prognosis may have been the principal reason patients were often dissatisfied with their Christian healers.

To the seemingly anachronistic minds of their many admirers and clients, Jewish physicians' mastery of the practical cabala and magical healing was another important asset.[41] Jewish healers practiced medicine in an era dominated by the antagonistic forces of magic and science. Galenic medicine was gradually losing its philosophical and theological aura, and only its scientific core survived. The great storm of witchcraft persecutions, the battle between the Galenic physicians and their astrological and Paracelsian competitors, the attacks of the Protestants and post-Tridentine Catholic Church on exorcists did not determine or change the allegiances of ordinary people or even of some intellectuals.[42] The influence of Christian theology waned as scientific materialism waxed. During this era of transition, the therapeutic vacuum was filled by the Jewish physician – the last Renaissance magus who seemed to unite all of his strongest interests, namely astrology, alchemy, ancient learning, and cabala.

Another advantage that Jewish physicians had over their Christian colleagues was their psychological appeal. Some patients, for example, justified their decision to consult a Jewish doctor by pointing out that they could speak to him more frankly about their problems than to a Christian doctor.[43] This argument illustrates some of the cultural barriers between learned Christian physicians and the majority of their potential patients. Communication barriers of this kind, however, did not exist between Christian patients and their Jewish healers, because the latter spoke the language of the common people. They also used therapeutic tools and procedures intrinsic to social relations and consistent with other symbols of contemporary social reality.

III

The widespread disenchantment with the available medical care before overall medicalization of society took place certainly helped the Jewish doctors find a niche in the medical marketplace during the late medieval and

---

41 See Hörnigk, *Juden Artzt,* 201–2. For the use of magic in Jewish folk medicine, see Herman Pollack, *Jewish Folkways in Germanic Lands (1648–1806): Studies in Aspects of Daily Life* (Cambridge, Mass., 1971), 113ff. For the place of magic in the medical practice of a sixteenth-century Jewish physician, see Ruderman, *Kabbalah,* 43ff.

42 For the anti-Semitic attacks by Paracelsus on Jewish physicians, see Fridolf Kudlien, "Some Interpretive Remarks on the anti-Semitism of Paracelsus," in Allen G. Debus, ed., *Science, Medicine and Society in the Renaissance: Essays to Honor Walter Pagel* (London, 1972). I would like to thank Dr. U. Benzenhöfer of Hanover for this reference.

43 See Hörnigk, *Juden Artzt,* 191.

early modern periods. It seems that Jewish healers, in particular, were known for satisfying their clientele, even though the service they had to offer was of low or dubious quality in the eyes of their antagonistic contemporaries. Although some patients complained to the authorities about medical malpractice or fraudulent behavior after unsuccessful treatment by a Jewish physician, most clients approved of their Jewish doctors and did everything to secure their tenure in the community. Satisfied patients often signed petitions on behalf of their Jewish physicians. Upper-class patients used their influence to convince the secular authorities that Jewish physicians should be allowed to continue to practice despite the various laws and measures passed by church councils and magistrates. When, in 1567, the local government of a town in East Prussia decided to appoint a Jew as town physician, despite the fierce protests of the local clergy, the town council replied that it was employing a physician, not a theologian.[44]

From the Middle Ages to the Enlightenment, the Jewish physician was a ubiquitous figure throughout the German principalities, in the towns as well as at court. These channels of contact broadened the scope of Jewish society beyond the walls of the ghetto. Unfortunately, almost no historian of the Jews regards these doctors as prime movers in what was happening in Jewish society at that time. Nevertheless, in addition to the few court Jews, whose influence is perhaps overestimated,[45] the numerous Jewish physicians, whose descendants entered German universities, were decisive for the later emancipation of German Jewry.

---

44 See Marcus, *Sick-Care,* 21. A similar liberal stance characterized the attitude of the town council of Regensburg toward Jewish physicians at the beginning of the sixteenth century. When barber-surgeons protested against their Jewish trade rivals, the case was brought before the imperial authorities in Innsbruck, who decided that "artzney [ist] ain freye kunst so gemayn, das alle mentschen, auch die alten weyber und die unvernünftigen their artzney treyben." Quoted in Raphael Straus, *Urkunden und Aktenstücke zur Geschichte der Juden in Regensburg, 1453–1738* (Munich, 1960), 360. This meant that everybody – even a Jew – was allowed to practice medicine.

45 See, e.g., Katz, *Out of the Ghetto,* 28ff.

11

Contacts and Relations in the Pre-Emancipation Period – A Comment

DEBORAH HERTZ

A student in a large lecture class of mine on the Holocaust once prefaced a question with the statement that "unlike you, we, after all, did not experience World War II." Since I was born several years after 1945, my student's remark obviously wounded my vanity! Reading the essays by Wexler, Guggenheim, and Jütte in Part III of this volume brought my student's remark to mind. All three essays are markedly postwar in theme and method. Each of the authors challenges and problematizes one or another strand in the classic, pre-1933 model of how to write the German-Jewish past. All three essays reflect a shift, sometimes a dramatic one, in our thinking about the German-Jewish past. All three essays reflect new subjects of research, new sources, and point toward fundamentally new conclusions about the vanished subculture that was German Jewry.

Perhaps it sounds odd, almost a half century after 1945, still to be contrasting new work with the picture of German Jewry presented by historians before the Holocaust. Surely that event was the most dramatic watershed imaginable, with huge implications for history writing, and it has also been over for quite a long time. No one would deny that German-Jewish history as it had been known ended at the hands of the Nazis. And that particular kind of ending to the story has, indeed, generated row upon row of books, whose authors aim to explain how things came to such a very bad end for the Jewish Germans. Much of this postwar scholarship is saturated with a retroactive pessimism – a tone, sometimes explicit, sometimes implicit, of inevitability.

The retroactive pessimism generated by Auschwitz has coexisted, however, with other, more old-fashioned methods and themes. German-Jewish historians, before and after the Holocaust, have emphasized how state officials affected changing social patterns and the importance of the rich and powerful. Both before and after the Holocaust, historians have been quite convinced that German Jewry was setting the trend for other Jewish communities in Europe. The emphasis on the state and on elites is an obvious parallel to what historians of the rest of the German past – with the Jews left out – have considered important. In brief, social history is still pale, both in the big world of German history and in the smaller world of German-Jewish history.

Each in their own way, these three scholars show how many strands of the old models are falling into eclipse. By taking us out of settled communities "onto the road," Yacov Guggenheim (Chapter 9) reconstructs the Jewish underclass. His is a necessary task at a time when we still know far more about the court Jews at the top of the Jewish hierarchy than we do about social relations at the bottom of the Jewish social structure. Robert Jütte (Chapter 10) writes a careful social history of a professional group whose members often enjoyed positive social relations with Christians. Jütte is convinced that Jewish emancipation is incompletely understood by concentrating mainly on economic achievements of court Jews and on government decrees. Rather, for Jütte, what we lack is a grasp of the slow preparation for emancipation by both Jews and Christians, going back into the early modern centuries. As for Paul Wexler (Chapter 8), he too challenges older models. Wexler suggests that the classic story of the evolution of Yiddish is wrong. The story that Wexler problematizes is that Jews departed Germany and went to settle in Poland in the late Middle Ages, bringing Yiddish with them. This made them, at least as seen by their historians, the "bearers and transmitters" of a "higher" linguistic culture. Wexler's challenge to the classic story will take scholars quite some time to evaluate. In the meantime, his work does uncover the subtle German–nationalist views of some Yiddish scholars. That Jews were often excluded from German society apparently did not prevent some of them from thinking that Germany was a "higher civilization" than civilizations in eastern Europe.

But let us end the quick tour and take a careful look at each chapter. We must be grateful to Yacov Guggenheim for focusing our attention on marginal and poor Jews. His essay reveals how restrictive early modern cities and states often were in their admission policies. As he shows, Jews were not the only ones classified as "undesirable." Guggenheim is also very clear that the internal class structure of Jewish society was extremely polarized in these centuries. Guggenheim has done thorough work in the primary sources and his anecdotal jewels will be appreciated by other historians.

However, he fails to define his central group, the *Schalantjuden* (road Jews), either in terminology, in time, in geographic space, or inside of either the Jewish or the overall social structure. Guggenheim does provide scattered quantitative evidence for various of his claims, but unfortunately these numbers do not actually substantiate his claims. Guggenheim's failure to define leads to confusions both small and large. He begins with the claim that the proportion of "marginal" Jews grew larger after the Black Death. A few pages later Guggenheim asserts that there were never more than "a few hundred" Jews on the road in Germany at any one time. He provides no evidence for his estimate. Moreover, we would need several other numbers to trust Guggenheim's initial claim about the increasing proportion of homeless Jews in the decades following the Black Death.

The eventual decline of the road Jews is confusing in Guggenheim's account. In a footnote he states a key theme that should have been highlighted in the text.[1] That claim is that the German term *Schalantjuden* was rarely heard once the sixteenth century began. According to Guggenheim, what he terms the "typographical heirs" of the *Schalantjuden* were the *Betteljuden* of the seventeenth and eighteenth centuries. This is confusing. It is fine for Guggenheim to concentrate on the fourteenth and fifteenth centuries, but most historians more familiar with the later centuries will legitimately wonder whether the *Schalantjuden* were basically similar to the *Betteljuden* or rather somehow quite different.

Guggenheim does a fine job of pointing out the variety of types of road Jews – including beggars, criminals, and roving physicians, some converted, some still Jewish. The Jewish criminals are a delicate and important subject. When he arrives at this issue, Guggenheim concludes that there was a "virtual absence of characteristic criminal behavior by the *Schalantjuden*." This claim sits uneasily with his failure to make clear what the relationship was between the medieval *Schalantjuden* and the early modern *Betteljuden*. A major theme of the work on the Jewish robber bands of the seventeenth and eighteenth centuries is that the line between legal and illegal commerce was more than a bit murky.[2] More knowledge about this touchy subject is obviously crucial. Anti-Semites often made harsh critiques of Jewish business practices. If beggars sometimes stole and then relied on "legitimate" Jewish traders to succeed in crime, there may have been some truth to the criticisms of anti-Semites. Guggenheim's cheery assessment that "characteristic criminal behavior" was "virtually absent" among the late medieval road Jews is intriguing but regrettably quite confusing. In spite of these various worries, Guggenheim's work is innovative. I especially like the evocative

---

1 See Guggenheim's essay in this volume (Chapter 9), note 6.
2 I am grateful to a former graduate student, Jason Sanders, now at Brandeis, for his research on this topic. See Rudolf Glanz, *Geschichte des niederen jüdischen Volkes in Deutschland* (New York, 1968), and, more recently, Uwe Danker, *Räuberbanden im Alten Reich um 1700* (Frankfurt/Main, 1988).

visual metaphor of "meeting on the road." We have much to learn about the preindustrial Jewish underclass, and Guggenheim has raised crucial questions that point us in the right direction.

One of the subclasses of roving Jews Guggenheim introduces us to is the "functional physician," someone with vague, if any, professional credentials who sold medical services to both Jewish and Christian patients. Robert Jütte provides a close-up portrait of Jewish physicians, whose expertise ranged from meager and practical to rigorously trained. Jütte's introduction to the place of Jewish physicians in medieval Germany, followed by his case study in fourteenth-century Cologne, are both polished and carefully researched. Jütte's decision to study doctors is based on a wise critique of the limits of much previous work on the period. In Jütte's view, medicine has not been given its due as an "integrationist" occupation. Medicine brought Jewish physicians into contact with Christian patients and their families, with city and state authorities, and, in a later period, with universities. The social networks created by these doctors existed for centuries before the emancipation process gathered speed in the late eighteenth century. Jütte, therefore, makes a solid contribution to the debate begun when Ezriel Schochat put forward the notion that emancipation in Germany was gradual and diffuse, rather than suddenly created by the intellectually and socially powerful.[3]

Jütte uses sources with extreme sophistication. His ultimate conclusion is provocative at several levels. Jütte thinks that there was a "therapeutic vacuum" in late medieval Germany, which Jewish doctors filled. The "magical science" of earlier centuries was still preferred by patients across the social hierarchy, even though elites from both churches had turned against the use of magic in medicine. He calls Jewish doctors the "last Renaissance magi," who united "astrology, alchemy, ancient learning, and cabala." Jütte's impressive essay opens up new directions for future research in the places in the past where Jewish history and the history of science meet.

In his own way and from within his own discipline of linguistics, Paul Wexler challenges the historic pedestal upon which historians and yiddishists alike have placed Germany Jewry. In Wexler's view, Yiddish is technically a Slavic language, which came to life in Sorbian-speaking eastern Germany between the ninth and thirteenth centuries. Wexler rejects the classic model, in which German was the linguistic "homeland" of Yiddish, which was then "exported" to eastern Europe as a "protective wall" against "Slavic barbarism." Rather, for Wexler, modern Yiddish was a

---

3 Schochat's book is *Im Hilufei Tekufot: The Beginnings of the Haskalah among German Jewry in the First Half of the Eighteenth Century* (in Hebrew) (Jerusalem, 1960).

Slavic contribution to European Jewish civilization. Wexler's colleagues within the field of linguistics will need to sift through the evidence and either confirm, reject, or modify his bold new view. Our tasks as historians are different. Our responsibilities are to dead humans, not their languages. Our task is to evaluate whether his version of the history of Jewish migration can support his linguistic thesis.

At the heart of Wexler's model is the idea that there were originally two versions of Yiddish, a western and an eastern version, which came to life on opposite borders of Germany. His story of the two Yiddishes is made more difficult to follow by his irritating habit of inconsistently using multiple labels to refer to the two regional dialects. But careful reading makes it possible to restate his argument. Western Yiddish began its life as Judeo-French, but Judeo-French died out and was eventually replaced by Eastern Yiddish. Eastern Yiddish, the eventual survivor dialect, began as Judeo-Sorbian, in eastern Germany. For Wexler, the reason that contemporary Western Yiddish is erroneously thought to be a Germanic language is because it does have many German words. Wexler does not dispute the proportion of German in Eastern Yiddish, but he maintains that the basic structure of the language is Slavic and that the German vocabulary was added later. One of Wexler's more elaborate arguments in favor of his thesis concerns the case of *Rotwelsch,* the underground criminals' language that most scholars label as a variant of Yiddish. Wexler focuses on the increasing proportion of Hebrew words in *Rotwelsch* over time. He concludes that early *Rotwelsch* had few Hebrew words, whereas Eastern Yiddish has much Hebrew in it. Wexler surveys a range of other linguistic evidence and concludes that, by the late seventeenth century, Western Yiddish had been "replaced" by Eastern Yiddish.

In a provocative summary, Wexler suggests that it was in the eastern regions of Germany that the version of Yiddish that eventually dominated was born. The Ashkenazic Jews from western Germany lost their dialect, Western Yiddish, but did succeed in imposing their religious practices on the eastern German Jews. (Wexler does not explain which practices he means here, from which centuries.) By the end of his essay, the eastern roots of Yiddish have become important enough to Wexler for him to conclude that "German Jews should now be viewed primarily as an outgrowth of an earlier Slavic Jewry."

This last comment sharply illustrates why Wexler's essay is bound to puzzle and even irritate historians. To my mind, the chief weakness of this learned and bold essay is that Wexler does not take migration patterns seriously enough. He makes strong claims about Jewish migration in an off-hand, erratic way. For me as a historian, Wexler's fascinating hypothesis requires a precise account of migrations to make real sense. In the classic account, German was brought to eastern Europe by German Jews after the eleventh century. Wexler argues against this interpretation, denying outright that there was a "large-scale Jewish migration eastward." This is confusing, since earlier in the essay he explains the high proportion of German words in Eastern Yiddish by the fact that "German moved eastward." How would Judeo-Sorbian/Eastern Yiddish become Germanized if Jewish speakers of German (or Western Yiddish, with a high content of German words) did not physically, and thus linguistically, mix with speakers of Eastern Yiddish?

Other equally serious confusions mount as we pursue Wexler's account. How was Western Yiddish replaced by Eastern Yiddish if Eastern Yiddish's presumably Polish speakers did not migrate westward? Wexler claims that Western Yiddish was popular as a literary language with speakers of Eastern Yiddish during the nineteenth century. This implies that two Yiddishes survived side by side until modern times. But the existence of two Yiddishes is inconsistent with his strong claims that Western Yiddish was replaced by Eastern Yiddish. Then there is the quandary of where Eastern Yiddish originated. Early on, Wexler situates the place as eastern Germany, but, later he switches the key birthplace of Eastern Yiddish to the Balkans. He slides from bold linguistic to bold geographic claims when he suggests that "some (or most) northern European Jews came from the Balkans in the sixth century." For historians, "come from" implies a chain of human movement, not just a particular language use. Balkan languages spoken in eastern Germany are quite different from the Balkan lands as a spot on a map. The final wild hunch, which Wexler slips in as if it were documented, is that Eastern Yiddish was born when Sorbian-speaking Balkan Slavs converted to Judaism in the ninth and tenth centuries.

In sum, Wexler may well have come up with a usefully provocative research program in the field of linguistics. That is not for historians to judge. We can only urge him to take the movement of real human beings as seriously as he takes their speech patterns. Historians can and do recognize bilingualism and language shifts on the borders between different lands. But we still need to write subtle, sophisticated national histories. Dethroning the Germanocentric model of modern Jewish history may well be a worthy goal, and Wexler's work may make a useful contribution to that goal. But, at least in this essay, he has not documented the radical conclusion that Slavic Jewry provided the linguistic and human foundations of modern German-Jewish civilization.

I began by observing that all three essays bring a much-needed new approach to the German-Jewish past. I also stressed how important it is to write social history and to question Germanocentrism. Now, in conclusion, let me turn to another way in which both Guggenheim's and Jütte's essays show a fresh kind of thinking about the German-Jewish past. That freshness lies in what I would call the "conceptual optimism" both reveal in their work, when they concentrate on positive social and professional ties between Jews and Christians in former times. It is rare, in our current post-Holocaust historiographic setting, to read of such ties. To my mind, focus on such ties means restoring some of the optimism that came so naturally to many German-Jewish intellectuals before 1933. The tilt away from blame and gloom should gain momentum, now that Jewish history has come into vogue in Germany. The field is currently thriving in three different national settings: the United States, Israel, and, at long last, in Germany again. Historians with quite diverse national experiences can now share their particular versions of the German-Jewish past. Imagining that Jewish–Gentile relations might have ended differently is clearly important to contemporary Germans. A retroactive pessimism about Jewish–Gentile relations has for too long been a lynchpin of Jewish identity in Israel and in the United States. It is time now to move away from that retroactive pessimism, not because it is politically immobilizing, which it is, but because it is a false, cheap, and misleading hindsight.

PART IV

Representations of German Jewry: Images, Prejudices, and Ideas

12

The Usurious Jew: Economic Structure
and Religious Representations
in an Anti-Semitic Discourse

R. PO-CHIA HSIA

This chapter analyzes the practice and discourse of Jewish moneylending in the Holy Roman Empire between the late fifteenth and early seventeenth centuries. Usury, as defined in the Old Testament was the taking of interest on loans to one's brethren;[1] Jewish usury, as defined by the Christian polemic of the late Middle Ages, referred to the excessive taking of interest on loans made by Jews to Christians.[2] The key word was "excessive," and it denoted the intermingling of economic and moral thinking in this anti-Jewish discourse. Usury was a form of immorality. According to the pamphlet, *A Faithful Warning to all good-hearted Christians,* published in 1531 by a certain Anthony B., German Jews took excessive interest (*überschwencklicher Wucher*) because, "as almost everyone knows, the Jews go around cheating from youth to old age."[3] The pamphlet provides a table of usurious interest to show that a debt of 1 Frankfurt gulden would, in twenty years, accumulate almost 2,593 florins in interest.[4] The pamphleteer urged Christians to help one another with interest-free loans, in order that Christian communities might remain pure and uncontaminated.[5]

Evidently the discourse against Jewish usury reflected broader problems in late medieval and early modern Germany. At issue was the morality of monetary exchange and the wider significance of this economic exchange for the totality of exchange structures between Jews and Christians.

---

1 Deuteronomy 23:19–20: "Non foenerabis fratri tuo ad usuram pecuniam, nec fruges, nec quamlibet aliam rem: sed alieno." From the Vulgate.
2 For a historic overview of the discourse on usury, see Benjamin Nelson, *The Idea of Usury: From Tribal Brotherhood to Universal Otherhood,* 2nd ed. (Chicago, 1969).
3 *Getrewliche Warnung an alle guthertzige Christen / sich für dem schnöden gesuch und überschwencklichen wücher der Juden zuverhëten. Zusampt einem klaren bericht / wie und mit welcher gestalt oder weyse / sie einfeltigen Christen von inen / durch ihre falsch listigkeit mit guthen worte verführt vnd betrogen werden. Nicht allein die bösen Juden / sondern auch die jenen so sich als from erzeyegen / betreffende* (n.p., 1531). On A1v, the author identifies himself as "Antony B." The citation reads (B1r–1v): "Es ist fast yederman kunt / dass die juden von jrer jugent an biss ins alter / mit betriegerey umb gehn."
4 Ibid., B3v–4r.   5 Ibid., A2r–2v, B3r–3v.

One can begin by positing two kinds of exchanges: in a commodity exchange, as defined by Marx, the thing exchanged, the alienable commodity, passed between independent social agents; in a gift exchange, as defined
by Marcel Mauss, the thing given, the inalienable gift, ritually affirmed ties
between interdependent social agents.[6] Contracting a loan between Christians, "brieff und sigel halten," to use the phrase of the period, represented
a commodity exchange. Giving charity to the poor, as the preachers admonished, was an example of the kind of exchange that affirmed the solidarity of Christian communities. Yet a third kind of exchange, Jewish
credit, threatened the very stability of the Christian community. The very
existence of economic exchanges between Jews and Christians, as the
Christian polemicists depicted, contaminated the moral purity of Christian
communities, reversed the superiority of Christians over Jews, and subverted the internal cohesion of Christian communities by aligning princes
and magistrates against the common folk.

In this essay, I analyze the practice of Jewish credit and the discourse on
the "usurious Jew" as parts of the larger structures of economic, religious,
and cultural exchanges in the society of late medieval and early modern
Germany. I first examine the relationship between the practice of Jewish
credit and the rhetoric of anti-Semitism. I argue that the declining importance of money lending by German Jews between the mid-fifteenth and
early sixteenth century and the rise of pawnbroking and retailing made little difference in the discourse of Jewish usury. Next I describe two different Christian discourses on Jewish usury. In one, the figure of the usurious
Jew represented the greedy Everyman; in this social critique, the actual Jews
became rhetorically marginalized and literally displaced by "Christian Jews"
and Christian usurers. In the other discursive tendency, the usurious Jew
was demonized. In place of a universal sign, the Jew was particularized and
assumed the attributes of greed, bloodthirstiness, and evil by virtue of his
essence. Finally, I shall argue that the emergence of Protestant Germany,
and its appropriation of Old Testament history, reified a nonreciprocal cultural exchange with Jews, even as it came to terms with the reality of day-
to-day economic transactions.

I

On February 25, 1519, the Jewish community of Regensburg, more than
800 adults and children, was expelled from this imperial city. Exploiting

---

6 See Marcel Mauss, *The Gift: Forms and Functions of Exchange in Archaic Societies,* trans. I. Cunnison
(London, 1966); Jonathan Parry and Maurice Bloch, eds., *Money and the Morality of Exchange* (Cambridge, 1989).

the death of Emperor Maximilian I, the Regensburgers rid themselves of the emperor's Jews, a goal that had been part of the city's political agenda since a ritual-murder trial in 1476. On the site of the demolished synagogue, a church was built to honor the Virgin Mary, an event commemorated in songs, woodcuts, and broadsheets.[7] The hero in these songs was the cathedral preacher, Balthasar Hubmaier, who acquired greater fame with his later martyrdom as an Anabaptist but whose sermons against Jewish usury, so the poet tells us, were indeed a message from God.[8]

Hubmaier's sermons against the Regensburg Jews are no longer extant. We can, however, reconstruct the major themes in a letter he wrote to the Emperor Maximilian in Innsbruck.[9] Composed in 1516 as a justification of his anti-Jewish sermons, Hubmaier boasted of his diligent sermons "on the case of usury, which touches on Christians and Jews, in order that such a great danger may be turned away from the soul." Basing himself on natural, biblical, canon, and imperial law, Hubmaier argued that usury was a sin "and although the Jewish community had given usurious loans, not without much detriment to Regensburg, we have hardly concerned ourselves with their usury." Moreover, Hubmaier warned Christian magistrates against pronouncing judgments on lawsuits regarding usury, lest they commit mortal sin.

Hubmaier's anti-usury sermons stirred up the citizens. Some refused to traffic with Jews; others declined to repay their debts.[10] But was usury the central issue? Apart from Hubmaier's sermons, the problem of usury hardly came up at all in the litany of anti-Jewish grievances presented by the city council and the guilds of Regensburg to Maximilian between April 1516 and June 1518.[11] The magistrates complained about the non-payment of moneys owed the city council, a debt which dated back to the settlement of the 1476 ritual-murder trial, and about the acceptance of

---

7 See, for example, *Wie die new Capell zu der schonen Maria in Regenspurg erstlich auff kommen ist nach Christi geburt M.CCCCC, vnd XIX Jar* (Nuremberg, 1519), a pamphlet in verse with woodcuts; this song-poem, together with four other folk songs celebrating the expulsion, was collected, albeit without woodcuts, and published in Rochus von Liliencron, *Die Historischen Volkslieder der Deutschen vom 13. bis 16. Jahrhundert*, vol.3 (Leipzig, 1867), 316–39 (nos. 336–40); the best-known visual representation is the single-leaf woodcut of the pilgrimage to the Schönen Maria by Michael Ostendorfer (ca. 1490–1550), a Regensburg artist, reproduced in Walter L. Strauss, *The German Single-leaf Woodcut, 1500–1550*, 3 vols. (New York, 1975).

8 *Wie die new Capell*, B1r–1v: "Got bald der stat ein Doctor sendt / Doctor Balthaser ist er genant / Verderbet pald der Judisch hundt / die priester hoben gen got in hendt / Got bald der stat ein Doctor sendt / Doctor Balthaser ist er genant / Der lernet Regenspurg zu handt / Wie man die sach solt greffen an / das selig worden fraw vnd man."

9 Hubmaier's letter is in a bundle of documents on the Regensburg expulsion, in the Tiroler Landesarchiv (hereafter cited as TLA), Innsbruck, Maximiliana XIV, 52a, 1516, fols. 285r–286r.

10 Raphael Straus, *Regensburg and Augsburg*, trans. Felix N. Gerson (Philadelphia, 1939), 155ff.

11 TLA, Maximiliana XIV, 52a, 1516, fols. 30r–41v, 60r–80r, 214r–220v.

stolen goods by Jewish pawnbrokers.[12] Submitting their grievances on June 28, 1518, twenty-six guilds accused the Jews, in a preamble, of ruining the livelihood of the Christian folk through "their dealings, goods, and merchandise, all manner of manipulations of a lavish, usurious, Jewish manner."[13] The metaphors of biological and social corporatism converged in the anti-Jewish language of the Regensburg guilds: they complained that the Christian folk were "sucked dry, injured in their body and goods, and without doubt, also blemished in their soul's salvation and all felicitous estate."[14]

In the articles of grievances of the individual guilds, however, it was not usury but Jewish competition that was at issue. By taking pledges, hawking merchandise, contracting with foreign artisans, and opening stalls, the Jews undercut the guild artisans by offering a greater variety of goods at cheaper prices. In other words, the Jews sold goods to the segment of Regensburg's population that also comprised their potential customers for credit. Primarily, those customers came from the lower and middle strata of urban society – the domestic maids, servants, laborers, bath maids, peasants, widows of artisans, journeymen, and poor craftsmen. A 1519 list of pledges and their owners, drawn up by the city council after the expulsion of the Jews, confirmed this picture.[15] A total of 300 Christians (176 men and 124 women, including couples) borrowed money from the Jews and deposited pledges. The social status of 59 men were identified: 1 nobleman, 2 physicians, 6 priests, 20 guild craftsmen, 5 weavers, 1 innkeeper, 1 miller, 1 soldier, 2 minor officials, 10 servants, 1 gardener, 3 fishermen, and 6 peasants. Most women were identified by their married names, and they seem to have been either the wives or the widows of craftsmen; others included 1 noblewoman, 8 weavers, 3 peasants, 1 fisherwoman, 1 prostitute, and a number of artisans. Although the amount of each loan was not indicated, they were most likely small consumer loans, a situation which was typical, for example, of the credit operation of the Nuremberg Jews between 1483 and 1499 as analyzed by Michael Toch.[16]

---

12 R. Po-chia Hsia, *The Myth of Ritual Murder: Jews and Magic in Reformation Germany* (New Haven, Conn., 1988), 81–2.
13 TLA, Maximiliana XIV, 52a, 1516, fol. 60r.
14 Ibid.: "all anstössend Christenvolckh, von den Juden daselbst, zue Regenspurg . . . ausgesaugt, an ere leib gut verletzt, unnd ungezweifflt, an der sel saligkait, unnd allem gluckhlichem zuestanndt befleckt werden."
15 Klaus Matzel and Jörg Riecke, eds., "Das Pfandregister der Regensburger Juden vom Jahre 1519," *Zeitschrift für Bayerische Landesgeschichte* 51 (1988): 767–806.
16 Michael Toch, "Der jüdische Geldhandel in der Wirtschaft des Deutschen Spätmittelalters: Nürnberg, 1350–1499," *Blätter für deutsche Landesgeschichte* 117 (1981): 283–310, here, 306–9.

The example of Regensburg allows us to draw four tentative conclusions about Jewish usury. First, the customers of Jewish credit, who represented the lower strata in urban society, did not directly agitate against the Jews, although they may well have responded to discourses against usury. Second, the people most vocal in articulating the anti-Jewish, anti-usurious discourse, in this case a part of the clergy and the politically organized craft corporations, were apparently not implicated in economic exchanges with Jews. Third, Jewish usury played a minor role in the specific economic grievances of the urban guilds, which furnished the mainstay of anti-Semitism in the cities. At issue was not only the figure of the usurious Jew embedded in a religious moral economy, but the real person of the Jewish business competitor. The charge of Jewish usury (as indeed with other anti-Jewish motifs) in mobilizing different grievances and focusing them on a single, visible target, therefore, functioned as an effective diversionary polemic. Four, because anti-Jewish rhetoric was potentially subversive of the urban ruling elites, who were both protectors of the Jews and practitioners of "Christian usury," city leaders concentrated on the Jews themselves, without regard for their actual economic practices. In championing the anti-Jewish cause of Balthasar Hubmaier and the guilds, the Regensburg magistrates defused an explosive crisis of a type that in the past had turned against the ruling regime itself.[17] Behind the 1519 Regensburg expulsion one can detect a configuration of political and religious forces similar to that which characterized the 1499 expulsion of Jews from nearby Nuremberg.[18] The rhetoric against Jewish usury was simultaneously a political language of subversion and resistance.

II

In 1541, Hans Obernaus published a long satirical song on usury, *Der Judenspiess* (the Jewish spear):

> Der Iudenspiess bin ich genant, ich fahr daher durch alle Landt/
> Von grossen Juden ich sagen will, die Schad dem Landt thun/ in der Still.
> Der Geistlichen fellt und wird zunicht/ Der Weltlich mechtig hoch auffgericht
> Und wandern umbher inn dem Landt/ Ihr wahr ist laster/ sündt und schandt.

17 Hsia, *Myth of Ritual Murder*, 83–5.
18 Cf. Michael Toch, " 'Umb Gemeyns Nutz und Nottdurfft willen.' Obrigkeitliches und jurisdiktionelles Denken bei der Austreibung der Nürnberger Juden 1498/99," *Zeitschrift für Historische Forschung* 11 (1984): 1–22.

(The Jewish spear is my name, traveling around is my game
Of the great Jews I say with poise, they ruin the land without a noise
The clergy falls and is no more, the secular mightily haughty tall
And around the land wandering, their ware of sin and shame a peddling.)[19]

As illustration for these opening verses is a small woodcut on the title page depicting a Jew carrying a spear. The rest of the satirical verses, ostensibly against Jewish usury, represented, in fact, a larger critique of greed in Christian society. The usurious Jew signified an Everyman:

Wer setzt sein endt inn zeitlich gut/ Und darinn sucht freud lust und mut/
Der greifft dem Juden nach dem hut/ Und ist ein Jud wie man ihm thut/
Er ist ein Jud wer samlet gut/ Und hat dabey kein rechten mut
Ein Jud verlert seiner freudn viel/ Sein Seel er nicht versorgen wil.
Geitz ist ein falsch betrigerey/ Der Teuffel gibt es dem Jüdn ein/
dass sie sollen wuchern und tobn/ Die bösen Christen das auch lobn.

(Whoever strives after worldly goods, seeking lust and joyous moods/
He grabs the hat of the Jews, and is treated like a Jew/
He is a Jew whoever collects goods, and thereby loses his true manhood
A Jew loses his joys to nought/ for his soul he cares not.
Greed is false treachery/ The Devil the Jews thus inspired/
in order [that] they may profiteer and rage/ This bad Christians also may praise.)[20]

The motif of the usurious Jew, as a figure of greed, allows Obernaus to attack the business practices of his day: the big merchants and monopolies who made bundles of profit from money exchange, bad coins, and usury. They were the ones, the poet declaimed, who took up the Jewish spear and drove the Jews themselves from moneylending.[21]

And now, Obernaus continues, everybody is running around with a Jewish spear; the usurers have moved out to the villages and are sucking the peasants dry.[22] The Common Man (*Gemeiner Mann*) is ruined.[23] Even the authorities have turned a blind eye to the *Juncker Judenspiess*.[24] The Holy Roman Empire, like the empires of old – the Persian, Assyrian, and Roman – will surely be destroyed by greed, for the natural order of the three estates, created by God, is being undermined by the fourth, the demonic estate of usurers.[25]

---

19 Hans Obernaus, *Der Judenspiess* (n.p.), 1541, British Library [11515.b.46], sig. A1r.
20 Ibid., sig. A2r–v.
21 Ibid., sig. B2r–3r: "Man hörte nicht so ein weklagen / Als man nur itzundt thut sagen. Man möcht es greiffen mit der hand / Die Juden sein vortrieben aussm land. Die bösn Christen habns genumen an / Manchen gar machen armen man. . . . Heist das nicht den Juden gesucht / Aber sie mögen nicht mehr bleiben. Die bösn Christen die Judn vertreiben / Mit dem Judenspiess thun sie rennen. Ich kenn ihr viel die ich nit nenne / Sie treiben wilde Kauffmanschafft."
22 Ibid., sig. B3r.   23 Ibid., sig. B3v.   24 Ibid., sig. B4v.
25 Ibid., sig. C1v–2r: "Gott hat die drey ding auch geschaffn / Die oberheit, Baurn und die Pfaffn. Das vierd seind Wucherer genant / Die schindn Burg / Stedt / dörffer und Land."

The *Judenspiess* is a surprising text. Invoked at the beginning, the figure of the usurious Jew suggests an association of anti-Semitic discourses. From usury, one would expect a litany of anti-Jewish tropes, perhaps in the vein of the vituperation of Conrad Celtis in his panegyric *Norimbergae* (1495): for the Jews not only sucked Christians of their wealth, but they also sucked the blood of their children; for they contaminated not only Christian communities, but they also desecrated the Christian Eucharist.[26] Instead, the rhetoric in the *Judenspiess* turns away from the Jews, who have been displaced by Christian usurers, the real villains in this morality tale.

A short pamphlet in verse, illustrated with woodcuts, the *Judenspiess* was a versatile text.[27] It could be read, in words and pictures; it could be sung. In fact, the text was probably published as a songbook for balladeers, who plied their trade in town squares and village commons.[28] A later edition of the *Judenspiess* (1580?), published by the Nuremberg printer Valentin Fuhrmann, appeared in a smaller pocket size, which could be bound with other songbooks of the sixteenth century.[29]

The most significant aspect of the figure of the Jewish spear, in its visual and textual representations, is not its character as a popular cultural construct, although the pamphlet *Judenspiess* was obviously meant for a popular market. Rather, the rhetorical trope of the usurious Jew as the avaricious Everyman reveals a tradition of textual transmission along a descending cultural and social axis. Several verses in the *Judenspiess* were taken verbatim from an anonymous illustrated broadsheet, *On Usury and Forestalling,* published in 1535 in Gotha.[30] In it, the theme of usury was secondary to the general critique of falsehood: "Betrieger seindt vnd felscher vil, wachen auff alle zeyt vnd zil, falsch lieb / falsch rat / falsch freind / falsch gelt, vol

---

26 Conrad Celtis, *Norimbergae* (Nuremberg, 1495). Facsimile edition, *Conrad Celtis und sein Buch über Nürnberg* (Freiburg, 1921). Speaking of the Jews, Celtis wrote: "Felices profecto urbes et terrae, quae hac hominum lue carent. . . . Videres ab illis Christianorum supellectilem, vestes, aurum, argentum, sacra etiam vasa, calices veluti proscriptam praedam sub hasta vendere, Christianorum pecunias non tantum, sed et sanguinem nostrum sitire, dum veteris suae superstitionis extispicia cum infantibus nostris, quos cruente mactant, celebrant et hoc divinationis genere futura perquirunt. Nullam Germaniae urbem immunem reliquere, quam hoc scelere non polluissent, sacris etiam hostiis et sacramentis nostris saepe ablatis contumeliaque et ignominia affectis," 198–9.

27 In addition to the woodcut of the Jewish spear on the title page, there is another on the following page showing Judas throwing the 30 pieces of silver back at the high priests.

28 On balladeers, printed songbooks, and anti-Semitism, see Hsia, *Myth of Ritual Murder,* 54. For general discussion of folk songs and the milieu of their performance, see Leopold Schmidt, *Volksgesang und Volkslied: Proben und Probleme* (Berlin, 1970); for an excellent study of balladeers in Renaissance Italy, the *cantastorii,* and their cultural milieu, see Ottavia Niccoli, *Prophecy and the People in Renaissance Italy* (Princeton, 1990).

29 The Fuhrmann edition in the British Library [11515.a.48(5)] is bound with other songbooks, including Hans Sachs's *Lobgesang Nürnberg.*

30 Reproduced in Strauss, *German Single-leaf Woodcut,* vol. 4. Compare the following verses to the *Judenspiess*: "Man leyhet yetzt ein müntz vmb golt. Fur zehen schreybt man eylff ins buch. Gar ley-

vntrew ist yetz die gantz welt." Even (or perhaps especially) the clergy was also seen as fraudulent. Falsehood was merely a step away from folly. Indeed, the motif of the Jewish spear can be traced back through the 1541 songbook, the 1535 broadsheet, and the 1531 *Faithful Warning* by Anthony B., to Sebastian Brant's *Narrenschiff* (1494).[31] The Jewish spear appears in two chapters of the *Narrenschiff*, "On Fame" (76) and "On Usury and Forestalling" (93), and some of the verses were copied word for word in the two 1535 and 1541 publications.[32] In short, the transmission of this social motif from the elevated text of Sebastian Brant to mass-produced broadsheets moved usury from the universal realm of morality to the specific sphere of political action.

Against this representation of the usurious Jew as Everyman, a generalized, figurative moral social critique, a second discourse represented Jewish usury as inherent in the demonic character of the Jewish people. *Juden Feind*, a polemical treatise published in 1570 by Georg Schwartz, a Lutheran pastor in Giessen, exemplified this tradition.[33] The polemic, dedicated to the landgraves Wilhelm, Ludwig, Philip, and Georg of Hesse, argued for expelling Jews. Schwartz repeated the familiar charges against Jewish moneylenders: the Jews were ruining Germany with usury, false coins, and goods. All usury should be forbidden, Schwartz advised, for it ruined the tradesmen. The pastor further suggested that the nobility and the officials tolerated Jewish usury because the Jews were obedient and gave large sums of

dlich wer der Juden gsuch. Aber sie mögen nit mer bleyben. Die Christen Juden / sie vertreiben. Mit Juden spiess die selben rennen. Ich kenn vil die ich nit will nennen. Die treyben doch wild kauffmanschatz."

31 *Getrewliche Warnung*, B2r–2v: "Es sein aber auch on zweyfel vil Christen / die auch ser mit dem judenspies stechen."

32 See the critical edition of Friedrich Zarncke, ed., *Das Narrenschiff* (Leipzig, 1854; reprinted: Darmstadt, 1964). Note in particular chap. 76, verses 6–12: "Mancher will edel syn, vnd hoch / Des vatter doch macht bumble bum / Vnd mit dem kuffer werch ging vmb / Oder hat sich also begangen / Das er vacht mit eynr stäheln stangen / Oder rant mit eym juden spyess / Das er gar vil zu boden stiess." And from chap. 93, verses 20–8: "Man lyhet eym yetz müntz vmb goltt / Für zehen schribt man eylff jnns buch / Gar lydlich wer der juden gesuch / Aber sie mögen nit me bliben / Die krysten juden, sie bertriben / Mit juden spiess die selben rennen / Ich kenn vil die ich nit will nennen / Die triben doch wild kouffmanschatz."

33 Georg Schwartz, *Juden Feind, Von den Edelen Früchten der Thalmudischen Iüden / so jetziger Zeit in Teutschlande wonen / ein ernste / wolgegründe Schrifft / darin kurtzliche angezeigt wird / Das sie die grösste Lesterer vnd Verechter unsers Herrn Jesu Christi / Darzu abgesagte vnd vnversündliche Feinde der Christen sind. Dargegen freunde vnd Verwande der Türcken / Uber das / Landschinder vnd Betrieger / durch jren Wucher vnd falsche Müntz. Die auch über das viel vnleidlicher böser stücke treiben. Derhalben sie billich von einer jdem Christlichen Oberkeit nicht geduldet werden solten / oder dermassen gehalten / wie in Gott selbs / die Weltliche vnd Geistliche Recht aufferleget / in zur Straffe / vnd allen Völckern / Sonderlich den Christen Menschen zum Exempel* (n.p., 1570). Under his Latin name, "Nigrinus," Schwartz had also published several polemical works against the Catholic Church and was the translator of Johann Georg Gödelmann's *Von Zäuberern, Hexen und Vnholden.*

protection money; he even claimed to know preachers who had been bribed by Jews.[34]

This suggestion of social critique, however, belied the true vehemence of Schwartz's polemic. For this Giessener pastor, the usurious Jew was not a sign of Christian greed but an embodiment of demonic character, who, second only to the Devil himself, represented the most bitter enemies of Christians.[35] As opposed to the symbolic representation of the Jew in *Der Judenspiess* tradition, Schwartz hated Jews for what they were, in essence:

Ich halte Juden für Juden/ Sie seyen getaufft oder beschnitten/
Sind sie nicht all einer Ankunft/ Gehören sie doch all in ein Zunft/
Sie dienen all gleich einem Gott/ Den Christus Mammon genant hat.
Welcher mit sein Dienern entlich gleich/ wird faren in des Teuffels Reich.

(A Jew is a Jew, baptized or circumcised, for all I care.
Even if they are of diverse origins, they belong to a guild.
They all serve one god, whom Christ named Mamon.
Who in the end with this servants, will go to the Devil's oven.)[36]

From the charge of usury, Schwartz easily leaped over to accusations of ritual murder, host desecration, and well poisoning.[37] Exhorting the Hessian princes to expel all Jews, the pastor stated that Christians should have no communion with nonbelievers, and tolerating Jews in their midst, in his words, "meant warming snakes in one's bosom and nurturing wolves in one's house" (das Heisset Schlangen im Büsem wermen / und Wölffe im Hause auffziehen).[38] The true cause of this deplorable state of affairs, wrote the Jew's enemy, was religious toleration, for confessional coexistence led to uprisings, treason, and civil war. Let the philo-Semite tolerate Jews, Catholics, Turks, Anabaptists, and heretics, let them tolerate witches, blasphemers, murderers, adulterers, thieves, and robbers, Schwartz thundered; he himself, however, must go to school again and learn anew the meaning of Christian love, when it required loving Jews and harming Christians.[39]

The *Juden Feind* incorporated two traditions. First, it inherited the motifs of medieval anti-Semitism, which had focused on the religion of the Jews. The charges of blasphemy, stubbornness, arrogance, and avarice were all based on the fundamental charge of false religion. But this was an anti-Semitism that held out the promise of acceptance through conversion. Second, it bore the fruit of a new form of anti-Jewish polemic, born out of the evangelical movement, which identified an innate, racial

---

34 Schwartz, *Juden Feind*, G2r–5v.   35 Ibid., F4r–v.   36 Ibid., H5v–6r.   37 Ibid., K1v–6v.
38 Ibid., L2v.   39 Ibid., L5r–7v.

character to the Jewish refusal to convert, no doubt a result of the evangelical clergy's anger with the fruitlessness of their Jewish missions. The older medieval anti-Jewish discourse, represented by the writings of clerics and Jewish converts, was amply cited by Schwartz. Among the converts he cited were Petrus Alfonsi,[40] Rabbi Samuel,[41] Nicolas de Lyra,[42] Paul Burgensis,[43] Victor von Carben,[44] Anton Margaritha,[45] and Johann Isaac of

40 Petrus Alfonsi, born Moses, an Aragonese Jew, converted in 1106. He composed the *Dialogus Petri et Moysi Iudaei* to justify his own conversion and to argue for the rational superiority of Christianity over Judaism. For Alfonsi, see Jeremy Cohen, *The Friars and the Jews: The Evolution of Medieval Anti-Judaism* (Ithaca, N.Y., 1982), 27–30. Alfonsi's polemic was available in a sixteenth-century edition, which was probably the text Schwartz consulted: Petrus Alfonsi, *Dialogi in quibus impiae Iudaeorum opiniones evidentissimis cum naturalis, tum coelestis philosophiae argumentis confutantur* (Cologne, 1536). Included in this text, published by Johann Gymnicum, is the *Libellus Rabbi Samuelis veri Messsiae parastasim continens,* a well-known medieval anti-Jewish polemic.

41 The *De adventu messiae praeterito liber,* attributed to the Morroccan Rabbi Samuel ben Judah ibn 'Abbas, was translated by Alfonsi into Latin from Arabic. For debates on the identify of Rabbi Samuel and the question of authorship and forgery, see Cohen, *Friars and the Jews,* 173 note 8. This text became one of the most widely reprinted anti-Jewish polemics in the Empire between 1485 and 1600. Latin editions appeared in 1485[?], 1493, 1497[?] in Cologne; 1498 in Nuremberg. The first German translation appeared in 1498 in Nuremberg, in 1524 in Augsburg, Colmar, in 1536 in Wittenberg, in 1583 in Heidelberg, and in Marburg in 1600. The reception of "Samuel Marochitanus" in Reformation Germany was predicated upon the evangelical fervor for Jewish conversion. The 1524 Augsburg Otmar edition, *Ain beweysung das der war Messias kommen sey, des die Iuden noch on vrsach zukünfftig sein warten,* was translated by Ludwig Hätzer, later a prominent Anabaptist. The 1524 Zwickau Gastel edition, *Das Ihesus Nazarenus der wahre Messias sey,* was translated into German by Wenzeslaus Linck, Luther's friend and an evangelical preacher in Nuremberg. The editions just cited can be found in the British Library, the Bodleian at Oxford, the Benecke at Yale, and in the Inter Documentation Company's microfiche collection, Hans-Joachim Köhler, ed., *Flugschriften des frühen 16. Jahrhunderts (1501–1530)* (Zug, 1978–87).

42 On the anti-Jewish polemic of Nicolas de Lyra, see Cohen, *Friars and the Jews,* 180–94.

43 On the fifteenth-century convert Bishop Paul of Burgos, see Cohen, *Friars and the Jews,* 130, note 2.

44 For an introduction to Victor von Carben, a Jewish convert and Catholic priest, see Heinrich Graetz, *Geschichte der Juden,* 11 vols. (Leipzig, 1873–1911), 9:42ff. For Carben's discourse on Jewish usury, see his *Dem durchleuchtigsten herren Ludwign Phaltzgrauen bey Rein, Hier inne wirt gelesen wie V. von Careben zu christlichem glaubn komen (Ein disputatz eynes Christen vnd eyns luden)* (Cologne, 1510?). This edition, written in dialect, was republished in a High German edition in 1550 (no publisher) that appended a short dialogue between Michael Kromer, pastor at Cunitz, and a Rabbi Jacob von Brucks. The 1550 edition was probably the one used by Georg Schwartz. The following anecdote is from the 1510 Cologne edition. Carben's discourse on Jewish usury was rather mild. He blamed rich Christians for secret dealings with Jewish usurers, citing one example of a rich merchant who, on his deathbed, could only cry out after his *Judengelt,* because he had recently lent a large sum of money to a Jew. When the merchant's servant went to the Jew, the latter said the merchant had in fact borrowed money from him. The dead merchant's family did not want this odious connection exposed and gave in to the Jew's blackmail. *Dem durchleuchtigsten,* chap. xxi, Eiv–2r.

45 Anton Margaritha, son of Rabbi Jacob Margolis of Regensburg, converted to Christianity in 1522. His 1530 work, *Der Gantz Judisch Glaub mit sampt eyner grundtlichtenn und warhasstigen anzeygung, aller satzungen, Ceremonien, gebetten, heymliche und offentliche gebreuch, deren sich die Juden halten, durch das gantz Jar, mit schonen untid gegrundten Argumenten wider jren glauben,* was published in Augsburg. It contains an attack on Jewish usury. Margaritha urged Christian magistrates to suppress usury rather than protect the Jews and allow the practice to flourish. If Jews were forced to perform manual work, their pride would be humbled, and they would no longer look down on Christians as their servants. Eventually they would convert (K1v–K3r). The practice of usury, according to Margaritha, was the central obstacle to the conversion of Jews (Cc1v–2v).

Cologne.[46] The new Lutheran anti-Semitism drew its sources from several writers of the first Reformation generation. Schwartz invoked the works of Johann Reuchlin, Paul Ricius,[47] Sebastian Münster,[48] Martin Bucer,[49] and, of course, Martin Luther. Although Lutheran anti-Semitism assumed many motifs from the medieval polemical texts, a new emphasis was given to the immutable, essentialist, and, to employ an anachronistic concept, the racial character of the German Jews.

III

It must not be forgotten that the agitation against Jewish usury occurred in the larger context of an intense debate in the empire on usury in general. As early as the *Reformatio Sigismundi* (1438–39), the idea of usury was broadly applied to and critical of many forms of unjust exchange – including simony, forestalling, and the taking of interest.[50] In the early sixteenth century, with the rise of the Fuggers and other large trading firms, an intense debate over usury and monopoly broke out between 1514 and 1525.[51]

46 Johann Isaac was the author of a *Sendbrief an die Juden zu Wetzler,* which I have not been able to locate (*Juden Feind,* D7r). Isaac and his family converted in 1546, according to evangelical rites. When the family moved to Louvain in 1547, they were baptized Catholic. Johann's son, Stephen Isaac, later became a priest in Cologne before he converted to Calvinism. For Stephen Isaac's story of his family's religious odyssey, see *Wahre und einfältige historia Stephani Isaaci* (1586), edited by Wilhelm Rotscheidt in *Quellen und Darstellunaen aus der Geschichte des Reformationsjahrhunderts* (Leipzig, 1910), vol. 14.

47 Contrary to Schwartz's categorization, Paul Ricius was a converted Jew, onetime professor of philosophy at Pavia, and later chief physician to Emperor Maximilian I. Ricius, who published Latin expositions of the cabala and the Talmud, repeated the conventional biblical injunction against usury in *De sexcentim et tredecim Mosaice sanctionis edictis* (Augsburg, 1515), C8v–D1r: "Pecuniam tuam non dabis ei fratri tuo ad usuram. Id est foenus non recipias. Fratrem appellat qui idola spernit, legemque amplectitur. Quum igitur insana iudaeorum turba christicolas idola colere ac legem subvertere existimet, hoc (ut paulo ante recensuimus) necquaquam in fraternam necessitudinem suscipiendos: ipsisque non iniuria foenerandum dejudicant."

48 The relevant work by Sebastian Münster was *Messias Christianorum et Iudaeorum Hebraice et Latine* (Basel, 1539). The work is discussed in Section III of this chapter.

49 The relevant work by Martin Bucer was the published memorandum to Landgrave Philip of Hesse urging him not to tolerate Jews. In *Von den juden ob / vnd wie die under den Christen zu halten sind / ein Rathschlag / durch die gelerten am ende dis buchlins verzeichnet / zugericht, Item, Ein weitere erklerung und beschirmung des selbigen Rathschlags* (Strasbourg, 1539), B2r–3r, Bucer argued that usury subverted the hierarchy between Christians and Jews. It was the duty of the Christian magistrate, Bucer wrote, to protect the poor Christian sheep against the wolfish Jews and false Christian merchants. Jews should be the tail (*Schwantz*), not the head; they should do the manual work and earn their salvation through humility.

50 The author of the *Reformatio Sigismundi* understood any action injurious to *aequalitas* as constituting usury. See Clemens Bauer, "Der Wucher-Begriff der Reformatio Sigismundi," in *Stadt-und Wirtschaftsgeschichte Südwestdeutschlands. Festschrift für Erich Maschke zum 75. Geburtstag* (Stuttgart, 1975), 110–17.

51 The major figures in this debate were Johann Eck, Martin Luther, and Jakob Strauss. See Nelson, *Idea of Usury,* 29–56; Heiko A. Oberman, *Werden und Wertung der Reformation* (Tübingen, 1977), 161–82; Thomas A. Brady, *Turning Swiss: Cities and Empire, 1450–1550* (Cambridge, 1985),

Only one theme in this well-studied development need concern us here: the generally conservative, anti-usury position of the evangelical movement and the participation of Jewish converts to Christianity in this debate, or, more succinctly, conversion and usury.

All Jewish converts of early sixteenth-century Germany attacked the practice of Jewish moneylending. Johannes Pfefferkorn identified usury as the main reason why Jews refused Christian conversion. He urged rulers to forbid usury, while allowing Jews to earn their livelihoods through honest work.[52] This chain of reasoning – that usury led to wealth, self-conceit, and arrogance among Jews – was forcefully stated by Anton Margaritha in *The Entire Jewish Faith* (1531), a work that would shape the anti-Jewish views of the Lutheran Church. If Jews were forced to do manual work to earn their living, Margaritha argued, their pride would be humbled. Eventually, they would convert to Christianity, because they would then know their true state of captivity. Christian magistrates should make Jews work, Margaritha urged, "out of mercy and brotherly love, according to the Gospels."[53] These prescriptions against Jewish usury, harsh as they may sound, aimed at conversion and social integration. However, after the initial fervor for missionary work had cooled, Protestant Germany appropriated only one part of this double anti-usury program. In Luther's anti-Jewish writings of the 1540s, one read of "the harsh mercy of forced manual labor," but not of the brotherly love urged by the Jewish converts. By the second half of the sixteenth century, usury was no longer a central issue in Lutheran anti-Jewish discourse. Since the reality of economic exchanges between Jews and Christians could not be moralized away, the figure of the usurious Jew was transformed and permanently fixed in the immutable world of a new racial theology.

Let us recall Schwartz's essentialist definition and compare it to the anti-Jewish discourses of the Jewish converts: "A Jew is a Jew, baptized or circumcised, for all I care." To be sure, this racial anti-Semitism reached back to earlier texts. In Sebastian Münster's *Messiah of the Christians and Jews* (1539) we can read a similar, astonishing stress on the purported physical appearance of the Jews. In this dialogue, a Christian greets a Jew in Hebrew. Surprised, the Jew asks the Christian whether he is one of them, and when

119–27; Jakob Strieder, *Studien zur Geschichte kapitalistischer Organisationsformen, Monopole, Kartelle, und Aktiengesellschaften im Mittelalter und zu Beginn der Neuzeit* (Munich, 1914), 60–4, 71–3.

52 For Pfefferkorn's writings against Jewish usury, see his *Speculum adhortationis iudaice ad Christum* (Speyer, 1507), C1r–2v; *Der Juden Veindt* (Augsburg, 1509), A4r–B2v; *Zu lob und Ere des aller durchleichtigsten und grossmechtigisten Fursten und herren, Herr Maximilian* . . . (Augsburg, 1510), A4v; *Handt Spiegel wider und gegen die Juden* (Mainz, 1511), F1v–2v.

53 Margaritha, *Der Gantz Judisch Glaub*, K1v–3v.

the Christian says no, goes on to ask how he could recognize a Jew. To this the Christian replies:

ex forma autem faciei tue cognovi te esse iudeum. Si quidem est vobis iudeis pe-culiaris quaedam faciei imago diversa a reliquorum mortalium forma et figura, quae res saepe in admirationem me duxit. Estis enim vos nigri et deformes, et minime albicantes more reliquorum hominum.[54]

(by the shape of your face, however, I can recognize you as a Jew. If indeed it is a particularity of Jews to differ in form and figure from other mortals, then this often leads me to admiration. Thus, namely, that you are black and deformed with little resemblance to other mortals.)

To which the Jew retorted, "If we are deformed, why do you Christians love our women so much, if they are not more beautiful than your women?" The Christian conceded as much but insisted Jewish women were better looking than the men.

This brief dialogue about Jewish physical characteristics, marginal to Münster's central concern of refuting the Talmud and the cabala, and of as-serting the universal messianic status of Jesus, was nevertheless revealing of a deep shift in anti-Jewish discourse. The crude anti-Semitism in the carni-val plays of a Hans Folz at the end of the fifteenth century found expression in the elite discourses of sixteenth-century Germany. And Sebastian Mün-ster's benign dialogue (the Jew and Christian parted on friendly terms and agreed to a future discussion) gave way in just a generation to Georg Schwartz's racial theology of anti-Semitism.

In the *Juden Feind* Schwartz argued that his contemporary Jews were un-worthy of their name because they were Talmudists. The Jews of the Dias-pora, he continued, were totally different from the Jews of the Old Testament from whom Jesus was descended. In almost fifteen hundred years of the Diaspora, many Jews had been killed, "therefore . . . I do not believe that there are many survivors who are descended from the pure Jewish seed of Abraham. They are likely to be bastards and half-breeds."[55] A bit farther in the text, Schwartz concludes that the Jewish religion and kingdom had long been destroyed, and what remained, in his day, were Jews in name but really "Talmudists, cabalists, and half Muslims."[56]

Judaism without Jews and the Old Testament without the Chosen People – this cultural transformation, a de-peopling of the Old Testament,

54 Münster, *Messias Christianorum et Iudaeorum*, A5v.
55 Schwartz, *Juden Feind*, B8v–C1r: "Darumb gleube er wer da wil / ich gleube nicht / das unter in [the Jews] viel ubrig seien / die aus unvermischtem Judischem Samen von Abraham herkomen. Es mögen wol Bastern und Mengling sein."
56 Ibid., C5r.

enabled Lutheran Germany to appropriate the idea of a New Israel for itself while preserving the discourse of anti-Semitism, even when the economic reality of Jewish usury (and other purported Jewish crimes) was being transformed during the sixteenth century. The simultaneous popularity of anti-Jewish writings and histories of Old Testament Israelites in the book market of sixteenth-century Germany reveals precisely this cultural dialectic.

Representations of Old Testament histories spanned a wide cultural spectrum. The simple folk could read a book of woodcuts and text on biblical, classical, and Christian history, *The Three Faiths* (1518), illustrated with good and bad Jews from the Old Testament.[57] The learned could consult Bartholomaeus Stenus's *Historical Method of the Dukes, Judges, Kings, and the Israelites* (1523), which offered a short summary of Old Testament history from Moses to Jesus.[58] The burgher could turn to Kaspar Turnauer's greatly popular history, *On the Jewish and Israeli People* (1528), which offered a chart of the patriarchs, kings, and prophets of Israel, in addition to a summary of Old Testament history, in order to show the example of the Jews, the first Chosen People who turned away from God, so that Christians might learn from their history and punishment.[59] For those unable to get Turnauer, which went out of print in a few short years, they could purchase the 1536 pamphlet by Wolfgang Russ, *The Book of the Patriarchs of the Israelites,* which was published in response to market demand.[60] In compiling the book from the Old Testament, Russ wanted to tell the story of how God chose the Jews to be his people, how they offended him and were punished, "and the reasons for the situation of our time, such as war, tyranny, uprisings, inflation, pestilence, etc., since everything that befell them [the Jews] is for us an example of their reward and punishment."[61] As a mirror of his time, and not forgetting his confessional polemic, Russ pointedly translated the word for the Israelite priests, *Kohenim,* as *Pfaffen.*

57 *Der dreien glauben, dz ist der Haiden, Iuden, vnd Cristen die frümbsten vnd pösten Mannen vnnd frawen* (Augsburg, 1518). Reprinted by H. Schobsser of Munich, 1520(?).
58 Bartholomaeus Stenus, *Docum / Iudicum / Regum / Israhelitici populi cum ex sacris tum prophanis literis hystorica Methodus* (Nuremberg, 1523).
59 Kaspar Turnauer, *Von dem judischen unnd Israelischen Volck unnd jren Vorgeern* (Augsburg, 1528), A2.
60 See "To the Christian Reader," (A1v) in Wolfgang Russ, *Das Buch der Altveter / des Israelitischen volcks / nemlich / woher die Synagog / das volck Gottes / oder die Kirche / jren ursprung habe. Aus Biblischen Historien vleissig gezogen* (Wittenberg, 1536).
61 Ibid., A2r–2v: "Und die ursach der leuffte / so sich zu unsern zeiten begeben / als krieg / Tyranney / auffruhr / thewrung / pestilentz, etc. deste besser erkennen / urteilen und vermeiden mögen / Denn alles was bey jnen ergangen und geschehen / ist uns zum Exempel / sampt seiner straff und belohnung geschehen."

This cultural appropriation was completed by the second half of the sixteenth century. There were isolated voices of dissent, notably from Jewish converts to evangelical Christianity. In 1555, Philipp Wolff, who had been baptized the previous year in Danzig, dedicated a work, *The Mirror of Jews*, to Danzig's city fathers and citizens. In the work, Wolff denied that Jews could be defined by race: strangers resided in Abraham's household; the Israelites lived among and married Gentiles in Canaan and Egypt; and the seed of Abraham was meant spiritually, not literally, to include all who accepted the true faith.[62]

As a commonplace in the self-expression of Lutheran Germany, the identity of New Israelites, internalized among broad segments of the evangelical pastorate, provided a language of self-critique. *The German Evangelical Judaism,* written by the dissident pastor Christian Hohburg (1607–75), was perhaps the best example.[63] In a prefatory address to the evangelical reader, Hohburg made explicit the identification between Protestant Germans and Israelites: "He has researched [the books] of all the holy prophets of God concerning the situation of the Jewish people from Solomon's successors to the Babylonian Captivity, all of which he has presented good-heartedly as an example to our Evangelical Germany."[64] There were numerous exact parallels between the Israelites and Lutherans: God led the Jews out of Egypt and led the Lutherans out of the Catholic Church; God punished the sins of the Jews with warfare and was punishing Lutheran Germans with the Thirty Years' War; God had helped Lutherans to withstand the onslaughts of Charles V, just as he had helped kings Abia and Assa; just as God had chosen the Jewish people above all others on earth, he also loved evangelical Germans more than other races (*Geschlechten*) on earth.[65]

To be sure, Hohburg was a dissident pastor who repeatedly ran afoul of consistorial authorities and ended up as a pastor to the Mennonites in

---

62 Philips Wolff, *Spiegel der Iuden. Darinnen menniglich zu ersehen wie die lieben patriarchen alle propheten / und Moses / so trostlich und klerlich anzeigen / das unnser Herr Jhesus Christus und Heilandt warhaffter Messias den Juden verheischen worden ist. Sampt der Juden Cabala und ihrem teglichem Gebett / aus Hebreyschen und Chaldeyschen Sprach verdeudscht. Neben angeheffter ausslegung ihres Semhamphoras / der 72 namen Gottes* (Danzig, 1555), P4r–v.

63 Christian Hohburg, *Teutsch-Evangelisches Judenthum, Das ist Auss den Heiligen Propheten Gottes / dass wir Evangelische in Teutschland grössten Theils / dem Jüdischen Volck im Alten Testament ietzo gleicht* (Frankfurt/Main, 1644).

64 Hohburg, *Teutsch-Evangelisches Judenthum,* "An die Leser" (A7–B5): "da ich den zustand dess Jüdischen volcks / von den Königen nach Salomo / biss zu der babylonischen gefängniss / aus dem sämptlichen heiligen Propheten Gottes habe aufgesucht / und solches unserm Evangeliischen Teutschland zum vorbild wolmeynentlich vorgestellet."

65 Ibid., 1–14, 48–50, 161–64.

Hamburg. The image of evangelical Germans as the New Israelites, however, remained a powerful cultural idea in Protestant Germany well
beyond the old regime. As to the Jews of the Holy Roman Empire, their
status, transformed by the Reformation and defined in accordance with
the matrix of Lutheran identity, was permanently sealed in a structure of
cultural signs, immune from the economic and political exchanges that
reshaped Jewish life.

13

Imagining the Jew: The Late Medieval Eucharistic Discourse

MIRI RUBIN

Any attempt to appreciate meaning and action in the past must see them as embodied through the working of meaningful images inserted into meaningful narratives. It is to recognize the fundamentally linguistic nature of our consciousness and of the construction of "reality," and to appreciate that life is never experienced as a raw, material sequence but rather that it is mediated through images and concepts that lend it meaning. To be a Jew, a woman, or a king was an experience arising from the interaction of (sometimes conflicting) expectations of the self and others as to what Jewishness, femaleness, kingliness were, as constructed within the salient narratives of the day. To take on board the symbolic nature of our apprehension of the world is not to draw a picture of historical actors reproducing defined narratives, blindly obeying preordained roles – quite the contrary. It is to see life as an ongoing engagement with available symbols inherited within a culture, as an application of them, through interpretation, to challenges and dilemmas.[1] However poignant, painful, and acute an experience may be, it is always the product of the work of symbols and narratives within the ever-changing circumstances of life, in a continuous engagement with questions of meaning and identity.

Yet when we address the question of Christian–Jewish relations, there is a strong attraction toward seeking and finding continuous, almost eternal, inevitable formulations of the nature and meaning of that relationship. Not least in these very years, as we meet again the cultures of eastern Europe after several decades of separation. As we encounter the (re)emergence of anti-Semitism, the expression of familiar anti-Jewish sentiments and fears, the morbid attraction of a static interpretation of the Jewish–Christian narrative is all too present. It is, therefore, particularly important for historians to resist the allure, to attempt a disaggregation of the forbidding whole of

---

1 For an interesting discussion of some of these issues, see Natalie Z. Davis, *Fiction in the Archives: Pardon Tales and Their Tellers in Sixteenth-Century France* (Stanford, Calif., 1987).

hate and fear into strands and contexts amenable to discussion and interpretation, even if not quite to understanding. It will be useful to remember
the variety of narratives of anti-Jewish sentiment, to recognize them as attempts to interpret the difference that Jews have represented. Difference, after all – be it of gender, race, creed – will always provide the ground for
identification of individuals and groups. Difference will always be an issue,
but it need not lead to persecution and death, nor has it invariably done so.
Only when difference is interpreted within a narrative that legitimates its
eradication, that constructs it as dangerous, harmful, evil, do the persecutions and killing follow. Such narratives are, furthermore, historical products; they are told and enacted by people, by agents who recount them anew
in ever-changing contexts. When such narration is credibly done, it can lead
to murder and death. Yet the story itself is only a potential, a resource; to
kill, it must be activated, narrated, brought to life.[2]

Most people take anti-Semitic narratives to be age-old, eternal. Many a
survey draws links between representations of Jews in the Gospels, through
the Middle Ages, through nineteenth-century radical thought, and to the
images of Nazism, drawing out the continuity of symbols: child-sacrifice,
the Jew as magician, the Jewish sow.[3] There is, of course, a measure of truth
in such a view; the gospels and early Christian apologetics in the early centuries of our era created a language of Jewish guilt. Yet from those early days
eleven hundred years passed before the birth of the myth of ritual murder,
and another seven hundred before the elaboration of the fantasy of a world-
wide Jewish financial conspiracy was elaborated. It is profitable to recognize
the historical variability of tales, and of their *Rezeption*.[4] I have, therefore,
chosen to examine the birth of such a narrative: of the host-desecration accusation against Jews that developed throughout the thirteenth century.[5] I
shall trace its symbolic construction, its power to move to wide-scale action, its spread, and its working in German lands through a number of cases
from the late thirteenth through the fifteenth century.

It is easy to make erroneous assumptions about the place of the Eucharist
in medieval culture, to assume that it had always been the center of cult, the
central symbol of a Christian sacramental worldview. But the Eucharist, an

---

2 Many of the issues discussed here have been considered in R. Po-chia Hsia, *The Myth of Ritual Murder: Jews and Magic in Reformation Germany* (New Haven, Conn., 1988).
3 I. Shachar, *The Judensau: A Medieval anti-Jewish Motif and Its History* (London, 1974).
4 On the decline of the ritual-murder accusation in Protestant areas of Germany, see Hsia, *Myth of Ritual Murder,* 136–62. On the development of and change in the image of the Jew as tormentor at the
Crucifixion, see W. C. Jordan, "The Last Tormentor of Christ: An Image of the Jew in Ancient and
Medieval Exegesis, Art, and Drama," *Jewish Quarterly* 78 (1987): 21–47.
5 For survey and basic outline, see P. Browe, "Die Hostienschändung der Juden im Mittelalter," *Römi-
sche Quartalschrift* 34 (1926): 167–97.

important ritual of early Christian communities, gained its emphatic power only through the close scrutiny accorded to it by theologians and liturgists from the eleventh century on. The full meaning of the Eucharist was quite unspecified in early centuries. It was a representation of Christ, but its nature was not clearly fixed, and the cultic and ethical relations of Christians to it were thus left open, undecided. But from the eleventh, and particularly from the twelfth century, the Eucharist grew in importance at the heart of a powerful sacramental-sacerdotal system. Its theology was clarified, its status scrutinized, and the working of transubstantiation in it was defined.[6] The claim was made that the thin and fragile round wheaten wafer consecrated at the altar was substantially transformed, becoming of the substance of Christ's historic body that had suffered the Passion, even under the enduring appearance of a wheaten wafer. This outrageous claim was conveyed to Christians through the ritual of the mass, in preaching and teaching, in illustrative tales, and through the news of the many miracles that the eucharistic body of Christ could perform in the world. Additionally, the eucharistic liturgy was enhanced and designed to accord the holy substance its proper veneration: the Eucharist was to be kept in precious vessels; it was to be handled carefully and only by priests; it was always to be marked by special lights and bells. So the Eucharist increasingly came to reside at the center of religious practice, annual communion was both obligatory and necessary, and many new devotions came to develop around it.[7] A whole cordon of protection was erected around it to save it from the indignities of accident and mishaps: falling off an altar, dropping out of an aged clerical hand, being rained upon when carried to the sick. There was thus a strong tension between the simplicity of the symbol – the fragile Eucharist – and the enormous claims made about it. This tension impressed and disturbed Christians and elicited an ongoing clerical attempt to protect the Eucharist while offering it as widely as possible.

But the Jew was central, too. It is therefore not surprising to find that as the eucharistic context of religious experience developed, this Christocentric interest drew in and defined a place for the Jew. In the early Middle Ages there were a number of widely told tales that juxtaposed Jew and Eucharist, and these adhered to the Augustinian representation of the Jew as witness to the truth of Christianity. Early medieval tales placed the Jew as a doubter of the Eucharist, whose doubts could be transformed into faith

---

6 On eucharistic theology, see G. Macy, *The Theologies of the Eucharist in the Early Scholastic Period* (Oxford, 1984), and on ideas and practices about the eucharist Miri Rubin, *Corpus Christi: The Eucharist in Late Medieval Culture* (Cambridge, 1991).

7 Rubin, *Corpus Christi*, esp. chap. 5.

through a vision or a miracle. Such a story appears in the earliest collection of eucharistic miracles, collated by Paschasius Radbert of the monastery of Corbie about 831 in order to bolster his arguments in a eucharistic debate.[8] This was the story of the Jewish boy[9] – a tale of Greek origin that had already been told by Gregory of Tours and that later traveled in a number of traditions until its incorporation, in the mid-twelfth century, into the repertoire of "Miracles of the Virgin," a collection of Marian tales compiled by Anselm, abbot of Bury Saint Edmunds, around 1140.[10]

It is the tale of a Jewish boy (in an Oriental city, in Burgos, in Bourges, in Pisa), who, after playing with his Christian friends at Christmas, followed his playmates into church and received communion with them. The story's eucharistic punch line comes when the boy, having returned home, told his parents what he had done, and, additionally, that he had seen the priest give every communicant a lovely little boy to eat. The angry Jewish father grabbed his son and threw him into the fire (the glazier-father's furnace,[11] the furnace for heating the Jewish ritual bath) where the child was protected by a lovely woman and was saved (Figure 13.1). The mother's cries summoned some Christian neighbors, who pulled the boy out of the oven to find him (miraculously) unscathed. The boy told them that a lovely lady (according to some versions, the lady he had earlier seen on the altarpiece in the church) had covered him with her mantle. The boy and his mother converted, with many other Jews, and, according to some versions, the father was thrown into the oven in turn.

This is a typical early medieval tale, with the hard-hearted Jewish father who fails to recognize truth, the innocent child to whom a divine truth is revealed, the wailing mother, and the Jews who convert after miraculous showing of Christian truth. The Eucharist is in the background; it is not abused. Once safely placed in the context of Marian legend, the story traveled widely, being translated in the thirteenth century into vernacular versions, such as Gautier of Coinci's *Miracles de Notre Dame* and the *Cantigas de Santa Maria* of Alfonso the Wise.[12]

---

8 Paschasius Radbert, "Liber de corpore et sanguine domini," chap. 9, no. 8, cols. 1298–9; B. Blumenkranz, *Le Juif médiéval au miroir de l'art chrétien* (Paris, 1966), 22–4.

9 T. Pelizaeus, *Beiträge zur Geschichte der Legende vom Judenknabe* (Halle, 1914); T. Nissen, "Zu den ältesten Fassungen der Legende vom Judenknaben," *Zeitschrift für französische Sprache und Literatur* 62 (1938–9): 393–403.

10 Gregory of Tours, "Libri miraculorum," bk. 1, "De gloria martyrum," chap. 10, cols. 714–15; R. W. Southern, "The English Origins of the 'Miracles of the Virgin,' " *Mediaeval and Renaissance Studies* 4 (1958): 176–216.

11 About the Jewish father as glazier, see M. Lillich, "Gothic Glaziers: Monks, Jews, Tax Payers, Bretons, Women," *Journal of Glass Studies* 27 (1985): 72–92.

12 On the dissemination of the tale, see E. Wolter, *Der Judenknabe* (Halle, 1879); Alfonso the Wise, *Cantigas de Santa Maria,* ed. W. Mettmann (Coimbra, 1959), vol. 1, no. 4, 11–14.

Figure 13.1. The miracle of the Jewish boy. Bibliothèque Royale Albert I / Koninklijke Bibliotheek Albert I, Brussels, ms 9229–30, fol. 12v. Reprinted by permission.

But a new tale was evolving in thirteenth-century Europe, the Europe of the Eucharist, of the Jewish–Christian disputations, of papal triumph, the century of inquisition, of elaborate state administrations, of the great councils, and of the greatest fears of heresy. The story was of a different type, with very different emphasis. It was geared not toward resolution but toward bloody confrontation, it was not merciful but violent, not revealing but damning, and it had no happy ending: it ended in torture and execution and death.[13] Its most famous elaboration is in the case of the rue des Billettes, the "Miracle of Paris" of 1290, by which time it was fully articulated, fully fledged. But before turning to it, let us consider some of the elements that were developing in the stories that related Jew and Eucharist early in the century.

Jewish encounters with the Eucharist gained in significance as the Eucharist rose in potency and came to symbolize the whole system of belief that the Jews were increasingly understood knowingly to reject.[14] Their rejection increasingly took the form of adversity in the present, in disputation, in harmful magic and murder, in abuse. It also touched upon the

13 B. Blumenkranz, *Juifs et chrétiens dans le monde occidental, 430–1096* (Paris, 1960), 144 note 76.
14 On the development of the idea of Jewish culpability, see J. Cohen, *The Friars and the Jews: The Evolution of Medieval anti-Judaism* (Ithaca, N.Y., 1982).

Eucharist.[15] Complex tales of new encounters were being constructed but still retained older elements. In 1213, Pope Innocent III wrote to Peter of Corbeil, the bishop of Sens, to recommend to him N., a young Jewish convert. He says that a Christian maid working for N.'s father had been deluded by Jewish error and was led to procure hosts at communion and to hand them over to the Jewish father. In haste, when called away, he mistakenly placed the host in a box containing 7 livres of Paris. When he returned and opened the box, he found that the coins had turned into hosts, and he could not distinguish the authentic ones from the others:

eam non utique denariies, sed hostiis, vidit plenam. . . . Quo eam discernere ab aliis non valente, circumstantes magnitudinem divini miraculi advertentes, deliberaverunt ad fidem accedere Christianam.[16]

(and he saw it full – not of coins – but of wafers. . . . When he was unable to distinguish this one from the others, the people standing about perceived the greatness of the divine miracle and decided to become converted to Christianity.)

The young man was among the witnesses to the miracle, and he went to Rome and received baptism. In his letter the pope was recommending N. for promotion and patronage at the hands of the bishop of Sens.[17] This tale recounts a eucharistic abuse by a Christian woman and the intention of further manipulation by the Jewish father. But the tone is neither fierce nor angry; this too has turned into a "happy-ending" tale of witnessing and conversion.

Much more dangerous than N.'s was another eucharistic encounter by a Cologne Jew, in a tale told by Herman (Hermannus) of Bologna.[18] Here, a Jew who was known for a propensity to discuss and argue on issues of religion with his Christian acquaintances disguised himself and approached the altar one day to receive communion from the priest's hands: "corpus Christi ore suo polluto de manu sacerdotis cum ceteris fidelibus sumpsit"

---

15 See the reasoning provided by the anonymous chronicler reporting the miracle of Paris of 1290: "De cujus eucharistiae ad animae vitam necessitate, ut olim, disserente Domino, venenati parentes offensi abierunt retrorsum, ita et de veritate illius dubii perstiterunt filii venenati Judaei," "De miraculo hostiae a Judaeo Parisiis anno Domini MCCXC multis ignominiis effectatae," in *Recueil des historiens des Gaules et de la France* (reprinted: Paris, 1968), 22:32.

16 "Innocenti III papae regstorum Lib. XVI," in J-P. Migne, ed., *Patrologiae cursus completus. Series Latina* (Paris, 1855), vol. 126, cols. 885–6; A. Grayzel, *The Church and the Jews in the Thirteenth Century* (Philadelphia, 1933), 137–40.

17 "Taliter facias in vitae necessariis provideri quod pro defectu temporalium retro aspicere non cogantur," "Innocenti . . . liber regestarum," col. 886. On the problem of financial support for converts, see J. Greatrex, "Monastic Charity for Jewish Converts in Thirteenth-Century England: The Requisition of Corrodies by Henry III," *Studies in Church History* 29 (1991): 133–43.

18 A. Hilka, ed., *Beiträge zur lateinische Erzählungsliteratur des Mittelalters,* vol. 3: *Das Viaticum Narrationum des Hermannus Bononiensis* (Berlin, 1935), no. 72, 100–1.

(he received Christ's body into his filthy mouth from the priest's hand with the other believers).[19]

He took the Eucharist out of his mouth and retired to a corner of the church and saw the host turn into a pretty little boy on the palm of his hand. A voice spoke to him (*in lingua Teutonica*), and when he tried to get rid of the host-boy by eating it, it hardened and fossilized and could not be chewed. The Jew tried to leave the churchyard, but every time he did so the devil appeared and threatened to accompany him. After (the usual) three repetitions, and in desperation, the Jew buried the child in the ground, but a voice followed him.[20] He called a passer-by and asked for the bishop, at whose feet he prostrated himself, begging for mercy.[21] The host was retrieved from the ground and was raised to heaven, while the Jew and many other Jews converted.[22] Again, a "happy ending," but the Jew was closer to abusing the host – not yet inflicting violence on it but receiving it falsely, handling it, burying it – many important breaches of the eucharistic code. In essence, this is still a story of witness, one that concentrates on the peculiar power of the Eucharist to encompass and demonstrate Christian truth.

As we progress in the century, stories of Jews and the Eucharist gain in their sense of danger and in the enormity of the transgression. We find evidence of the anxiety that exposure of the Eucharist to the Jewish gaze could evoke, in a variety of sources. A canon of the council of Vienna of 1267 required that Jews stay at home and close their windows and doors, after the sounding of the bells that announced the passage of a eucharistic procession to the sick.[23] In 1275, Bishop Giffard of Worcester sent a mandate to the deans of Westbury and Bristol to excommunicate some Jews of Bristol who had committed iniquities upon the body of Christ when it was being carried by the parish priest of Saint Peter's, in Bristol, to a sick person who resided *in placea iudaismi*.[24] Henry of Heimburg reports that in 1281 in Vienna, King Rudolf passed judgment in the case of a Jew who was alleged to have thrown stones at a priest carrying Christ's body.[25] At its most vul-

---

19 Ibid., 100.   20 The voice of the centurion: "Vere filius Dei erat iste," (Matthew 25:7).

21 "Domine, episcope, quaeso, miseremini mei," *Beiträge . . . Viaticum Narrationum,* 102.

22 "Propter quod multi Iudei crediderunt," ibid.

23 C.-J. Hefele and H. Leclercq, *Histoire des conciles* (Paris, 1914), chap. 6, no. 1, p. 138; on the council and its many canons relating to Jews, 133–9.

24 J. W. Willis Bund, ed., *Register of Bishop Godfrey Giffard* (Oxford, 1902), 1:71. See later examples in the records of the papal justices of the Avignon region in France, in the 1370s, in cases of Jews who refused to kneel before the passing eucharist; J. Chiffoleau, *Les Justices du pape: Délinquance et criminalité dans la région d'Avignon au quatorzième siècle* (Paris, 1984), 204.

25 "Rodulphus Romanorum rex post pasca inter alia iudicia, que fecit Wienne, fecit Iudeum quendam lapidibus obrui, qui fertur sacerdotem cum corpore dominico euntem luto nescio vel lapide vulnerasse"; "Heinrici de Heimburg Annales," in G. H. Pertz, ed., *MGH. Scriptores* (Hanover, 1861), 717.

nerable, when out of doors, when carried in the hand of the priest passing through muddy lanes, sometimes in the rain, at these moments, any movement, gesture, even the mere presence of Jews could irritate and kindle doubts and anxieties, tensions that were inherent in the very nature of the Eucharist.[26]

An early and short version, in a fragment from the Church of Saint Denis in Paris, simply stated that on Easter 1290 one of the city's Jews had procured a host and, with other Jews, put it into hot water, then cut it, only to see a flow of blood issue from it:

Quidam Judaei hostiam sacram a quodam pessimo habuerunt, quam in aquam calidam positam cum cultello percusserunt: de qua, virtute divina, sanguis copiose effluit in tantum, quod tota aqua rubefacta est.[27]

(Some Jews got the sacred host from some bad person and having put it in water they struck it with a knife: from it, by divine power, blood flowed copiously, until all the water became red.)

A later, longer version told of a Jew of the parish of Saint-Jeanen-Grève who procured a consecrated host from a Christian woman who had pawned clothes with him. He tempted her to exchange her clothes for the host and meant to test the power of the Eucharist:

cum muliercula quaedam tenuissimae fortunae vestes suas pignoris nomine pro summa xxx solidorum Parisiensium apud Judaeum quendam deposuisset, et ab eo ut inter vicinas cultior appareat, reposceret, gratis redditurum se Judaeus pollicetur, si rem illam, quam mulier Deum suum asserebat, afferet.[28]

(Since a certain woman of very slender means had deposited her clothes with a Jew as security for a loan of 30 shillings, and demanded them from him, so that she could look prettier among her neighbors; the Jew promised that he would return it to her for free if she were to bring to him that thing which she claimed to be her God.)

The Jew went on to abuse the host:

Corripit ergo cultellum pennarium que sacrosanctum Corpus arcae superpositum, diris transfigit ictibus, et ex ipso sacrum sanguinem copiose fluere conspiciens, uxori et filiis factum aperuit.[29]

---

26 These fears continued: see accusations against Jews in sixteenth-century Rome, N. Davidson, "The Inquisition and the Italian Jews," in S. Haliczer, ed., *Inquisition and Society in Early Modern Europe* (London, 1987), 40 note 39.

27 Under the year 1289, "Ex brevi chronico ecclesiae S. Dyonisii," in *Recueil des historiens des Gaules*, 23:145–6.

28 "De miraculo hostiae," 32. On the tale, see W. C. Jordan, *The French Monarchy and the Jews: From Philip Augustus to the Last Capetians* (Philadelphia, 1989), 193–4, and on women and moneylending, see W. C. Jordan, "Women and Credit in the Middle Ages: Problems and Directions," *Journal of European Economic History* 17 (1988): 33–62.

29 "De miraculo hostiae," 32.

(He snatched a penknife with which he pierced through Christ's sacrosanctum body, with terrible blows, and seeing that holy blood issued from it copiously, he disclosed the fact to his wife and children.)

The host then turned into a crucifix. The Jew's son informed the Christian congregation, rushing to see the Eucharist in the parish church, that Christ was in fact in his own house:

frustra in ecclesia illa Christianos Deum suum quaerere ait, quem flagellatum, injuriis affectum et male tractatum, modo pater suus occidisset.[30]

(he said to the Christians, "You seek your God in this church in vain, since after it was struck, injured, and maltreated, my father has just killed him.")

A woman came to check the house and took the host to the church; the bishop was summoned, the Jew was burned and his family converted, along with many other Jews.

A few years later, Pope Boniface VIII allowed a chapel to be built on the site of the Jew's house, and it was constructed at the expense of one of the richest men of Paris, Renier de Flamenc.[31] The "holy knife" with which the abuse was allegedly perpetrated became an object of veneration and was also kept in the chapel.[32] The story was reported in the major French chronicles of the Ile-de-France and soon in Flemish ones too.[33] Writing in 1294, John of Thilrode, monk of Saint Bavo, Ghent, could report from Parisian documents that the woman was the Jew's maid and that the Jew meant to test the host:

quidam Iudeus commorans Parisius christianam habebat ancillam, erga quam hostiam emit pro 10 libras consecratam. Ipso vero hostiam consecratam suo domino presentavit; quo facto, predictam hostiam posuit in mensam ac alios Iudeos fecit convocari, dicens: "Numquid non sunt stulti christiani in hanc hostiam credentes?" Accipientes cultellos et stilos ac instrumenta alia hostiam delere volebant; quod facere non potuerunt.[34]

(a Jew living in Paris had a Christian maid, and it is she who bought a consecrated host for 10 pounds. She presented the host to her master. After that he put the same host on a table and assembled other Jews, saying, "Are not the Christians stupid to believe in this host?" Taking knives and stakes and other instruments, they wished to destroy the host, but this they could not achieve.)

30 Ibid.
31 S. Simonsohn, ed., *The Apostolic See and the Jews: Documents, 492–1404* (Toronto, 1984), no. 175, 283–4.
32 See description of the cult in A. Tuetey, *Journal d'un bourgeois de Paris, 1405–1449* (Paris, 1881), 372; P. Perdrizet, *Le Calendrier parisien à la fin du moyen-âge d'après le breviaire et les livres d'heures* (Paris, 1933), 158–60.
33 P. Hidiroglou, "Les Juifs d'après la littérature historique latine de Philippe Auguste à Philippe le Bel," *Revue des études juives* 133 (1974): 419–21.
34 "Iohannis de Thilrode Chronicon," in J. Heller, ed., *MGH. Scriptores* (Hanover, 1880), 25:578.

Figure 13.2. The Miracle of Paris. From Giovanni Villani, "Chroniche di Giovanni,
Matteo e Filippo Villani," Biblioteca Apostolica Vaticana, Chigi ms LVIII 296, fol.
149v. Reprinted by permission.

The story spread quickly, through a variety of media. When working in
the Low Countries in the 1320s, Giovanni Villani probably picked it up and
later inserted it into his chronicle, under the year 1290, as "D'uno grande
miracolo ch'avvenne in Parigi del corpo di Cristo" (Figure 13.2).[35] This
version now told of a Jewish usurer who procured the host by compelling
a Christian woman who had pawned her clothes with him: "Se tu mi rechi
il corpo del vostro Cristo, io ti renderò i tuoi panni senza denari" (If you
bring me the body of your Christ, I shall return your clothes to you free of
charge).[36]

The *semplice femmina* did so, and the Jew proceeded to boil the host in a
cauldron, stab it with a knife until it bled, and throw it into cold water, only
to see it bleed. Christians coming to borrow money discovered the crime,
the Jew was caught and burned, and the host was taken to a church built
on the site of the Jew's home. Villani's version provided the basis for a *sacra
rappresentazione* by the mid-fifteenth century. This in turn inspired the

35 *Croniche di Giovanni, Matteo e Filippo Villani* (Trieste, 1857), chap 143, 166. For an illustrated manuscript of the chronicle, see L. Magnani, *La cronaca figurativa di Giovanni Villani* (Vatican City, 1936),
   Figure xl.
36 *Croniche di Giovanni, Matteo e Fillipo Villani*, chap. 143, 166.

Figure 13.3. The profanation of the host. *Predella* (scene 2) of the altarpiece by Paolo Uccello. Galleria Nazionale della Marche, Palazzo Ducale, Urbino. Reprinted by permission.

choice of scenes, and mis-en-scène, by Paolo Uccello when he painted his six *predelle* for the altarpiece of the Corpus Christi confraternity of Urbino in 1465–8 (Figure 13.3).[37] There was a fifteenth-century French version, *Le Jeu de la Sainte Hostie,* and an English version of about 1461, the Croxton *Play of the Sacrament.*[38]

During the very late thirteenth century, a well-known case involved a Jew who was accused and found guilty of procuring the host through manipulation of a Christian woman, of repeated and various abuses, and of inflicting pains on the Eucharist. All his pains could produce was the unequivocal miraculous demonstration of the substance of Christ's blood in the Eucharist, and they brought about his arrest and death. As in earlier cases, the wife and daughter converted, but this is an element that will be transformed throughout the Middle Ages; by the mid-fifteenth century, at

37 M. A. Lavin, "The Altar of Corpus Christi in Urbino: Paolo Uccello, Joos Van Ghent, Piero della Francesca," *Art Bulletin* 49 (1967): 1–10; M. A. Goukovsky, "A Representation of the *Profanation of the Host:* A Puzzling Painting in the Hermitage and Its Possible Author," *Art Bulletin* 51 (1969): 170–3.

38 L. Muir, "The Mass on the Medieval Stage," *Comparative Drama* 23 (1989–90): 317; S. Beckwith, "Ritual, Church and Theatre: Medieval Dramas of the Sacramental Body," in D. Aers, ed., *Culture and History, 1350–1600* (London, 1992).

Uccello's hand, the whole family will burn for a crime that was obviously committed by its head.

It is difficult to determine the exact trails of dissemination of a story; we find versions in many forms and all over Europe. For its use in the German-speaking realm, it need not have arrived as a version of the Miracle of Paris; it probably developed quite independently, in ways that we have already discerned. It would also have been received against the background of cases of ritual-murder accusation. By the later thirteenth century, Germany knew the cases of Margaret of Pforzheim (1267), Little John of Cologne, and Werner of Oberwesel (both, 1287).[39] News of an accusation could travel through preachers, merchants, within a religious order, and it could become authoritative, written down to be told and retold, and it could have motivated further action. The news of the host desecration in Büren (Westphalia), in 1292, was probably the event referred to at the foundation of the new feast of Corpus Christi in the diocese of Paderborn, as stated in an episcopal indulgence for the support of the new shrine: "maxime propter varias negligencias, quae in diocesi nostra contiguerunt, heu per Judaeos quam per alios, qui hoc sanctissimum viaticum indigne tractaverunt" (above all because of various negligences which occurred in our diocese, both by Jews and by others, who treated irreverently this most sacred viaticum).[40]

It traveled through the mediation of preachers, like Giordano da Rivalto (da Pisa) who in Florence, in 1304, preached about the recent events that had followed a host desecration by Jews (probably the Rintfleisch massacres):

io era in quelle contrade quando fu che un Guideo mandò una sua fante alla chiesa de'cristiani e fece e procurò sì o per pecunia o per altra malizia, che si fece venire il Corpo di Cristo.

(I was in that region when it came to pass that a Jew sent his maid to the Christian church and made it happen, either by the offer of money or by some other evil, that she brought Christ's body.)

He goes on to tell of the appearance of a little child (*un fanciullo*) after the abuse and the subsequent revenge taken by a pious layman (*ispiritual persona*), who put to death twenty-four thousand Jews.[41] The authority of the host-desecration tale developed as it entered a variety of contexts, as it formed

---

39 G. R. Schroubek, "Zur Verehrungsgeschichte des Andreas von Rinn," pts. 1–2, *Tiroler Kulturzeitschrift: Das Fenster* 38 (1985): 3845–55, 39 (1988): 3766–74; E. Iserloh, "Werner von Oberwese: Zur Tilgung seines Festes im Trierer Kalender," *Trierer theologische Zeitschrift* 72 (1963): 270–85. There was soon to be the case of Konrad of Weissensee in 1303.

40 F. Fürstenburg, "Zur Geschichte der Fronleichnamsfeier in der alten Diözese Paderborn," *Theologie und Glaube* 9 (1917): 316; P. Bauerreiss, *Pie Jesu* (Munich, 1931), 59.

41 Giordano da Rivalto (da Pisa), *Prediche*, ed. D. Moreni (Florence, 1831), 2:227–8. On Giordano, see C. Delcorno, *Giordano da Pisa e l'antica predicazione volgare* (Florence, 1975).

part of "local knowledge" – the taken-for-granted truths about the world.[42] Thus, in a collection of legal precedents from the town of Brünn of the early fourteenth century, there is a section "De poena subtrahantis sacramentum eucharistiae," which reports the case of two scholars who stole four consecrated hosts from the parish church and attempted to sell them to the Jews. The (wise) Jews refused to do business and reported the scholars to the authorities. The legal point that was being made here was that the scholars should be liable not simply for the crime of theft but for the intention to sell the Eucharist.[43]

Before we go on to examine some of the accounts of the host-desecration tale in German towns, it would be useful to remember that while looking at the construction of the accusations we must bear in mind a variety of factors that constituted the experiences of Jewish–Christian relations. It is important to remember the encounters between Christian artisans and laborers and the Jewish providers of subsistence loans, and the economic straits that the gentry and those with aspirations to gentility encountered when land values fell. We must bear in mind a political system that placed towns and territorial lords in an adversarial position but that sometimes permitted collaboration in a struggle against imperial ambitions.[44] These were the somewhat similar but always divergent elements that created the context for the unfolding of an accusation, for each exercise in the collective mounting of an accusation. Going against the grain and resisting the force of the tale, we will attempt, when possible, to unearth divergences and dissents from the tale, the imperfect telling of an accusation, and the saving of lives.

The first great massacre in German lands related to an accusation of host desecration has come to be named after its leader, Rintfleisch, whom some will have an urban butcher but who was most probably a member of the lower-Franconian gentry.[45] The massacres began in Röttingen on the river Tauber in April 1298 and continued in three waves over two years, rav-

---

42 J. Berlioz, "Le Récit efficace: L'exemplum au service de la prédication (xiiie–xve siècle)," *Mélanges de l'Ecole français de Rome. Moyen-âge – temps modernes* 92 (1980): 113–46.

43 "Voluntas venditionis gravior est judicando, quam actus furti," in the town's *Schöffenbuch*. See E. F. Rossler, ed., *Deutsche Rechtdenkmäler aus Böhmen and Mähren*, vol. 2: *Die Stadtrechte von Brünn aus den XIII. u. XIV. Jahrhundert* (Prague, 1852), no. 544, 258–9.

44 See S. Jenks's analysis in "Judenverschuldung und Verfolgung von Juden in Franken im 14. Jahrhundert," *Vierteljahresschrift für Sozial- und Wirtschaftsgeschichte* 56 (1978): 309–56.

45 For an authoritative study of the sources and establishment of the sequences, see F. Lotter, "Hostienfrevelvorwurf und Blutwunderfälschung bei den Judenverfolgungen von 1298 (Rintfleisch) und 1336–1338 (Armleder)," in *Fälschungen im Mittelalter* (Munich, 1988), 5:548–60, and on the sources, see 550 note 57. F. Graus, *Pest – Geissler – Judenmorde: Das 14. Jahrhundert als Krisenzeit* (Göttingen, 1987), 290–2. For a map of the itinerary of the massacres, see *Germania Judaica*, vol. 2, no. 1 (Tübingen, 1968).

aging Franconia and spilling into Bavaria, destroying some 146 Jewish communities and at least three thousand people.[46]

Besides the rather laconic entries in many of the chronicles, there is an unusual source of information on these massacres and their aftermath. This is a book of tales composed by a Dominican friar, Rudolf, who was prior of the house of Schlettstadt from 1294.[47] It is a collection of stories of extraordinary events, prodigies that occurred in the fin de siècle: of Jews, witches, spirits, demons, knowledge transmitted to him by knights and other members of his order.[48] The fifty-six tales tell of events that supposedly occurred in the years 1284 through 1303, and they include a number of cases related to Rintfleisch, as well as a story of ritual murder and one about the murder of a Jew.[49] The book explored the world of religious tales, of beliefs and rumors, that circulated in the area where this persecution took place and attempted to give it meaning and justification. This is a very readable account, in lively and simple Latin; a book for young scholars, parish priests, and even townsmen with some Latin training.

According to Rudolf, the beginning of the massacres was this: having procured the host from a "perverse" Christian, a Jew put it on a table and "tested" it with a knife, but when he wounded it, it bled. He tried again, and it started crying like a little boy "trium circiter annorum" (of about three years). He hurt it again, and it cried again. The Jew continued to cut the host into three and again heard the lamenting voice of a child. Female neighbors were surprised to hear a child's voice from a house in which no child was living and sent one of their own children to check. They also called the butcher Rintfleisch to check whether or not a child was being killed by the Jews. He approached the door but was not let in, cried out, and the poor of the neighborhood came to him, caught the Jew, brought him to justice, and finally put him to death. When people from the vicinity heard of this event, they fell upon their Jews and burned their houses and their bodies.[50]

For Rudolf of Schlettstadt, the killing was intuitively executed by people who only later were to find proof of the justness of their cause. In their destroyed Jewish houses, remains of hosts that had been procured by the Jews were discovered:

---

46 *Germania Judaica*, vol. 2, no. 2, 719–20; S. Salfeld, ed., *Das Martyrologium des Nürnberger Memorbuches* (Berlin, 1898), 164–200 and 231–6. News had reached Bohemia, too, and the fearful Jewish community was pressured into paying King Wenzel protection money, just in case; F. Graus, *Struktur und Geschichte. Drei Volksaufstände im mittelalterlichen Prag* (Sigmaringen, 1971), 49.

47 On Rudolf, see E. Kleinschmidt's introduction to his edition of Rudolf of Schlettstadt, *Historiae memorabiles* (Cologne, 1974), 9–12.

48 Ibid., 14–15.   49 Ibid., 18.   50 Ibid., chap. 6, 49–51.

[Iudei] furati sunt plus quam centum hostias consecratas, que postea in domibus eorum in destructione. . . Nam in pluribus locis sacramentum Cristi diversis modis obtinuerint et illud in locis turpissimis absconderunt.[51]

([The Jews] stole more than one hundred consecrated hosts, which were later found in the ruins in their houses. . . . Since in many places they had obtained Christ's sacrament by various means, and hid it in the most filthy places.)

According to the Chronicle of Saint Peter's in Erfurt, ongoing revelations provided fresh reasons to go on with the killing:

Christiani namque, ut dicitur, post interfectionem ipsorum ipsa secreciora eorundem purgantes invenerunt corpus Christi plurimis locis confossum, illudque pro sacramento habentes loca eadem dicunt miraculis choruscare.[52]

(Because, as it is said, after the killing [of the Jews], the Christians who cleared out their most secret places found Christ's body, which they took to be the sacrament, buried in numerous places, and in those places they say that miracles take place.)

To act out the story of host desecration was to relive stories heard in the past; it was to become part of a chain of events that fell in neatly with religious practice, supernatural assumptions, and the expression of an aggression: against Jews, the town council, the emperor. The narrative had to be chosen and to fit at least some of the circumstances at hand, and the most authoritative tellers of tales of this kind were priests. In many cases reported by Rudolf, a neighbor (often a woman) reports the first signs to a priest who is called in to advise. In Iphofen, the house of a Jew who had fled because of the rumors of massacres in the region was left empty, and two boys played around it as they always had done. Looking into the house, they saw a lovely boy (*puer pulcherrimum*), but when they called their father he could see nothing (again, the *topos* of a child's privileged vision), so he went back to work in his garden. The boys then saw a beautifully dressed lady, whom again their father could not see. But things were strange enough for the neighbors to decree: "Sine dubio in hac domo est absconditum dominicum sacramentum. Vocamus igitur sacerdotem" (Without doubt, the Lord's sacrament is hidden in this house. Let us then call a priest.)[53] The priest came and found three hosts and gave orders for a proper ritual setting to be created: torches to be brought, hangings, and a bell to ring the host's presence.[54]

These were violent and insecure days. The imperial throne was being contested by Albert of Habsburg and Adolf of Nassau, a struggle concluded at the battle of Göllheim on July 2, 1298, with Albert's ascendancy. It meant

---

51 Ibid., chap. 5, 49.
52 "Cronica S. Petri Erfordensis," in O. Holder-Egger, ed., *MGH. Scriptores rerum germanicarum* (Hanover, 1899), 42:319.
53 Rudolf of Schlettstadt, *Historiae memorabiles*, chap. 8, 52.   54 Ibid., chap. 8, 53.

that proper procedures for protection of the Jews and proper episcopal attention to the authorization of cults did not function as they might have done at other times. A few years later, an interesting Austrian case shows that the very question of authority over interpretation of the eucharistic findings could be contested. In the autumn of 1305, in Klosterneuburg, not far from Vienna, we are told that ten Jews had been killed following a host-desecration accusation some six to seven years earlier.[55] The bishop of Passau instituted an investigation into the affair, and the report of Ambrose of the Holy Cross, the Cistercian examiner, has survived. A bloodied fraction of a host, found on the threshold of a Jew's house, was taken to church as a miraculous relic, just as the Jew was led to the pyre:

Ante vi vel septem annos ... in domo quadam iudeorum deprehensum fuit et inventa est quedam oblata, immo tercia tantum particula unius oblate involuta panniculo et sanguine conspersa.[56]

(Some six or seven years earlier ... in a Jewish house a certain [Jew] was seized, snatched away, and a certain host was found, at least a third of a single host, wrapped in a cloth and sprinkled with blood.)

The initiative here had been taken by the citizens ("cives civitatis"), who summoned the parish priest and his clerks ("plebanus et cleric venientes"). The crucial question was not whether the Jew should be blamed for a host found near his house but whether the host particle had indeed been consecrated. The investigator was thorough in his questioning of the many witnesses who rushed to him when he came to investigate the three-year-old case, and he heard stories of blind people gaining their sight, the curing of the lame and paralytic, the liberation of the possessed, and of candles that spontaneously lit up when near the miraculous particle. But Ambrose was still doubtful; he insisted that "de cuius tum consecracione nil poenitus sciebatur" (nothing about its consecration was decisively known). Thus he incurred the wrath of the townsfolk:

Exorto quoque contra me odio Civium prefatorum, quas ego apponerem iudeis et processum negocii impedirem reversus sum ad Claustrum et pro excusacione mea sequens opusculum compilavi.[57]

(Having incurred the said citizens' wrath, as if I sided with the Jews and impeded the course of justice, I returned to Klosterneuburg and, to justify myself, have compiled this little work.)

---

55 As added to the Salzburg Annals for the year 1305: "Item eodem anno inventum est corpus Christi in Neuburga a parte fori contemptum a Iudeis, feria sexta quatuor temporum ante festum michahelis, et Iudei ibidem omnes cremati sunt," in "Continuatio Zwetlensis III," in W. Wattenbach, ed., *MGH. Scriptores* (Hanover, 1851), 9:662.
56 H. Zeibig, ed., *Urkundenbuch des Stiftes Klosterneuburg bis zum Ende des vierzehnten Jahrhunderts* (Vienna, 1868), 2:172–5, 174.   57 Ibid., 175.

In his report he insisted that the issue should be dealt with finally by a papal investigation.[58] In Klosterneuburg, then, the narrative was far from straightforward.

The recommendation to pass such difficult issues of deciphering to papal authority was followed, by the next bishop of Passau, in dealing with a difficult case of suspected fraud in Pulkau (Upper Austria) in 1338. Suspicions moved Duke Albert II to write to the pope with a request for an investigation of the events in a year when Easter coincided with the Jewish Passover.[59] In his mandate, Benedict XII reminded the bishop of recent cases of dubious attribution of miraculous status to hosts desecrated by Jews, mentioning the case "in opido Newmburch" (Klosterneuburg) as notorious:

quedam hostia non consecrata madefacta cruore, per quemdam clericum in ecclesia dicti opidi posita fuit.[60]

(a certain unconsecrated host drenched in blood was put in the church of the said town by a certain priest.)

In Pulkau, in 1338, the accusation was

Pulka in quodam opido, nomire quedam hostia cruore conspersa ante domum cuiusdam Iudei extra tamen limites eius, in strata sub paleis a quodam laico fuit inventa, quam populus dicti opidi, verum corpus Dominicum fore credentes, per manus sacerdotis loci tollere fecerunt, et in eccelsiam transportarunt.[61]

(in a town by the name of Pulkau . . . a certain host sprinkled with blood was found by a layman in front of a Jewish house, albeit outside on its threshold, in the street under some straw; and because the people of the said town thought it to be the Lord's real body, they had it carried in the priest's hand and transported to the church.)

The chronicler John of Winterthur also laid the deceit on an indigent priest:

Iudeorum tribulatio orta est propter quendam sacerdotem nimia inopia oppressum, qui hostiam sanguine aspersit et a se proiectam iuxta Iudeos ipsos suspectos reddidit et graviter infamavit. Que cum reverencia maxima ad ecclesiam predicti malefici prespiteri delata et deducta fuisset et ibi collocata, a populo tocius terre circomposite frequentabatur sacrificiisque et oblacionibus devotissime venerabatur.[62]

(The tribulation of the Jews was occasioned by a certain priest of very slender means, who had sprinkled a host with blood and then thrown it near the Jews, ren-

58 See K. Lohrmann, *Judenrecht und Judenpolitik im mittelalterlichen Österreich* (Cologne, 1990), 105; Lotter, "Hostienfrevelvorwurf," 559–60.
59 *Germania Judaica,* vol. 2, no. 2, 665–6.
60 Simonsohn, ed., *Apostolic See,* no. 354, 372–4, at 372.
61 Ibid. The pope wrote to the duke and informed him of the action taken; Simonsohn, ed., *Apostolic See,* no. 355, 374–5.
62 C. Brun and F. Baethgen, eds., *Die Chronik Johanns von Winterthur* (Berlin, 1924), 142–3.

dering those Jews as suspects and gravely defaming them. And since that host was borne and led with greatest reverence to that evil priest's own church and was placed there, it was visited by people from the whole surrounding region and was venerated most devoutly with offerings and oblations.)

He thus totally exonerates the Jews and sees the simple folk as the real victims of the fraud:

Qui postquam populum christianum diu delusisset sub specie simplicis panis pretendentis verum corpus Christi et consecratum . . . perpetravit in sue anime et innumerabilium animarum periculum et perdicionem . . . dum supersticionis et ydolatrie causam scienter motus avaricia, que est ydolarum servitus, dedisset.[63]

(And after this the Christian people were deceived for a long time, simple bread under the appearance of simple bread pretending to be the real and consecrated body of Christ, perpetrated in the people's heart and in the heart of many others danger and perdition . . . as it gave cause to superstition and idolatry, because of avarice, which is the servant of idols.)

In fact, the bishop of Passau had been so concerned that the host might be nothing but bread painted red that, to avoid idolatry on the part of its worshipers, he placed an authentic consecrated host beside the "found" (*inventa*), "miraculous" one, for simultaneous adoration:

veniens quoque episcopus Pataviensis, in cuius erat diocesi propter maiorem cautelam a tergo circa hostiam inventam aliam hostiam cosecratam apponi mandavit, timens ne populus idolatriae commiteret crimen.[64]

(and the bishop of Passau, whose diocese it was, arrived, and for the sake of greater safety he ordered that another, consecrated host be placed behind the "found" one, fearing lest the people commit the crime of idolatry.)

The presence of such scrutiny could sometimes make a difference in allowing an accusation to succeed or to be thwarted. But the examiner sent to Pulkau was not of the disposition of Ambrose of the Holy Cross. Frederick, Doctor of Canon Law and canon of Bamberg Cathedral, wrote his report in 1341.[65] The tract is a dialogue between doctor and pupil in ten points. The first five points deal with the nature of the Eucharist in general. He states forcefully that those who are loath to avenge offenses against it are as bad as the Jews and are motivated by greed (an argument we found veiled in complaints against Ambrose of the Holy Cross in 1305):

63 Ibid., 143. Also, see Lotter, "Hostienfrevelvorwurf," 578–9.
64 J. Loserth, ed., *Die Königsaaler Geschichts-Quellen mit den Zusätzen und der Vorsetzung des Domherrn Franz von Prag* (Vienna, 1875), 559.
65 Austrian National Library, ms 350, fols. 1ra–17vb; this manuscript originally belonged to Salzburg Cathedral. I owe my acquaintance with this work to an article by M. Anselgruber, who has treated it very closely (see following footnote).

Sed principes et magnates, quos seva cupiditas, que est radix omnium viciorum, ex-cecavit . . . nec, heu, malicia istorum blasphemorum pena condigna plectitur.[66]

(But the princes and the magnates, whom raging cupidity, the root of all evils, had blinded . . . and alas, the malice of these blasphemies was not fittingly punished.)

He was obviously railing against magnates such as Duke Albert, whom he saw as being committed to the Jews through financial dependence, an accusation that recurred in other contexts. At the eighth point Frederick reached the heart of the matter; he recounted the accusation that Christ's body had been found in Pulkau under a manure heap, where it had been hidden by Jews once blood issued from it:

factum fuit, quia corpus Christi a Iudeis attractatum sub sterquilinio fuit inventum in Pulcha et fimo contectum et perfidi Iudei ibi proiecerant et fimum superiecer-ant, et, ut sic obtegerent et occultarent sanguinem defluentem.[67]

(It so happened, because Christ's body, which had been brought by the Jews, was discovered in a dung heap in Pulkau, hidden in dung, and the perfidious Jews threw it there and had covered it with dung, in order thus to cover and hide the flowing blood.)

This version differs from the one reported to and by Benedict XII, and from other contemporary accounts, like that of the annals of nearby Zwettl:

reperta est in Pulka in domo cuiusdam Iudei hostia tota cruentata, et multis mira-culis approbata, et non solum ab indigenis, verum etiam ab omnibus circumquaque terrarum populis humiliter visitata et devote venerata. Propter quod factum chris-tiani zelo divino permoti . . . omnes Iudeos in Pulka, Retz, Znoyma, Horn, Egen-burga, Neunburga, Zwetl occiderunt et combusserunt et in pulverem redegerunt.[68]

(A host was found in the house of a Jew of Pulkau, totally stained with blood, and shown to be true by many miracles, and it was humbly visited and devoutly ven-erated not only by the poor, but truly by all the people of surrounding lands. And the zeal of Christians was so moved by this fact . . . that they killed and burned all the Jews in Pulkau, Retz, Znoyma, Horn, Egenburg, Neuenburg, and Zwettl, re-ducing them to dust.)

But even without the evidence of the latrine, to Frederick the fact that miracles had followed was sufficient evidence of the previous abuse inflicted on the hosts. We know nothing of the subsequent actions of the papacy or

---

66 M. Anselgruber, "Die angebliche Hostienschändung in Pulkau 1338," unpublished paper (1990), 7 note 15 (fol. 1va). This type of accusation against magnates, protectors of Jews, is an old one; see A. Abulafia, "Christian Imagery of Jews in the Twelfth Century: A Look at Odo of Cambrai and Guibert of Nogent," *Theoretische Geschiedenis* 16 (1989): 383–91.

67 Anselgruber, "Die angebliche," 12 note 26.

68 "Annales Zwetlenses," in Wattenbach, ed., *MGH. Scriptores* (1851), 9:683; *Germania Judaica*, vol. 2, no. 2, 665–6, and see map of massacres on 667.

the bishop. This is the version that in fact held, since Pulkau became a great pilgrimage center and from 1396 boasted a new chapel, the Blood Chapel (Blutkapelle).

The episodes of Klosterneuburg and of Pulkau are cases in which divergent authorities clashed over the stories of host desecration. These struggles usually took place well after the killing of Jews, but at least they indicate that for some the stories did not work. The accusations offered other sensibilities and other interests: ducal prerogative in deciding the fate of his Jews, and clerical anxiety about expressions of misguided religious sentiments. The former context was created in Saint Pölten, just a year after the report from Klosterneuburg.[69] Here the duke, at the instigation of his father, King Rudolf, responded swiftly to the massacre of Jews at the hand of the burgesses following the accusation of host desecration:

Nam cum apud Sanctum Ypolitum inimici crucis Christi Iudei comperti fuissent, ut antea perpluries impune fecerant alias, blasphemiam et ludibrium sacramento dominici corporis irrogasse, fideles fidei zelo accensi, commoto in eos impetu aliquos trucidaverunt.[70]

(Since in St. Pölten the enemies of the cross, the Jews, were found out, and before that they had frequently committed other things with impunity, inflicting blasphemy and mockery on the sacrament of the Lord's body, the faithful, burning with zeal for the faith and moved by a force within them massacred them.)

Duke Rudolf laid siege to the town ("crudelissima obsidione affixit"), an enclave of episcopal jurisdiction within his territory. He succeeded in forcing on the lord of the town, the bishop of Passau, a fine of 3,500 pounds for the offense against the Jews. But the chronicler could tell that the duke's untimely death, soon after this, was his punishment for having protected the Jews. These had returned to the town in 1309, only to be decimated again in the aftermath of the Pulkau accusation.

Imperial authority could also be tested in the wake of such events. Rudolf of Schlettstadt reports that after his coronation and during the events of the Rintfleisch uprising, King Albert sent a representative, the lord of Rinsperch, to Würzburg to defend the Jews there. The emissary consulted local allies as to the best strategy to follow. But he suffered a bad accident while in the neighborhood, and Albert, a Dominican friar, was sent to hear his confession. The friar promised him life after confession. He confessed that his mission had been "Defensio Judeorum, que michi in animo et consciencia mea plurimum contradicit" (the defense of the Jews, which was ex-

69 *Germania Judaica*, vol. 2, no. 2, 735–6.
70 "Continuatio Zwetlensis III," 663; Lohrmann, *Judenrecht und Judenpolitik*, 118.

ceedingly objectionable to me, in my mind and conscience), and the friars suggested "quod eam subito resignetis et servire vos deo fideliter promittetis" (that you resign it quickly and promise to devote yourself to God faithfully).[71] The royal servant recovered, but this story highlights the sort of local pressures that could be brought to bear on a royal representative working against local sentiment (whipped up by the local Dominicans). This may explain why action by King Rudolf had been so slow, even after the resolution of the dynastic contest.

In the face of accusations against Jews and the attendant uprising to which they had led, town authorities had to take a position on the events and on the underlying accusations. In the wake of the Rintfleisch massacres, Rothenburg had been attacked on June 25, when a large number of Jews had escaped with some help from townsfolk.[72] When it was attacked again on July 18, the majority of Jews hid in the castle, but this fell four days later, and 370 Jews were killed.[73] In the next large town on the attack route, Würzburg, there was full collaboration with Rintfleisch: "Judei cum Herbipoli a carnifice Rintflaisch interficerentur" (the Würzburg Jews were butchered by Rintfleisch), and when a Jewess was found "convocato Rindflaisch eam sibi comiserunt" (having called Rintfleisch, they handed her over).[74] The Jews of the town had obviously understood how hopeless their situation was, since they started to kill their families and themselves rather than fall into the hands of the famous butcher. The behavior of the town here was obviously directed by the burghers' long-standing conflict over rights with their lord, the bishop. These struggles often centered on the duty to collect Jewish taxes or to spend money on their protection.[75] In 1337, the townspeople would withstand the attack of the Armleder mob.[76]

As the murderers of 1298 moved farther into the Jagst Valley, refugees had congregated in the town of Wildstein, and here the Jews received help from the townspeople before the town fell to the besiegers. The events of Nuremberg followed, on August 1, and were even more distinctive: here the mayor and the castellan let the Jews into the castle, but townsmen (and their names suggest artisan status) fell on the Jews and murdered them. Here

---

71 Rudolf of Schlettstadt, *Historiae memorabiles,* chap. 14, 62.

72 *Germania Judaica,* vol. 2, no. 2, 707.

73 The town was obviously divided on the issue. See the evidence of a Jewish tombstone, F. Lotter, "Die Judenverfolgung des 'König Rintfleisch' in Franken um 1298. Die endgültige Wende in den christlich-jüdischen Beziehungen im Deutschen Reich des Mittelalters," *Zeitschrift für historische Forschung* 15 (1988): 385–422; 406 note 71.

74 Rudolf of Schlettstadt, *Historiae memorabiles,* chap. 11, 58.

75 Lotter, *Die Judenverfolgung,* 410.

76 K. Arnold, "Die Armledererhebung in Franken 1336," *Mainfränkisches Jahrbuch für Geschichte und Kunst* 26 (1974): 35–62, 48.

the king was quick to fine the town and order the banishment of the culprits; this was facilitated by the help of royal officials in the town, who had defended the Jews.[77] Regensburg and Augsburg, next, were able to resist successfully.

Even in the heat of a popular uprising under the banner of revenge on the Jews, some killings were contested, and other courses of action could suggest themselves as powerfully as the call for blood. The burgesses of Regensburg had decided to resist the killers, in the name of the town's honor, as put by Eberhard, archdeacon of Regensburg:

Cives tamen Ratisponenses, suam volentes honorare civitatem, ipsos Iudeos absque iudicio occidi et destrui vetuerunt, dicentes, quod voluntati Dei in Iudeorum interfectione nollent resistere, sed expectare, donec de hoc, quod hec vindicta esset a Domino, eis fieret maior fides. Et sic Iudei Ratisponenses, licet, cum multa difficultate, usque hodie incendium evaserunt.[78]

(The citizens of Regensburg, wishing to honor their city, refused to kill and destroy these Jews without trial, saying that they did not wish to resist God's wish in the killing of Jews, but rather to wait and see, up to the time when this be revenged by the Lord, when it would be of greater faith to them. And so the Jews of Regensburg, not without much difficulty, have avoided the fire until this very day.)

In Augsburg the Jews were saved, defended by the townsfolk, on the condition that they maintain a section of the town wall.

A look at some of the events of 1298, the year of the greatest regional massacre since the First Crusade, one that might have spread all over the empire had the succession crisis not been resolved, reveals elements that recurred in many late medieval persecutions. The impulse to avenge host desecration was always mediated in local contexts but was also universal. The story told about the Jews and the Eucharist could fit anywhere; it was made of the building blocks of Christian dogma and popular religious practice. Accordingly, we find that the spread, application, and reenactment of this impulse in whole regions followed the universal logic of revenge. The universal applicability of the accusation of host desecration made it everyone's issue. When some refugees from Franconia reached Constance, they were asked by a knight where they had come from, and they answered that they had escaped from Rintfleisch. The knight pressed them for the reason for their persecution. When they could not offer one, he had the older Jew burned and turned to the younger, who duly "confessed."

77 A. Müller, *Geschichte der Juden in Nürnberg, 1146–1945* (Nuremberg, 1968), 23.
78 "Eberhardi archidiaconi Ratisponensis annales," in Pertz, ed., *MGH. Scriptores,* (1861), 597; H. Fischer, *Die Verfassungsrechtliche Stellung der Juden in den deutschen Städten während des dreizehnten Jahrhunderts* (Breslau, 1931), 57–8.

Anni quindecim transierunt, quod nos Judei in diocesi Herbipolensi comperavimus hostiam, quam sacerdotes Cristianorum consecrant in Jhesum Cristum. Quam cum habuissemus, supremus noster nos congregavit et coram nobis stantibus hostiam manu levavit et manu secunda cultellum tenens in eam fixit. Et continuo ex ea sanguis largiter emanavit.[79]

(Fifteen years have passed since we, the Jews of the diocese of Würzburg obtained a host, which Christian priests consecrate into Jesus Christ. . . . When we had it, our leader assembled us and standing there in front of us lifted the host in his hand, took a knife in the other, and struck it into the host. Blood started to emanate from it without end.)

They tried to hide it, but it turned into flesh, and then into a child, and then into a crucifix (the Parisian sequence). So Jews, too, could tell the famous tale that made sense everywhere.

The great potential for exultation of the popular religious interest in the abused host is revealed in these cases, the power derived from which led to fraud and contests over authentication. There was much to be gained from a local bleeding host – pilgrims, offerings, fame. One of the cases that followed the Armleder massacres of 1336–8, which occurred in the town of Deggendorf in Lower Bavaria, is a good example.[80] A local knight, Hertmann of Degenberg, and a large following fell on the Jews of the town and of neighboring towns like Straubing. Afterward, Heinrich, duke of Bavaria, received the appeals of the town to forgive the excess, and he handed over to them the Jewish goods and even exempted Straubing from paying taxes on those quarters that had been burned.[81] By 1360, a church dedicated to the Holy Sepulcher (*zum heiligen Grab*) had been consecrated as a memorial for the local story of desecration, and there we find the inscription

> wurden die Juden erslagen
> die sdat si anzunden
> do bard Gotes Laichenam funden
> daz sahen frauen und man
> Do huab man daz gotshaus ze baun an.[82]

(The Jews were killed,
The city was burned,
God's body was found there.
This was seen by women and men
And therefore God's house built there.)

79 Rudolf of Schlettstadt, *Historiae memorabiles,* chap. 15, 63.
80 *Germania Judaica,* vol. 2, no. 2, 157; Bauerreiss, *Pie Jesu,* 95–100.
81 K. Geissler, *Die Juden in Deutschland und Bayern bis zur Mitte des vierzehnten Jahrhunderts* (Munich, 1976), 224.
82 G. Krotzer, "Der Judenmord von Deggendorf und die Deggendorfer 'Gnad,' " in W. P. Eckert and E. J. Ehrlich, eds., *Judenhass – Schuld der Christen?!: Versuch eines Gesprächs* (Essen, 1964), 309–27, at 311–12; Lotter, *Hostienfrevelvorwurf,* 569–70.

Here was perfect collusion between count, town, and church; they all stood to gain from their town's newly won fame.

By the end of the fourteenth century, chronicles brimmed and *exempla* books burst with stories about host desecration by Jews and the harsh punishment meted out by zealous knights and townsfolk. Empty quarters, blackened houses, new chapels, and preached reminders (culled from books such as *Historiae memorabiles*) all told the tale of host desecration by Jews and its aftermath. These narratives were worked out, when occasion arose and when passions were high, in a drama played out by emperor, dukes, bishops, town councils, parish priests, townspeople, and, of course, the Jews. Forty years after the Rintfleisch massacres, there was another great wave within a similar region, playing on similar sentiments, and in another period of political unrest, that is, the troublesome years of Ludwig of Bavaria.[83]

This wave was called the "Armleder Uprising," after the leather body protection they wore when fighting, as put by the Swiss chronicler John of Winterthur: "hac de causa, quod in brachio corio pro ferro utebatur" (for this reason, because leather was used on the arm in place of armor).[84] The massacres covered Franconia, Alsace, and Swabia but overflowed into Bavaria (Deggendorf) and Austria (Pulkau).[85] This movement of men was initially led by a member of the lower gentry, a knight of Ussingheim. The chronicle of Saint Peter of Erfurt describes the instigation as coming during a court hearing attended by some knights and some Jews (Were they involved in a lawsuit for debt?):

interfecti fuerunt Iudei in civitate Rotingen, item in civitate dicta Augia, item in Bischofsheym et in multis civitatibus aliis et villis; quarum persecucionum iniciator et capitaneus fuit quidam miles de Ussinkeim, qui stans in civitate Rotinburc cum multis aliis nobilibus in quodam placito cum Iudeis, cum corpus Christi deferebatur in platea, et Christiani, ut dignum est, genu flecterent coram sacramento, Iudei iniqui ad domum quandam declinantes, prefato milite audiente, blasphemando proruperunt in hec verba seculis inaudita: "Sustineamus, quousque canis impudicus deferatur." Que verba ut audivit miles prefatus, per ipsum corpus Christi iuravit omnibus viribus se laborare velle pro morte Iudeorum; quod ita factum est.[86]

(Jews were killed in the city of Röttingen and in the city of Auga, also in Bischofsheim and in many other towns and villages; and the instigator and leader of their persecution was a certain knight of Ussingheim, who, while standing in the town of Röttingen with many other nobles in a trial with some Jews. Just then Christ's body was being carried in the street, and Christians were kneeling in front of it, as is fitting. Some iniquitous Jews, turning aside into a certain house, and within earshot of the said knight, rushed forth to blaspheme in these words, unheard for

---

83 For a thorough study of the movement and identification of its leader, see Arnold, "Die Armledererhebung."

84 *Die Chronik Johanns von Winterthur,* 140.   85 See map in Arnold, "Die Armledererhebung," 45.

86 "Chronicae S. Petri Erfordensis continuatio III," 375–6.

centuries: "Let us wait until the shameless dog is carried past." When the knight heard these words, he swore by that very body of Christ to strive with all his might for the death of the Jews. And that is what in fact happened.)

So the knight, probably Arnold of Ussingheim,[87] was moved to action because he had overheard some blasphemies about Christ's body; some other chronicles will tell that he acted in revenge for the death of his brother at the hands of a Jew. After a year's action, an offering of 400 pounds heller by the Jews prompted Count Gottfried of Hohenlohe to arrest Arnold, who was taken to Kitzingen and executed.[88] He soon became a martyr, and at his tomb in his village church miracles took place.[89] But Arnold was quickly succeeded, and the Armleder men had a new leader, a taverner named John Zimberlin.[90] When he visited the area in the next year, King Ludwig of Bavaria exacted compensation from the towns and demanded banishment of troublemakers and that surviving Jews be restored to their quarters.[91]

There is a striking geographic match between the events of 1298 and 1336.[92] But the later massacres were more brutal, and they were executed by an organized knightly troop and met little imperial resistance. Voices of the clergy were less evident, but chronicles appeared to be more shocked and disturbed. An interesting comment is the *Planctus ecclesiae in Germaniam*, written by Master Konrad of Megenberg about the recent troubles.[93] Writing to a colleague, he complained that lawless violence perpetrated by knights had swept towns and the lands around them and that it was targeted not only at Jews but at all exploitative idlers: bishops, clerks, monks, nuns, and scholars.[94] Jews were persecuted for their usury, parish priests for their depredations:

> Nitentur layci, credas, velut audio dici,
> Quod male presbiteri simul et perdantur Hebrei;
> Nam bona prespiteri sua devastant et Hebrei.
> Hii nimis usura, primi perimant sua iura.[95]

---

87 Arnold, "Die Armledererhebung," 51–3.   88 Ibid., 49; Lotter, "Hostienfrevelvorwurf," 563.

89 "Sed heu! tandem in civitatem Kyczingen deductus ibidem decollatus est; qui in suam villam, scilicet Ussenkeym, delatus in ecclesia sepultus innumeris claruit miraculis," in "Chronicae S. Petri Erfordensis continuatio III," 376.

90 Arnold, "Die Armledererhebung," 39–41.

91 For example, see M. Wiener, ed., *Regesten zur Geschichte der Juden in Deutschland während des Mittelalters* (Hanover, 1862), no. 123.

92 Lotter, "Hostienfrevelvorwurf," 562–3.

93 Konrad of Megenberg, "Planctus ecclesiae in Germaniam," in *MGH. Staatsschriften des späten Mittelalters* (Leipzig, 1941), 2;1; Graus, *Pest – Geissler – Judenmorde*, 295.

94 Cited in Graus, *Pest – Geissler – Judenmorde*, 295 note 84.

95 Konrad of Megenberg, "Planctus," 46, lines 602–5. The clergy could also be implicated, on suspicion of selling the host to Jews, as in the case of Pulkau and in Sternberg (Mecklenburg) in 1492, when a priest was executed for such a crime; E. Schnitzler, *Das geistige und religiöse Leben Rostocks am Ausgang des Mittelalters* (Berlin, 1940), 56.

(The laity desired, would you believe, I say it as I heard it,
That bad priests and Jews should be lost together.
Because the priests waste their goods and the Jews do just the same;
The latter ruin them by usury, and the former – by their rights.)

The emperor was engaged in his campaigns, and this left the field open
to expression of aggression against perceived oppressors.[96] The chronicle of
the dukes of Bavaria claimed that Ludwig (and others) had tried to defend
the Jews: "quia principes et omnes eorum officiales pro eorum defensione
seriose laborabant nec tamen eos poterant defendere."[97] It was finally a
coalition of lords, clergy, and towns that put down the last wave of Armleder forces in Alsace.

The accusation of host desecration was one of many stories told about
Jews, one that could be made to justify robbery and killing on a vast scale
with relative impunity. Other stories coexisted, ones that stressed the manipulation of magic, like the poisoning of wells and ritual murder, the con-
spiratorial element becoming increasingly familiar.[98] As Jews moved
eastward, in the wake of expulsions, the accusation traveled with them, to
Bohemia and Poland.[99] Prague and Breslau are interesting cases of later authoritative narratives of host desecration.[100]

Bohemia had escaped unscathed the widespread massacres of the plague
years (1348–50). Only Eger had suffered, in 1350, following the fervent
preaching of a Franciscan friar.[101] But this region, too, was finally drawn
into the circle of narration in 1389, when a host-desecration accusation was
enacted – or was it that?[102] The Limburg Chronicle tells us, in rather controlled language, that during Holy Week Jews were killed:

Daz qwam also, daz ein prister drug daz heilige sacrament . . . nit ferre von der juden gassen. Da wart von eime [*sic*] Juden ein klein steinichen geworfen uf di mon-

96 The emperor was able to intervene in some cases. See Konrad of Megenberg, "Planctus," 46–7,
   lines 614–24, and 53, lines 783–7.
97 "Chronica de ducibus Bavariae," in G. Leidinger, ed., *Bayerischen Chroniken des XIV. Jahrhunderts*
   (Hanover, 1918), 167.
98 Recently discussed in Carlo Ginzburg, *Ecstasies: Deciphering the Witches' Sabbath* (London, 1990),
   33–62. On the accusations made during the Black Death and the massacres that followed in Germany, see Alfred Haverkamp, "Die Judenverfolgungen zur Zeit des Schwarzen Todes im
   Gesellschaftsgefüge deutscher Stadt," in Haverkamp, ed., *Zur Geschichte der Juden im Deutschland des
   späten Mittelalters und der frühen Neuzeit* (Stuttgart, 1981), 27–93.
99 The first Polish accusation was made in Cracow in 1347. See L. Poliakov, *The History of anti-Semitism,* trans. R. Howard (London, 1974), 248.
100 See also the interesting case of Vienna in 1421, which will not be discussed here, in Lohrmann, *Judenrecht und Judenpolitik,* 300–3.
101 *Germania Judaica,* vol. 2, no. 1, 185–8; Graus, *Struktur und Geschichte,* 50.
102 *Germania Judaica,* vol. 2, no. 2, 659–62.

strancien. Daz sagen di cristen. Da wart ein gerufe unde ein geschrei ober di juden, daz si smelichen doit bleden.[103]

(It so happened that a priest carried the Holy Sacrament . . . not far from the Jewish quarter. And there a little stone was thrown at the monstrance by a Jew. This is what Christians say. And there was an outrage and an outcry against the Jews, so that they could no longer remain there.)

To this tame description we may juxtapose a highly embellished satirical account of the events, written by a priest whose pen name was Johannes Rusticus Quadratus.[104] He gives a detailed account of the event, treating it as a story of the Jews' Passion, "Passio Judaeorum Pragensium secundum Johannem," couched in biblical language and descriptions of Christ's Passion, to describe the Jewish crime against Christ and the "Passion" which they suffered in consequence in later-day Prague:

Vespere autem sabbati . . . ingressus sacerdos cum corpore Jesus in Judaeam. Judaei sibi obviam exierunt et portantes lapides in manibus suis clamabant dicentes: "Lapidetur iste, quia filium Dei se fecit." Deinde pueri Hebraeorum tollentes saxa platearum obviaverunt sacerdoti clamantes et dicentes: "Maledictus quem portas in tuis manibus."[105]

(On the even of the Sabbath . . . the priest entered with Christ's body into Judaea. The Jews moved out of his way and, carrying stones in their hands, they shouted, saying: "Stone him, because he has made himself the Son of God." From there Jewish boys carrying paving stones stood in the priest's way, shouting and saying: "Cursed is he whom you carry in your hands.")

Although other accounts describe the stone as hitting the priest's hand or the monstrance, this account inverts the events that led to Christ's Passion: the entry into Jerusalem heralded by boys, the greeting. The Jews were then dragged to the *praecon* as Christ had been (in this case the town court), while preachers in Prague churches incited their audiences: "super iniuria Jesu illata vindictam feceritis, omnes scandalum patiemini anno isto" (to take vengeance for the injuries suffered by Jesus; all of you suffer the scandal this year).[106] A leader offered himself, Ješek (*Gesco*). He and the multitude were armed with a powerful argument that God's wrath would fall on them if they failed to take revenge:

103 "Die Limburger Chronik des Tilemann Elhen von Wolfhagen," in A. F. W. Wyss, ed., *MGH. Deutsche Schriften* (Hanover, 1883), 4:1, 79.
104 P. Lehmann, *Parodistische Texte: Beispiele zur lateinischen Parodie im Mittelalter* (Munich, 1923), 36–41.
105 Ibid., 36.　　106 Ibid., 37.

Ab illa ergo hora cogitaverunt interficere omnes Judaeos, dicentes: "Ne forte ve-
niat ultio Dei super nos, tollamus eorum bona, et gentem perfidam de terra viven-
tium disperdamus."[107]

(From that time on they thought about killing the Jews, saying to themselves: "Lest,
indeed, God's anger fall upon us, let us take away their goods, and destroy the perfidious people from the land of the living.")

They did just that, killing their Jews and burning their quarter.

The town authorities became anxious and ordered people to stay indoors
on the next day. Townsfolk were then ordered to collect the stolen Jewish
goods, which found their way as a fine to the coffers of King-Emperor
Wenzel.[108] The naked bodies of Jews strewn in the streets of Prague were
finally moved away and burned by poor Christians, for a fee, and for good
sanitary reasons:

innumera Hebraeorum nuda cadavera per domos et plateas in stantionibus iacentia
et in suis membris diversimode mutilata pariter et adusta, inito consilio, ne ex
usuraria pingwedine aeris corruptio inficeret civitatem, statuerunt, ut quidam indi-
gentes et egeni Christiani, tamen pretio appretiati eadem in cineres redigerent igne
forti.[109]

(Numerous nude corpses of the Hebrews lay thrown in houses and streets in public, mutilated variously in their limbs and also burned. After consultation, and lest
the corruption of the air arising from the usurious body fats infect the town, they
decided, and some poor and needy Christians, hired at a price, reduced them to
ashes in a blazing fire.)

Prague, health-conscious as so many towns became after the Black Death,
could not take the risk of infection from the usury-infested air that arose
from the Jewish bodies.

So the new authoritative narrative, couched in visual representation and
in oral traditions, was used, applied, and interpreted. It became part of the
history of many towns after 1298.[110] It could have universal appeal, as long
as a priest or another knowing person could start the telling, and whenever
a Rintfleisch, a Jesek, a count of Degenberg, came along to lead it. The instigator could be a powerful preacher, one who raised the temperature in a
town and stirred its passions. Such was John of Capistrano (1386–1456), the
famous Franciscan, who had led the movement of revival and enthusiasm
in northern Italian towns that resulted in the establishment of *monti di*

---

107 Ibid.   108 Graus, *Struktur und Geschichte,* 57.   109 Lehmann, *Parodistische Texte,* 41.
110 On Jews in urban historiography, see the case of Cologne, discussed in A.-D. von den Brincken,
   "Die Juden in der Kölnischen Chronistik des 15. Jahrhunderts," in J. Bohnke-Kollwitz, W. P. Eckert, F. Gokzewski, and H. Greive, eds., *Köln und das rheinische Judentum: Festschrift Germania Judaica,
   1959–1984* (Cologne, 1984), 63–74.

Figure 13.4. The host desecration at Sternberg (1492). Contemporary woodcut.

pietà.[111] John was delegated by the papacy to preach in those areas that had been influenced by Hussitism, and he mounted a preaching tour of Germany, Austria, and Poland in the early 1450s. Soon after his preaching in Breslau, during the Feast of the Exaltation of the Holy Cross, a host-desecration accusation against the Jews was made (Figure 13.4). The local account, *De expulsione judaeorum,* says that on May 22, the Thursday after the feast, a solemn eucharistic procession was held *quadam necessitate,* which exposed Christ to Jewish eyes.[112] It was raining and Christians fell to their knees in the mud, in devotion. Seeing this, the Jews mocked them and planned to procure some hosts and mock them too. Some days later they tempted the custodian of the Church of Saint Matthew to give them God's body, to be tested: "utrum illa hostia quam Christiani adorent Deus sit, utrum quoque panis ille, materia, re, forma et natura reclamantibus in carnem transeat et sanguinem?" (whether this host, which the Christians adore, is God, whether this bread – its material, substance, form and nature notwithstanding – is transformed into flesh and blood).[113]

111 B. Pullan, *Rich and Poor in Renaissance Venice* (Oxford, 1971), 606–9.
112 "De expulsione judaeorum," *Monumenta poloniae historica* (Lvov, 1878), 786.   113 Ibid., 786.

The custodian resisted awhile and then relented (after consulting his wife!) and sold them the host. The Jews went on to desecrate it in the house of the Jew Mayr: they broke and struck it, only to see it bleed, and frightened, they cried out in terror. This alerted Christians, who knelt to venerate the host and then took it to their church.[114] A trial ensued a few weeks later, at which John of Capistrano, in his inquisitorial powers, presided. The ten Jews involved were sentenced to death, the Jewish community was expelled, some were baptized, and some one hundred fifty Jews were killed. This too became a story to be retold, and it appears in a fifteenth-century collection of *exempla* by a Dutch compiler, the *Speculum exemplorum,* as a famous tale "noviter conscripta" for further edification of others.[115]

Such stories lost their particular allure in areas that became *judenrein,* but other narratives about the Eucharist continued to live on. The stories also declined as changes in the apprehension of the holy, in understandings of the miraculous, and the magical, changed in this and the later period.[116] The appeal of the host-desecration tale was reinforced by other images that townsmen would have encountered. Particularly striking were the late medieval dramatic renditions, in the vernacular, of scenes of the Passion, which stressed Jewish fellowship with the devil.[117] But even in this powerful field of drama, there were various images to pursue, with significantly divergent nuances. Even in the work of a single playwright, like the Nuremberger Hans Folz in the 1470s and 1480s, one observes a change in tenor and in choice, according to the audience and in relation to the town's mood. If his *Kaiser Constantinus* of 1474 represented scenes of quite learned and bookish exchange between *ecclesia* and *synagoga* figures, his slightly later *Spiel vom Herzog von Burgund* was nastier, strongly stressing the polluting effect of usury, the scatological associations with Jews, in a whole gamut of fiendish names and characterizations.[118] Folz was creating and being created by the mood of a town, which was applying in the 1490s for permission to expel

114 Ibid., 787.
115 B. Geremek, "L'Exemplum et la circulation de la culture au moyen-âge," *Mélanges de l'Ecole français de Rome. Moyen-âge – temps modernes* 92 (1980), 169–70. *Speculum exemplorum,* editio princeps (1481), X, 2.
116 See Hsia, *Myth of Ritual Murder,* 136–62, on the decline of ritual-murder accusations in the sixteenth century.
117 J. Trachtenberg, *The Devil and the Jews* (New Haven, Conn., 1943), 22; E. Wenzel, "*Synagoga* und *ecclesia.* Zum Antijudaismus im deutschsprachigen Spiel der späten Mittelalters," in H. O. Horst, ed., *Judentum, Antisemitismus und europäische Kultur* (Tübingen, 1988), 62–3. For French material, see G. Dahan, "Les Juifs dans le théâtre religieux en France du XIIe au XIVe siècles," *Archives juives* 13 (1977): 1–10.
118 Wenzel, "*Synagoga* und *ecclesia,*" 64–70.

its Jews.[119] Product and producer, he moved between the tracts and the authorities, constructing one type of image when he was addressing the patricians and a different one for playing in the streets under the demands of popular humor and aggression. But this distance was becoming increasingly narrow in the fifteenth century. We must see Folz's choices as conscious and knowing ones, as were those of the tellers of host-desecration tales that we have encountered.

We have looked at the host-desecration accusation as it was told, reported, recorded, and retold, leaving aside, for now, the emphasis on death and destruction that surrounded it. By concentrating on the ways in which people told and retold a story in which Jewish protagonists acted to inflict pain and shame on the Christian Savior, we have also discerned some of the fragility of the tale. Host-desecration accusations, which often also described a childlike figure of Christ bloodied, chewed, and tortured, existed in that shady domain in which horrors are told, stories of transgression, breaches of the most binding taboos: child abuse and god killing. But their telling was also an act of assertion of truths that were all too fragile, of beliefs all too ridden with doubt: the claims of sacramentality, the promise of salvation, the mediation of the clergy, the logic of spirit working in matter for the well-being of believers. We can easily understand those moments of interaction, of communication, of coexistence; the dark moments of abuse are the ones that call for careful unfolding.

We observe a frequent transfer of some of the clinging tensions of social life and religious ambivalence onto the Jew, whose identification as tester of the host, as its abuser, made him also the potential guarantor of its truth and power, the summoner of its miracles. In many ways heretics did the same, but neither were they as vulnerable nor was their status so ambiguous as the age-old tormentors of Christ that filled the inquisitorial courts. Inasmuch as aggression and stifled expectations could sometimes provide the framework for social confrontations, the narrative, ubiquitous and terrible, could be used and reused.

Perhaps one learns from the telling of host-desecration stories, above all, that there was choice and deliberation in the act of narration; that there was always the moment at which it was decided or suggested by someone that such a tale fit the circumstances at hand. To take part was to participate in a social event, to expect some financial benefit, or perhaps to

---

119 Granted finally in 1499. On the late medieval expulsions, see M. Wenninger, *Man bedarf keiner Juden mehr. Ursachen und Hintergründe ihrer Vertreibung aus den deutschen Reichsstädten im 15. Jahrhundert* (Vienna, 1981).

feel virtuous. We have met knights, parish priests, women, a doctor of canon law, all intent on telling the tale, for a variety of reasons, and perhaps simply because it was available and gave meaning to a whole number of other ideas and aspirations. But we have also seen a frustrated emperor, a doubtful pope, some skeptical chroniclers, an embarrassed monk, and towns – all of which preferred the narrative of good government to that of vengeful fury. As deeply as we are committed to the understanding of the past, we must always come up against the fact that there were those who chose to accept and others who were able to resist the story that gave license to violence.

14

Representations of German Jewry: Images, Prejudices, Ideas – A Comment

CARLO GINZBURG

Commentators are usually asked to compare essays in order to stress convergences and divergences between them – an intellectual exercise that is sometimes a bit contrived, if not overtly artificial. This is certainly not the case with the two challenging essays I have been asked to comment on. They shed light upon each other and, in a very real sense, they supplement each other. The aim of my comment is to make explicit some of the suggestions resulting from reading the two essays side by side.

Miri Rubin's essay brilliantly explores the emergence and diffusion of a well-known anti-Jewish topos: the desecration of the sacred host. Rubin rightly remarks that in the early medieval story focusing on the Jewish boy, the host is not defiled. She says, however, that "the ambiguous feeling raised by the Jewish father has the potential to worry and unsettle or merely foretells other tales which will develop side by side but with very different consequences."[1] In those later tales, the Jews that have desecrated the host are finally put to death. I would suggest, however, that the Jewish boy story also points toward a different albeit related sequence centered on another notorious slander against the Jews: the ritual murder.

In his valuable study of this topic in late medieval and early modern Germany, R. Po-chia Hsia emphasizes that "in the 1470s legends of ritual murders and host desecrations began to converge, resulting in a standardized type of ritual murder discourse in which prepubescent boys and Eucharistic devotion play the crucial roles."[2] In fact, the early medieval story analyzed in Rubin's essay suggests that the connections between the two accusations are much older. On the one hand, we have a Jewish boy who, having received communion with the Christians, has been in a sense assimilated to Christianity. Only the Virgin's miraculous intervention will save him from his father's murderous intentions. On the other hand, we

---

1 This comment, not in Chapter 13, is from Rubin's original address at the conference.
2 R. Po-chia Hsia, *The Myth of Ritual Murder* (New Haven, Conn., 1988), 52.

have lurid tales about Christian boys being killed by Jews who wanted to commemorate the crucifixion of Christ. Needless to add, little girls are never mentioned in this context. The common morphological link between the two narratives had been provided, presumably, by the little boy, who emphasized the presence of Christ in the sacrament, a well-known iconographic device, duly mentioned in the Jewish boy story. But a connection between this story and the emergence of ritual murder accusations probably existed on a historical level as well. Rubin mentions the study in which R. W. Southern convincingly ascribed the influential English version of the "Miracles of the Virgin," which included the Jewish boy story, to Anselm, the abbot of Bury Saint Edmunds, who died in 1148.[3] The earliest version of the ritual murder allegedly performed by Jews was recorded in a text written not far from Bury Saint Edmunds some years later. It was recorded in the first book of *The Life and Passion of Saint William the Martyr of Norwich* by Thomas of Monmouth, written between 1149 and 1150, according to the chronology suggested by Gavin Langmuir.[4]

Morphologically related elements were rearranged in order to create two different narratives, having different meanings. The aggressive anti-Jewish features, which became so prominent in the tales on the desecration of the host throughout the thirteenth century, are obviously related to the growing emphasis on the real presence of Christ in the host, proclaimed in 1215 by the Fourth Lateran Council. Rubin rightly speaks of the enormous vulnerability of the Eucharist, which was therefore "to be kept in precious vessels." This widespread feeling produced objects like the enameled eucharistic doves from Limoges, of which at least forty-two, ranging in date between 1200 and 1220, have been preserved.[5] These splendid works of art had a bloody counterpart: the innumerable stories about Jews either desecrating the host or performing the ritual murder of Christian boys. Rubin's essay shows the role played by these narratives in anti-Jewish persecution. Some deep anxieties triggered by the extraordinary claim that Christ was really present in the host were therefore projected onto the Jews.

But the growing emphasis on Christ's real presence in the sacrament is only one among many historical forces that gave a new, aggressive twist to the old Jewish boy story. Not less crucial is another force that has

3 R. W. Southern, "The English Origins of the 'Miracles of the Virgin,' " *Medieval and Renaissance Studies* 4 (1958): 176–216; E. W. Williamson, ed., *The Letters of Osbert of Clare* (Oxford, 1929), 191–200.
4 G. Langmuir, *Towards a Definition of Antisemitism* (Berkeley, Calif., 1990), 209–36, 284–7.
5 P. Williamson, *The Thyssen–Bornemisza Collection: Medieval Sculpture and Works of Art* (London, 1987), 148–51.

been dealt with in R. Po-chia Hsia's essay, in which he carefully analyzes the tension between two different images of the usurious Jew in sixteenth-century Germany. Either he was regarded as the avaricious Everyman, as in Hans Obernaus's *Der Judenspiess,* or he was regarded as the product of an evil attitude intrinsic to Jews as in Georg Schwartz's *Juden Feind.* I am not able to follow Hsia's suggestion that Schwartz "identified . . . a racial character to the Jewish refusal to convert." Race as such, in the modern sense of the word, is, I suspect, quite out of place here. On the contrary, I think he is absolutely right in saying that "at issue was not merely the figure of the usurious Jew embedded in religious moral economy." I am much less convinced, however, by his conclusion that at issue was "the real person of the Jewish business competitor." The "usurious Jew" was, and has until today been, above all a mythical figure, to be understood on a metaphorical rather than a literal level. As Abram Leon brilliantly suggested fifty years ago, the growing polemical attitude toward the usurious Jew was the paradoxical result of the diminishing role of Jews in the late medieval economy.[6] I would suggest, therefore, that the split attitude toward the usurious Jew in sixteenth-century Germany must be connected to a deep widespread anxiety concerning the effects and implications of a monetary economy. Behind the usurious Jew lurked the Jew as Everyman.

The analogy with the psychological mechanism triggered by the emphasis on Christ's real presence in the sacrament is, I think, striking. In both cases, largely unspoken social anxieties were projected onto Jews. Being at the same time external and very close, they were the ideal candidates for playing the role of scapegoats – a category that needs, I believe, further analysis.

Furthermore, the two anxieties were closely connected. As far as I can judge from Rubin's essay and Hsia's book, nearly all narratives focusing on host desecration and ritual-murder accusations share a common theme. They show Jews buying, rather than stealing, both sacred hosts and Christian boys. When a Christian maid steals a sacred host from the communion, as in Pope Innocent III's letter of 1213 mentioned in Rubin's essay, the emphasis on the extraordinary power of money is only symbolic but in a sense even more vivid. Having "mistakenly placed the host in a box containing 7 livres of Paris," the Jew finds "that the coins had turned into hosts." The miracle has a bitter, albeit repressed, implication. Money can transform itself into the body of Christ only because it can buy everything, including the body of Christ:

6 A. Leon, *The Jewish Question: A Marxist Interpretation* (New York, 1970).

By possessing the *property* of buying everything, by possessing the property of appropriating all objects, *money* is thus the *object* of eminent possession. The universality of its *property* is the omnipotence of its being. It is therefore regarded as omnipotent . . . Can it not dissolve and bind all ties?

You have certainly recognized the voice of the German Jew who, in a youthful essay, had powerfully developed the theme of the usurious Jew as Everyman: I mean, of course, Karl Marx.[7]

7 Karl Marx, *Economic and Philosophic Manuscripts of 1844,* vol. 3, in *Collected Works,* (New York, 1975), 323–4.

PART V

The Pattern of Authority and the Limits of Toleration: The Case of German Jewry

15

German Territorial Princes and the Jews

ROTRAUD RIES

I

The prerequisites and conditions that shaped the relations between territorial princes and Jews in the early modern period lay in the territorialization and commercialization of Jewish protection rights (*Judenschutzrechte*), which were characteristic of the late Middle Ages. By grant or assignment of interest, or through purchase, the territorial princes as well as cities gained possession of these rights, which permitted them to admit and expel Jews, to impose taxes on them, and to "use" them. Although the emperor continued to claim the right to be the Jews' highest patron and to collect taxes accordingly, cities and territorial princes were the de facto political authorities that determined the conditions of life for Jews in the late Middle Ages.[1]

Until far into the fifteenth century, the large economically and politically powerful cities played the leading role. These were usually imperial cities (*Reichsstädte*), where the larger Jewish communities had developed. Before the start of the sixteenth century, however, most of these cities chose to terminate their relations to the Jews by expelling them and thus gave up their potential influence in the shaping of Jewish policy.[2]

The territorial princes, in contrast, often had to rely on the cooperation and support of the cities in forming their protective relationship to the Jews. They deliberately settled individual families where the economy needed them and utilized their economic potential to the advantage of the regional

---

Alice Eve Kennington of College Park, Maryland, provided the English translation of this chapter.

1 See Friedrich Battenberg, "Zur Rechtsstellung der Juden am Mittelrhein in Spätmittelalter und früher Neuzeit," *Zeitschrift für Historische Forschung* 6 (1970): 129–83, 137–40, 145–56; Friedrich Battenberg, *Das Europäische Zeitalter der Juden. Zur Entwicklung einer Minderheit in der nichtjüdischen Umwelt Europas,* 2 vols. (Darmstadt, 1990), 1:111, 136–40, 144–5.

2 See Markus J. Wenninger, *Man bedarf keiner Juden mehr: Ursachen und Hintergründe ihrer Vertreibung aus den deutschen Reichsstädten im 15. Jahrhundert* (Vienna, 1981); for statistical material on the expulsions, see Arye Maimon, ed., *Germania Judaica,* vol. 3: *1350–1519,* no. 1 (Tübingen, 1987).

centers of power.[3] In addition to these individual families, entire Jewish communities received privileges or protection documents specific to a particular location.

By the time the Jews had been forced from the large cities to small towns and villages in the countryside, as a consequence of expulsions and of the process of economic displacement, territorial princes had gained new political opportunities. The consolidation of areas of authority and the development of these areas into territorial states cleared the way for Jewish policy to have a territorial base. The early modern territorial state understood the right to exercise protection of the Jews to be an integral component of territorial rule, independent of the Jewish royal prerogative (*Judenregal*) awarded by the emperor,[4] and asserted this against the important provincial cities, which had hitherto been autonomous but were now losing influence.

In the following centuries, urban policy toward Jews, apart from the policy of ejection, remained limited to exceptions like Frankfurt am Main, Worms, and Hamburg. In contrast, the local aristocracy pursued a policy of protecting the Jews (*Judenschutzpolitik*), guided by financial self-interest, far into the eighteenth century. Their policy was one that often competed with that of the respective territorial prince and took the sting out of the latter policy by offering alternatives.[5]

Although in the fifteenth century some princes had already followed the example set by the cities in expelling Jews, by the age of the Reformation and the Counter-Reformation they were systematically using their increased latitude for action to drive the Jews from their realms, often in collusion with religious authorities. By 1570, out of all of the more important territorial states and imperial cities, only Hesse and Frankfurt am Main still allowed Jews to live within their boundaries.[6]

This was the time when the dispute between Catholics and Protestants reached a deadlock, marking the beginning of an era of doubt and modification of Christian views and values. In this era, politics assumed a new, secular role, one oriented to well-being in this life, in which stability and the general welfare were guaranteed by the power of the state, independent of

---

3 Battenberg, *Europäisches Zeitalter,* 1:126.

4 Friedrich Battenberg, "Assenheimer Judenpogrome vor dem Reichskammergericht: Die Prozesse der Grafschaften Hanau, Isenburg und Solms um die Ausübung des Judenregals, 1567–73," in *Neunhundert Jahre Geschichte der Juden in Hessen. Beiträge zum politischen, wirtschaftlichen und kulturellen Leben* (Wiesbaden, 1983), 123, 141.

5 A. Eckstein, *Geschichte der Juden im Markgrafentum Bayreuth* (Bayreuth, 1907), 22; Wilhelm Volkert, "Die Juden im Fürstentum Pfalz-Neuburg," *Zeitschrift für bayerische Landesgeschichte* 26 (1963): 560–605, 564.

6 Jonathan Israel, *European Jewry in the Age of Mercantilism, 1550–1750* (Oxford, 1985), 10, 23.

religious demands. In this context, the role of the Jews was also redefined.[7] The high regard for commerce that was part and parcel of the rise of mercantilistic thinking also caused a positive reevaluation of Jewish economic activity and resulted in the Jews' advancement through the granting of generous privileges.

The tendency toward a change in Jewish policy is documented by the unrestricted readmission of Jews to Bohemia by Emperor Maximilian II (1565–76) and the generous Jewish policy of his successor, Rudolph II (1576–1612). The expansion of potential for economic growth, especially in the realm of commerce, caused a dramatic increase in the size of the Jewish communities in Prague and in Frankfurt am Main. New and important Jewish settlements also came into existence in Fürth, in East Friesland, and in Hamburg and its environs. This development continued apace at the beginning of the seventeenth century, though admittedly the success of this resettlement was limited until the time of the Thirty Years' War.[8]

The special political, economic, and financial circumstances of the war offered the Jews, particularly the court Jews, the opportunity to prove their important, even indispensable role in the continental European system of trade and credit. By extending credits, some of which were nonrepayable, and by organizing supplies for the various armies, they succeeded in buying protection and privileges from all the warring parties. Jews obtained permission to resettle and more advantageous rights in trade and religion as well. But they remained strictly barred from Brandenburg, Pomerania, Mecklenburg, and Electoral Saxony.[9]

With the end of the war and the withdrawal of the Swedes and the French, however, a new debate flared up over toleration of the Jews. The cities in particular, and there specifically the mayors, the Catholic or Protestant clergy, and the guilds, took the lead in anti-Jewish demands. A few princes gave in to this pressure and expelled the Jews. The most prominent

---

7 See Alex Bein, *Die Judenfrage. Biographie eines Weltproblems,* 2 vols. (Stuttgart, 1980), 1:157; the analysis of Israel in his *European Jewry,* 36–8, 56–7, is excellent, but he does not sufficiently distinguish the Jewish policy of secular and ecclesiastical territorial princes. Generally, research for this period focuses mainly on prominent Jews, i.e., on the court Jews and the well-to-do. On Jews under absolutism, see Felix Priebatsch, "Die Judenpolitik des fürstlichen Absolutismus im 17. und 18. Jahrhundert," in *Forschungen und Versuche zur Geschichte des Mittelalters und der Neuzeit. Festschrift für Dietrich Schäfer* (Jena, 1915), 564–651; Peter Baumgart, "Die Stellung der jüdischen Minorität im Staat des aufgeklärten Absolutismus. Das friderizianische Preussen und das josephinische Österreich im Vergleich," *Kairos,* n.s. 22 (1980): 226; Peter Baumgart, "Zur Geschichte der Juden im absoluten Staat," *Vierteljahrsschrift für Sozial- und Wirtschaftsgeschichte* 51 (1964): 101. The only detailed study of the relations between territorial princes/states and Jews is Selma Stern, *Der preussische Staat und die Juden,* 4 vols. (Tübingen, 1962–75).
8 Israel, *European Jewry,* 58, 65, 87.
9 Ibid., 88–103, 170, 272; Bein, *Judenfrage,* 1:157–60.

example is certainly that of Emperor Leopold I (1658–1705), who banished the Jews of Vienna – victims of their lessening economic importance and of the militant Counter-Reformation of 1669–70. Neither this nor any other expulsion, however, lasted very long.[10]

Other territorial princes ignored the anti-Jewish efforts and, for reasons of economic policy, relied on their perception of authoritarian rule to disregard the complaints of the cities. Thus, Elector Friedrich Wilhelm I of Brandenburg-Prussia (1640–88) gradually expanded settlement and development opportunities for Jews. Through the granting of concessions, some of them quite generous, Jewish settlement was also promoted in Mannheim in 1660, in Baden-Durlach in the 1670s, in Denmark in 1673 (later extended to include Oldenburg), and in Hanover at the end of the seventeenth century. Existing Jewish communities stabilized and expanded. By and large, the second half of the seventeenth century is characterized by an enormous growth in Jewish communities, owing to the expansion of economic activities, in contrast to the relatively stable Christian population.[11]

From the beginning of the eighteenth century on, however, this development gradually was reversed, as economic expansion no longer kept pace with the growth in population. Jewish trade was restricted by protectionist measures, and, at the same time, Jews profited little from the new direction in economic policy, namely the promotion of manufactories. This change in direction of economic policy was accompanied by further restrictions that limited the number of Jewish families everywhere, forbade marriage of any but the first-born son, and generally tightened control over the Jews. Once again, migration from the urban centers into the countryside began, and the growth of the Jewish population leveled off relative to the Christian population. As economic opportunities were cut back, the Jews became increasingly impoverished. More than half were reduced to peddlers, beggars, and small-time crooks.[12]

Beyond this general line of development of princely policies concerning Jews between 1350 and 1750 that I have just sketched, scholars agree only that the specifics of the relationships between territorial princes and Jews exhibit great regional variation. Research on this topic remains highly unsatisfactory; hence a useful comparative analysis of this relationship for the various regions is not possible at this time.[13] For that reason, in Section II I examine the structures of Jewish policy, the factors conditioning it, and the

10 Israel, *European Jewry*, 145.   11 Ibid., 149, 169.   12 Ibid., 239.
13 See Alfred Haverkamp's excellent study, "Erzbischof Balduin und die Juden," in Franz-Josef Heyen, ed., *Balduin von Luxemburg, Erzbischof von Trier – Kurfürst des Reiches, 1285–1354. Festschrift aus An-*

forms in which it was expressed, citing examples as illustration. Here, too, we will find that available knowledge allows clear answers to only a few questions; other questions can only be addressed insufficiently or not at all. Following the structural analysis, in Sections III and IV I illustrate Jewish policy in its regional and chronological context, using the Guelph territories of Braunschweig-Calenberg and Braunschweig-Wolfenbüttel as examples.[14] In view of the fact that Jewish settlement was concentrated in the southern and southwestern regions of the empire, these examples would seem, at first glance, to be atypical. But upon closer examination, it will be seen that they are well suited to serve as paradigmatic examples of the essential elements of Jewish policy in the context of late medieval and early modern times.

II

All political action, including that taken by a prince who has become increasingly wedded to the ideas of absolutism, arises within a context shaped by individual and social factors. The differing weight given these factors beyond the disparity of conditions determines the specific contours of policy.

Let us first consider the individual attitude of the prince. For the Jews, this element was relatively important politically within the power structures of the state in the late Middle Ages and early modern times. This element encompassed the presuppositions and interests of the territorial prince, his needs and his ability to assert himself, as well as the extent to which he had internalized common stereotypes about Jews. These personal principles determined the prince's subjective assessment of political measures, and thus his policy stance toward the Jews; they were cofactors influencing the other

---

lass des 700. Geburtsjahres (Mainz, 1985), 437. Although we lack such studies for most of the territorial princes, examples we do have include Hermann Arnold, *Von den Juden in der Pfalz* (Speyer, 1967); S. Haenle, *Geschichte der Juden im ehemaligen Fürstentum Ansbach* (Ansbach, 1876); Josef Kirmeier, "Aufnahme, Verfolgung und Vertreibung. Zur Judenpolitik bayerischer Herzöge im Mittelalter," in Manfred Treml and Josef Kirmeier, eds., *Geschichte und Kultur der Juden in Bayern*, 2 vols. (Munich, 1988), 1:95–104; Holger Lemmermann, *Geschichte der Juden im alten Amt Meppen bis zur Emanzipation (1848)* (Meppen, 1975); Leopold Löwenstein, *Geschichte der Juden in der Kurpfalz. Nach gedruckten und ungedruckten Quellen dargestellt* (Frankfurt/Main, 1895); Stefan Schwarz, *Die Juden in Bayern im Wandel der Zeiten* (Munich, 1963); Raphael Straus, "Judenpolitik Herzog Heinrichs des Reichen von Landshut," *Zeitschrift f. d. Geschichte der Juden in Deutschland* 1 (1929): 96–118; Aaron Taenzer, *Die Geschichte der Juden in Württemberg* (1937; reprinted Frankfurt/Main, 1983); Helmut Teufel, "Zur politischen und sozialen Geschichte der Juden in Mähren vom Antritt der Habsburger bis zur Schlacht am Weissen Berg, 1526–1620," Ph.D. diss., Universität Erlangen, 1971. Other references can be found in the footnotes to the present chapter.

14 See Rotraud Ries, "Strukturen frühneuzeitliche Judenpolitik in Braunschweig-Calenberg," in Rainer Sabelleck, ed., *Juden in Südniedersachsen* (forthcoming); and Ries, "Soziale und politische Bedingungen jüdischen Lebens in Niedersachsen im 15. und 16. Jahrhundert," Ph.D. diss., Universität Münster, 1990.

conditions of the prince's Jewish policy. For this reason, it is not always possible to distinguish this element clearly from others.

Individual conditions and differences rooted in the personality of the territorial prince are evident in the various policies toward Jews, which ranged from vigorously administered protection, to pragmatic solutions, to arbitrary measures. In the middle of the fifteenth century, Margrave Albrecht Achilles of Bayreuth (1457–86) championed his Jews as fully as had Ruprecht I of the Palatinate (1353–90) before him or, later, the counts of Hanau and the patrons of the Fürth Jews in the seventeenth century.[15]

Pure pragmatism characterizes the attitude of the electors of the Palatinate at the beginning of the sixteenth century. They considered expulsion of little effect with respect to the Jews in the areas ruled by the imperial knights.[16] The Jewish policy of Elector Friedrich III of Brandenburg-Prussia can be characterized as indecisive, inconsistent, capricious, and easily influenced.[17]

Count Ernst of Schaumburg (1595–1622) chose the path of least resistance by settling Jews, at the beginning of the seventeenth century, only in those places where he could expect no protest. Moreover, he "toyed" with the instruments of Jewish policy by first driving out the Jews in 1601, merely in order to get an idea how many there were and to acquire a "gift" of money. Then he issued them new letters of protection having no restrictions at all. After the middle of the seventeenth century, his successors arbitrarily decreed a series of smaller expulsions.[18] In general, one can assume a certain degree of arbitrariness, when the expulsions are many, without necessarily being able to substantiate this in specific cases. The motivation for expulsion is often insufficiently evident from the sources, but this also has not been adequately investigated.

We find a more specific category of individually based conditions of Jewish policy in the sphere of personal religious intensity. As will be seen, this is closely related to the question of the religious affiliation of the territorial prince. It was not until after the Reformation that territorial princes began to concern themselves independently with the religion of the Jews. Landgrave Philipp of Hesse (1509–67) still took a relatively unemotional view in this regard. When, in 1538, Bucer and six other Hessian clerics submit-

15 Eckstein, *Juden in Bayreuth*, 10–11; Gerhard Renda, "Fürth, das 'bayerische Jerusalem,'" in *Geschichte und Kultur der Juden in Bayern*, 1:225, 229; Berthold Rosenthal, *Heimatgeschichte der badischen Juden seit ihrem geschichtlichen Auftreten bis zur Gegenwart* (Bühl, 1927), 36–7; Ludwig Rosenthal, *Zur Geschichte der Juden im Gebiet der ehemal. Grafschaft Hanau* (Hanau, 1963), 31, 52, 57.
16 Volkert, "Juden in Pfalz-Neuberg," 564.   17 See Stern, *Der preussische Staat*, 1:75–6.
18 Hans-Heinrich Hasselmeier, *Die Stellung der Juden in Schaumburg-Lippe von 1648 bis zur Emanzipation* (Bückeburg, 1967), 3, 92–5.

ted in writing their position on the toleration of Jews, Philipp did not consider their recommendations to be adequately grounded in the Bible, and he substituted his own biblical interpretation. In contrast to the clerics, he did not attempt to enforce his desire to convert the Jews by imposing rigorous economic constraints.[19]

The Jewish stereotype typical of the sixteenth century proved to be explosive. Independent at first of denominational adherence, it held that the Jews were harmful, both because of their economic activity and because of their religion. Then, out of religious zeal, some of the Protestant princes absorbed this stereotype with greater gusto and translated it into policy. Count Palatine Ottheinrich of Pfalz-Neuburg (1506–59), for example, who had converted to Lutheranism in 1542, began to expel Jews shortly after returning to his territories in 1552–3, and in his will he successfully stipulated a rigorously anti-Jewish course to be followed by his successors, who were likewise strict Lutherans.[20]

Personal contacts with Jews also belonged to the sphere of individual influences on Jewish policy. This occurred throughout this period, usually sporadically, whenever individual Jews entered into close business relations with their ruling territorial lord. But it was not until the sixteenth century that the phenomenon of the court Jew began to appear, as, for example, in the close tie between Count Simon VI of Lippe (1563–1613) and Isaac and his son Israel in Salzuflen. The count recruited these two for economic and political enterprises, held his ground that they be tolerated, against the massive opposition of the territorial estates, and granted Isaac's wish that his numerous relatives (as many as thirty families) be taken in.[21] After the Thirty Years' War, court Jews became such a widespread phenomenon that nearly all courts maintained contacts with them. Independent of the economic functions of court Jews, this resulted in personal relationships of unprecedented intensity, which enabled prejudices to be broken down into biases that both parties could manipulate politically. The court Jew could intercede with the prince to advocate the interests of his coreligionists, whereas the prince could use the court Jew to organize and control the Jewish com-

19 Siegmund Salfeld, "Die Judenpolitik Philipps des Grossmütigen," in *Philipp der Grossmütige. Beiträge zur Geschichte seines Lebens und seiner Zeit* (Marburg, 1904), 519–44, 528–41; Wilhelm Maurer, "Martin Butzer und die Judenfrage in Hessen," *Zeitschrift d. Vereins f. hessische Geschichte und Landeskunde* 64 (1953): 29–43, 35–42; Ernst-Wilhelm Kohls, "Die Judenfrage in Hessen während der Reformationszeit," *Jahrbuch der hessischen kirchengeschichtlichen Vereinigung* 21 (1970): 87–100; Battenberg, *Europäisches Zeitalter*, 1:197; Battenberg, "Reformation, Judentum und landesherrliche Gesetzgebung," in Andreas Mehl and Wolfgang C. Schneider, eds., *Festschrift für Lothar Graf zu Dohna zum 65. Geburtstag* (Darmstadt, 1989), 315, 330.
20 Volkert, "Juden in Pfalz-Neuburg," 577.
21 Michael Guenter, *Die Juden in Lippe von 1648 bis zur Emanzipation 1858* (Detmold, 1973), 12.

munity and to utilize it in the economy. Thus the court Jew functioned as a bridge between the territorial prince and the Jewish community.

As orthodox Christian theological values relating to Jews became relativized and, concurrently, Jewish commerce was reevaluated within the framework of the mercantile system after the decade of 1570, a change was wrought in political attitudes. At first only a few princes adhered to these new ideas and, like the young Count Philipp Ludwig II of Hanau (1595–1618), granted the Jews far-reaching rights. He predicated this on the benefits accruing to himself and his country from Jewish commerce, and he also accepted members of the Reformed Church in Hanau. The Jews were permitted the public exercise of religion in their synagogues.[22] As the seventeenth century progressed, this positive assessment of Jewish trade became much more attractive to many territorial princes, for whom the potential of exploiting the Jews financially was an added incentive.

After this period, the conditions of Jewish policy based on the individual views of the rulers began to concentrate around these two poles. That development may be seen, for example, in Brandenburg, where Elector Friedrich Wilhelm placed the Jews under his direct administration as one of his financial resources in order to mitigate the Jewish royal prerogative. At the same time, he pursued his Jewish policy as part of a larger plan to transform the country from an agrarian economy into a modern mercantile entity by fostering immigration and encouraging a systematic policy of commerce, manufacturing, and the trades.[23] His son, King Friedrich I, on the other hand, clearly regarded the Jews primarily as a financial resource that could be exploited to meet the monetary needs of his indebted court and a squandering camarilla.[24] The attitude of his successor, King Friedrich Wilhelm I (1713–40), toward the Jews can be characterized as ranging from uninterested to negative. He did not pursue his financial policy at the cost of the Jews, but then neither did he attach much importance to commerce or to promoting it, and he had no reservations about imposing restrictions on the economic activity of the Jews.[25] Jewish welfare fell increasingly to his officials, and through the *Generalprivilegium* of 1730 the Jews were made directly subordinate to the state. This development indicated the decline in the influence of individual princely attitudes on Jewish policy, a general tendency of the eighteenth century.[26] Reasons of state gradually superseded personal attitudes, and the right of Jews to claim protection was no longer at issue. State utilitarianism now advanced as the prevailing motive in Jewish policy. This guaranteed a more generous policy toward the Jews when-

22 Rosenthal, *Juden in Hanau,* 31.   23 Stern, *Der preussische Staat,* 1:22, 33–6, 44–7.
24 Ibid., 1:80–1; 2:3.   25 Ibid., 2:3, 37–9, 56–62.   26 Ibid., 2:3, 20.

ever such a policy appeared to benefit the state, even when the attitude toward Jews was negative, for example, that of Empress Maria Theresia (1740–80) and King Friedrich II of Prussia (1740–86).[27]

Among the social factors that influenced the rulers, the financial situation and the financial interests of the territorial prince or the country always represented an important parameter of Jewish policy. These are among the policy criteria that can be determined objectively, but when looked at in the interrelated context of the other conditions, they could well be evaluated differently and have varying political consequences.

The financial exploitability of the Jews had been an essential component of the Jewish royal prerogative, and it very rapidly developed into a constitutive element in the protective relationship between the territorial princes and the Jews as well. In the late Middle Ages, the structures of power and administration, as well as the fact that the prince's relationship was limited to individual Jews or to individual Jewish congregations, had greatly limited any continuous productive use of taxes on the Jews for the benefit of the princely purse. Periodic appropriations by confiscation or through cancellation of debt, the transfer of rights over the Jews in exchange for a one-time payment, these seemed to offer the requisite, though necessarily short-sighted way out. The fiscally determined behavior of some patrons of the Jews just prior to the pogroms of 1348–50 and the two big debt cancellations of King Wenzel (1378–1400) speak for themselves.[28]

A further aspect of the financial determinants of Jewish policy in the late Middle Ages is the fact that the wealth of the Jews kept diminishing, as a result of economic repression and of periodic exploitation. Especially the Jews who were settling in the small towns and villages of the prince's realm tended to present little opportunity for productive exploitation because of their poverty. Only where a greater number of Jews lived were there significant sums of money to be had. The fact that toleration of Jews offered only a slight financial incentive contributed in more than a minor way to the expulsions of the late Middle Ages. In places where Jews were tolerated, their taxes and special payments, though higher than those levied on Christians, represented only a small portion of the prince's budget until far into the sixteenth century, assuming that the territorial prince had authority over these at all. To

---

27 Baumgart, "Jüdische Minorität," 239; Manfred Agethen, "Die Situation der jüdischen Minderheit in Schlesien unter österreichischer und unter preussischer Herrschaft," in Peter Baumgart, ed., *Kontinuität und Wandel: Schlesien zwischen Österreich und Preussen. Ergebnisse eines Symposiums in Würzburg vom 29.–31. Oktober 1987* (Sigmaringen, 1990), 307, 319, 329.

28 In particular, see František Graus, *Pest – Geissler – Judenmorde: Das 14. Jahrhundert als Krisenzeit* (Göttingen, 1987), 227; Arthur Süssmann, *Die Judenschudentilgungen unter König Wenzel* (Berlin, 1907); Wenninger, *Man bedarf*, 38–53.

be sure, even a small sum could be of considerable interest in times when money was urgently needed and debts were high.

Only with the intensification of territorial rule and Jewish policy beginning in the sixteenth century and the modest beginnings of economic advancement by individual Jews was there a change in the financial conditions and forms of Jewish policy. It has been verified, for example, that, beginning in this period, not only were Jews admitted for financial reasons but also that improved administration and tighter control permitted a more thorough and intensified taxation of Jews by means of uniform protection fees and the introduction of additional taxes.[29] As the rights of particularistic sovereignty were reasserted and financial administration became more centralized, the interest of the territorial princes in the Jews' taxes naturally increased as well. Where the Jews were exploited beyond their economic capacity, however, their numbers and financial productivity diminished very rapidly.[30]

After the Peace of Westphalia (1648), the expenditures of the absolutist princes rose sharply, owing to the cost of reconstruction and the lavishness of their courts. As a result, they used the growing number of Jews and the growth of the Jews' economic clout, levying old and new taxes on them, to increase the proceeds obtained from them. In contrast to the rest of the taxes, which were usually administered by the estates, taxes from Jews were at the princes' direct disposal. This went so far that people began to regard the Jews at that time as saviors of the state in times of financial distress.[31]

Although there was a great range of variation in how Jewish taxes were organized, the amount of individual taxes to be paid and the number of taxes levied continually increased, especially after about 1700.[32] Within the framework of restrictively applied Jewish policy, increased attention was paid to exploiting the Jews financially. Regulations about the minimum

29 Considering the small number of Jews admitted, it remains unclear whether or not the financial motives assumed here were really that strong. Only detailed investigations into the finances and taxation in specific territories could further elucidate the Jews' importance for state finances. Eckstein, *Juden in Bayreuth,* 19; Renda, "Fürth," 226; Rosenthal, *Heimatgeschichte,* 36–7; Rosenthal, *Juden in Hanau,* 49; Volkert, "Juden in Pfalz-Neuburg," 590.
30 For the case of Baden-Baden since 1594, see Renate Overdick, *Die rechtliche und wirtschaftliche Stellung der Juden in Südwestdeutschland im 15. und 16. Jahrhundert* (Constance, 1965), 110.
31 Peter Baumgart, "Der deutsche Hof der Barockzeit als politische Institution," in August Buck et al., eds., *Europäische Hofkultur im 16. und 17. Jahrhundert* (Hamburg, 1981), 1:25–43, 29; Stern, *Der preussische Staat,* 1:36–8, 80–3.
32 For figures, see Volkert, "Juden in Pfalz-Neuburg," 591; Guenter, *Juden in Lippe,* 18, 21–4, 28–32; Rosenthal, *Juden in Hanau,* 52, 81–5; Rosenthal, *Heimatgeschichte,* 59–69, 101, 117, 121; Hasselmeier, *Juden in Schaumburg-Lippe,* 57, 65–6; Stern, *Der preussische Staat,* 1:38–43, 83–6; 2:40–5, 52–3.

amount of wealth required for residence were intended to maintain the capacity for taxation and, at the same time, to reduce the number of Jews.[33] The poorer families were driven out to economically less interesting territories and to rural areas, where a distinction had to be made, after that, in the amount of the protection fee for rich and poor Jews.[34]

A regular component of the Jews' financial burden was the protection fee (*Schutzgeld*), typically in the form of concessions, refurbishments, or free-passage fees to be paid at ten- to twelve-year intervals or on the occasion of a change of ruler. Smaller amounts were assessed for marriages, births, deaths, and as regional payments; sometimes fees had to be paid for moving away or for marrying outside the country. The house of Brandenburg was particularly inventive, for example, in obligating the Jews to finance the military and to sell the products of the royal porcelain factory.[35]

The Jews also made a significant contribution to regular state and municipal taxes and assessments, as well as customs duties and excise taxes, and they were sometimes assessed for these at a higher rate.[36] Finally, they were burdened with sometimes arbitrary fines and, above all, with special assessments levied at various intervals, often in sizable amounts.

The dependence of the territorial princes on income from the Jews, around 1700 and after, has been acknowledged as a contributing factor in stabilizing the rights of residency for this minority. Moreover, in Prussia, the reform of the Jewish tax system in 1728 made the relationship between the state and its Jewish subjects more objective, that is to say, the Jews became "taxpayers of the state instead of a royal prerogative of the crown."[37]

Let us now consider a second social factor that affected rulers' individual decisions. Economic presuppositions and influences were closely related to the financial conditions and forms of Jewish policy. For clearly, if the Jews had no place in the economic life of the country, no opportunity to earn money, a tax policy designed to produce financial yields would not be possible. Thus, directly as well as indirectly, the policy toward Jews was aligned with the attractiveness of Jewish economic activity for the territorial prince and/or for the overall economy of the country.

No true economic policy planning with respect to the Jews can be identified in the late Middle Ages, in view of the general lack of capacity for political planning and the rather unattractive economic position of the Jews at

33 Rosenthal, *Heimatgeschichte*, 118; Volkert, "Juden in Pfalz-Neuburg," 591.
34 For example, see Hasselmeier, *Juden in Schaumburg-Lippe*, 57; Volkert, "Juden in Pfalz-Neuburg," 591.
35 Stern, *Der preussische Staat*, 1:83; 2:40–1; Agethen, "Jüdische Minderheit," 323.
36 This happened in Brandenburg-Prussia. Stern, *Der preussische Staat*, 1:40–1.   37 Ibid., 2:45–6.

this time.[38] Economic ties were formed, like the protection relationships, at an individual level or with small groups. Within this framework, individual Jews worked for the territorial prince himself or for his appointees, and, as a rule, the Jews were in the credit business. These, however, remained exceptional instances.

In the sixteenth century, too, this picture changed very little at first. Between expulsions sanctioned by the territorial prince, or despite them, individual Jews were accepted or given privileges for economic reasons. Since they often lacked the necessary capital, their role and significance in the credit business changed, and they worked primarily as credit facilitators.[39] At the same time a new sphere for various commercial activities unfolded very gradually, and these activities appear to have played the decisive role in all granting of privileges. There is noticeably more said about Jewish commerce in this context, both in general and in particular; for example, there are references to trading in gold and silver, to money changing, dealing in armor and guns, and to horse trading.[40]

The first indications of a more comprehensive economic policy with respect to the Jews are seen as part of the gradual change in Jewish policy that can be traced in the years after 1570. This policy shift reflects the positive evaluation of commerce in the mercantilistic thinking that was gradually gaining ground and extends it to the commerce of Jews as well, which various territorial princes now judged to be fruitful for the country and fostered accordingly.[41] In economic policy, a bipolar structure developed, which on the one hand continued to turn to those individuals who worked predominantly in the immediate interest of the territorial prince, such as court Jews, Jews engaged in minting money, or Jews holding princely monopolies, and on the other hand gradually included the business of the Jewish community as a whole in its calculations.

The sector of economic policy directed at individuals was an extension of the policies of the sixteenth century. It continued the arrangement whereby certain individuals were admitted and given privileges because their work was of interest – not infrequently as exceptions to the norms of Jewish policy otherwise in effect. Thus, for example, the emperor settled a few Jews in Breslau as lessees and managers of the minting operations. In

---

38 Territorial economic policy since the fifteenth century was, for a long time, restricted to regulation and was not yet concerned with process. See Herbert Hassinger, "Politische Kräfte und Wirtschaft, 1350–1800," in Hermann Aubin and Wolfgang Zorn, eds., *Handbuch der deutschen Wirtschafts- und Sozialgeschichte* (1971; Stuttgart, 1978), 1:608.

39 Volkert, "Juden in Pfalz-Neuburg," 567.   40 Rosenthal, *Heimatgeschichte*, 66–8, 72–3.

41 Examples in Israel, *European Jewry*, 40–4; Rosenthal, *Juden in Hanau*, 31.

the margraviate of Bayreuth, the Jews were appreciated for their usefulness, particularly in the "tides of war"; in Pfalz-Neuburg and in Lippe, individual Jews received privileges as dealers in precious metals and as entrepreneurs in coin minting, during and after the Thirty Years' War.[42] Even King Friedrich Wilhelm I of Prussia, who, at the very outset of his reign, had discharged the Jewess named Liebmann who had been in charge of minting coins, had little luck in making himself independent of the Jews engaged in minting, since they monopolized the silver trade. He therefore had to rehire Jews to run the mint.[43]

The preeminent role among the various privileged Jews was taken by the court Jews, who made themselves indispensable during the Thirty Years' War and were able to expand their positions at the German princely courts into an institution resembling a civil service. The court Jews fulfilled the requirements of the absolutist state and court by supplying the military after the war; by playing an increasing role in minting, state finances, and the international payments business; by working as trade and political agents; and by purveying diamonds and other jewels to the court.[44] Hence the function of the court Jews was not primarily concerned with the economy of the country as a whole; instead it concentrated on the prince and his court. The court Jews enabled him to be less dependent financially on the estates, facilitated the establishment of a loyal civil service and a standing army, and serviced the desire for luxury and ostentation. In so doing, they played an important role in developing the political structures of the early absolutist principality.

Through their far-flung business involvements, their traffic in precious metals and luxury goods, and their role in supplying the army, the court Jews did at the same time have an effect on the entire economy of the country. Their business association with a great number of other Jewish merchants, some of whom sooner or later also settled in the vicinity of the princely residence and engaged in trade, likewise had a stimulating effect on the economy. This kind of gradual Jewish resettlement of a territory in

42 Agethen, "Jüdische Minderheit," 310; Eckstein, *Juden in Bayreuth,* 24; Guenter, *Juden in Lippe,* 53–5; Volkert, "Juden in Pfalz-Neuberg," 582.

43 Stern, *Der preussische Staat,* 2:115.

44 Peter Baumgart, "Joseph Süss Oppenheimer: Das Dilemma des Hofjuden im absolutistischen Fürstenstaat," in Karlheinz Müller and Klaus Wittstadt, eds., *Geschichte und Kultur des Judentums* (Würzburg, 1988), 91–110, 92–3; see also Bernd Schedlitz, *Leffmann Behrens: Untersuchungen zum Hofjudentum im Zeitalter des Absolutismus* (Hildesheim, 1984), 91; Israel, *European Jewry,* 123; Battenberg, *Europäisches Zeitalter,* 1:245; Heinrich Schnee, *Die Hoffinanz und der moderne Staat: Geschichte und System der Hoffaktoren an deutschen Fürstenhöfen im Zeitalter des Absolutismus,* 6 vols. (Berlin, 1953–67); for a critique of Schnee's work, see Francis L. Carsten, "The Court Jews: A Prelude to Emancipation," *Leo Baeck Institute Year Book* 3 (1958): 140, 155–6.

the wake of a court Jew, which can be observed, for example, in Hanover after the end of the seventeenth century, was one way to demonstrate to the prince the usefulness of Jewish commerce and to prompt him to relax his Jewish policy.[45]

Another way – and here the individual differences of various territorial princes clearly come to bear – also presupposes, even without the prince's personal experience, the usefulness of Jewish commerce. This development was in keeping with the tenets of the mercantile system and followed, in part, the example of the Netherlands. It encouraged the settlement of Jews and facilitated their activity by liberalizing the prevailing structural conditions. The duke of Braunschweig-Wolfenbüttel followed this course, for example, as did the counts of Hanau, the territorial princes in Lippe, the elector of Brandenburg and the electors of the Palatinate.[46]

It is no coincidence that all of these examples come from the period between 1570 and 1700, for in 1700 a change of emphasis began within the mercantile system with a turn away from commerce and toward a more protectionist policy with stronger advocacy of manufacturing. The role of Jews in long-distance commerce lost immediacy, since the states were trying to provide for manufacturing all necessary products within their own borders. This resulted in a great number of export bans on raw materials and import bans on finished goods. Only trade with Poland, the importation of spices and unprocessed foodstuffs (raw sugar, tobacco leaves) remained open to the Jews.[47] Only a few Jews were able to distinguish themselves as factory owners, publishers, or franchise holders of state monopolies.[48] There were upheavals within the Jewish economic system as well, since the importance of the court Jews had withered in the long period of peace following the Treaty of Utrecht (1713), and they had begun to loosen their ties and their commitments to the Jewish community as well as to cooperation with their coreligionists.[49] Moreover, this period as a whole is characterized by a managed economy, which prescribed exactly what kind of goods the Jews could

---

45 Schedlitz, *Leffmann Behrens;* on Electoral Saxony, see Fritz Költzsch, "Kursachsen und die Juden in der Zeit Brühls," Ph.D. diss., Universität Leipzig, 1928.

46 Rosenthal, *Juden in Hanau,* 31, 49, 57; Guenter, *Juden in Lippe,* 17; Stern, *Der preussische Staat,* 1:33–8, 49–51, 79–80; Stefi Jersch-Wenzel, *Juden und "Franzosen" in der Wirtschaft des Raumes Berlin/Brandenburg zur Zeit des Merkantilismus* (Berlin, 1978), 40; Rosenthal, *Heimatgeschichte,* 101; Heinz Duchhardt, "Judenpolitik am Mittelrhein nach dem Dreissigjährigen Krieg," *Jahrbuch für westdeutsche Landesgeschichte* 8 (1982): 13–24, 18–20.

47 Israel, *European Jewry,* 247–9; Stern, *Der preussische Staat,* 1:133, 138; 2:60–6.

48 Stern, *Der preussische Staat,* 1:130; 2:89–105; Jersch-Wenzel, *Juden und "Franzosen,"* 196–200; Leopold Donath, *Geschichte der Juden in Mecklenburg von den ältesten Zeiten (1266) bis auf die Gegenwart (1874)* (Leipzig, 1874; reprinted 1974), 85–6; Guenter, *Juden in Lippe,* 78–83; Hasselmeier, *Juden in Schaumburg-Lippe,* 44; on craft policy, see Hassinger, "Politische Kräfte," 615, 635.

49 Israel, *European Jewry,* 243.

supply and trade as well as where they could reside, for the purpose of controlling competition among them or competition with Christian merchants. This *dirigisme* also selectively fostered commercial activity in certain cities or regions by providing favorable conditions there. It affected Silesia and East Prussia, for example, with emphasis on Königsberg or Frankfurt on the Oder, where the Jews were put to use in maintaining the important trade links with the east, which were handled almost exclusively by Polish and Russian Jews.[50] As a part of this flexible policy totally committed to the utilitarian ends of the state, restrictions were also relaxed in order to increase population in the wake of the wars, to rebuild cities, and to stimulate the establishment of factories, or, as in Prussia, where the financial system was still backward, to further Jewish currency trade.[51]

Within the framework of mercantile policies directed toward the financially robust Jewish merchants in the cities, the high-volume trade in agricultural products, particularly cattle, in which the Jews engaged played almost no role. Depending on the basic attitude underlying Jewish policy, this trade was tolerated, to a greater or lesser extent, as a by-product of Jewish settlement. Peddling met with still less political approval, since only in isolated instances was it considered useful,[52] and, particularly in the eighteenth century, it was saddled with ever more numerous restrictions. Finally, the regulations excluding Jews from artisanal occupations were scarcely eased at all. Mannheim remains a laudable exception to this.[53] Other than that, Bohemia, with its different kind of political and economic structure, and the area near the Polish border were the only places where Jewish artisans could be found.[54]

All of this shows that the economic elements of Jewish policy were applied in an exclusive manner and that the policy was still assigning a stopgap function to the Jews. As long as the trade they engaged in was appreciated in the context of economic policy, the Jews were wooed and granted

---

50 H. Heider, "Die Rechtsgeschichte des deutschen Judentums bis zum Ausgang des Absolutismus und die Judenordnungen in den rheinischen Territorialstaaten," LL.D. diss., Universität Bielefeld, 1973, 142; Overdick, *Stellung*, 127–8; Stern, *Der preussische Staat*, 1:124; 2:67–73, 82, 91; Hasselmeier, *Juden in Schaumburg-Lippe*, 53; Agethen, "Jüdische Minderheit," 319.

51 Agethen, "Jüdische Minderheit," 322; Stern, *Der preussische Staat*, 2:108.

52 Agethen, "Jüdische Minderheit," 324.

53 Rosenthal, *Heimatgeschichte*, 101.

54 See Anna M. Drabek, "Die Juden in den böhmischen Ländern zur Zeit des landesfürstlichen Absolutismus," in *Die Juden in den böhmischen Ländern. Vorträge der Tagung des Colloquium Carolinum in Bad Wiessee 27.–29. November 1981* (Munich and Vienna, 1983), 123–43; Vladimir Lipscher, "Jüdische Gemeinden in Böhmen und Mähren im 17. und 18. Jahrhundert," in *Die Juden in den böhmischen Ländern*, 73–86; Helmut Teufel, "Juden im Ständestaat: Zur politischen, wirtschaftlichen und sozialen Geschichte der Juden in Mähren zwischen 1526 und 1620," in *Die Juden in den böhmischen Ländern*, 57–71.

generous rights. After this line had been discarded, however, it quickly became evident that the position of the Jews had not fundamentally changed, and they were once again, indeed now more than ever, forced into a tight economic and social corset.

The significance of a third social factor, the political structures and decision-making processes of a particular state (or city), for Jewish policy has been underestimated, although recently some scholars have emphasized this aspect more.[55] The importance of this factor is immediately obvious where, for example as in Fürth or in Assenheim, several princes either shared local sovereignty or fought over it. This rivalry was capable of working to the advantage of the Jews when the local lords offered favorable privileges in order to attract Jews into their spheres of power. It could also veer to the opposite, however, if all the parties were merely attempting to exploit the Jews financially.[56]

In addition, however, the potential intervention of the emperor as the supreme protector has to be counted among the political conditions of the territorial princes' policy toward Jews. The constitutional structures within the territory devolving from the secular or ecclesiastical status of the respective prince, the articulation of demands on the part of the cities and/or the territorial estates, and the attempts by such societal groupings as the church or churches and the guilds and companies to exert influence must also be considered. For the sake of completeness, it should be noted that the guilds and companies, together with oppositional groups within the cities, played the decisive role in influencing urban Jewish policy.

The emperor's acts of intervention were usually limited to reacting to political decisions that had already been made and often already implemented, unless, of course, he saw his sovereign interests as being directly impacted. His intervention was usually initiated in response to persistent complaints from the Jews. The emperor perceived intervention to be called for when his own rights were being massively infringed upon,[57] as in the case in which Albert II of Mainz attempted the supraterritorial expulsion of Jews, or when the matter involved imperial prerogatives. In this latter function the emperor was, from the sixteenth century onward, gradually supplanted

55 Haverkamp, "Erzbischof Balduin," 451; R. Po-chia Hsia, "Die Juden im Alten Reich: Forschungsaufgaben zur Geschichte der Juden im späten Mittelalter und in der Frühen Neuzeit," in Georg Schmidt, ed., *Stände und Gesellschaft im Alten Reich* (Stuttgart, 1989), 211, 216.

56 See Battenberg, "Assenheim," 124; Renda, "Fürth," 225.

57 See Arye Maimon, "Der Judenvertreibungsversuch Albrechts II. von Mainz und sein Misserfolg (1515/16)," in Alfred Haverkamp, ed., *Zur Geschichte der Juden im Deutschland des späten Mittelalters und der frühen Neuzeit* (Stuttgart, 1981), 205, 218.

by the highest courts of the empire.[58] As a rule, it was the expulsions against which the Jews protested, but since the Jews' legal situation was so shaky that no territorial prince could be compelled to tolerate them, the emperor's opportunities to intervene were limited to demanding to know the legitimacy of the circumstances of the expulsion and making sure that the Jews were not also prohibited free passage through a territory. As a whole, the emperor's means of intervening in the Jewish policy of the territorial princes remained modest; as a power factor he was completely eliminated by the time the rights to Jewish protection had become fully territorialized, no later than in the seventeenth century.

In contrast to this, the political structures and negotiating mechanisms within the territories carried significant weight in shaping the policy toward Jews, since, until far into the modern period, many of the territorial princes did not yet possess the political autonomy we associate with the notion of an absolutist principality. In carrying out their political goals, especially in financing them, the princes were dependent on the consent and cooperation of political forces within the country, and therefore they were obliged again and again to make concessions.[59]

The ecclesiastical or secular status of the territorial prince must also be mentioned in this connection, if only for the sake of completeness, as one of the factors affecting territorial Jewish policy. In the late Middle Ages this appears to have had much less political relevance than, for example, the individual presuppositions and interests of the respective prince.[60] In the sixteenth century, the religious affiliation of the prince became one of the factors defining the specific Jewish policy of the time.

By the seventeenth and eighteenth centuries, however, there were two differences distinguishing the Jewish policy of ecclesiastical princes from that of secular princes.[61] First, the political structure of ecclesiastical states did not permit an egotistical, dynastically centered policy, and it tied political action to the electoral conditions set by the cathedral chapter. Second, although some of the ecclesiastical princes exercised an absolutist style of rule, they did not change over to a mercantile economic system that would have dealt with the Jews solely from the aspect of utility to the state. Hence,

---

58 See especially Sabine Frey, *Rechtsschutz der Juden gegen Ausweisungen im 16. Jahrhundert* (Frankfurt/Main, 1983).
59 See Rudolf Vierhaus, *Deutschland im Zeitalter des Absolutismus, 1648–1763* (Göttingen, 1978), 117.
60 Cf. Haverkamp, "Erzbischof Balduin."
61 See the contribution of J. Friedrich Battenberg in this volume (Chapter 16). For a regional comparison between Jewish policy of ecclesiastical and secular territorial princes, see Duchhardt, "Judenpolitik."

their policies toward the Jews tended to remain traditional and bound to canon law. The multiplicity of authorities and those entitled to play a political role, as well as the broad distribution of ecclesiastical and secular powers, opened up political space in which Jews could exist.[62] Although the Jews enjoyed fewer rights under the ecclesiastical princes, they did occupy a place in society as a defined and segregated community, not only exclusively as interesting individuals.

The cities, the estates, and the largely Protestant clergy, none of them involved in protecting Jews nor in the profits accruing from such protection, formulated anti-Jewish demands for political, economic, or ideological reasons. Within the cities, the guilds and the merchant class bore the responsibility for these efforts, and the cities in turn set the tone of hostility to Jews on the part of the territorial estates. The demands of all three groups were mainly aimed at an expulsion of the Jews, or, if this did not appear feasible, they limited themselves to asking for far-reaching restrictions on the number of Jews, their commercial opportunities, or their religious liberty.[63]

Although in the sixteenth century the clergy were frequently able to exert influence on Jewish policy, after the seventeenth century they were largely denied any direct political impact.[64] They possessed no means of power to get their way, but their propaganda did nonetheless indirectly affect the political atmosphere with regard to Jews, and this in turn was articulated by the estates.

To date, little is known about policy negotiating and decision-making strategies with respect to the demands made by the cities and the estates. But in some places it is evident that the territorial prince and his officials succeeded in forging compromises. Thus, for example, Count Bernhard of Lippe (1536–63) bought the approval of the cities to admit Jews by con-

---

62 Cf. Heider, "Rechtsgeschichte," 85–121, 134; Ismar Elbogen and Eleonore Sterling, *Die Geschichte der Juden in Deutschland: Eine Einführung* (Frankfurt/Main, 1966), 105.

63 On cities, see Donath, *Juden in Mecklenburg,* 111; Guenter, *Juden in Lippe,* 12–13, 19, 58–60; Hasselmeier, *Juden in Schaumburg-Lippe,* 3, 41–3, 92; Rosenthal, *Heimatgeschichte,* 103–7; Stern, *Der preussische Staat,* 2:75–8; Leo Trepp, *Die Oldenburger Judenschaft. Bild und Vorbild jüdischen Seins und Werdens in Deutschland* (Oldenburg, 1973), 20; Volkert, "Juden in Pfalz-Neuburg," 585. On the estates, see Eckstein, *Juden in Bayreuth,* 24; Guenter, *Juden in Lippe,* 12–14; Költzsch, "Kursachsen," 294–300.

64 This subject has so far been dealt with insufficiently. For now, see Battenberg, "Reformation," 330–3; Salfeld, "Philipp der Grossmütige," 528–43; Maurer, "Martin Butzer," 35–43; Kohls, "Judenfrage"; Rotraud Ries, "Zur Bedeutung von Reformation und Konfessionalisierung für das christlich-jüdische Verhältnis in Niedersachsen," in Leonore Siegele-Wenschkewitz, ed., *Als Minderheit in einer christlichen Gesellschaft. Beiträge zum Verhältnis von Juden und Christen in der Reformationszeit* (Neukirchen, 1992). More generally, see Israel, *European Jewry,* 10–13; for observations on the seventeenth and eighteenth centuries, see Eckstein, *Juden in Bayreuth,* 33, 38–41, 48–52; Guenter, *Juden in Lippe,* 56–7; Rosenthal, *Juden in Hanau,* 56–7.

ceding to them the right to collect a domicile tax from the Jews.[65] In 1653, shortly after he assumed rule, Philipp-Wilhelm of Pfalz-Neuburg (1653–90) permitted the city of Lauingen its long-desired expulsion of Jews in spite of current covenants, but obligated the city to reimburse the Jews for the protection money they had already paid in advance and also to see to it that all debt claims of the Jews were satisfied.[66]

A widespread reaction to the demands of the estates was represented also by concessions on individual points and by promises for the future, for example, the promise to allow the covenants with the Jews to lapse and to motivate them to an earlier departure. Promises of this kind were frequently not kept, but they had the function of providing an anti-Jewish facade, behind which the prince retained a relatively free hand to make decisions that enabled Jews to be admitted and given privileges; deliberately ambiguous formulations in the covenants and laws played the same role.[67]

Admittedly, the many measures carried out at the wish of the estates and under the pressures they exerted show that their anti-Jewish political potential was nevertheless effective.[68] Even territorial princes who were relatively friendly toward Jews were sometimes induced, for political reasons, to pursue an anti-Jewish policy – for instance, Emperor Rudolph II in Silesia, in 1582 – or to react with flexibility to the respective regional balances of power and thus to exhibit a Jewish policy that at first glance seems self-contradictory – for example, Elector Friedrich Wilhelm I of Brandenburg-Prussia.[69]

The pressure exerted by the estates on Jewish policy did, however, gradually diminish. Their claims to political codetermination were rejected by the absolutist princes, whose political goal was to gain exclusive authority over finances, the army, and the bureaucracy.[70] The inclusion of Jewish policy in the basic political line directed at the estates and its simultaneous liberation from the influence of the estates can be followed with particular clarity in Brandenburg-Prussia, thanks to the research conducted by Selma Stern.[71] The power complexes differed so greatly in the various territories,

65 Guenter, *Juden in Lippe*, 10–11. For a similar event, which took place in Schaumburg-Lippe in 1666, see Hasselmeier, *Juden in Schaumburg-Lippe*, 64.

66 Volkert, "Juden in Pfalz-Neuburg," 585.

67 Rosenthal, *Heimatgeschichte*, 72; Donath, *Juden in Mecklenburg*, 119; Költzsch, "Kursachsen," 299–300, 306.

68 For examples, see Eckstein, *Juden in Bayreuth*, 16–19; Overdick, *Stellung*, 102; Paul Sauer, *Die jüdischen Gemeinden in Württemberg und Hohenzollern: Denkmale, Geschichte, Schicksale* (Stuttgart, 1966), 2; Guenter, *Juden in Lippe*, 13, 58–60; Heider, "Rechtsgeschichte," 150; Donath, *Juden in Mecklenburg*, 94–5, 110; Volkert, "Juden in Pfalz-Neuburg," 597.

69 Agethen, "Jüdische Minderheit," 309; Stern, *Der preussische Staat*, 1:60–1, 66–75.

70 Baumgart, "Hof der Barockzeit," 28.

71 Stern, *Der preussische Staat*, 1:21, 47–8, 60–1, 65–79, 95–8, 154; 2:22–9.

however, that the development in Prussia, essentially completed by the Great Elector, cannot be simply extrapolated to other regions, where the estates might from the outset have had fewer chances to exert influence, or where perhaps the process of repressing the estates lasted until far into the eighteenth century.

The fact that the estates, especially the territorial princes and the nobility, were capable of pursuing a policy friendly to Jews when they themselves profited by it is demonstrated by the situation in the eastern and southeastern parts of the empire. In East Prussia, Pomerania, and Silesia, and particularly in Bohemia and Moravia, the powerful nobility protected a great number of Jews in the countryside and on their manors and used them in pursuing an economic policy to compete with the cities. Such a nobleman had little interest in expelling or restricting Jews; consequently he fought against any anti-Jewish policy of the territorial prince and boycotted it.[72]

Even in absolutist princely states, political negotiations and decision-making processes were not exclusively the concern of the ruler; the territorial bureaucracy also played a role. The bureaucracy not only was involved in formulating the content of policy toward the Jews but also participated in translating it into concrete administrative action. The treatment of Jews was thereby subject, among other things, to the organization and development of territorial administrations. Only the territorial bureaucracies, most of which were established in the sixteenth century, were organizationally in a position to register a large number of Jews on their own and to keep an eye on the Jews and to "use" them in the immediate interest of the prince.[73] This consolidation and centralization of administrative activity with regard to the Jews continued in the seventeenth and eighteenth centuries.

In small, easily managed territories like Schaumburg-Lippe, this led to a situation in which the central administration monopolized all decisions concerning the Jews – for example, for collecting protection money or granting dispensation or respite from payment thereof – and in legal matters only the highest court of the country had jurisdiction.[74] In the larger territories, whose composition was more complex, such as Brandenburg-Prussia, or the areas ruled from a distance, such as the county of Hanau or Bohemia and Moravia, the local governments and administrative bodies remained involved in Jewish policy, and thus they developed perceptions and interests that diverged from those of the central power. Because of their more in-

---

72 Ibid., 1:135–8; Agethen, "Jüdische Minderheit," 314; Drabek, "Juden in den böhmischen Ländern"; Lipscher, "Jüdische Gemeinden"; Teufel, "Juden im Ständestaat," 57, 61–3.
73 See Ries, "Judenpolitik in Braunschweig-Calenberg."
74 Hasselmeier, *Juden in Schaumburg-Lippe,* 83–6, 91.

tensive knowledge of local details and also for the sake of political calm, their opinions were taken into account (at the discretion of the ruling power) in making policy decisions.[75] In the wake of the various administrative reforms in Prussia, the elimination of the influence of the estates and of urban autonomy, and the centralization and standardization of policy, Jewish affairs were also completely reorganized (ultimately in the *Generalprivilegium* of 1730). Jewish matters were placed under the directorate general and the chambers for war and for the crown lands, an administration that was uniform for all parts of the country.[76] Since that time the particularistic entities of the estates and the cities that were largely hostile toward Jews were prevented, for the most part, from exercising influence and from administrative chicanery.

Moreover, Jewry profited from this situation in which a bureaucracy imbued with the ideas of the Enlightenment now had exclusive responsibility for them, a bureaucracy that gradually developed a benevolent humanitarian interest in the Jews, as happened, for example, with the members of the Jewish Commission by virtue of their intensive preoccupation with the matter. This was also the case with the ministers of King Friedrich Wilhelm I, who influenced him and contradicted him when he violated the tenets of *Staatsräson*. They were opponents of the small, particularistic state controlled by the estates, as well as of Lutheran orthodoxy, and were instead adherents of natural rights and the enlightened welfare state. And it was true of civil officials, who, in practical administration, brought some of the king's anti-Jewish regulations into harmony.[77]

Two other factors – the need to set norms for the coexistence of Christians and Jews, and the reception of general developments in jurisprudence – are among the elements of social reality that shaped Jewish policy in the long term. Christian theology excluded those of a different faith, the kings and emperors placed Jewish merchants in a protected position, Jewish economic competition was throttled by urban commerce and trades – all of these fostered the emergence of a body of Jewish law over the centuries that was available to every territorial prince as he shaped his Jewish policy.[78] The general conditioning factors of Jewish policy described here determined the need for standardization and with it also the rules and regulations

75 Rosenthal, *Juden in Hanau,* 73; Lipscher, "Jüdische Gemeinden," 74; Stern, *Der preussische Staat,* 1:18, 20–1; on the administration of Jewish affairs, see ibid., 13–17, 23, 88–94, 98–101.

76 Stern, *Der preussische Staat,* 2:12–29.

77 Ibid., 1:99–101; 2:10; Agethen, "Jüdische Minderheit," 326; Baumgart, "Minorität," 240.

78 On the process of setting norms for the Jews, see Rotraud Ries, "Juden: Zwischen Schutz und Verteufelung," in Bernd-Ulrich Hergemöller, ed., *Randgruppen der spätmittelalterlichen Gesellschaft. Ein Hand- und Studienbuch* (Warendorf, 1990), 232–76, 233–46.

that were actually applied. Since these were different for each territorial lord, this led to substantial regional and chronological differences in territorial Jewish law. Provided that Jewish settlement had existed more or less continuously, a matrix of norms was formed specific to the territory, and these solidified into traditions.[79] On the other hand, when Jewish policy was aligned to particular local economic circumstances, the body of Jewish law that emerged could well be inconsistent and vary according to locality.[80]

The establishment of Jewish rights through letters of protection and privileges issued by the territorial princes, which began in the fourteenth century, reveals that the need for standardization was still slight. A greater need became more apparent in the course of the sixteenth century, when the territorial princes consolidated Jewish policy. From that point on, there was a growing tendency for legal provisions affecting Jews to be included in the national or police ordinances or in special Jewish ordinances, all of which were then emerging.[81] Like other inhabitants of the country, the Jews then became victims of the standardization and control endeavors typical of early modern times, but they profited at the same time from the concurrent stabilization of their rights. Despite persisting regional differences, the Jewish law, which affected every sphere of life for the Jews, tended to exhibit a greater uniformity. This was probably owing to improved conditions of communication and, above all, to the fact that the development of law in the larger territories functioned as a model for the rest.

Beyond the difference in the relationship of ecclesiastical and secular princes to the Jews, the Reformation and denominational schism in the sixteenth century altered the conditions of Jewish policy; the religious denomination of the territorial prince also became a significant social factor influencing Jewish policy. The general religious confrontation of the time played a role in this at first: It led to an atmosphere of aggression and a more radical policy toward all those who believed in a way different from oneself. This also meant the Jews.[82] In the course of this worsening climate, which the theologians were not the last to foment, the territorial princes who had now become Protestants perceived themselves to have been put in a new position of responsibility for the spiritual salvation of their subjects; they internalized the religious arguments of the theologians and made them the maxims of their policy. Foremost consideration was given to the alleged blasphemy of the Jews. Since blasphemy was outlawed everywhere, it served,

79 See, e.g., the multitude of specific taxes in the county of Hanau. Rosenthal, *Juden in Hanau,* 27.
80 On Lippe, see Guenter, *Juden in Lippe,* 62–3.
81 Battenberg, "Rechtsstellung," 140, 165; Battenberg, "Judenordnungen der frühen Neuzeit in Hessen," in *Neunhundert Jahre Geschichte der Juden in Hessen,* 83–122.
82 Hsia, "Juden im Alten Reich," 219.

along with the charge of usury, as the most accessible argument for expulsion.[83] By and large, previous scholarship has left the connection between the religious affiliation of the prince and his policy toward the Jews quite vague. Conclusions have been limited to statements like these: The Elector of the Palatinate had attempted since the introduction of the Reformation to expel the Jews; Margrave Georg Friedrich of Baden-Durlach (1604–22), a strict Lutheran, expelled the Jews on religious grounds at the beginning of the seventeenth century and sought to prevent their readmission by means of appropriate provisions in his will.[84] The role that Luther's anti-Jewish recommendations played in this context has never been adequately examined. For it was precisely the theological changes of the Reformation period that permitted the princes to assume personal responsibility in response to the demands of the theologians and gave them the autonomy to choose between religious and worldly goals. This is evident in the Jewish ordinance of 1539 in Hesse, in which Landgrave Philipp embraced the religious provisions from commentaries by Bucer and other clerics, thus adopting religious constraint and conversion of the Jews as his own goals, but at the same time ignored the clerics' insistence on banning usury and commerce. In so doing, he enabled the Jews to retain a certain economic latitude and made it possible for them to remain in the country.[85] After the middle of the seventeenth century, the issue of religious affiliation gradually lost its political relevance.

The last two factors affecting territorial Jewish policy are even less capable of being fleshed out than the points discussed earlier. They should therefore be understood only as indicators. The first to be mentioned is the spatial component, which involves the geographical position of the territory in relation to the imperial ruler (*Königsnähe*) and to neighboring areas, especially those areas belonging to other lords located within one's own borders. Both aspects determined the prince's scope for political action and influenced policy beyond any direct competition for the rights over Jews, since the settled presence of Jews and especially their commerce in the immediate vicinity had to be taken into account in forming policy.[86]

The unfolding pattern of Jewish settlement, its concentration in the southern and southeastern parts of the empire and its gradual advance to the north and east, along with the number of Jews and the age of the Jewish community, also created differing presuppositions for Jewish policy. It is evident, for example, that in a territory with merely a handful of Jewish fam-

---

83 See, e.g., Eckstein, *Juden in Bayreuth*, 20.
84 Rosenthal, *Heimatgeschichte*, 63–6, 72–3; Overdick, *Stellung*, 102.
85 Battenberg, "Reformation," 330; Battenberg, *Europäisches Zeitalter*, 1:197; Salfeld, "Philipp der Grossmütige," 528.
86 Eckstein, *Juden in Bayreuth*, 22–5; Volkert, "Juden in Pfalz-Neuburg," 564.

ilies there would be less objective need for establishing norms for coexistence with Christians than in a territory in which the Jewish population was comparatively large.

The age, and especially the size, of the Jewish presence seem to have influenced the forming of regional attitudes toward them. The greater the number of Jews, the more alienation, rivalry, and envy were felt among the populace. An even stronger influence on attitude might well have been the frequency and intensity of Jewish persecutions, the public efficacy of discriminatory Jewish policy, and very importantly, the anti-Jewish incitement articulated mostly by clerics.

Even if the princes did not necessarily share the attitude of their people toward Jews, they still could not entirely avoid the political pressures that emanated from that and under some circumstances were challenged to react. At the level of territorial bureaucracy there was, moreover, a close relationship between popular attitude and policy.

III

The region examined here is southeastern Lower Saxony, lying between Hanover, Hildesheim, Braunschweig, Helmstedt, Hameln, Göttingen, and Goslar. Here there had been Jews since about the middle of the thirteenth century.[87] The lords who ruled in this area were the dukes of Braunschweig-Lüneburg in the lines of Wolfenbüttel, Calenberg-Göttingen, and Grubenhagen, as well as the bishops of Hildesheim.[88]

There is no record of a transfer of Jewish protection rights from the emperor to the dukes of Braunschweig-Lüneburg, although Duke Ernst of Braunschweig-Lüneburg (1345–67) refers to this in 1348.[89] What was decisive for the Jews was that the territorial princes exercised these rights. Yet already by the end of the thirteenth century the princes could no longer pursue an autonomous policy toward the Jews, because the Jews were pouring into the larger towns and commercial centers of the country, which were already well on their way to wresting a certain autonomy from their territorial lords. Thus it happened that the princes requested towns like Braunschweig and Göttingen to admit Jews and involved the town coun-

---

87 For articles on the cities in Lower Saxony mentioned here, see Ismar Elbogen, Aaron Freimann, and H. Tykocinski, eds., *Germania Judaica,* vol. 1: *Von den ältesten Zeiten bis 1238* (Breslau, 1938), 118; and Zvi Avneri, ed., *Germania Judaica,* vol. 2: *Von 1238 bis zur Mitte des 14. Jahrhunderts,* 2 vols. (Tübingen, 1968).

88 Hermann Kleinau, "Überblick über die Gebietsentwicklung des Landes Braunschweig," *Braunschweigisches Jahrbuch* 52 (1972): 9–48.

89 Gustav Schmidt, ed., *Urkundenbuch der Stadt Göttingen,* 2 vols. (Hanover, 1863–67), 1:163–4, no. 172.

cils in the protection of the Jews (1296 and 1348).[90] This trend corresponds to the increasing autonomy, though not legalized, of urban Jewish policy.

Aside from specially protected individuals, the Jews of the country in general stood under the unwritten and open-ended protection of the territorial prince. For the Jews of Braunschweig and Göttingen, however, the prince did confirm this protection in writing prior to the persecutions associated with the Black Death.[91]

In the quarter century after the plague, the Guelph princes sold their Jewish protection rights in Braunschweig, Göttingen, and Hanover to the town councils, and thus limited their opportunities for political influence on the Jewish communities of smaller towns within their spheres of authority. Hameln was already able to decide freely about its Jews after 1277.[92]

We know of only a few scattered instances of connections between territorial princes and Jews up to the end of the fifteenth century. No letters of protection have come down to us at all; tax payments, business contacts, and interventions on behalf of individual Jews are only occasionally documented.[93] The potential for activity by the dukes in Jewish policy thus appears to have been relatively slight, even when one takes into account the distortions resulting from the transmission of historical materials. The practice still current in the sixteenth century leads one to think that there were individual Jews under the special protection of the princes but that the majority of them, the "common Jews" (*Gemeine Juden*), enjoyed general protection.

Only in the beginning of the sixteenth century does the Jewish policy of the territorial princes become more visible, so for this reason we will now distinguish among the various lines of the house of Braunschweig-Lüneburg.

The partitioned dukedom of Calenberg had existed since 1495 in its divided form, with the land between the Deister and the Leine in the north and the province of Göttingen in the south.[94] Until the family died out in 1584, this territory was ruled by the dukes Erich I (1495–1540) and Erich II (1540–84). It then fell to Wolfenbüttel. Between 1540 and 1546, Duchess

---

90 Ibid.; Ludwig Hänselmann and Heinrich Mack, eds., *Urkundenbuch der Stadt Braunschweig,* 4 vols. (Braunschweig and Berlin, 1873–1912), 2:201, no. 418.

91 Hänselmann and Mack, eds., *Urkundenbuch Braunschweig,* 1:42, no. 35; 42–3, no. 37; Schmidt, ed., *Urkundenbuch Göttingen,* 1:163–4, no. 172.

92 Hermann Sudendorf, ed., *Urkundenbuch zur Geschichte der Herzöge von Braunschweig und Lüneburg und ihrer Lande,* 11 vols. (Hanover and Göttingen, 1859–83), 3:137, no. 212; 4:62–3, no. 55; Peter Wilhelm, "Die jüdische Gemeinde in der Stadt Göttingen von den Anfängen bis zur Emanzipation," Ph.D. diss., Universität Göttingen, 1973, 22; Otto Meinardus, ed., *Urkundenbuch des Stiftes und der Stadt Hameln* (Hanover, 1887), 1:57–9, no. 79.

93 For information on individual cities, see the articles in volume 3 of *Germania Judaica.*

94 Kleinau, "Überblick über die Gebietsentwicklung," 35–6.

Elisabeth controlled policy-making as regent for her son, Erich II.[95] The central towns of the two land parcels were Hanover and Göttingen.

The Jewish policy of the Calenberg dukes reveals itself in the areas of the economy, finances, law, and measures of protection. In addition to these, an important matter for the Jews was the kind of relationship that existed between the territorial princes and the towns with respect to Jewish policy.[96]

Economy. Business contacts were a constant element in the relation of the Calenbergs to local and foreign Jews. Duke Erich I repeatedly obtained credit from Jews and had business dealings in particular with Michel von Derenburg and his relatives living in Lower Saxony.[97] The proportion of Jews among the creditors of Erich I remained small, on the whole, since the duke primarily employed them to negotiate credit; their own capital would not have covered the sums needed.[98] Duke Erich II likewise had Jews do business for him and take business trips, but nothing more is known about the purpose of these activities. In addition, he utilized the commercial contacts of the Jews to the advantage of the ducal mint. In 1562, one Jew was put under contract to supply silver for the mint in Münden, and in 1565 another was installed as the lessee of the mint in Wunstorf. All the Jews in the country were enlisted to supply raw material for the new mint. The Christian overseers of the Wunstorf mint either proved to be dishonest or else gave up the job very quickly, hence the mint was closed again in 1569.[99]

Finances. For the deeply indebted Calenberg dukes, the financial aspect of Jewish policy played a significant role; at least they made good use of the fact that there were Jews in the country. It is not clear from the documents whether they also admitted Jews on financial grounds. The tax requirements encompassed Jewish protection money, contributions to the country's treasury and other taxes imposed on all the inhabitants of the country, special levies and more or less special payments on the occasion of marriages and similar events. Before the middle of the sixteenth century, the protection money ranged between 1 florin (gulden) and 5 talers; after 1575 this was

---

95 See especially Albert Brauch, "Die Verwaltung des Territoriums Calenberg-Göttingen während der Regentschaft der Herzogin Elisabeth 1540–46," Ph.D. diss., Universität Leipzig, 1930.

96 For details, see Ries, "Judenpolitik in Braunschweig-Calenberg."

97 Brauch, "Verwaltung," 249; for archival evidence, see Ries, "Judenpolitik in Braunschweig-Calenberg."

98 Brauch, "Verwaltung," 249, 256.

99 Eduard Fiala, *Münzen und Medaillen der welfischen Lande,* pt. 5: *Das mittlere Haus Braunschweig, Linie zu Calenberg* (Prague, 1904), 15–24; Heinrich Ohlendorf, *Geschichte der Stadt Wunstorf* (Wunstorf, 1957), 67–72; Hauptstaatsarchiv Hannover, Cal. Br. 13, no. 13, fol. 33.

standardized to 6 talers.[100] More oppressive than the taxes that were imposed (not very systematically) were the special levies that were mentioned several times; there was one amounting to 1,200 florins in 1515, for example, that was extorted by arresting all the Jewish men in the Göttingen section of the country.[101] In 1553, Duke Erich II proclaimed the expulsion of all Jews from the country, only to have his officials bargain with each Jew on the price for extending protection.[102] Something similar happened in 1574–5, although this time Erich may at first have actually intended to expel the Jews. He allowed his mind to be changed quickly by his councilors when they reminded him of the extra tax on the Jews that could be demanded.[103]

Law. The few extant letters of protection were issued only to those Jews who were under the duke's special protection or whose acceptance into the group of "common Jews" required special arrangements.[104] The majority of the Jews were included in a corporation under the general protection of the territorial prince, at least until 1574. There was very little need to formulate a special body of Jewish law by standardizing legal norms. Up to 1575, only the position of Jews in courts of law had been spelled out; in a letter of protection of the same year, some trade provisions were issued for the first time. A Jewish ordinance proclaimed by Duchess Elisabeth in 1543 was never instituted.[105] Just like the Christian inhabitants, the Jews were subject to the jurisdiction of the ducal court and had the same procedural opportunities. Unequal treatment, which can be assumed in only a few instances, was not the result of any political handicap but rather of the discretionary latitude of individual ducal officials.[106]

Protective measures. The stabilization of law and the fairly affirmative basic posture toward the Jews can be most clearly seen in the numerous measures that served to protect the Jews and their rights. Besides Duchess Elisabeth herself and several officials, it was the ducal councilors who distinguished themselves in particular. Because of the frequent absence of the territorial

100 For further evidence, see Ries, "Judenpolitik in Braunschweig-Calenberg."
101 Staatsarchiv Wolfenbüttel, 2 Alt 1611, fols. 1–3.
102 Meir Wiener, "Geschichte der Juden in der Residenzstadt Hannover, vorzugsweise während des 16. Jahrhunderts," *Monatsschrift f. d. Geschichte und Wissenschaft des Judentums* 10 (1861): 121, 161, 241, 281, and suppl. 6, 170; an interpretation can be found in Ries, "Judenpolitik in Braunschweig-Calenberg."
103 See Ries, "Judenpolitik in Braunschweig-Calenberg."
104 Hauptstaatsarchiv Hannover, Cal. Br. 23, No. 546, fol. 23–24, 28; Cal. Br. 23, no. 548, fols. 16–19.
105 Hauptstaatsarchiv Hannover, Cal. Br. 8, no. 171.
106 Cf. Ries, "Judenpolitik in Braunschweig-Calenberg."

lord, they were already quite involved, mostly autonomously, with Jewish policy.[107]

The relationship between the dukes and those cities that exercised rights of Jewish protection on their own (Hanover, Göttingen, Hameln, Northeim) was founded on compromise and consensus. Because of this, the Jews did not become victims of political strife between the territorial lords and the cities. The situation was different in the small towns that did not participate in the protection of Jews; here there developed an unambiguously anti-Jewish attitude.[108]

The Wolfenbüttel part of the country was ruled in the sixteenth century by the dukes Heinrich the Elder (1495–1514), Heinrich the Younger (1514–68), Julius (1568–89), and Heinrich Julius (1589–1613). The duchy's main town was Braunschweig, which enjoyed economic and political dominance over the entire region. The city was de facto independent of the territorial lord, and until the expulsion of 1546 the largest Jewish community in the region existed there.[109]

The Wolfenbüttel Jewish policy was divided into the same elements as the Calenberg policy. Since it exhibits many breaks in continuity, however, owing to the personalities of the rulers, it will be presented chronologically rather than systematically.

Like their Calenberg cousins, the Wolfenbüttel dukes maintained business contacts with a few rich Jews from whom they repeatedly obtained credit during the second half of the fifteenth century and at the beginning of the sixteenth.[110] There is no information about how the protective relationship was formed under Heinrich the Elder and Heinrich the Younger. One can only surmise that there were parallels to the policy in Calenberg, that is, that both general and special protection of Jews were practiced at the same time. Heinrich the Elder did, however, display some interest in having and using the rights to Jewish protection, for in 1494 he took advantage of a temporary weakness of Braunschweig to try to regain these and other rights – but he did so in vain. Only twelve years later he acquiesced in the legally impugnable Jewish policy of Braunschweig, certainly not without receiving money to do so, and granted the city the right to expel its Jews.[111]

---

107 Ibid.   108 Ibid.
109 See Hans-Heinrich Ebeling, *Die Juden in Braunschweig. Rechts-, Sozial- und Wirtschaftsgeschichte von den Anfängen der jüdischen Gemeinde bis zur Emanzipation (1282–1848)* (Braunschweig, 1987); Rotraud Ries, "Zum Zusammenhang von Reformation und Judenvertreibung. Das Beispiel Braunschweig," in Helmut Jäger et al., eds., *Civitatum Communitas: Festschrift Heinz Stoob zum 65. Geburtstag,* 2 vols. (Cologne and Vienna, 1984), 2:630–54.
110 Ebeling, *Juden in Braunschweig,* 65, 75.
111 Ibid., 13–14; Gustav Hassebrauk, "Herzog Heinrich d.J. und die Stadt Braunschweig, 1514–1568," *Jahrbuch des Geschichtsvereins für das Herzogtum Braunschweig* 5 (1906): 1–61, 10.

Heinrich the Younger, one of the most prominent personalities among the Catholic princes of his time, had little interest in Jewish policy, since his country was beset by conditions resembling civil war and he himself was ultimately driven out by the Schmalkaldic League. The position of Jews in a court of law, comparable to that in Calenberg, demonstrates the incorporation of the Jewish minority into the existing legal system of the early modern state that was typical of the period, whereas the protection money of 1 or 2 florins per family, which had remained constant since the fifteenth century, and the absence of special levies document a relatively low level of interest in exploiting the Jews. What was decisive in Wolfenbüttel's Jewish policy was ultimately the personal attitude of Heinrich the Younger in the decade of the 1550s and perhaps the attitude of his councilors as well. Convinced of the perniciousness of Jewish commerce, against which the Wolfenbüttel mining ordinance (*Bergordnung*) of 1551 was also directed, the duke allowed himself to be lured into collectively criminalizing the Jewish minority, after two crimes happened to be committed at the same time by Jews, and in 1557 he expelled all the Jews from his country.[112]

When Heinrich's unloyal son Julius, a merchant on the ducal throne,[113] began to rule in 1568, the Jews renewed their hopes. In 1569, they approached Julius in Prague, and somewhat later they motivated Emperor Maximilian II to write a letter requesting Julius to once again offer the Jews safe-conduct for passage through his lands.[114] In the following years, business dealings with the duke's officials smoothed the way for the initial contacts between the duke and a few Jews, prior to holding secret negotiations in 1577 and 1578 about readmitting the Jews. Israel Schay from Bodenwerder negotiated on the Jewish side about the intention of several distinguished and wealthy Jews to settle in Wolfenbüttel. The prerequisite for this project was that Jews were to be permitted safe passage through the principality once again.[115] Not until August 1578 did Duke Julius finally decree such a general safe-conduct, and later selected Jews were allowed to take up domicile. The duke had a settlement built in Melverode (between Braunschweig and Wolfenbüttel) expressly for this purpose.[116]

112 *Bergordnung* Heinrichs d.J. from 1551, printed in 1552. Hauptstaatsarchiv Hannover, Bergordnung. On mandates, see Wiener, "Residenzstadt," suppl. 8, 173; on crimes, see Staatsarchiv Wolfenbüttel, 1 Alt 8, no. 258; 8 Alt, no. 258, fols. 14–23.

113 Albert Neukirch, *Niedersächsische Adelskultur der Renaissance* (Hanover, 1939), 19; Fritz Redlich, "Der deutsche fürstliche Unternehmer, eine typische Erscheinung des 16. Jahrhunderts," *Tradition* 3 (1958): 17–31, 98–112, 18, 21.

114 Staatsarchiv Wolfenbüttel, 1 Alt 9, no. 372, fol. 26; Wiener, "Residenzstadt," suppl. 9, 248.

115 Staatsarchiv Wolfenbüttel, 1 Alt 9, no. 27; 1 Alt 9, no. 372, fols. 4–7, 10.

116 Wiener, "Residenzstadt," suppl. 16, 254; Staatsarchiv Wolfenbüttel, 2 Alt 8489, fols. 19–21.

It is evident from this general safe-passage decree that in admitting Jews, Julius was pursuing goals of economic policy. The Jews were to import useful goods, engage in trade with the subjects and particularly with ducal officials, and see to the marketing of products from the ducal mines and quarries in other countries. The passage and residence of the Jews was organized down to the last administrative detail, and a multitude of economic, legal, social, and religious norms constrained their conduct and at the same time secured their rights. Protection money was made uniform at 6 gold florins, in addition to which there were rather considerable sums for rent, permission for slaughter, circumcision, and marriages, plus contributions to the state treasury and other extraordinary taxes.

The readmission of Jews released a wave of protest that was articulated especially by the country's theologians in written commentaries and in sermons. The territorial estates kept demanding the expulsion of the Jews, and in the ducal council people were very critical of the fact that Jews were again being tolerated. Nonetheless, Duke Julius held firmly to his policy; he saw to it that the Jews were protected and had fair trials in court; he rejected wholesale accusations against them.[117]

This massively anti-Jewish mood exploded immediately after Julius's death in 1589, when the court council imposed a ban on the Jews' exercise of their religion and the synagogues were closed.[118] This was followed, in January 1590 and in June 1591 by the expulsion of Jews from the country and renewed withdrawal of safe-passage. Not until the emperor had intervened several times was passage permitted once again in 1594.[119]

In contrast to his father, Heinrich Julius had no economic interest in the Jews. In the unstable political situation at the time when rulership changed hands, he had to rely on consensus with the most important social forces in the country, and so he caved in to the demands for expulsion. After he had admitted individual Jews once again twenty years later, the same thing happened when his successor took over the government.[120]

IV

The Guelph territories were among those regions remote from the king where Jews settled sparsely and relatively late. The attitude toward them

117 For now, see Ries, "Zusammenhang," 641, 645; Hauptstaatsarchiv Hannover, Cal. Br. 23, no. 552, fols. 82–4; Cal. Br. 21, no. 1021, fols. 3–5; Cal. Br. 23, no. 194, fol. 211.
118 Hauptstaatsarchiv Hannover, Cal. Br. 23, no. 552, fol. 7; Cal. Br. 21, no. 2389, fol. 4v–5; Staatsarchiv Wolfenbüttel, 1 Alt 22, no. 94, fol. 13v–14r, 15r.
119 Wiener, "Residenzstadt," suppl. 19, 293; suppl. 20, 295; Johannes H. Jung, "Tractatio juridica de iure recipiendi Judaeos . . . in terris Brunsvico-Luneburgicis," J.D. diss., Universität Göttingen, 1741, § 8, 103.
120 Wilhelm, "Jüdische Gemeinde," 44–5.

seems to have been less hostile than elsewhere. There were no pogroms at all, with the exception of persecutions during the Black Death, which are hard to document in the sources. The political posture of the territorial lords until far into the sixteenth century can be characterized as predominantly authoritarian: They accepted the Jews as subjects as a matter of course; the toleration of Jewish communities, not only economically interesting individuals, was not questioned. One did business with them and imposed taxes on them, but beyond that saw no cause to institute a special policy nor any heightened need to establish a special body of laws.

In the sixteenth century, this fundamental attitude gradually lost force. In order to exploit the Jews financially to a greater degree, the Calenberg dukes in the Guelph territories employed methods that had not been common up to then, measures such as arrest or announcing expulsions. Their policies were erratic and showed little planning, but the financial pressure on the Jews was alleviated by the imperfections in administering these policies. The occasionally anti-Jewish policy of the duke was mitigated by the Jews' secure position in the courts and by the comprehensive protective measures, especially those of the councilors. As a whole, much of the Jewish policy of the Calenbergs remained bound to medieval categories.

In addition to this, Wolfenbüttel exhibits the range of variation in princely policy toward the Jews: Heinrich the Younger shows how politically effective individual prejudices were; Julius shows the positive assessment of Jewish commercial activity as well as the ability to assert himself politically; the easily influenced Heinrich Julius, who caved in to political pressure against the Jews, displays conduct varying from indifferent to hostile.

At the same time, under Duke Julius we see an early example of the principles of the early modern policy toward Jews that had been in practice since about 1570, even though these were not applied for long – the economic motives of (early) mercantilism caused Jews to be admitted and their commercial activity to be judged positively. There were extensive covenant negotiations and detailed norms for administering Jewish affairs, religious liberties were granted, and Jewish self-administration was authorized by the territorial prince; there were also anti-Jewish demands on the part of the rural estates and the clergy. In the context of his time, Duke Julius proved to be decidedly innovative. In the Guelph policy toward Jews, however, we see gathered together the essential elements and conditions of the relationship between the territorial prince and the Jews in late medieval and early modern times.

16

Jews in Ecclesiastical Territories of the Holy Roman Empire

J. FRIEDRICH BATTENBERG

I

At first glance, an investigation of "Jews in ecclesiastical territories" does not necessarily promise meaningful scholarly reward. Publications of the later eighteenth century[1] regarded these territories as the embodiment of backwardness.[2] In 1785, Philipp Anton von Bibra, a canon of Fulda, called for an inquiry into the current state of the ecclesiastical territories in the Holy Roman Empire. The information he collected from respondents amounted to a devastating assessment. When these territories were secularized in 1803, an act which abolished ecclesiastical states in Germany, it aroused little sustained opposition.[3]

One of the harshest critics of the ecclesiastical territories was the legal scholar and former secretary of state of Hesse-Darmstadt, Friedrich Karl von Moser, son of the famous scholar of constitutional law, Johann Jakob Moser.[4] In *Über die Regierung der geistlichen Staaten in Deutschland,* published in Frankfurt am Main and Leipzig in 1785,[5] the younger Moser described the problem as follows:

If one wants to shed light on the deficiencies of ecclesiastical government, then one has to realize that many stem from the religious and hierarchical system of the Catholic Church, and, therefore, are common to both ecclesiastical and secular

---

The original German-language text of this essay is to be published in an extended and partly revised version in the journal *Aschenas*. Elisabeth Battenberg and Damien Heylings worked on the translation of the text; the volume editors translated the quotations (originals retained in footnotes).

1 Peter Wende, *Die geistlichen Staaten und ihre Auflösung im Urteil der zeitgenössischen Publizistik* (Lübeck and Hamburg, 1966).

2 Peter Hersche, "Intendierte Rückständigkeit: Zur Charakteristik des Geistlichen Staates im Alten Reich," in Georg Schmidt, ed., *Stände und Gesellschaft im Alten Reich* (Stuttgart, 1989), 133–49, 134.

3 Karl Otmar Freiherr von Aretin, *Heiliges Römisches Reich 1776–1806. Reichsverfassung und Staatssouveränität,* vol. 1 (Wiesbaden, 1967), 372.

4 Hans-Erich Kaufmann, *Friedrich Carl von Moser als Politiker und Publizist (vornehmlich in den Jahren 1750–1770)* (Darmstadt, 1931), 130–1.

5 Wende, *Die geistlichen Staaten,* 13–14.

Catholic governments. Other deficiencies, however, owe their cause to the origins, longevity, incurability, and, if you will, the inviolability derived from the inherent constitution of ecclesiastical rule.[6]

In other words, he ascribed the major shortcomings of the ecclesiastical territories of the ancien régime chiefly to their internal constitutions, which, as his other writings reveal, he did not consider capable of reform.

According to publicists of the late eighteenth century, Jews in the ecclesiastical territories had no choice but to suffer the shortcomings of ecclesiastical government. Even a well-meaning ecclesiastical imperial estate (*Reichsstand*) was prevented from doing good by the *Wahlkapitulationen,* capitulations – the agreements candidates made in order to be elected to the office of prince-bishop.[7] In addition, lasting reforms were difficult, if not impossible, to effect, since any planning was limited to the reigning ruler's life span.[8] Moreover, owing to the "differences in laws and possessions of territorial states and cathedral chapters, as well as the pronounced inequality of the aims and outlooks of both, and so many other named and unnamed weaknesses," as Moser put it, the constitutions of the ecclesiastical territories could not be standardized.[9] That archbishops and bishops, abbots and other prelates, were ecclesiastical territorial princes (*Landesherren*), combining ecclesiastical dignity with the authority of secular office, proved particularly awkward. Thus, an ecclesiastical prince had become, again using Moser's formulation, "coruler, copossessor of the legislative and executive power."[10] If we judge the policies of the ecclesiastical *Landesherren* from this perspective, then we can assume that the linkage of the two viewpoints – secular "duty to mission" and "retaining the purity of the Catholic faith" – must have had a deleterious effect on the Jews' fate, at least when general perspectives such as "welfare of the state" and "common good" (*Gemeiner Nutzen*) were suppressed.[11] Pope Gregory IX's *Liber extra* of 1234, a doctrine established in canon law stating that the Jews were to be kept in

---

6 "Beleuchtet man nun die besondere[n] Mängel geistlicher Regierung, so fliessen viele derselben aus dem Religions-und Hierarchischen System der Catholischen Kirche, welche daher mit diesem stehen und fallen, und allen, so[wohl] geist[lichen] als weltlichen Catholischen Regierungen gemein sind. Andere aber erhalten ihre Entstehung, Dauer, Unheilbarkeit und, wenn man will, Unverletzbarkeit aus der den geistlichen Regierungen eigenen innern Verfassung." Friedrich Carl Freiherr von Moser, *Über die Regierung der geistlichen Staaten in Deutschland* (Frankfurt/Main and Leipzig, 1787), 37. One copy of this publication is housed in the Staatsarchiv Darmstadt, Bibliothek H 719/25.

7 Moser, *Über die Regierung,* 60.   8 Ibid., 71.

9 "Verschiedenheit der landesherrlichen und (dom-) capitularischen Rechte und Besitzungen und der ebenso starken Ungleichheit beyderseitiger Zwecke und Absichten, und so vielen anderen genannten und ungenannten Gebrechen." Ibid., 88.

10 "Mitherrscher, Mitteilhaber an der gesetzgebenden und vollziehenden Gewalt." Ibid., 25.

an inferior yet dignified condition, legitimated their exploitation when they became the regulatory focus of ecclesiastical legislation.[12]

There were, in fact, references to this notion of inferior status in the Jewish ordinances (*Judenordnungen*) promulgated in ecclesiastical territories. In the preface of an ordinance from 1700, for example, Elector Joseph Klemens of Cologne stated literally that "a noticeable distinction must also be maintained between Christian liberty and Jewish servitude."[13] This "noticeable distinction" must have had an especially negative effect on Jewish trade, handicraft production, and business, in a state based on a clerical ideology. Such a state had more than sixty holidays a year, excluding Sundays,[14] was infused with religious symbolism, and was animated by the official agenda of the Counter-Reformation. Thus, for more than three months each year Jews were prevented from engaging in commercial activity. Furthermore, this did not include their Sabbath, which, as a day of rest, restricted them even further. The Münster Jewish Ordinance of 1662, proclaimed by the prince-bishop Christoph Bernhard, gives us an impression of the kind of limits imposed on the Jews.

As regards those Jews who have been given safe-conduct to reside and pursue proper manual labor according to the custom of other, neighboring lands, our proper disposition, and imperial laws, . . . they should live peacefully and quietly and without causing any annoyance among our subjects, they should not commit blasphemy, scold or detest the Catholic religion or faith, they should not try to convert any Christian either by deeds or words to the Jewish community, they should not live in places where our subjects make their processions or services, like churches or cemeteries, they should not be in the streets on Sundays or other holy days before vespers or on Easter and the three days before nor on the high holy days and should keep their doors closed and windows locked, nor should they live in the same houses with Christians nor should they hire Christian wet nurses or servants.[15]

---

11 See. J. Friedrich Battenberg, "Obrigkeitliche Sozialpolitik und Gesetzgebung. Einige Gedanken zu mittelrheinischen Bettel- und Almosenordnungen des 16. Jahrhunderts," *Zeitschrift für historische Forschung* 18 (1991): 33–70, 43.

12 J. Friedrich Battenberg, *Das Europäische Zeitalter der Juden. Zur Entwicklung einer Minderheit in der nichtjüdischen Umwelt Europas,* vol. 1: *Von den Anfängen bis 1650* (Darmstadt, 1990), 104.

13 ". . . auch zwischen der Christlichen Freyheit und Jüdischen Dienstbarkeit ein mercklicher Unterscheidt gehalten werden möge." Manuscript copy, Landes- und Hochschulbibliothek Darmstadt, Sammlung Alfter, vol. 56, 221.

14 Hersche, "Intendierte Rückständigkeit," 140.

15 "Soviele nun aber auch weiters diejenige[n] Juden, welche zur Wohnung und gebührlicher Handesarbeit nach dem Gebrauch anderer benachbarten Landen, unserer fernerer Disposition und der Reichsabscheiden gemessener Handthierung in unserem Stift von uns vergleidet worden sein . . . ,dieselbe[n] sollen sich bey unsern Unterthanen . . . friedlich, still und unaergerlich ohne Gotteslästerung und Schmähung oder Veracht[ung] der Catholischen Religion und Glauben ver-

Not every ordinance was so clearly steeped in Catholicism. But within these ordinances concerning Jews, the protection of Christians' religious freedom was always paramount, and usually at the Jews' expense. This can be seen in the example of Elector Lothar of Trier's order of 1619.[16] At the very least, Jews were to comport themselves "on important holidays and on Good Friday, when processions are held, very quietly and out-of-sight." Considering the limitations on their freedom, the restrictions on their economic activity, and the general biases they faced in such a state, would it not have made more sense for Jews in the empire to avoid the ecclesiastical territories altogether?

In contrast to all the difficulties facing Jews in these territories, a bon mot from the beginning of the eighteenth century states that one could "live well under the bishop's crosier" (unter dem krummen Stabe gut wohnen).[17] In the mid-eighteenth century, Johann Friedrich Eisenbart commented on this saying: "The bishops' mild way of governing brought their subjects many advantages that cannot be found in the secular states. And this provided a reason for the common proverb. . . . Many of the public burdens, to which the subjects of a secular state are subjected, cannot be found in bishoprics."[18]

In a recent article, Peter Hersche demonstrates that this view of the circumstances obtaining in seventeenth- and eighteenth-century ecclesiastical states had indeed a basis in fact.[19] The ecclesiastical state was nearly the antimodel of the absolutist, enlightened, and "modern" secular state. That enlightened contemporaries viewed the ecclesiastical state as backward and in need of dissolution highlights only one aspect of the problem. "Backward-

---

halten, keinen Christen zu ihrer Judenschaft mit Worteren oder Wercken verleiten, ihre Wohnungen an den Ortheren, wo unsere Underthanen ihre Processiones und Andacht gemeintlich verrichten, alss bey Kirchen und Kirchhöven, nicht haben, auf den Heiligen Sonn[tag] und anderen Heiligen Tagen sich zuhauss und vor Abgang der Vesper auf den Gassen nicht finden lassen und auf den Heiligen Ostertag und negst vorhergehenden dreyen Tagen in der Heiligen Carwochen wie auch anderen hohen Jahrlichen Feyrtagen ihre Laden finster und [ihre] Häusser versperrt halten, sonsten auch mit kleinen Christen zugleich in einem Hausse wohnen noch darvon Saug-Ammen oder Gesinde bey sich haben." Staatsarchiv Münster/Westfalen, Fürstbistum Münster, Edikte A2 und J2.

16 ". . . auf grossen Feyertagen und [an] Charfreytag, wan man Processiones hält, in aller Still und unverweisslich." Landeshauptarchiv Koblenz, Abt. 10, no. 1218, fols. 240–43v.

17 Hersche, "Intendierte Rückständigkeit," 146. See Roman Brauser, *Disquisitio juridica paroemiae: Unter dem krummen Stabe ist gut wohnen* (1712; reprinted: Jena, 1720).

18 "Die gelinde Regierungsart der Bischöfe hat ihren Untertanen viele Vorteile verschafft, welche in einem weltlichen Staate nicht angetroffen werden, und diese haben zu dem gegenwärtigen Sprüchwort Gelegenheit gegeben. . . . Viele öffentliche Lasten, denen die Untertanen eines weltlichen Staates unterworfen sind, finden in einem bischöflichen Land nicht statt." Johann Friedrich Eisenbart, *Grundsätze der deutschen Rechte in Sprückwörtern* (1769; reprinted: Leipzig, 1823), 655. Quoted in Hersche, "Intendierte Rückständigkeit," 146.

19 Hersche, "Intendierte Rückständigkeit," 146.

ness" is a relative concept, however; it can be seen only within the context of the contemporary situation. The notion of backwardness contrasts with that of modernity – likewise a relative judgment – as embodied in the age's absolutist princely state (*Fürstenstaat*).

The difference between these models from the ancien régime, namely, the model of the ecclesiastical state and the model of the secular princely state, can be described using different standards of social regimentation (*Sozialdisziplinierung*). In the secular princely state, *gemeiner Nutzen* was the exclusive "state aim" (*Staatszweck*) of the authorities and the subjects. The pursuit of the common good tended to promote united political action as well as the formation of a rationally functioning institutional system. In the ecclesiastical state, a competition existed between at least two different and mutually exclusive aims: as spiritual leaders and, thus, pastors, the territorial rulers of ecclesiastical states were responsible for the souls of their subjects and yet, in typical fashion, subordinated the common good to the "aim of government" (*Regierungszweck*). If the priests were at the same time rulers ("die Priester zugleich Regenten sind"), as it was memorably asserted in 1798, in an anonymous publication on the characteristics of ecclesiastical territories,[20] the goal of the absolutist state, namely, the regimentation of all subjects, could be only partly achieved.

Obviously, a comparison of the levels of social regimentation might suggest that in ecclesiastical states the Jews enjoyed better living conditions. When they relinquished the goal of total regimentation, ecclesiastical territorial princes probably created a certain freedom of movement for Jews, enabling them to establish a separate community life. Within the framework of such a state, the Jews were not merely objects of fiscal and exploitative policies. Rather, they were targets of a message of salvation that respected other lifestyles in the hope of eschatological conversion on Judgment Day.

Under these circumstances, we should not be surprised that Jonathan Israel emphasizes in his recent study the comparatively favorable situation of the Jews in the Holy Roman Empire's ecclesiastical territories. He asserts that the Jews in these states were much less threatened by expulsion than those living in secular territories.[21] Following an increasing ideological intransigence and the hardening of state aims, a process usually called "confessionalization," secular states had no more room for the Jews, expelled them for being impossible to discipline, and restricted them occupation-

20 Wende, *Die geistlichen Staaten*, 5.
21 Jonathan I. Israel, *European Jewry in the Age of Mercantilism, 1550–1750* (Oxford, 1985), 23.

ally.[22] In contrast to their more sensible rulers, even theologians at the princely courts advocated expulsion of the Jews.[23] Since the late sixteenth century, however, ecclesiastical princes were much more prepared to tolerate Jews. On account of the *reservatum ecclesiasticum,* which Emperor Ferdinand I of Habsburg had granted in 1555 at the Peace of Augsburg, the bishops and other imperial prelates enjoyed protection from threatening confessional changes. Their positions were not jeopardized in the same way as those of the secular territorial princes,[24] even if Emperor Ferdinand I had granted this right, unacceptable to the Protestants, only to Catholics.[25] It is striking that after the 1570s the Jews were readmitted to many ecclesiastical states but not to a single secular one. The following observation by Israel could easily apply to similar cases.

Here and there, where Jews had been expelled altogether during or before the Reformation, they were now readmitted, on the initiative of the ecclesiastical princes. Thus, the Jews were recalled to the bishopric of Hildesheim in 1577, to the abbey principality of Essen in 1578 and, slightly later, to the bishopric of Halberstadt.[26]

Seen from this perspective, we can also redefine the function of the Jewish ordinances in ecclesiastical territories. If the ordinances regulated and stabilized the legal relations between Jews and Christians, then the ecclesiastical princes served a legitimating purpose. But the creation of valid, enduring law that would also remain untouched by social and economic changes necessitated the limitation of Jewish activity.[27] Through these ordinances, the basic ideological position of the territorial princes in relation to the estates (*Stände*) and the cathedral chapters (*Domkapitel*) was established. As Rosenkranz observed, with regard to conditions in the bishopric of Paderborn, such ordinances were an expression of Christian worries, not of Jewish ones.[28] In short, their only intent was to preserve the purity of the Catholic faith and guard it against outside influences. In addition to Jewish ordinances

22 J. Friedrich Battenberg, "Reformation, Judentum und Landesherrliche Gesetzgebung. Ein Beitrag zum Verhältnis des Protestantischen Landeskirchentums zu den Juden," in Andreas Mehl and Wolfgang Christian Schneider, eds., *Reformatio et Remationes. Festschrift für Lothar Graf zu Dohna zum 65. Geburtstag* (Darmstadt, 1989), 315–46, 334.
23 Rotraud Ries, "Zum Zusammenhang von Reformation und Judenvertreibung: Das Beispiel Braunschweig," in Helmut Jaeger, Franz Petri, and Heinz Quirin, eds., *Civitatum Communitas. Festschrift für Heinz Stoob zum 65. Geburtstag* (Cologne and Vienna, 1984), 630–54, 631; Battenberg, "Reformation," 330–1.
24 Heinrich Lutz, *Das Ringen um deutsche Einheit und kirchliche Erneuerung. Von Maximilian I. bis zum Westfälischen Frieden, 1490–1648* (Berlin, 1983), 307.
25 Horst Rabe, *Reich und Glaubensspaltung. Deutschland 1500–1600* (Munich, 1989), 296–7.
26 Israel, *European Jewry,* 42.
27 J. Friedrich Battenberg, *Judenverordnungen in Hessen–Darmstadt. Das Judenrecht eines Reichsfürstentums bis zum Ende des Alten Reiches. Eine Dokumentation* (Wiesbaden, 1987), 35.
28 G. J. Rosenkranz, "Über die früheren Verhältnisse der Juden im Paderbornschen. Ein Fragment," *Zeitschrift für vaterländische Geschichte und Alterthumskunde* 10 (1847): 259–80, 264.

as regulatory instruments, the territorial prince possessed an even easier means of intruding on the lives of Jews living in his territory. Partly contrary to and in competition with such ordinances, the prince also had police ordinances (*Polizeiverordnungen*), decrees (*Dekrete*), privileges (*Privilegien*), and singular instructions (*Einzelverfügungen*) at his disposal. Many scholars hold the view that the commercial life of the Jews was not built upon restrictive measures but rather was determined by a well-meaning bureaucracy (*Beamtenschaft*), that was acquainted with the Jews' local needs and problems.[29]

The question remains, however, whether or not the happier – as Israel maintains – situation obtaining for the Jews living in ecclesiastical territories after the 1570s was merely based on accidental conditions. That is, was this situation determined more by a well-meaning or capricious prince than the legal or constitutional structure of his state? Were there objective conditions that allowed the Jews to dwell and engage in trade more favorably in ecclesiastical territories so that they, as contemporaries expressed it, "unter dem Krummstab gut wohnen konnten?"

Two lines of argumentation will help us here. First, we need to establish the essential characteristics of ecclesiastical territories, particularly those relevant to the Jews. Second, we must investigate institutions within ecclesiastical territories that were involved in the day-to-day reality of Jewish existence. Considering the large number of ecclesiastical territories in the ancien régime, only a few basic traits, which together do not necessarily give us a complete picture, can be explored. Because too many questions remain unanswered, construction of an ideal type regarding policies toward the Jews in the ecclesiastical territories is not possible at this juncture. Moreover, we cannot exclude developments in ecclesiastical territories that appear deviant.

Historians have analyzed Jewish policies in only a very few ecclesiastical territories. These include the bishoprics of Bamberg and Würzburg, in the southeastern corner of the empire within the imperial circle (*Reichskreis*) of Franconia. The histories of both have been relatively well researched: see the older monographs by Adolf Eckstein (1898 and 1899),[30] David Weger (1920),[31] and Markus Bohrer (1922),[32] as well as Manfred Agethen's as yet

29 Hans-Joachim Behr, "Judenschaft, Landstände und Fürsten in den geistlichen Staaten Westfalens im 18. Jahrhundert," in Peter Freimark and Helmut Richtering, eds., *Gedenkschrift für Bernhard Brilling* (Hamburg, 1988), 121–35, 129.

30 Adolf Eckstein, *Geschichte der Juden im ehemaligen Fürstbistum Bamberg* (Bamberg, 1898); Adolf Eckstein, *Nachträge zur Geschichte der Juden im ehemaligen Fürstbistum Bamberg* (Bamberg, 1899).

31 David Weger, "Die Juden im Hochstift Würzburg während des 17. und 18. Jahrhunderts," Ph.D. diss., Universität Würzburg, 1920.

32 Markus Bohrer, "Die Juden im Hochstift Würzburg im 16. und am Beginne des 17. Jahrhunderts," Ph.D. diss., Universität Freiburg, 1922.

unpublished study.[33] Both territories were also somewhat atypical in that they did not form unified entities in the center of the ancient royal province of Franconia. Each was frequently in conflict with a strong knightly nobility, composed of the imperial knighthood (*Reichsritterschaft*) and the territorial nobility (*Landadel*). The knighthood was organized partly into imperial corporations of the knightly cantons (*Ritterkantone*) and partly into territorial estates (*Landstände*) of both bishoprics. In their doctoral theses, Siegfried Bachmann[34] and Ernst Schubert[35] examine the peculiarities of the constitution of territorial estates, which influenced the bishops' policies toward the Jews.

In counterpoint to the Franconian bishoprics stood the two bishoprics of Münster and Paderborn, situated in the northwestern corner of the Holy Roman Empire. Each succeeded in achieving relative unity of their territorial borders and in integrating the freehold nobility into the structure of their territories. No *Reichsritterschaft* of the kind found in Franconia existed. The so-called *Erbmännerschaft,* in the bishopric of Münster, a haughty knighthood originating with merchants in the region, could not break up the territory.[36]

Many books and essays have been written about both territories. In 1906, Carl Rixen wrote his doctoral thesis on Münster;[37] G. J. Rosenkranz wrote an essay on Paderborn over one hundred years ago (1847);[38] and in 1938 Hildegard Kraft wrote her dissertation on Paderborn, albeit from an anti-Semitic perspective.[39] Nearly a half century later, in 1985, Rudolf Muhs wrote a brief but excellent survey on the same bishopric.[40] A recently published study by Hans-Joachim Behr catalogs the most important features of the ecclesiastical policies toward Jews in Münster, Paderborn, and the duchy of Westphalia[41] – all examples of areas at the periphery of imperial influence.

With the help of supplementary sources, the following discussion can reflect only the works just mentioned. The numerous other bishoprics and

33 Manfred Agethen, "Die Juden im deutschen Fürstenstaat des konfesionellen Zeitalters" (provisional title), chap. 6 in *Judenpolitik im Hochstift Würzburg,* to be published.
34 Siegfried Bachmann, *Die Landstände des Hochstifts Bamberg. Ein Beitrag zur territorialen Verfassungsgeschichte* (Goslar, 1962).
35 Ernst Schubert, *Die Landstände des Hochstifts Würzburg (Würzburg, 1967).*
36 Cf. Karl-Heinz Kirchhoff, "Die Erbmänner und ihre Höfe in Münster," in Kirchhoff, ed., *Forschungen zur Geschichte von Stadt und Stift Münster* (Warendorf, 1988), 53–76.
37 Carl Rixen, *Geschichte und Organisation der Juden im ehemaligen Stift Münster* (Münster, 1906).
38 G. J. Rosenkranz, "Über die früheren Verhältnisse der Juden im Paderbornschen."
39 Hildegard Kraft, "Die rechtliche, wirtschaftliche und soziale Lage der Juden im Hochstift Paderborn," *Westfälische Zeitschrift. Zeitschrift für vaterländische Geschichte und Alterthumskunde* 94 (1938): 101–204.
40 Rudolf Muhs, *Zwischen Schutzherrschaft und Gleichberechtigung. Die Juden im Hochstift Paderborn um 1800* (Paderborn, 1985).
41 Behr, "Judenschaft, Landstände und Fürsten."

abbeys of the Old Reich must, at least for the time being, remain unexamined. One important reason for setting them aside has to do with the fact that many were often under the influence of secular territorial rulers and therefore were unable to pursue a totally independent Jewish policy. That is especially clear in the case of the bishopric of Hildesheim, which Israel uses as an example in his study. This bishopric remained dependent on the Guelph dukes of Braunschweig, the ancestors of the later electoral princes of Hanover and monarchs of Great Britain, so that independent expressions of political will were possible only in combination with the representatives of that dynasty. One of the most famous prelates in the eighteenth century and a member of the Wittelsbach family, Duke Klemens August of Bavaria (d. 1761), united all of these bishoprics in his own person. He was variously prince-bishop of Münster, Paderborn, Osnabrück, and Hildesheim, as well as archbishop and electoral prince of Cologne.[42] As a consequence, his influence on Jewish policies during this time was immense, and it is possible to demonstrate this influence with the examples of Münster and Paderborn.

This analysis must, however, limit itself to the era of confessionalism, that is, between the late sixteenth through the late eighteenth centuries. Independent of the question of the extent to which confessionalization influenced Jewish policies in ecclesiastical territories,[43] a limitation to this time span is necessary, because only during this time did this kind of state, based on the principles agreed upon at the Council of Trent, come into being. With this newly found identity, they could clearly set themselves apart from Protestant and also Catholic secular princely rule. Even if, as in the case of the Federation of Princes of 1658 (*Fürstenbund*), a common policy between ecclesiastical and secular territories was possible, as in the so-called Third Germany, the atypicality of policies toward Jews in ecclesiastical states remained. This continued within the framework of regional organizations as well, where unanimous political action vis-à-vis the Jews took place – for example, regarding the policies of the imperial circles toward Jewish beggars (*Betteljuden*).[44] Confirmed at the Peace of Westphalia (1648), the *superioritas territorialis*[45] granted ecclesiastical rulers the right to independent

42 Erwin Gatz, "Clemens August Herzog von Bayern," in Gatz, ed., *Die Bischöfe des Heiligen Römischen Reiches 1648–1803. Ein Biographisches Lexikon.* (Berlin, 1990), 63–66.

43 Cf. R. Po-chia Hsia, "Die Juden im Alten Reich," in Schmidt, ed., *Stände und Gesellschaft im Alten Reich*, 211–22, 219.

44 Bernhard Post, *Judentoleranz und Judenemanzipation in Kurmainz 1774–1814* (Wiesbaden, 1985), 121–22; Rudolf Glanz, *Geschichte des niederen jüdischen Volkes in Deutschland. Eine Studie über historisches Gaunertum, Bettelwesen und Vagantentum* (New York, 1988), 128.

45 Dietmar Willoweit, *Rechtsgrundlagen der Territorialgewalt. Landesobrigkeit, Herrschaftsrechte und Territorium in der Rechtswissenschaft der Neuzeit* (Cologne and Vienna, 1975), 121.

organization of their states, even when they were constituted only as an imperial estate with princely authority.[46]

II

Ecclesiastical rule (*geistliche Herrschaft*), as mentioned earlier, was founded with the religious leaders – namely archbishops, bishops, provosts, and abbots – serving a double function, as clergymen and, simultaneously, as holders of secular power. Unique in German constitutional history,[47] this system had its roots in the *Reichskirchensystem* of Otto I, combining, in an especially intensive way, noble rule (*Adelsherrschaft*) with church politics. Access to ecclesiastical power was reserved for the lower and upper nobility, which in this way could provide for its younger sons, for whom there was no place in secular government. This nobility filled the benefices (*Pfründen*) of the cathedral and other chapters, as well as the convents of the prince abbeys.[48] Prince-bishops and prince-abbots were elected out of the nobility's own social circles.[49] The area of ecclesiastical activity, the diocese, extended in most cases much beyond the secular dominion; thus it was possible for the bishop to use ecclesiastical sanctions (for example, excommunication) to influence the secular side of politics. The *Reichskirche,* which was an essential bulwark of imperial rule in Germany, consisted of the archbishoprics of Mainz, Cologne, Trier, and Salzburg (a fifth, Magdeburg, had been secularized by the electors of Brandenburg), the twenty prince-bishoprics of Bamberg, Würzburg, Worms, Eichstätt, Speyer, Strasbourg, Constance, Augsburg, Hildesheim, Paderborn, Freising, Regensburg, Passau, Trent, Brixen, Basel, Münster, Osnabrück, and (since 1752) Fulda, and the forty-four imperial abbeys and provosts, such as Kempten, Ellwangen, Berchtesgaden, Weissenburg, Prüm, Stablo, and Corvey.[50] The *reservatum ecclesiasticum* protected them from the ever-present threat of secularization and tied them closely to imperial central authority.

With regard to the ecclesiastical states' policies toward Jews, the imperial police ordinances (*Reichspolizeiordnungen*) of 1548 and 1577 had special rel-

46 Ibid., 134.
47 Fritz Kallenberg, "Geistliche Herrschaft und kirchlicher Besitz. Die Säkularisation von 1803 und ihre Folgen," in Alois Gerlich, ed., *Vom Alten Reich zu neuer Staatlichkeit. Alzeyer Kolloquium 1979. Kontinuität und Wandel im Gefolge der Französischen Revolution am Mittelrhein* (Wiesbaden, 1982), 76–92, 76.
48 See Harm Klüting, "Reichsgrafen – Stiftsadel – Landadel. Adel und Adelsgruppen im niederrheinisch–westfälischen Raum im 17. und 18. Jahrhundert," in Rudolf Endres, ed., *Adel in der Frühneuzeit. Ein regionaler Vergleich* (Cologne and Vienna, 1991), 17–54, 40.
49 Erich Feine, *Die Besetzung der Reichsbistümer vom Westfälischen Frieden bis zur Säkularisation* (Stuttgart, 1921; reprinted: 1964).
50 Kallenberg, "Geistliche Herrschaft," 79.

evance. It was stated here "that from now on no one could accept Jews or allow them to stay except those who have received that privilege from us (namely, the emperor) and the Holy Roman regalia."[51] In this way, not only was the imperial origin of all Jewish rights of residence established,[52] but the royal prerogative as the constituting principle for the imperial princes was also maintained.[53] This prerogative regarding Jews, or *Judenregal,* which had entirely replaced the older system of imperial serfdom (*Kammerknechtschaft*),[54] supplemented territorial princely rule and was removed from the hands of third persons, as can be demonstrated with the example of Assenheim in Upper Hesse.[55] For ecclesiastical rulers this royal prerogative was relevant in that through it imperial authority could be legitimated vis-à-vis the territorial estates, especially vis-à-vis those cathedral chapters that claimed their own protection rights over the Jews. For this reason, the bishops had their *Judenregalien* (Jewish prerogatives) repeatedly reconfirmed by the emperor.

The case of the bishopric of Münster is a good example of this situation. In 1337, Emperor Ludwig the Bavarian enfeoffed Count Heinrich of Waldeck with the *Judenregal,* although he was not the holder of the territorial power.[56] By the sixteenth century, at the latest, the bishop of Münster was holder of this *Judenregal* and, therefore, supreme protector of the Jews in his land.[57] Even though we have imperial *Judenregalien* only for the period after 1624,[58] after 1568 the bishops of Münster issued escort and protection letters in which they repeatedly pointed out such imperial rights.[59] In 1688, Bishop Gottfried of Würzburg issued a mandate against the intermediate estates, referring to his territorial rights over the Jews.[60] The bishops of Bamberg and Würzburg had acquired the imperial *Judenregalien* much earlier. Albrecht of Hohenlohe, bishop of Bamberg, was granted a similar right by King Ruprecht in 1401.[61] But these grants did not stop the Reich

---

51 *Reichspolizeiordnungen* from June 30, 1548, and November 9, 1577, in *Neue und vollständigere Sammlung der Reichsabschiede,* vol. 2 (1747; reprinted: Osnabrück, 1967), 587–606, and vol. 3 (1747; reprinted: Osnabrück, 1967), 379–98. Additionally, see J. Friedrich Battenberg, "Zur Rechtsstellung der Juden am Mittelrhein in Spätmittelalter und früher Neuzeit," *Zeitschrift für historische Forschung* 6 (1979): 129–83, 139.

52 Battenberg, "Zur Rechtsstellung," 139.

53 Willoweit, *Rechtsgrundlagen der Territorialgewalt,* 47.

54 J. Friedrich Battenberg, "Des Kaisers Kammerknechte. Gedanken zur rechtlich-sozialen Situation der Juden in Spätmittelalter und früher Neuzeit," *Historische Zeitschrift* 245 (1987): 545–99, 572.

55 J. Friedrich Battenberg, "Assenheimer Judenpogrome vor dem Reichskammergericht. Die Prozesse der Grafschaften Hanau, Isenburg und Solms um die Ausübung des Judenregals, 1567–1573," in Christiane Heinemann, ed., *Neunhundert Jahre Geschichte der Juden in Hessen. Beiträge zum politischen, wirtschaftlichen und kulturellen Leben* (Wiesbaden, 1983), 123–50, 141.

56 Rixen, *Geschichte und Organisation,* 15.   57 Ibid.

58 Staatsarchiv Münster, "Fürstentum Münster, Landesarchiv," 1o–9b.

59 Rixen, *Geschichte und Organisation,* 70.   60 Weger, "Die Juden im Hochstift Würzburg," 72.

61 Ludwig von Oberndorff and Manfred Krebs, eds., *Regesten der Pfalzgrafen am Rhein 1214–1508,* vol. 2: *Regesten König Ruprechts* (Innsbruck, 1939), 59, no. 861 (May 11, 1401).

from regularly reserving several "rights of use" (*Nutzungsrechte*), based on the *Kammerknechtschaft*. This had happened, for example, in 1415, when King Sigmund of Luxembourg secured the use of 50 percent of the tax on Jews, as well as half of the so-called *Goldener Opferpfennig,* from the Jews living in the Bamberg and Würzburg dioceses.[62]

At the same time the close relationship between the episcopal protection rights over the Jews and imperial power, as can be shown especially with regard to the *königsnahe Landschaft* of Franconia,[63] limited the actual exercise of these rights. In the bishoprics of Bamberg and Würzburg, this state of affairs became demonstrably relevant at the moment when they found themselves in an era of self-confident consolidation within the framework of post-Tridentine Catholicism.[64] When, in 1560, the bishop of Würzburg, Friedrich of Wirsberg, intended to expel the Jews from his territory by referring to his *Judenregal* and imperial authorization, Emperor Ferdinand I interfered, as a mediating supreme protector of the Jews.[65] Later, Bishop Veit of Würzburg tried to expel the Jews from his diocese, using the same claims. But the expulsion was prevented by Emperor Maximilian II of Habsburg by means of his mandate of 1566,[66] which was based on the privilege of the Jews and the constitution of the Holy Roman Empire.[67] The lawsuits in the Imperial Chamber Court (Reichskammergericht), and the Imperial Privy Council (Reichshofrat), which were brought by the Jews in both bishoprics, partly achieved the continued protection of the Jews at the imperial level.[68] These suits established the idea that the *Judenregalien,* which had been given to the bishops, could not be permitted to be substantially undermined.

Another constant of Jewish policies in ecclesiastical states was based on the fact that prince-bishops were not members of a unified dynasty (the

---

62 Wilhelm Altmann, ed., *Regesta Imperii,* vol. 11: *Die Urkunden Kaiser Sigmunds (1410–1437),* pt. 1: *1410–1424* (Innsbruck, 1897; reprinted: Hildesheim, 1967), 121, no. 1849 (July 19, 1415).

63 Peter Moraw, "Franken als königsnahe Landschaft im späten Mittelalter," *Blätter für deutsche Landesgeschichte* 112 (1976): 123–38, 125.

64 Ludwig Huettl, "Geistlicher Fürst und geistliche Fürstentümer im Barock und Rokoko. Ein Beitrag zur Strukturanalyse von Gesellschaft, Herrschaft, Politik und Kultur des alten Reiches," *Zeitschrift für bayerische Landesgeschichte* 57 (1974): 3–48, 8.

65 Sabine Frey, *Rechtsschutz der Juden gegen Ausweisungen im 16. Jahrhundert* (Frankfurt/Main, 1983), 115.

66 Ibid.

67 See the privilege of Kaiser Karl V from April 3, 1544, in J. Friedrich Battenberg, *Quellen zur Geschichte der Juden im Hessischen Staatsarchiv Darmstadt,* vol. 1: *1080–1650* (Wiesbaden, 1993), 1285. Cf. J. Friedrich Battenberg, "Die Ritualmordprozesse gegen Juden in Spätmittelalter und Frühneuzeit. Verfahren und Rechtsschutz," in Rainer Erb, ed., *Blutbeschuldigungen gegen Juden* (Berlin, 1993), 1–29.

68 Frey, *Rechtsschutz der Juden,* 115.

temporary domination of the bishopric of Münster by the house of Wittelsbach had other causes), but rather owed their governing authority itself to election. Since the Concordat of Worms (1122), the cathedral chapters that existed at that time had the right to elect the bishop. The chapters elected either persons from their own ranks or foreign candidates from both the lower and upper nobility. On the one hand, this means of acquiring legitimacy resulted in relatively stable governing authority. Niccolo Machiavelli was right when he wrote in his *Il Principe* (1515) that the rulers of ecclesiastical territories obtained authority by election, did not have to defend them, and got subjects they did not really govern.[69]

On the other hand, this stability corresponded to a dependency on electoral committees. Thus, like the emperor, prince-bishops had to subject themselves at their inauguration to so-called "election agreements." Moreover, cathedral chapters supervised the implementation of the latter.[70] Although Pope Innocent XII canonically forbade such treaties (1695), in accordance with the ideas of Emperor Leopold I, the tradition of reaching election agreements was maintained until the end of the ancien régime.[71] Restrictions with respect to the exercise of ecclesiastical territorial rights were expressly banned in a papal rescript of 1698, issued to the cathedral chapter of Würzburg in order to prevent creation of ecclesiastical condominiums. The rescript prohibited the arrival at such settlements for future vacancies of the see (*Sedisvakanzen*), which were said to refer to "circa temporalia regalia, nempe iura territorialia, cameralia et politica," and thus included the *Judenregalien*.[72] However, because the cathedral chapters held the entire governmental power and territorial jurisdiction, as well as the exclusive right to vote during vacancies of the see, and also looked after the administration of the episcopal holdings and derived from this a right of participation in the government, it was only logical that, during episcopal elections, they demanded guarantees concerning the exercise of government by future rulers of the territory.[73] With this they confronted the bish-

---

69 Niccolo Machiavelli, *Il Principe* (*Der Fürst*), ed. Rudolf Zorn (Stuttgart, 1978), chap. 11.
70 Huettl, "Geistlicher Fürst," 21; Günter Christ, "Selbstverständnis und Rolle der Domkapitel in den geistlichen Territorien des Alten Deutschen Reiches in der Frühneuzeit," *Zeitschrift für historische Forschung* 16 (1989): 259–328, 259, 281.
71 Huettl, "Geistlicher Fürst," 22; Rudolf Vierhaus, "Wahlkapitulationen in den geistlichen Staaten des Reiches im 18. Jahrhundert," in Huettl, ed., *Herrschaftsverträge, Wahlkapitulationen, Fundamentalgesetze* (Göttingen, 1977), 205–19, 205. For a fuller treatment, see Christ, "Selbstverständnis," 304. Also, Michael Kissener, *Ständemacht und Kirchenreform. Bischöfliche Wahlkapitulationen im Nordwesten des Alten Reiches* (Paderborn, 1993), 195.
72 Vierhaus, "Wahlkapitulationen," 209; Christ, "Selbstverständnis," 281.
73 Vierhaus, "Wahlkapitulationen"; Christ, "Selbstverständnis."

ops, especially when they were foreigners and not members of the cathedral chapter, as representatives of the territories, since they wanted to obligate candidates to consider their interests.[74]

In 1787, Friedrich Karl von Moser was therefore able to describe the typical situation of the ecclesiastical ruler.

Only he – in the literal sense of the word – can claim the name of public prosecutor, because he cannot tolerate bad, disadvantageous, impulsive actions like a secular sovereign, because he has the watchful eye of his chapter over and around him and even in what he considers, according to his own insight, good, useful, and necessary, he has to fight with many more obstacles than a secular prince, because he has to overcome and rise above the special prejudices of his own ecclesiastical status.[75]

Thereby, however, an additional element of uncertainty entered into episcopal Jewish policies, which produced in some respects incalculable factors. Since the canons, who claimed the right to cogovernance, could not also claim a greater degree of rationality, they therefore did not initially refer to the common welfare (*Gemeinwohl*) in the electoral agreements.[76] Rather, as Manfred Agethen points out, they were exposed to a twofold conflict: between their personal interests as members of the imperial nobility and their corporate obligations in the chapter, on the one hand, and between the secular and ecclesiastical needs of their bishoprics, which were put in their charge, on the other.[77]

One hardly needs to explain that these contractual limitations of episcopal power, which since the thirteenth century were common, must have had consequences for policies aimed at the Jews, even if the cathedral chapters, in the course of the eighteenth century, scarcely had the power to insist on fidelity to electoral agreements. The relevance for the episcopal right to protect the Jews may be analyzed with the help of the well-documented example of Würzburg.[78]

The bishops of Würzburg had acquired the *Judenregalien* very early, be-

---

74 Huettl, "Geistlicher Fürst," 25; Christ, "Selbstverständnis."

75 "Denn nur ihm kommt in buchstäblicher Bedeutung des Worts der Name eines Staatsanwaltes zu, weil schlechte, nachtheilige, unbesonnene Handlungen ihm nicht so, wie einem weltlichen Souverain, ungenossen hingehen, weil er das wachende Auge seines Capitels über und um sich hat und selbst in dem, was er nach seiner Erkänntnis als gut, nützlich und nötig erachtet, mit weit mehr Hindernissen als ein weltlicher Fürst zu kämpfen hat, weil er sich selbst über manche Vorurteile seines geistlichen Standes hinwegsezen und erheben . . . muss." Moser, *Über die Regierung,* 149.

76 Vierhaus, "Wahlkapitulationen," 213; Christ, "Selbstverständnis," 288; Kissener, *Ständemacht,* 11.

77 Agethen, "Judenpolitik im deutschen Fürstenstaat."

78 Joseph Friedrich Abert, "Die Wahlkapitulationen der Würzburger Bischöfe bis zum Ende des XVII. Jahrhunderts," *Archiv des Historischen Vereins von Unterfranken und Aschaffenburg* 46 (Würzburg, 1904), 27–186, 175.

cause of a privilege granted in 1247 by King Heinrich Raspe.[79] About three hundred years later, a bishop of Würzburg was, for the first time, limited by the cathedral chapter in his traditional and previously unopposed rights over the episcopal Jews.[80] The reason for the intervention of the chapter, with which should be linked the new episcopal candidate, Melchior Zobel von Giebelstadt, was given as follows; that

for some time now, many Jews have slipped into our city Würzburg and elsewhere in our ecclesiastical lands, and they molested the subjects and associates of our lands with usury, forbidden business, buying, selling, and in other ways, and they also dress in a way that one cannot distinguish them from Christians.

For these reasons the bishop had to promise in the election agreement

to try hard to prevent and see to it that no additional foreign Jews should be admitted to our lands; rather, to diminish by as many as possible the number already there.

Furthermore, the bishop should decree

that all Jews and Jewesses . . . young and old, should carry recognizable signs so that they can be distinguished from Christians. Moreover, from now on Jews should not lend money on usury, buy, sell, or do commerce in any other way. Wherever such happens, they should not be paid for it, nor should the courts help them in their financial business.[81]

Bishop Melchior's successors, Friedrich von Wirsberg and Julius Echter von Mespelbrunn, had to swear on the occasion of their elections in 1558 and 1573, respectively, to agree verbatim to electoral agreements. In the same way, bishops Philipp Adolf von Ehrenberg and Franz von Hatzfeld also had to swear the same oath in the years 1623 and 1631, respectively.[82] Behind these capitulations stood complaints lodged by the town guilds in

---

79 Johann Friedrich Böhmer and Julius Ficker, eds., *Regesta Imperii*, vol. 5: *Die Regesten des Kaiserreichs unter Philipp, Otto IV, Friedrich II, Heinrich (VII), Conrad IV, Heinrich Raspe, Wilhelm und Richard 1198–1272* (Innsbruck, 1881–82; reprinted: Hildesheim, 1971), 919, no. 4884 (February 5, 1247); cf. Bohrer, "Die Juden im Hochstift Würzburg," 9.

80 Bohrer, "Die Juden im Hochstift Würzburg," 50.

81 ". . . ain zeitlang her etwa vil Juden in unser Stadt Wirtzburg, auch sunsten hin und wider in unsrem Stifft Orbrigkeit und Gebiete untergeschlaift und die armen unsere und gemelten unsres Stifts Unterthane[n] und Verwanten mit Wucher, verbotenem Gesuche, Handtierung, Kaufen, Verkaufen und in andere Weg heftig beschwerdt, sich auch mit irer Cleidung dermassen halten, dass man dieselben vor den Christen nit wol erkennen mag"; "mit Vleiss zu verhuten und darvor zu sein, das kein auslendige Juden mehr in unserm Stift an- und eingenommen, sodern sovil moglichen, derjhenigen Zal, her darinnen sein, geringert und eingezogen werde"; "dass alle Juden und Judinnen[n] . . . jung und alt, offentliche kundliche Zeichen tragen, damit sie vor den Christen erkennt weden. Dergleichen, dass sie hinfur nit mer auf Wucher leihen, kaufen, verkaufen oder in andere Weg hantieren. Wo aber solchs beschee, dass inen darfur nichts gegeben, noch zu Einbringung desselben inn- und ausserhalf Gerichts geholfen werden solle." Abert, "Die Wahlkapitulationen," 177.

82 Ibid., 178.

Würzburg about the Jews' damaging interest rates. The cathedral chapter got hold of these complaints and tried, by way of a compromise between the maximum anti-Jewish demands and the financial interests of the state in maintaining its tax base, to limit the number of Jewish families in the bishopric, as well as to ban the collection of interest on loans. They also tried to reactivate the regulation that obligated Jews to wear distinguishing badges. In existence since the Fourth Lateran Council (1215), this regulation had meanwhile been all but ignored. Its renewal was aimed at marking the special position of this class and to achieve the latter's complete social segregation.[83]

As a matter of course, the bishops did not keep to these conditions of the electoral agreements. Since the Jews continued to charge interest for capital loans, individual orders of expulsion were indeed issued. But these served only a legitimating function and were carried out very hesitantly. Because the town of Würzburg, in particular, complained about the unwelcome economic competition of the Jews, Bishop Johann Philipp of Schönborn, who had been elected in 1642, was compelled, by a supplement to his capitulation, to expel the Jews from the town and diocese "within a half or an entire year's time."[84] The expulsion was then carried out in the same year, as the result of a common mandate from the bishop and the cathedral chapter.[85] But, as on previous occasions, this expulsion was not entirely successful. And so Bishop Johann Hartmann von Rosenbach, who was elected in 1673, was obligated "to expel and remove Jews and Jewesses within half a year."[86] Furthermore, officials also even wanted to forbid trade between Jews living elsewhere and the Christian subjects of this ecclesiastical territory. It was defined literally:

Moreover, regarding the deceitful matter with the expelled Jews, should they attempt in the future to come under the protection of other lords in our bishopric and attempt to provide for themselves from our bishopric, we shall want to discuss ways and means [of prevention] with the advice of the cathedral chapter.

Because the Jews were indispensable for the financial health of the episcopal treasury, the authorities finally came to terms with them. They could remain in the bishopric, as long as they took up residence outside the walls of the city of Würzburg. The last electoral agreements of the seventeenth century, those of 1675, 1683, and 1684, expressed the motivation for this regulation explicitly:

---

83 Battenberg, *Das Europäische Zeitalter, 103.*   84 Abert, "Die Wahlkapitulationen," 179.

85 Robert Flade, *Die Würzburger Juden. Ihre Geschichte vom Mittelalter bis zur Gegenwart* (Würzburg, 1987), 56.

86 ". . . die Juden und Judinne[n] inner[halb] eines halben Jahres Frist auszugebieten und wegzuschaffen." From the Wahlkapitulation of 1673, chap. 67, cited in Abert, "Die Wahlkapitulationen," 179.

Although in previous capitulations our princely predecessors and our cathedral chapter had thought it well to expel the Jews from our bishopric and to uphold the privilege of not tolerating Jews, now the prince's government is of the opinion that they should be tolerated a while longer, owing to our special mercy and according to our whim. Therefore, if it be pleasing to both parties, we and the cathedral chapter would either expel the Jews or by special grace tolerate them for now until some further date.[87]

Nothing in this situation changed in the eighteenth century, and with the foundation of the episcopal Judenamt, or Jewish Office, by 1719, at the very latest, the intention to expel the Jews, which theoretically continued to exist, faded into the background.[88]

Changes in government were of course used in secular territories as well to redefine the existing rights of the Jews. The town guilds, in particular, used the inauguration of a new government as an opportunity to lodge complaints against the Jews and to demand their expulsion or at least their circumscription. The maintenance of a dynasty, and the implicit obligation toward related predecessors in office, however, ensured a large measure of continuity. Nonetheless, if the demands of the territorial estates to alter the rights of Jews in the territory were met, it was more likely owing to a change of attitude in the territorial court than to a change in a ruler's legal relationship with the territorial estates.

The example of the bishopric of Würzburg shows clearly that electoral agreements in the ecclesiastical territories of the ancien régime indeed created a basis for expulsions of and discrimination against the Jews. But this example also demonstrates that, owing to the legitimating function of these actions, the position of the Jews stabilized. With declarations of their intent to expel the Jews, they created one-sided existential uncertainties for the latter. Through the real ties between them, which the bishops rejected and the popes and emperors forbade, they managed, however, to create a safe space for Jews, one upon which members of the cathedral chapter could hardly imposed limits.

---

87 "In übrigen, wie die betrugliche Handlung mit denen ab- und ausgeschafften Juden innskünftig, wann sie im Stift sich unter anderer Herschaften Schutz nehmen sollten und auss unserm Stift sich zu ernehren begehren, begegnet werde wollen wir uff gewisse Mittel und Weeg mit unsers Dombcapituls Rat bedacht seinn"; "Obwohlen unser [hochfürstlichen] Vorfahren sambt unserm Dombcapital in vorigen Capitulationen für gut angesehen, die Judenschaft auss unserm Stift ausszuschaffen und das privilegium de non recipiendis iudaeis zu manutenirn, nun aber die fürstliche Cammer dafür gehalten, dass sie noch ein zeitlang und zwar auss besonderen Gnaden undt nach Belieben zu tolerieren wehren; alss haben wir sambt unserm Domcapitul sie, die Juden, wann es unss beederseits beliebig sein würdt, entweder auszuschaffen order ex speciali gracia gleich jetzt undt zur Zeit noch geschiehet, ad interim undt ihr Wohlbehalten zu tolerieren." Abert, "Die Wahlkapitulationen," 180.
88 Weger, "Die Juden in Hochstift Würzburg," 5, 57.

If one discusses the cathedral chapter, then one must also discuss the territorial estates in ecclesiastical lands. As long as they were not driven out by the chapter, they were organized in basically the same way as in secular territories. For example, in the bishopric of Bamberg we find the prelate estate, which represented the abbotts and provosts; the knighthood, which consisted of the territorial lower nobility; and finally the corporation of the "cities, markets, and commoners," normally characterized by the word *Landschaft*.[89] All were represented in the territorial diet (*Landtag*). Likewise, in the bishopric of Würzburg we find the three curiae: the priesthood, the knighthood, and the *Landschaft*, representing the cities and *Ämter* (offices).[90] When the imperial knighthood, which had since the 1540s reorganized itself into an independent organization within the Franconian knightly circle (*Ritterkreis*), detached itself from the bishoprics, the result was a reduction in the size of both diets.[91]

The situation looked quite different in the bishopric of Münster. The three curiae here were set up in a much more concentrated and uniform way. The first estate was formed by the cathedral chapter for the priesthood and the second by the freehold knighthood.[92] The cathedral chapter played the dominant role; the government sought its advice preemptively on all proposals; and the chapter presented official proposals to the knighthood only after it had reached final agreement on the matter. Only then, when the two bodies had come to an agreement, were towns contacted and their opinions sought.[93] In the end, it was the cathedral chapter of Münster, which had a strong lower nobility, that determined estate politics.[94]

The meaninglessness of the Würzburg diet was already demonstrated by the fact that the towns introduced their complaints about the Jews into the electoral agreements by means of the cathedral chapter. They were not active in the diet in a corresponding fashion. Even earlier, the comparable Bamberg committee was a forum wherein the towns acted against the Jews. It is known that during the diets of 1588, 1638, and 1652, the towns of Höchstadt, Forchheim, Kronach, Vilseck, and Pottenstein demanded the

---

89 Bachmann, *Die Landstände des Hochstifts Bamberg,* 94; cf. Christ, "Selbstverständnis," 315.
90 Schubert, *Die Landstände des Hochstifts Würzburg,* 123.
91 Volker Press, *Kaiser Karl V., König Ferdinand und die Entstehung der Reichsritterschaft* (Wiesbaden, 1980), 40; Press, "Kaiser und Reichsritterschaft," in Endres, ed., *Adel in der Frühneuzeit,* 163–94, 169; J. Friedrich Battenberg, "Zwischen Reich und Territorialstaat. Zur rechtlichen Situation der Reichsritterschaft im 17. Jahrhundert," *Zeitschrift für Neuere Rechtsgeschichte* 7 (1985): 129–59, 131.
92 Friedrich Keinemann, *Das Domkapital zu Münster im 18. Jahrhundert. Verfasung, persönliche Zusammensetzung, Parteiverhältnisse* (Münster, 1967), 60; Rudolfine Freijin von Oer, "Landständische Verfassung in den geistlichen Fürstentümern Nordwestdeutschlands," in Dietrich Gerhard, ed., *Ständische Vertretungen in Europa im 17. und 18. Jahrhundert* (Göttingen, 1974), 94–119.
93 Keinemann, *Das Domkapital,* 60.   94 Klüting, *Reichsgrafen,* 40.

expulsion of the Jews.[95] The towns played a similar role within the diet of Münster as well as the diet of Paderborn. Even here the towns, which claimed the right to participate in protecting the Jews (*Mitvergleitungsrecht*), demanded expulsions and settlement limitations within the framework of the proceedings of the diet.[96] They made their case especially vehemently during the Paderborn diets of 1606 and 1651.[97]

In 1729 and 1730, the electoral prince-bishop of Cologne, Duke Klemens August of Bavaria, who simultaneously held the sees of Münster and Paderborn, told the territorial estates in both territories that he was willing to expel the Jews completely and to renounce his use of the *Judenregalien,* if they reimbursed "the amount that the Jewry annually contributed."[98] The estates, however, could not accept the bishop's proposal that they themselves compensate for the lost Jewish taxes, and so things remained as they were. Perhaps it was exactly this attitude of the ruler, who wanted to show proof of his willingness to cooperate with the estates through this not very serious offer, that stabilized the Jews' situation in Münster and Paderborn.

The special situation in the bishoprics of Bamberg and Würzburg was the result of the presence of a strong and knightly nobility, subject directly to imperial authority (*reichsunmittelbar*), at least since the middle of the sixteenth century. To a large extent, this nobility followed the teachings of the Protestant faith. In this respect it was closely tied to the episcopal freehold nobility, possessing *Reichsherrschaften* and *Mediatherrschaften* with the office (*Vogtei*) and lower jurisdictions (*Niedergerichtsbarkeit*), which were subordinate to episcopal territorial rule.[99] This nobility was even partly in charge of independent residential rights (*Schutzrechte*) for the Jews, which the emperors had lent to it.[100] For the bishopric of Würzburg it can be shown that the number of so-called knighthood Jews was equal to the number of episcopal resident Jews (*Schutzjuden*).[101] Using their feudal positions as lords, the bishops were interested in extending their influence regarding the Jews over the dominions of the knighthood as well, independent of whether these were parts of the territory or immediately subject to the empire. Because the knights had independent policies vis-à-vis the Jews, based on the *Judenregalien* as well as the authority of the *Reichspolizeiordnung* of 1548, which

95 Bachmann, *Die Landstände des Hochstifts Bamberg,* 150.
96 Behr, "Judenschaft, Landstände und Fürsten," 122.
97 Rosenkrantz, "Über die früheren Verhältnisse," 261.
98 Behr, "Judenschaft, Landstände und Fürsten," 125, 128.
99 Agethen, "Judenpolitik im deutschen Fürstenstaat."
100 Weger, *Die Juden im Hochstift Würzburg,* 74; Eckstein, *Geschichte der Juden,* 59.
101 Eckstein, *Geschichte der Juden,* 60, 323.

authorized them "to take in and protect Jews in our noble lands," conflicts arose.[102] This gave hope to the Jews who were partly expelled from the cathedral areas or who were limited in their commercial activities.[103] This situation made the Würzburg chapter admit, in 1570, "that in Franconia no such territorial princely authority – or a common law in the whole province – could be implemented, since there are many princes, counts, lords, cities, and the knights who were not subordinate to one another."[104] An argument between the cathedral chapter and the knighthood regarding the protection of the Jews,[105] which broke out in the diet of 1570, remained unresolved at the end of the ancien régime.[106] The Jews most likely benefited from this conflict of interests.

In order to characterize the peculiarities of the ecclesiastical territories of the Holy Roman Empire with respect to the Jews, we must comprehend the following: the double competence of bishops and other imperial prelates did not necessarily disadvantage the Jews. Indeed, since the Catholic Church viewed its mission to the Jews as a matter of special concern, the ecclesiastical orientation of a government may have led the Jews to maintain their faith more fervently.[107] One example of this trend was the establishment in 1543 of an educational institute in Würzburg for Jews who expressed a willingness to convert.[108] Another was the subjection of the Jews, since the early eighteenth century, to *Bussgerichtsbarkeit* (atonement via penance) at the archdeaconry tribunals in Paderborn and Münster.[109] The mission to the Jews also guaranteed their very existence and livelihood, because it contained and limited their repression. The extent to which the pressure to convert was increased in ecclesiastical territories after the late sixteenth century cannot be ascertained. But it is likely that the ecclesiastical regime, which had been strengthened by the Council of Trent, was prepared to diminish the pressure on the Jews to convert and thereby stabilize their situation.

The close connection between the ecclesiastical princes and the imperial central authorities, which came about through church rule (*Kirchenherrschaft*) and the efficacy of the *Judenregalien,* likewise advantaged the Jews. The em-

---

102 *Reichspolizeiordnung* of 1548; cf. note 51 of this chapter.
103 Agethen, "Judenpolitik im deutschen Fürstenstaat."
104 ". . . dass in dem Land zu Francken keine solche Landsfürstliche Obrigkeit oder ius in tota provincia könte angezogen werden, sintemal viel Fürsten, Grafen, Herrn, Stätte und die Ritterschaft darinnen wohnten, deren keiner dem anderen unterworfen." Schubert, *Die Landstände des Hochstifts Würzburg,* 141.
105 Ibid.   106 Bohrer, "Die Juden im Hochstift Würzburg," 75.
107 Agethen, "Judenpolitik im deutschen Fürstenstaat."
108 Ibid.   109 Rixen, *Geschichte und Organisation,* 50; Kraft, "Die rechtliche . . . Lage," 128.

peror remained active as the supreme protector of the Jews and, with the help of the Reichskammergericht and the Reichshofrat, exerted his influence against expulsions of the Jews, insofar as there was a fear that the *Judenregalien* were being undermined and that his feudally derived authority was being flaunted.

Similar conclusions can be reached regarding the consequences of the electoral system in the ecclesiastical territories. The frequent vacancies in episcopal offices indeed created regularly recurring insecurity, and the collection of new taxes by the cathedral chapter, on account of these vacancies, meant additional suffering for the Jews.[110] Nevertheless, the electoral agreements created the possibility for contractual ties and/or a certain amount of freedom. The reduction in the bishop's room to maneuver was usually compensated for by ties to the cathedral chapters, which had to be content with contractual agreements. Within the context of territorial power, however, the cathedral chapters could not exert influence on the political enforcement of these agreements.

In the bishoprics of Bamberg and Würzburg, especially, and to some degree in the cathedral chapters in northern Germany, the Jews' existential room to maneuver was enlarged accordingly. To the extent that they were carried out at all, expulsions remained largely ineffective, owing to the lack of a consensus on the part of the territorial states in question. On fiscal grounds, moreover, knightly rulers were prepared to receive Jews on a regular basis.

Thus, we can conclude that it was not the benevolent and open-minded attitude of imperial prelates, particularly the ecclesiastical princes, that was responsible for the comparatively favorable situation of the Jews in the ecclesiastical territories. Rather, it was the variety of rulers and the wide distribution of ecclesiastical and secular jurisdictional authority that were decisive. The desire to expel the Jews, the animus for which came especially from the towns, was limited by the divided rule. Here, authority was parceled out to the bishop, as spiritual leader and as secular prince, the cathedral chapter, the territorial estates, and the knighthood, part of which came from outside the territory.

III

We now need to ask whether or not the special structures of the ecclesiastical territories had a stabilizing effect on the communal institutions of the

110 Kraft, "Die rechtliche . . . Lage," 44.

Jews. Of course, we cannot expect such a stabilization before the late seventeenth and eighteenth centuries, following the failure, once and for all, of attempts at expulsion. A peaceful coexistence between Jews and other subjects within a Christian atmosphere and within the framework of an absolutist government, however, was possible only if the Jews were recognized as a legitimate social group – and that group's activity fell within the purview of government.[111] This contact could happen via governmental delegates, clerical supervisors, or inspectors at the *Landjudenschaften*. The latter were pseudoparliamentary assemblies of Jews that regulated intra-Jewish affairs and allotted the local taxes demanded by the territorial administration. Such assemblies existed as early as 1619 in the bishopric of Bamberg.[112] In the other German bishoprics analyzed here, and commensurate with the general trend at this time, *Landjudenschaften* operated since the middle of the seventeenth century.[113]

Sometimes the territorial princes interfered with these organizations in a regulatory way in order to secure control over them. This interference took place, for example, in the bishopric of Münster in 1651, when the newly elected bishop, Christoph Bernhard von Galen, decreed: "We have found it necessary that the Jews who live in our ecclesiastical land Münster, within our jurisdiction and safe conduct, should have a commander and a leader, so that our interests could be observed more diligently and that no fraud could occur."[114]

Appointed as Jewish leader (*Judenvorgänger*), Nini Levi was given the order at this time "to collect diligently the yearly residence taxes and to turn them over promptly to officials for proper receipts."[115] To maintain the Jews' ability to pay taxes, Levi not only had to provide for the timely payment of the residence tax (*Schutzgeld*), but he also had to stand guard over the territorial Jewry's rights and privileges. In order to achieve the regimentation of the Jews, Levi was appointed an assistant officer of episcopal administration, with the following words: "should someone dare, without our gracious special order, to ask from Jews levies, taxes, contribution, or the like under any name other than at the request of Nini Levi, officials

111 Battenberg, "Obrigkeitliche Sozialpolitik," 43.   112 Eckstein, *Geschichte der Juden,* 62.

113 Weger, "Die Juden im Hochstift Würzburg," 6, 8; Muhs, *Zwischen Schutzherrschaft,* 8; also see Behr, "Judenschaft, Landstände und Fürsten," 121; Rixen, *Geschichte und Organisation,* 33.

114 "Demnach wyr vor notigh befunden haben, uber die in unserem Stift Münster vermögh unser[er] Regalien vergleideten Juden einen Befelchaberen und Vorgänger zu verordnen, damit unser hierunter habendes Interesse desto besser und fliessiger beobachtet [werden kann] und kein Unterschleif geschehen wird." Rixen, *Geschichte und Organisation,* 33.

115 ". . . das jährliche Schutzgeldt bestens fleissig beyzutreiben [und] unsern darzu Verordneten gegen gebuerliche Quittungh zur rechten Zeit einzuliefern." Ibid.

should remedy this and not permit it."[116] According to Carl Rixen, Levi and his successors occupied the office of Jewish leader (*Vorgängeramt*) in the mutual interests of both Jews and the territorial administration of the territorial ruler.[117] As court Jews (*Hofjuden*), these leaders performed a critical mediating function, and thus they neutralized pressures exerted, for the most part, by the Christian territorial estates on other Jews.

In institutional and personal contact with the territorial princes, court Jews could be found in secular and ecclesiastical territories during the ancien régime. In this regard, ecclesiastical territories shared in the general trends of the period. Something new, however, was added in the transfer of jurisdictional authority over internal Jewish conflicts to Jewish leaders. These conflicts had otherwise been subject to the arbitrary legal jurisdiction of the territorial ruler, who regulated them centrally, as long as they did not fall within the rabbi's jurisdiction. According to the above-mentioned decree, it was therefore ordered, in 1651, that "the same [Jews] will be sent first to this Nini Levi, and he will be herewith commanded to name a rabbi who will decide such quarrels."[118] This meant that, mediated by the office of the Jewish leader, the territorial rabbi in the bishopric received an official function. The territorial rabbi could now decide intra-Jewish quarrels (*Jude contra Jud*) on behalf of the territorial ruler. On the one hand, this gave the rabbis more authority; on the other hand, they were now subject to more control.

The effect of this regulation, which was attained by means of the above-mentioned decree, was reinforced by the creation of independent oversight bodies like the Jewish Commission (Judenkommission) and the Jewish Office (Judenamt) in Paderborn and Würzburg.

In ecclesiastical as well as secular territorial states, quarrels between Jews and Gentiles normally fell within the competence of secular Christian courts, with the provision that the territorial court of justice would arbitrate all appeals. The traditional jurisdiction of the emperor as supreme protector of the Jews worked the same as before, as exemplified by numerous Jewish trials at the Reichskammergericht in Speyer (later in Wetzlar), the Reichshofrat in Vienna, and the Imperial Court Tribunal (Reichs-

---

116 ". . . daferner auch einige sich unterstehen werden, ohne unseren habenden gnedigsten Spezialbefelch von den Juden einige Schatzungh, Steuer, Bruchten oder Contribution, wie die Nahmen haben mögten, zu fordern, sollen unsere Beamten solches auf sein, Nini Levi, gepürendes Ansuchen remedy[r]en und nicht gestatten." Ibid., 33.

117 Ibid., 34.

118 ". . . dafern dieselben [Juden] an diesen Nini Levi zuvorderst verwiesen werden, und wird er hiermit befehligt, einen Rabbiner, solche Streitigkeiten zu entscheiden, zu benennen." Ibid., 47.

hofgericht) in Rottweil.[119] Intraterritorial quarrels, however, had long since been transferred to the jurisdiction of the territorial courts, either through the granting of imperial privileges or through custom. With regard to the Jews in Westphalia, Emperor Ludwig the Bavarian (1342) and King Karl IV (1349) affirmed the juridical responsibility of the defendant's hometown court ("in quo resident manifesto").[120]

Regardless of this fact, many attempts were made to subject the Jews to ecclesiastical jurisdiction through a broad interpretation of the requirements of the Christian mission. Attempts of this kind can be seen since the late medieval centuries, especially within the bishoprics of the Holy Roman Empire. Therefore, since the fourteenth and fifteenth centuries, the Jews within the jurisdiction of the prince-archbishop and elector of Mainz let themselves be assured by the archbishop – within the framework of protection – that Gentiles could sue Jews only at secular courts and that only there could they win convictions.[121] But the problem remained acute, and the archdeaconries of the bishoprics of Münster,[122] Paderborn,[123] and those in the duchy of Westphalia[124] (a territory belonging to the electoral archbishopric of Cologne) claimed jurisdictional authority over Jews, which represented an ongoing danger for the Jews in the respective territories.

Under these circumstances, the creation of a secular intermediary (*Zwischeninstanz*) that could take care of Jewish interests seemed to be a way out. For that reason, the prince-bishop of Paderborn, Franz Arnold Wolf von Metternich, who later also became the bishop of Münster, established an independent Jewish Commission in 1705 that would manage the legal affairs of the Jews in cooperation with two court councilors.[125] Initially, this commission failed to achieve any notable successes. But in 1719 the newly elected prince-bishop of Münster, Klemens August, the duke of Bavaria,[126] strengthened this judicial body, which had fallen into disuse by this time.[127] The commission became the court of original jurisdiction in all civil law-

---

119 Battenberg, "Des Kaisers Kammerknechte," 574; Battenberg, *Das Reichskammergericht und die Juden des Heiligen Römischen Reiches. Geistliche Herrschaft und korporative Verfassung der Judenschaft in Fürth im Widerspruch* (Wetzlar, 1991); Battenberg, "Juden am Reichskammergericht in Wetzlar. Der Streit um die Privilegien der Judenschaft in Fürth," in Bernhard Diestelkamp, ed., *Die politische Funktion des Reichskammergerichts* (Cologne, 1993), 181–213.

120 J. Friedrich Battenberg, *Die Gerichtsstandsprivilegien der deutschen Kaiser und Könige bis zum Jahre 1451,* vol. 1 (Cologne and Vienna, 1983), 255, no. 442a (May 1, 1342), and 296, no. 531a (July 16, 1349).

121 For examples of such privileges, see Battenberg, *Quellen zur Geschichte der Juden,* index under "Gerichtsstand."

122 Rixen, *Geschichte und Organisation,* 50.   123 Kraft, "Die rechtliche . . . Lage," 29.

124 Maria Holthausen, "Die Juden im kurkölnischen Herzogtum Westfalen," *Westfälische Zeitschrift. Zeitschrift für vaterländische Geschichte und Altertumskunde* 96 (1940): 48–152, 75.

125 Kraft, "Die rechtliche Lage," 133.   126 Gatz, "Clemens August," 63.

127 Muhs, *Zwischen Schutzherrschaft,* 16.

suits for all Jews, both in the towns and in the territory of the bishopric of Paderborn (but not in Münster). In his position as supreme commissar (*Oberkommissar*) of the Jews, the prince-bishop retained the right to mete out heavy penalties. The territorial supreme court continued to have jurisdiction over the aforementioned appeals. The comprehensive responsibility of the Jewish Commission in civil lawsuits between Jews and Christians – as between Jews – was reaffirmed in a decree from 1745:

> In all cases affecting the resident Jewry, whether they are raised by other Jews or by Christians, our lower courts should not act but should send these court cases to the special commission which I have installed and which should decide all such cases concerning resident Jews.[128]

When this regulation was incorporated into Paderborn's legal practice (*Justizordnung*) in 1764, the Judenkommission became a constitutionally valid court of justice within this bishopric. The Jewish Commission continued its work until the bishopric was abolished at the beginning of the next century.[129]

The Judenamt had a similar function in the prince-bishopric of Würzburg. The newly elected bishop, Johann Philipp Franz Graf von Schönborn[130] established this office in 1719 as an intermediate link between the episcopal administration and the territorial Jewry.[131] The holder of this office, the *Judenamtmann*, was a member of the princely court council; he was assisted by a supernumerary officer (*Aktuar*), who was simultaneously subordinate to the court treasury and thus formed the connection to the territorial fiscal administration.[132] His responsibility, however, extended mainly to the internal affairs of the Jews but went beyond mere legal jurisdiction. He particularly had to make decisions about complaints and appeals against the sentences of the head rabbi, the *Oberrabbiner,* as well as the seven territorial Jewish leaders, the *Landvorgänger,* who were responsible for the administration of the Jews in the different precincts.[133] But if the amount in litigation (*Streitwert*) was less than 12 florins, he could not act as the court of first jurisdiction. His activity, for which he was paid 120 florins a year, tied

---

128 "In denen die begleidete Judenschaft betreffenden Angelegenheiten sowohl von seinen Glaubensgenossen als den Christen, so dürfen sich die Untergerichte keiner Gerichtsbarkeit unterziehen, sondern sie sollen alle Vorfallenheiten bey der von unss zur begleydeten Juden gnädigst angeordneten Commission angängig machen, alss dero allien die begleydete[n] Juden in allen obigen Fällen unterwürfig seyn sollen." Kraft, "Die rechtliche . . . Lage," 134.

129 Ibid.

130 On the Schönborns, see Friedhelm Jürgensmeier, "Die Schönborn. Ihr Aufstieg von nassauischen Edelleuten zu Reichs- und Kreisfürsten," in Endres, ed., *Adel in der Frühneuzeit,* 1–16.

131 Weger, "Die Juden im Hochstift Würzburg," 57.   132 Ibid., 64.   133 Ibid., 31.

him as much to the episcopal government as to its subjected Jews. Finally, he had to put into practice orders and ordinances of the bishop; for example, the granting of letters of residence (*Schutzbriefe*), the assessment of just tax demands, as well as petitions from Jews.[134]

Nevertheless, the Judenkommission of Paderborn, as well as the Judenamt of Würzburg, neither of which had a counterpart within the bishoprics of Bamberg and Münster,[135] were typical creations of early modern absolutism. First and foremost, they were the territorial ruler's instruments of regulation and control (*Disziplinierungsinstrumente*). The combined positions of the court Jew and the Jewish leader, as we have witnessed in the bishopric of Münster, fit into this context. Simultaneously, the commissioners and clerks, who were in close communication with the Jews, helped to promote within the central administration an understanding of the special existential situation of the Jews. In this way, a certain sense of social responsibility was instilled,[136] which later on, in fact, led to the formation of enlightened concepts of Jewish emancipation.[137] The course of Jewish emancipation in Mainz in the late eighteenth century, under the electoral prince-bishop Friedrich Karl von Erthal, is another example of an ecclesiastical territory that supports the thesis but could not be examined in detail in the present analysis.[138]

IV

In light of the preceding structural analysis, when one considers the problem of the existential condition of Jews in the ecclesiastical territories of the Holy Roman Empire, we can confirm Jonathan Israel's observation about the comparatively favorable conditions of life for the Jews who lived under the bishop's crosier.[139] This thesis is supported by demographic developments as well. Although the Jews of the Holy Roman Empire never exceeded 1.5 percent of the population,[140] their percentage in the ecclesiastical territories was significantly higher. Precise figures are available for the prince-bishopric of Paderborn, where almost 2,000 Jews lived just before the abolition of this ecclesiastical state – nearly 2 percent of the popula-

---

134 Ibid., 5.
135 Eckstein, *Geschichte der Juden,* 191; Rixen, *Geschichte und Organisation,* 50.
136 Behr, "Judenschaft, Landstände und Fürsten," 131.
137 J. Friedrich Battenberg, "Gesetzgebung und Judenemanzipation im ancien régime. Dargestellt am Beispiel Hessen–Darmstadt," *Zeitschrift für historische Forschung* 13 (1986): 43–63, 58; Battenberg, "Judenverordnungen in Hessen–Darmstadt," 29.
138 Post, *Judentoleranz,* 76.   139 Israel, *European Jewry,* 23, 42, 64.
140 J. Friedrich Battenberg, *Das Europäische Zeitalter der Juden,* vol. 2: *Von 1650 bis 1945* (Darmstadt, 1991), iii.

tion.[141] For the area of middle and lower Franconia, which consisted primarily of the bishoprics of Bamberg and Würzburg[142] but also included the regions of the imperial knighthood and some smaller countries and dominions, we find Jews to comprise nearly 3 percent. Altogether, about 20,000 Jews lived in these areas.

The rapid increase of the Jewish population, which had quadrupled from the seventeenth century, can be observed in all of these ecclesiastical territories. The growth of the Jewish population in the ecclesiastical principalities is evidence that they were increasingly attractive to Jews. It is also evident that crucial for the settlement of Jews was the economic character of these territories, which until the end of the ancien régime were much more agrarian than their secular counterparts.[143] Such circumstances were propitious for the Jews because Gentile guilds and corporations, which normally provided strong commercial competition, were absent. As a result, additional areas of economic activity were open to the Jews.

More decisive, however, were the institutional peculiarities of these territories: the special relevance of the *Judenregalien* and the close ties to the center of imperial power; the consequences of the electoral system, established by canon law, with the praxis of the election agreements; and the effectiveness of the cathedral chapter's and the territorial estates' rights to participate in the system. Finally, it was also important that ecclesiastical territories had been relatively open to the lower knighthood, which was partly freehold and partly *reichsunmittelbar.*

All of this created constraints on development and idiosyncratic laws that enabled the Jews to form a stronger corporate structure as well as an institutional connection to the absolutist government. Perhaps it was precisely this fact that explains why the ecclesiastical territorial ruler remained dependent, to a greater extent than his secular colleagues, on participatory governmental rights of the cathedral chapter and the territorial estates. Thus, he had to make additional efforts to establish cooperative links to the Jews. With the help of commissars, clerks, and court Jews – as *Vorgänger* – he could relate better to this social group and give them protection, in the hope of collecting considerable taxes and of creating a homogeneous community of Jewish and Christian subjects.

Among the secular rulers, there certainly were some who protected the Jews in a similar fashion. There were also bishops who, in the course of con-

141 Muhs, *Zwischen Schutzherrschaft,* 37.
142 Agethen, "Judenpolitik im deutschen Fürstenstaat."
143 Hersche, "Intendierte Rückständigkeit," 139; Huettl, "Geistlicher Fürst," 33.

fessionalization, strove to make their territory completely Catholic, naturally at the expense of the Jews. It can be established from the sources presented in this analysis, however, that the structural preconditions in
ecclesiastical territories were generally more favorable for the Jews than in
the secular territories.

17

Jews in the Imperial Cities: A Political Perspective

CHRISTOPHER R. FRIEDRICHS

The two hundred years from the mid-sixteenth to the mid-eighteenth century represented in some ways the nadir of Jewish life in the imperial cities
of Germany. The great Jewish communities that had existed in so many of
these cities in the Middle Ages had mostly disappeared. By 1550, the Jews
had long since been expelled from Augsburg, Colmar, Cologne, Heilbronn,
Lindau, Nördlingen, Nuremberg, Ravensburg, Regensburg, Rothenburg,
Strasbourg, Ulm, and a host of smaller imperial cities.[1] Nor was the wave
of successful expulsions over by then: the Jews were expelled from Dort-
mund in 1596 and from Aachen in 1629. Increasingly, as is well known,
Jewish life in Germany was centered in towns or villages of the territorial
states.

But Jewish life was not entirely extinguished in the imperial cities. Major Jewish communities survived, during the early modern period, in Frankfurt, Worms, and Friedberg. A significant Jewish community – or rather,
Jewish communities – emerged in Hamburg in the course of the seventeenth century. Smaller Jewish communities survived in Goslar, Speyer, and
Wetzlar. By the seventeenth century, Jews began to return to some of the
imperial cities from which they had been expelled, notably Regensburg. In
many other cities, Jews were familiar as day visitors or temporary inhabitants in time of war.

To be sure, the fact that an individual Jew might occasionally be seen on
the streets of Cologne or Nuremberg is not particularly interesting, from
the political point of view. But the fact that vigorous Jewish communities

---

1 For the late medieval expulsions, see Markus J. Wenninger, *Man bedarf keiner Juden mehr: Ursachen und
Hintergründe ihrer Vertreibung aus den deutschen Reichsstädten im 15. Jahrhundert* (Vienna and Cologne,
1981). Since the volumes of the *Germania Judaica* have not yet been extended beyond the early sixteenth century, there exists no systematic survey of the status of Jewish communities in German towns
of the early modern era. For introductory information and basic bibliographic references on Jewish
communities in the major German cities, see the relevant entries in the *Encyclopaedia Judaica*, 16 vols.
(Jerusalem, 1971–2).

continued to exist in some imperial cities is indeed noteworthy. In fact, the Jewish communities of Frankfurt and Worms did not just survive the era of expulsions; they grew steadily in the sixteenth century and, despite attempts to banish them in the years 1612 to 1616, they maintained their presence throughout the seventeenth century. The Jewish community of Worms, like the city itself, was somewhat reduced in size when Worms was reestablished after being destroyed by the French in 1689.[2] But Frankfurt and Hamburg continued to be major centers of German-Jewish life in the eighteenth century. In all three of these cities, the Jewish communities experienced a vigorous political life during the early modern era.

It is worth giving some thought to the nature of this political life. For neither the internal politics of the Jewish communities nor the role of Jews in the political life of their host communities has, I think, received sufficient emphasis in recent discussions of the Jewish experience in early modern Germany.

Most discussions of the political relationship between Jews and Gentiles during this period are built around certain familiar concepts: toleration, exclusion, autonomy. Toleration was something granted by the Christian authorities. The first dimension of toleration was, of course, to grant the Jews permission to live in a particular place; further dimensions of toleration involved permission for the Jews to carry out their religious and communal activities without restriction. Exclusion involved the separation of Jewish life from the life of the host communities. Unlike toleration, which was determined entirely by the host community, the degree and character of exclusion could be determined partly by the wishes of the Jews themselves. Inevitably, both toleration and exclusion were linked to the issue of Jewish autonomy, or self-government – the way in which Jews regulated their own communal affairs with a minimum of interference from the Christian authorities. In the late eighteenth century, toleration came to involve the possibility of assimilation and civic emancipation. But before that time, the extent of toleration would normally have been measured by the degree to which Jews were given the opportunity to live in a particular place with a minimum of interference and a maximum of self-government.

Every student of the subject will recognize the importance of these concepts in any discussion of Jewish – Christian relations of the early modern era. The extent and especially the limits of toleration are, for example, the themes around which Joachim Whaley builds his admirable treatment of re-

---

2 Fritz Reuter, *Warmaisa: 1000 Jahre Juden in Worms* (Worms, 1984), 120–42, esp. 139.

lations between Jews and Gentiles in seventeenth- and eighteenth-century Hamburg.[3] The concepts of exclusion and autonomy are no less central to our understanding of early modern Jewish history. It has been argued, for example, that among Ashkenazic Jews the degree of separation from Christian society in the early modern era was even greater than it had been in medieval times.[4] Jonathan Israel emphasizes the exclusion of Jews from the mainstream of European civilization as a key factor in the flowering of Jewish self-rule in the early modern period. "It is curious," Israel argues,

that . . . so little sympathy should be shown to the forms and procedures of early modern Jewish self-government. It may be that Jewish self-rule was oligarchic and that its zeal for regulating life-style ill accords with twentieth-century ideas on personal freedom. It is also true that early modern Jewish autonomy was partly a product of enforced segregation and the fiscal convenience of the state. But the positive side of its influence deserves attention also.

Israel differs from some other authors in regretting the decline of Jewish autonomy that began during the Enlightenment. For him, the isolated and cohesive character of Jewish self-rule during the early modern era contributed to a rich social, economic, and cultural system that fell apart as toleration grew in the eighteenth century.[5] This is in some ways an unusual point of view, but Israel shares the widespread assumption that Jewish communities of the sixteenth and seventeenth century were sharply separated from the life of their host communities.

No doubt this was generally true. It is worth asking, however, whether this assumption applies fully to the German imperial cities of the early modern era. For by treating the Jews as members of a separate, encapsulated community, one may overlook the degree to which they were part of a city's entire political system. We can see an extreme case of this, for example, in Matthias Meyn's important study of Frankfurt on the eve of the Fettmilch Uprising in the early seventeenth century. Meyn analyzes the society of Frankfurt in terms of four "systems": the "constitutional and administrative system," the "economic system," the "social system," and the "cultural-religious system." The Jews of Frankfurt, who made up some 10 percent of the total population, are seen by Meyn as part of only the

---

3 Joachim Whaley, *Religious Toleration and Social Change in Hamburg, 1529–1819* (Cambridge, 1985), 70–110.

4 Jacob Katz, *Exclusiveness and Toleration: Studies in Jewish – Gentile Relations in Medieval and Modern Times* (Oxford, 1961), 131–4.

5 Jonathan I. Israel, *European Jewry in the Age of Mercantilism, 1550–1750* (Oxford, 1985), esp. 255. The quoted passage has been dropped from the second edition of the book (Oxford, 1989) but the essential argument is preserved.

"cultural-religious" system. They were the objects of political conflict among the Christian population, but they were not themselves part of the city's political system – nor, in fact, of its economic or social systems.[6]

Such an approach is in some ways understandable. One of the central themes of German-Jewish history, after all, is the gradual admission of the Jews to civic rights in the various German states during the first two-thirds of the nineteenth century. In Frankfurt, for example, the Jews received civic rights briefly during the Napoleonic period, lost them after 1813, were granted the status of *israelitische Bürger* (Jewish citizens) in 1824, and received complete equality with other citizens in 1864. This process is described by conventional history as resulting from the "struggle of the Frankfurt Jews for their emancipation."[7] The same story, with obvious differences in detail and chronology, was repeated for Jews all over Germany between the French Revolution and the founding of the German Empire in 1871.

The implications of the traditional approach are clear. Through the process of emancipation, the Jews were finally admitted to a political system from which they had long been excluded. Membership in the system was defined, at least in cities, by possession of the *Bürgerrecht* (rights of citizens). In some cities, such as Worms, Jews had in fact enjoyed the status of *Bürger* as late as the fourteenth century.[8] Then they were excluded. Half a millennium later, they were readmitted to that status and thus, it is implied, to participation in the political system. This seems to mean that for five hundred years they had not been part of the political life of a city like Worms.

What is misleading about this approach, however, is the assumption that participation in the political system of the imperial cities in the late Middle Ages and early modern era was limited to those persons who were *Bürger* – or, to put it another way, that political life was confined to members of the *Bürgerschaft*. There is no question, of course, that possession of the *Bürgerrecht* conferred special rights. Often the most important advantages of citizenship had to do with residential and occupational rights, but every *Bürger* of a German town was also conscious of belonging to a group that had the real or latent power to participate in certain types of decision making. Occasionally, the failure of oligarchical leaders to adequately consult or consider their fellow citizens could lead to a violent civic uprising.[9] But did this mean that only the *Bürger* were part of a community's political system?

---

6 Matthias Meyn, *Die Reichsstadt Frankfurt vor dem Bürgeraufstand von 1612 bis 1614: Struktur und Krise* (Frankfurt/Main, 1980), 9–22, 167–236.

7 Eugen Mayer, *Die Frankfurter Juden* (Frankfurt/Main, 1966), 47. 8 Reuter, *Warmaisa*, 57.

9 For a brief survey and references to the literature, see Christopher R. Friedrichs, "German Town Revolts and the Seventeenth-Century Crisis," *Renaissance and Modern Studies* 26 (1982): 27–51.

Even the citizens themselves participated in political life only rarely, through elections or public assemblies, and only a handful ever held public office. The most customary form of political activity was the application of political pressure on city councils by specific interest groups. Pressure was applied by submitting petitions, by demanding negotiations, by launching legal cases, and by appealing for support from outside the community. The citizens applied all of these methods, either through their guilds or through other associations. But all of these methods of political action were also open to other groups within the community – including, in cities like Frankfurt and Worms, the Jews.

Certainly the Jews were not the only noncitizens who participated in the political process as recognizable interest groups. In many German cities, for example, organizations of journeymen – the *Gesellenvereinigungen* – exerted considerable power on behalf of their members. Bolstered by their solidarity with similar organizations in other communities, the journeymen's associations in certain trades often controlled the terms of employment for their members. When journeymen in a particular trade felt aggrieved, they might boycott the master, the guild, or even the whole city concerned. In the fifteenth century, the magistrates of numerous southern German cities tried to undertake collective measures to reduce the power of these organizations. Yet as late as the seventeenth century the *Gesellenvereinigungen* in certain trades were still a force to be taken seriously in many southern German cities.[10]

The Jews, like the journeymen, were not citizens – yet they too were capable of pursuing their interests effectively within the community. Indeed, the Jewish community could, where it existed, be an even more powerful political entity than the *Gesellenvereinigungen*. This became evident in Frankfurt and Worms when, in the early seventeenth century, the expulsionist impulse was again manifested there. In both cities, after two years of anti-Jewish agitation the Jews were banished by the citizens, only to be restored to their homes and rights shortly thereafter. A number of factors accounted for the failure of these attempted expulsions of the Jews in Frankfurt and Worms.[11] But among these factors was an apparent growth in the Jews' own capacity for effective political action.

---

10 Knut Schulz, *Handwerksgesellen und Lohnarbeiter: Untersuchungen zur oberrheinischen und oberdeutschen Stadtgeschichte des 14. bis 17. Jahrhunderts* (Sigmaringen, 1985), 58–162; Kurt Wesoly, *Lehrlinge und Handwerksgesellen: Ihre soziale Lage und ihre Organisation vom 14. bis ins 17. Jahrhundert* (Frankfurt/Main, 1985), 347–90.

11 Christopher R. Friedrichs, "The Anti-Jewish Movements in Frankfurt and Worms, 1612–1617: Local Crisis and Imperial Response," in *Proceedings of the Tenth World Congress of Jewish Studies,* division B, vol. 2 (Jerusalem, 1990), 199–206.

The Jews of the Holy Roman Empire had learned, for example, to take advantage of the emergence of new imperial courts – the Reichskammergericht, after 1495, and the Reichshofrat in the course of the sixteenth century. The right of the Jews to appear as plaintiffs in either of these tribunals was unquestioned, and Jews became accustomed to appeal to the imperial courts for protection in cases of illegal expulsion.[12] But like other plaintiffs, they decided whether to appeal – and if so, to which court – on a selective basis. What was really important was to know how the constitutional system worked and to seek, in any given situation, the most politically advantageous solution.

There were, for example, attempts to maintain the unity of Jews throughout the empire by strengthening the bonds that connected Jews across territorial lines. The special links between the Jews and the emperor were increasingly vitiated, in the fifteenth and sixteenth centuries, by the tendency of individual territorial rulers to place the Jews under their protection and control and to regulate Jewish affairs through territorial *Judenordnungen* (regulations regarding Jews).[13] But the Jews did not fully accept the proposition that their only, or even primary, political allegiance should be to the territorial price or overlord. It was, in fact, partly to counteract this tendency that German Jews of the sixteenth century attempted to strengthen their organizational links in the series of rabbinical synods that culminated in the famous Frankfurt meeting of 1603.[14]

The conference of 1603 has traditionally been seen as a relatively innocuous attempt to regulate internal Jewish affairs, particularly with regard to taxation, and the subsequent efforts made to punish the participants are held to reflect irrational anti-Jewish sentiments. But in his significant reinterpretation of these events, Volker Press has argued convincingly that if the synod had succeeded it could have paved the way toward the emergence of the Jews as a distinct transterritorial group within the empire, analogous in some ways to the imperial knights or the Hanseatic League. Seen in this light, the efforts to undo the synod's decisions can be seen as a realistic political response by some territorial rulers, notably the elector of Cologne, to what was recognized as an authentic political threat.[15] Obviously the Jew-

---

12 Sabine Frey, *Rechtsschutz der Juden gegen Ausweisungen im 16. Jahrhundert* (Frankfurt/Main, 1983).
13 Friedrich Battenberg, "Zur Rechtsstellung der Juden am Mittelrhein in Spätmittelalter und früher Neuzeit," *Zeitschrift für historische Forschung* 6 (1979): 129–83, esp. 138–43, 149–71.
14 For an overview of the meetings between 1542 and 1603, see Eric Zimmer, *Jewish Synods in Germany during the Late Middle Ages (1286–1603)* (New York, 1978), 67–100.
15 Volker Press, "Kaiser Rudolf II. und der Zusammenschluss der deutschen Judenheit: Die sogenannte Frankfurter Rabbinerverschwörung von 1603 und ihre Folgen," in Alfred Haverkamp, ed., *Zur Geschichte der Juden im Deutschland des späten Mittelalters und der frühen Neuzeit* (Stuttgart, 1981), 243–93.

ish leaders overreached themselves in 1603, but the attempt itself suggests that the Jews had the potential to become a real political force on the imperial level.

Of course this did not happen. But the concept of a united *Judenschaft deutscher Nation* (Jewry of the German nation) remained strong, and the Jews did not rely only on their territorial or local rulers for protection. The Jews of Frankfurt and Worms, for example, were by no means confined to a local perspective in their response to the crisis of 1612–16.

Consider the case of Worms.[16] As soon as the threats to their communal existence emerged, the Jews of Worms began to send petitions and delegations to the imperial court to press the emperor to uphold their rights. Indeed, more than once the emperor received his first news about the latest developments in Worms from the Jews, and he responded repeatedly by insisting that Jewish rights that had been granted by imperial authority had to be upheld. Like the citizens themselves, the Jews of Worms tried to use those institutions of the empire that worked in their favor, while ignoring institutions that worked against them. In the fall of 1614, for example, the citizens of Worms secured a preliminary mandate from the Reichskammergericht in Speyer, authorizing a reduction in the interest rates that Jews could charge on their loans. The citizens immediately attempted to force the Jews to settle outstanding accounts at the new rate. But the Jews firmly resisted this procedure. Though Jews at other times had depended on the Reichskammergericht to uphold their rights, the Jews of Worms resented the court's decision in this case – and they suspected, quite rightly, that the mandate would be hard to enforce. So they refused to comply. Some Jews were reported – admittedly by a hostile source – to have declared contemptuously: "We would not give 3 farthings for such an imperial mandate; we have the real, living emperor on our side, and we will leave to you citizens the dead emperors in Speyer."[17] The Jews' calculation of the political realities in this case was entirely sound. The citizens' case got mired in further proceedings, and the decree was never enforced. To be sure, at one point the Jews were forcibly banished from Worms by the citizens. But this only heightened their efforts to seek redress from the imperial court. Soon the emperor intervened to insure their return to Worms.

In the case of Frankfurt, once the emperor had appointed an imperial commission to deal with the political crisis, the Jews directed most of their

---

16 A full treatment of this episode is provided by my article "Anti-Jewish Politics in Early Modern Germany: The Uprising in Worms, 1613–17," *Central European History* 23 (1990): 91–152.

17 Haus-, Hof- und Staatsarchiv, Vienna: Reichshofrat Antiqua 1145/11, no. 3, art. 29. The phrase "dead emperors" presumably referred to the famous tombs of the Salian emperors in Speyer.

petitions and addresses to the imperial commissioners or their subdele-gates.[18] An attempt to submit their complaints directly to a meeting of the Reichstag in Regensburg was deflected by the city council.[19] But the imperial commission persistently upheld the Jews' rights. After the Jews were expelled from the city, the imperial commissioners acted to reaffirm their rights and supervised their eventual restoration to the *Judengasse,* or ghetto, of Frankfurt.

The Jewish communities of Hamburg never experienced such a dramatic expulsion as occurred in Frankfurt and Worms, but there were constant threats to their presence from citizens whose anti-Jewish sentiments were persistently fanned by the city's rigidly Lutheran clergy. In 1649, the Ashke-nazic Jews were in fact banished from Hamburg – but the wealthier Sephardic Jews were not, and within a few years the Ashkenazim began to return.[20] For, despite some temporary setbacks, as a whole the Jews of Hamburg effectively defended their right to remain in the city, typically by making clear that the city would lose more by their departure than they would themselves. Confident of their economic value to the community and bolstered by protection from the kings of Denmark, whose territory abutted Hamburg and who claimed sovereignty over the city itself, the Jews were able to overcome any fundamental challenge to their presence in Hamburg.[21]

There is no question, then, that the Jews of these imperial cities were well equipped to function politically within the institutional framework of the empire as a whole. But the political vigor of Jewish communities is illustrated not only by their ability to defend their collective interests in a time of crisis but also by the character of their internal political life. Indeed, to assume that the Jewish communities always functioned in a united or collective manner would be highly misleading, for it would mask the political character of these communities. Politics, after all, is primarily a process of conflict resolution – but it is conflict, rather than its resolution, that truly defines a community as political.

When it comes to Worms, we know much about the way in which the Jewish community was administered but little about the way in which internal conflict was regulated. In seventeenth-century Worms, the work of the rabbi and a few other salaried communal functionaries was supple-

18 Isidor Kracauer, "Die Juden Frankfurts im Fettmilch'schen Aufstand, 1612–1618," *Zeitschrift für die Geschichte der Juden in Deutschland* 4 (1890): 127–69, 319–65; 5 (1892): 1–26.
19 Ibid., 4:322–3.
20 Max Grunwald, *Hamburgs deutsche Juden bis zur Auflösung der Dreigemeinden 1811* (Hamburg, 1904), 8–11.
21 Whaley, *Religious Toleration,* esp. 74, 81–82.

mented by a vast structure of volunteer positions that were established to administer the religious, educational, and charitable concerns of the community. Jewish affairs were directed by a communal council, the *parnasim*. The rules under which the council was elected and its procedures for conducting business were recorded in elaborate detail.[22] In fact, these practices were strikingly reminiscent of the procedures followed by German city councils of the same era. But how effectively these communal leaders functioned in their relations with the rest of the community is still unclear.

We know much, however, about the internal political life of the Frankfurt Jewish community in the early modern era. In the seventeenth century, the Jews of Frankfurt were characterized by great extremes of wealth and poverty.[23] As Isidor Kracauer showed, in his great history of the Frankfurt Jews, the community was characterized by political inequality as well. By the early seventeenth century, power within the Jewish community had come to be concentrated in the hands of a highly oligarchical council – the Zehner, or Ten – and there was growing discontent among those Jewish householders who were excluded from political participation. The tensions could not be contained within the Jewish community. Complaints against the high-handed rule of the Zehner were made to the emperor. Even at the height of the Fettmilch Uprising, when the very existence of the Jewish community was at stake, the internal tensions did not abate. The imperial commissioners who were appointed to settle the political situation in Frankfurt also received petitions and requests to settle the internal disputes within the Jewish community. But their attempt to solve things did not satisfy opponents of the Zehner. In 1617, the Frankfurt city council appointed a panel of rabbis to mediate the conflict – but again, to little avail. New complaints were addressed to Vienna. In 1622, the city council radically restructured the constitution and voting procedures of the Jewish community. Some of the Jews were dissatisfied with this settlement and submitted their complaints both to the Council of the Four Lands – the great Jewish synod of Poland – and to the celebrated Rabbi Yom-Tov Lipmann Heller in Prague. Yet attempts by the council and by Rabbi Heller to intervene in the dispute proved ineffective. It was only when members of the Jewish community complained once again to the emperor that the conflict was finally resolved. For, in order to forestall further intervention from

---

22 Leon J. Yagod, "Worms Jewry in the Seventeenth Century," Ph.D. diss., Yeshiva University, 1967, 78–134, esp. 83–9. This work is based chiefly on the minhag book of Juspa Shammes of Worms (1604–78).

23 Isidor Kracauer, *Geschichte der Juden in Frankfurt a. M. (1150–1824)*, 2 vols. (Frankfurt/Main, 1925–7), 2:31–2.

Vienna, the city council pressured the Jews to reach an agreement on other changes, which the magistrates then endorsed. By 1628, relative peace was at last restored.[24]

Though the internal struggles then abated, a new round of conflicts broke out in the later seventeenth century. These conflicts were centered on the personality of Abraham zum Drachen, or Drach, one of the most prominent members of the Frankfurt Jewish community. A group of his enemies within the community accused Drach of high-handed and tyrannical practices in regulating the community's affairs. Their accusations were referred first to the city council, then to the archbishop of Mainz, who claimed some jurisdiction over the synagogue of Frankfurt, and finally to the emperor. In response, Drach and his wife hired lawyers, who appealed to the council, to the archbishop, and to the Reichshofrat in Vienna. Eventually Drach secured a favorable judgment from the Reichshofrat, and his opponents were severely fined. At times the city council was virtually excluded from dealing with the affair. Indeed, at one point, when the magistrates had tried to reduce tensions by changing the rules for election to the Jewish council, the Jewish leaders put aside their differences long enough to appeal to the Reichskammergericht to overturn the city council's action. The court did so by ordering new elections, in accordance with rules of its own devising.[25]

These struggles within the Frankfurt Jewish community are strikingly reminiscent of the conflicts that took place among the Christian citizens of Frankfurt and countless other German cities during the same epoch. In the history of German cities in the early modern era, the recurrent struggles by ordinary citizens against the oligarchical tendencies of authoritarian magistrates are normally seen as a sign of political vigor.[26] But these struggles never were or could be confined to the community itself. In territorial cities the citizens could appeal to the prince for a resolution of the conflict. In an imperial city there were many more options; in fact, there was an entire array of imperial institutions to which aggrieved parties might appeal in hope of advice, support, or direct intervention: the emperor, the Reichskammergericht, the imperial diet, the diet of cities, the governments of other cities, university law faculties, or perhaps, if applicable, the city's own "pro-

24 Kracauer, *Geschichte,* 1:399–410, and "Beiträge zur Geschichte der Frankfurter Juden im dreissigjährigen Kriege," pts. 1–2, *Zeitschrift für die Geschichte der Juden in Deutschland* 3 (1889): 130–58, 337–72; 4 (1890): 18–28; esp. 3:344–57; I. Halpern, "A Dispute over the Election of the Community Council of Frankfurt am Main and Its Repercussions in Poland and Bohemia" (in Hebrew), *Zion,* n.s. 21 (1956): 64–91. I am grateful to Rahel Halabé for assistance in translating this last article from the Hebrew.
25 Kracauer, *Geschichte,* 2:47–72.
26 See Otto Borst, "Zur Verfassung und Staatlichkeit oberdeutscher Reichsstädte am Ende des alten Reiches," *Esslinger Studien* 10 (1964): 106–94.

tective lord" or *Schutzherr*.[27] Aggrieved citizens rarely shared the magistrates' concern that excessive dependence on outside intervention might ultimately weaken the city's political autonomy as a whole. In much the same way, in their disputes of the seventeenth century, different parties among the Jews of Frankfurt willingly reached out to whatever non-Jewish sources of authority might settle the conflict in their favor: the city council, a great regional prince, the imperial courts, or the emperor himself.

An old tradition, strongly reasserted by the German rabbinical synods, forbade Jews to bring any litigation against each other before Gentile courts.[28] But this principle, which may have been honored in personal disputes, certainly did not apply to political conflicts. There was apparently little concern that submitting such disputes to the Christian authorities might diminish the degree of autonomy or self-government that the Jewish community as a whole enjoyed. The object of each party was to win the struggle at hand. Any external institution that might help in the pursuit of this goal was readily approached and brought into the conflict.

All this should suggest the degree to which the Jewish community in a city like Frankfurt was in fact integrated into the larger political system of the city, and indeed of the empire as a whole. The Jews were skilled participants in the political arena. Acting for their community as a whole, they knew how to use political institutions to protect the rights and privileges they held as a group. Acting at other times to promote individual or factional interests within their own community, Jews were no less able to manipulate political institutions in their pursuit of personal or group advantage.

Of course, the lives of Jews in Frankfurt and Worms – as indeed in all German cities where they were found – were sharply circumscribed by the terms of the *Judenordnungen* that regulated countless aspects of their existence. Such ordinances were, after all, the characteristic instrument by which the authorities of early modern Germany regulated Jewish affairs in every territory where Jews lived.[29] But Jews were not the only group that experienced this form of control. Since the later Middle Ages, after all, not only each occupational group but also numerous other recognized groups within every urban community came to be regulated by *Ordnungen* of one sort or another. Indeed, the volume, scope and detail of such ordinances grew steadily after the mid-sixteenth century. To the countless *Zunftordnungen* (guild regulations) of earlier times were added *Polizeiordnungen* (po-

27 Christopher R. Friedrichs, "Urban Conflicts and the Imperial Constitution in Seventeenth-Century Germany," *Journal of Modern History* 58, suppl. (1986): 98–123.

28 Zimmer, *Jewish Synods*, 79–80.

29 Battenberg, "Zur Rechtsstellung der Juden," 140–3, 163–70.

lice regulations) of every description, all of them designed to regulate the economic and social conduct of an entire community or, more often, of specific segments of the community's population. We must not forget that alongside the *Judenordnung* of a city like Frankfurt or Worms we are likely to find a *Bettelordnung* (begging regulation), *Spitalordnung* (hospital regulation), *Hochzeitsordnung* (marriage regulation), and countless other manifestations of the "well-ordered police state" of early modern Germany.[30]

None of this, of course, can obscure the huge religious and cultural differences that separated the Jews of Frankfurt am Main, Worms, Hamburg, and other cities from their Christian inhabitants. Nor, of course, can it minimize the significance of anti-Jewish sentiment that accounted for so much Jewish suffering in early modern Germany. Indeed, the *Judenordnungen* themselves have long been regarded as a prime source of evidence for the anti-Jewish prejudices of the host populations. Heinrich Graetz described the Frankfurt *Stättigkeit* of the early seventeenth century, with its stringent clauses designed to reduce the amount of physical contact between Jews and Christians, as being among the "most repugnant and absurd" pieces of legislation ever passed.[31] Certainly many of its well-known clauses – forbidding Jews, for example, to appear in the streets of Frankfurt on a Sunday or to touch farm produce that Christians might want to buy – suggest an obsessive concern with avoidance of physical contact. But the fear of pollution from contact with members of another religious group was not confined to Christian–Jewish relations in early modern Europe. We are familiar enough with comparable obsessions that emerged in relations between Protestants and Catholics, notably in France during the wars of religion.[32] But in discussing German cities of the seventeenth century, the prohibition on physical contact between Jews and Christians must be seen as part of a much broader system of stringent taboos that were by no means only religious in character. There were, for example, severe restrictions on physical and social contact between ordinary inhabitants and members of the dishonorable trades. Executioners, gravediggers, carrion flayers, and their families were subjected to avoidance taboos that had much in common with those imposed on the Jews of Frankfurt and other communities.[33]

30 See Marc Raeff, *The Well-ordered Police State: Social and Institutional Change through Law in the Germanies and Russia, 1600–1800* (New Haven, Conn., 1983), 43–179.
31 Heinrich Graetz, *Geschichte der Juden von den ältesten Zeiten bis auf die Gegenwart,* 11 vols. (Leipzig, 1853–76, frequently republished), vol. 10 (2nd ed., 1882), 30.
32 Natalie Z. Davis, "The Rites of Violence: Religious Riot in Sixteenth-Century France," *Past and Present* 59 (1973): 51–91, esp. 57–60.
33 Rudolf Wissell, *Des alten Handwerks Recht und Gewohnheit,* 2nd ed., 6 vols. (Berlin, 1971–88), 1:146–52, 186–215.

Of course, there is no question that Jews experienced a socially segregated existence in those few imperial cities in which they were even permitted to live in early modern Germany. But social separation was not the same as exclusion from the political arena – particularly where numerous groups of noncitizens coexisted in the same community. Indeed, it is striking that the three imperial cities with the largest Jewish communities in seventeenth-century Germany were also multiconfessional, from the Christian point of view. Jews were not present in significant numbers in uniconfessional imperial cities, nor in those southern German cities where parity between Catholics and Lutherans came to be rigidly regulated by the Peace of Westphalia. But Frankfurt, Hamburg, and Worms had a different character. All three cities were ruled by Lutheran oligarchies that had found it impossible to impose religious uniformity. Frankfurt had a small but economically and politically aggressive Calvinist population, and a smaller but well-entrenched Catholic presence. Hamburg had both Calvinist and Catholic minorities. In Worms a Catholic minority was strongly protected by the bishop of Worms; at times the city had Calvinist inhabitants as well.[34] In this multiconfessional environment, a Jewish population may well have been less conspicuously variant than it would have been in an overwhelmingly uniconfessional community like Cologne or Nuremberg. Salo Baron once argued that, in general, "if a state embraced a number of ethnic groups, the 'alien' character of the Jews was much less pronounced."[35] The same, of course, could apply to a city-state that embraced a variety of religious groups. In fact, in Frankfurt, Hamburg, and Worms influential members of the Lutheran majority perceived the Jews as being only one of numerous objectionable minority groups. What happened in Hamburg in the late 1640s is suggestive. The *Oberalten* – one of the city's governing bodies – was struggling to expel the Jews, or at least to restrict their right to worship in the city. But some political leaders countered that the Jews were in fact much less bothersome in religious matters than the Calvinists, who, unlike the Jews, were always seeking converts.[36]

Certainly the conditions under which Jews lived in the imperial cities were largely determined by the attitude of the host communities. But even

34 For Worms, see Fritz Reuter, "Mehrkonfessionalität in der Freien Stadt Worms im 16.–18. Jahrhundert," in Bernhard Kirchgässner and Fritz Reuter, eds., *Städtische Randgruppen und Minderheiten* (Sigmaringen, 1986), 9–48.

35 Salo W. Baron, "Changing Patterns of Anti-Semitism: A Survey," *Jewish Social Studies* 38 (1976): 5–38, esp. 15. I am grateful to Gershon D. Hundert for alerting me to this reference.

36 "Wegen der Juden sei keine Seduction zu befürchten, aber der Calvinismus reisst ein": Grunwald, *Hamburgs deutsche Juden*, 8–9, attributes this sentiment to Hamburg's Senate; Whaley, *Religious Toleration*, 76, citing the same document, attributes it to the *Oberalten* themselves.

so, if the Jews of Frankfurt, Worms, and Hamburg had remained entirely passive in the face of efforts to banish them or drastically restrict their activities in the seventeenth century, it is unlikely that they would still have been found in those cities a hundred years later. It was their capacity to function effectively as political actors in these three cities that accounted, at least in part, for the survival of any Jewish presence in the imperial cities of early modern Germany.

18

Germans with a Difference? The Jews of the Holy Roman Empire during the Early Modern Era – A Comment

THOMAS A. BRADY, JR.

Perspective is everything in history, and I want to open my comment on the three essays in Part V with an observation about their common perspective. The authors' common framework and point of departure is the institutional, legal, political, economic, and social history of the Holy Roman Empire from the sixteenth through the eighteenth century. Their common narrative is the gradual integration of the Jews into the structures of the Holy Roman Empire during the last three centuries before emancipation. The common conclusion is that the empire's Jews were a "minority" in the modern sense and that their integration into a gradually secularizing society was a good thing. I first comment on each essay in detail, before looking at the common questions they raise and the research agendas they suggest.

I

Christopher Friedrichs's story (Chapter 17) is the most coherent, partly because his theme is limited to three leading free cities – Frankfurt am Main, Worms, and Hamburg – whose Jewish communities benefited from their multiconfessional atmospheres. He argues convincingly that the Jews both participated, as other townsfolk did, in civic and supralocal politics through petitions and legal suits, and conducted their own internal political life, the procedures of which are "strikingly reminiscent of the procedures followed by German city councils of the same era." His argument rests heavily on his procedural view of politics as "primarily a process of conflict resolution." In his eyes, the Jews of these cities were German townsfolk with a difference. Friedrichs regards the barriers between Jewish and Christian politics as much more permeable than, for example, Jonathan Israel does, and his account is on the whole a positive story of skillful political management by Jews in a hostile but not alien world.[1]

Rotraud Ries's essay on the lay principalities (Chapter 15) supplies some interesting elements of the chronology and motivation of the treatment of Jews by princely governments. The first three-quarters of the sixteenth century seem to have continued the late medieval pattern of expulsions – by 1570, only Hesse, among the larger territories, still tolerated Jews – but the isolated expulsions thereafter, for example, in Vienna in 1669–70, were ineffective. About this time began the reception of Jewish migration in the northeastern territories, which had previously excluded Jews. Generally, princely governments signaled a more positive attitude toward them. In lay territories, unlike the cities, the Jews could not count on interventions on their behalf by the emperor or the imperial courts. The first step in the more positive treatment of Jews seems to have come because the court Jews made themselves "indispensable" during the Thirty Years' War. The subsequent amelioration is laid chiefly to fiscal and commercial considerations, grouped as "mercantilist" policy, as well as to a waning interest in the religious component of early modern "social discipline."

There is some discrepancy between this picture and Friedrich Battenberg's account (Chapter 16) of the ecclesiastical territories. He concludes that there was much truth in the saying "Life is good under the crosier," precisely because the prince-bishops were constrained by cathedral chapters, electoral capitulations, territorial estates, and close ties to the emperor. Jews were thus protected from aggressive absolutism. However seriously the bishops took their duties in the area in which discrimination against the Jews was rooted, namely, religion, they could not escalate fiscal exploitation of Jewish dependence, as the lay princes could.

II

Taken together, these essays raise some important issues for political and social historians of the Holy Roman Empire. One issue is the effect of the Reformation and confessionalization on the existential condition of the Jews. Both Rotraud Ries and Friedrich Battenberg suggest that the atmosphere of religious conflict boded ill for the Jews, the former by reference to the Lutheran clergy, the latter to the Catholic bishops' missionary duty. Yet they also indicate that the coming of multiconfessionalism created, by analogy, more room for the Jews. Indeed, the onset around the 1570s and 1580s

---

1 It seems inadvisable to follow Friedrichs in calling the cities the Jews' "host communities," for "host" suggests as its counterpart either "guest" or "parasite."

of confessionalization – a process that may be seen less as an intensification of religious sensibility than as more effective management of an already intensified sensibility – seems to have coincided with the early slackening of expulsions, which had been typical of the preceding era. The full consequences of this tendency, as with almost all other aspects of confessionalization, emerged only after 1650.

A second issue concerns the role of the court Jews, who, along with the Jewish notables of Friedrichs's imperial free cities, appear as potential political representatives and even brokers between Jewish communities and their rulers. If this is correct, their informal role was transitional to the institutionalized forms of governance of Jews in the eighteenth century such as Paderborn's Judenkommission (Jewish Commission) and Würzburg's Judenamt (Jewish Office).

A third point concerns the effects of absolutism on the living conditions of Jews. Did absolutist regimes favor the Jews by giving them greater protection, for fiscal reasons, as Ries contends? Or did the Jews fare better under the old-fashioned, dualistic regimes of the prelates, as Battenberg argues? Indeed, is such a contrast valid at all? Did the Jewish communities gain greater internal cohesion and a stronger identity from their exclusion from Christian political society, as Israel has argued, or did either fiscally minded absolutist tolerance or routinized political involvement, as Friedrichs suggests, better prepare the Jews for emancipation?

These questions all point up the vastness of our ignorance about the Jewish communities, their ways of life, and their internal organization. This is true, most of all, for the Jews of the late medieval Diaspora, when much of Ashkenazic Jewry was pushed out of the major cities and into the small towns and villages, but it is true for most of the early modern era as well. This is why these essays throw much light on governmental regulation of Jews but little, with the possible exception of Friedrichs's piece, on the Jews themselves. It is not surprising to learn from Friedrichs that in the larger urban communities Jews made use of the courts and petitions to guard their liberties; rather more revealing is the argument that the internal organization of Frankfurt Jewry resembled the corporate organization of Frankfurt itself. But what was happening to the small Jewish communities in fragmented landscapes such as Franconia and Alsace?

These essays contribute important information and some clarity toward a satisfactory social history of the Jews as a religious minority in the Holy Roman Empire. There is still much to do. First, such a history must center on the middling and dwarf states, the small towns, and the rural areas of the southern and western parts of the empire, on the milieu in which the over-

whelming majority of Jews lived. Second, it must treat the regulation, treatment, and mistreatment of Jews by Christians and the ways of Jews living
among Jews. Third, it must cover both the Christians' attitudes toward Jews
and those of Jews toward Christians. As these essays show, it is clearly not
the case that the Jews were always the passive objects of Christian action nor
that the emotional relationships were always of a single kind. Fourth, such
a history must treat the passage of Jews into Christian society and determine
whether there was movement in the other direction as well. Finally, it must
approach the subject of the Reformation and the Jews from a starting point
that recognizes that the major areas of Jewish settlement did not much over-
lap with the heartland of the Lutheran Reformation.

III

A history written with these desiderata in mind may come closer than we
are at present to a satisfactory picture of the Jews and the Holy Roman Empire in the early modern era. It will of course not satisfy the quite different
vision of Jewish history in the empire before emancipation as "a multicol-
ored and sordid reality" that presents "an enormous multitude of local variations of a basically uniform and universal theme."[2] That is as it must be,
for in the social history of the Holy Roman Empire during the early modern era the Jews form a series of minority segments in many regions and localities; in Jewish history they form the first stage of the long lull between
the fourteenth-century persecutions and those of the twentieth. Seen one
way, in which Jews are Germans with a difference, the strands fuse into the
story of emancipation and assimilation; seen from another, improvement,
emancipation, and assimilation form but a treacherous introduction to the
great storm. To put it another way, the history of the empire's Jews forms
a plausible prehistory for the story of Jewish emancipation in the nineteenth
century, but it does not and cannot prepare for the story of Jewish catastrophe in the twentieth. Each of these stories – the Jews as Germans with a
difference; the Ashkenazim as a doomed branch of the Jewish nation – has
its own claim on us. I must confess, however, that I see no possibility for
satisfying both claims in a single, unified history.

---

2 Salo W. Baron, "Emphases in Jewish History," in Baron, *History and Jewish Historians: Essay and Addresses,* ed. Arthur Hertzberg and Leon A. Feldman (Philadelphia, 1964), 68.

PART VI

Through the Looking Glass: Four Perspectives on German-Jewish History

19

Germany and Its Jews: A Changing Relationship (1300–1800)

JONATHAN I. ISRAEL

The study of German Jewry in the late medieval and early modern eras is of central importance for our grasp of European Jewish history more generally. Germany was the only country in western and central Europe, apart from the northern half of Italy, where Jewish existence and Jewish culture were continuous from the High Middle Ages to the Enlightenment. Whereas from the eighteenth century onward Italian Jewry became more or less a secondary component of European Jewry, German Jewry was crucially and centrally significant throughout this period.

The essays collected in this volume reveal that much disagreement still exists about the nature of the transition that German Jewry underwent in the fifteenth, sixteenth, and seventeenth centuries. Several of the essays concentrate on the religious and theological drama, emphasizing the unique character and intensity of the confrontation between Christianity and Judaism in Germany when compared with other major European countries. This intensity and complexity of the Christian–Jewish encounter in the German lands was partly owing to the continuity of the Jewish presence throughout the long period under consideration. But it was also a consequence of the crisis that beset Christianity in Germany itself, that is, a consequence of the tensions and fragmentation of the Reformation.

In his introductory essay to this volume, Jacob Katz has eloquently drawn attention to the acuteness of the encounter between Jews and Christians throughout the pre-Reformation, Reformation, and post-Reformation eras. Elsewhere, Amos Funkenstein has put forward the arresting, important, but in my view fundamentally mistaken argument that the broad restructuring of the Christian–Jewish confrontation in Germany resulting from Luther's Reformation led directly to an easing of tensions and gradually to a less antagonistic relationship.[1] Clearly, the Reformation did entail a basic re-

---

1 See Amos Funkenstein, *Perceptions of Jewish History* (Los Angeles, 1993).

structuring of the Christian–Jewish relationship. But I would argue that the basic shift in the form and terminology of Christian anti-Jewish polemics and discourse in the early and mid-sixteenth century occurred without reducing the tension or the negative repercussions of the theological encounter on German-Jewish life. Anti-Jewish preaching and religious writing in six-teenth-century Germany arguably was changed by a Lutheran Reformation that stripped the anti-Jewish fervor of the past of much of its magical and sacramental content and set out to "disenchant" – as R. Po-chia Hsia ex-pressed in his recent book as well as in his essay here – the Jew, Jewish rit-ual, and the Hebrew texts, without lessening the momentum of the drive to restrict, squeeze, and reduce the Jewish role in German life.[2]

The essays in this volume can be thought of as falling into three main groups. The first group emphasizes the diversity and complexity of the de-mographic and economic development of German Jewry between the late Middle Ages and the eighteenth century. Discussion of these issues is linked to the discussion of the theological confrontation between Jews and Chris-tians by revealing a basic shift in the general structure and distribution of German-Jewish life. This structural shift took place precisely at the time when the great religious crisis, brought on by the onset of Christian Hu-manism and the Protestant Reformation, was under way. Several essays, in-cluding Alfred Haverkamps's discussion of the relocation of Jewish quarters in late medieval German cities (Chapter 1), confirm our picture of the gen-eral deterioration of the Jewish position in Germany and the progressive narrowing of the economic role of the German Jews during the fifteenth century.[3] Illustrating this point, Haverkamp demonstrates that a marginal-ization of German-Jewish urban life preceded the great expulsions from the major cities in the late 1400s.

Another group of contributions, including Friedrich Battenberg's analy-sis of the comparatively favorable situation of the Jews in the ecclesiastical principalities in the sixteenth century (Chapter 16), focuses on the political and social elements of continuity that bridged the late medieval and early modern periods.

A third set of essays, including Otto Ulbricht's on Jewish criminality (Chapter 3), demonstrates the radically changed demographic, economic, and more general social situation of German Jewry by the eighteenth century.

---

2 R. Po-chia Hsia, *The Myth of Ritual Murder: Jews and Magic in Reformation Germany* (New Haven, Conn., 1988), 131–37, 151, and Chapter 12 of this volume.

3 For recent data and observations on this process, see Michael Toch, "Der jüdische Geldhandel in der Wirtschaft des deutschen Spätmittelalters: Nürnberg, 1350–1499," *Blätter für deutsche Landesgeschichte* 117 (1981): 283–309.

A central issue in the socioeconomic debate that is directly connected to the discussion about Luther, the impact of the Protestant Reformation, and the subsequent easing of Christian–Jewish relations is the sharp and enduring geographic split. The volatile situation in the north contrasts the quite different and relatively static pattern of Jewish life in much of central and southern Germany. It is undoubtedly the case, as Michael Toch forcefully argues in his essay (Chapter 5), that the great expulsions of the late fifteenth century left the Jewish population of the central and southern regions of Germany both widely and thinly dispersed in a great number of minuscule communities, which became – and after the Reformation remained – tightly restricted in all respects: religious, economic, and demographic. Many of the tiny rural congregations scattered across Hesse, the Palatinate, Franconia, and even more sporadically farther south exhibited a high degree of continuity for the next two or three centuries. Although they slowly grew larger (in some cases only slightly so), these settlements otherwise played much the same socioeconomic role in local rural life. But should we agree with Toch's conclusion that this "deeply entrenched pattern," dominant in these localities from the late Middle Ages onward, was the prevailing model of German-Jewish development and, at the same time, also "little connected" with what was happening in the major cities as well as with the pattern of rapid, even dramatic change characteristic of Jewish life in Hamburg, Berlin, and the small communities of Brandenburg, the Lower Rhine, East Friesland, Westphalia, Hanover, and Silesia? I think that the answer has to be no on both counts.

If it is true that developments in the two geographic zones sharply diverged and were "little connected," then it follows that regional factors, legal contexts, and tradition counted far more than general factors of change such as the Reformation, the post-Reformation relaxation of Christian–Jewish tensions, and the rise of mercantilism, at least in the parts of Germany where the majority of German Jewry lived. But it is surely the case that the negative impact of Luther's anti-Judaism, and that of the German Reformation generally, on Jewish life manifested itself in all parts of Germany, wherever sizable Jewish communities were found. In Luther, Bucer, and other leading Reformers, as indeed in Erasmus, who shared much of their hostility toward the Jews, there was a restructuring of the Christian–Jewish encounter, stripping it of its previous magical and sacramental character but not lessening its theological intensity. In Luther – as in Erasmus – the notion that Christianity and Judaism were fundamentally and necessarily at odds, irreconcilable, and essentially antagonistic was central to the whole structure of his thought. It may be that in the early years after his break with Rome Luther adopted a more tolerant, conciliatory stance toward the Jews. But the fact that Luther's more strident anti-Semitism was a product of his later, especially post-1530 development, does not mean that the intensity of Luther's later anti-Judaism was "incidental," as Funkenstein calls it, rather than inherent in the Lutheran Reformation.

On the contrary, the whole of Luther's development after his break with Rome divides into an early, tolerant phase, in which his theology and social thought were in a state of flux, and a later, longer phase in which his theology and outlook became not only more structured and confessionally oriented but also dogmatic and authoritarian. The onset of this second phase tended to reduce Luther's influence markedly in regions adjoining Germany, such as the Low Countries, where the early Luther had exerted a powerful appeal; the subsequent hardening of his thought shifted attention to other reformist influences. But as far as Germany was concerned, it was precisely this later Luther, taking shape from the late 1520s onward, that determined the lasting contours and most of the political, social, and cultural characteristics of the Reformation in that region.

The general impact of the Protestant Reformation on Jewish life in Germany was essentially threefold. First, a powerful new impetus, theological as well as economic, emanating from Bucer as well as from Luther, emerged to drive the Jews out.[4] In 1538, Bucer and his colleagues urged Landgrave Philipp of Hesse to expel the Jews from his territories. Secular authorities resisted these pressures, primarily for financial reasons. But at Luther's instigation, and that of the Lutheran clergy, the Jews were driven out of Electoral Saxony, Braunschweig, Hanover, and then later from Brandenburg and Silesia.[5] Second, the restructuring of the terms of the theological encounter of Christianity and Judaism, previously mentioned, led to a process of demystification of the Jews, Jewish ritual, and the Hebrew language. Third, where Jewish life continued within a predominantly Protestant context, as in Hesse and the Palatinate, authorities tightened restrictions and further isolated the Jews, with the aim of preventing, as much as possible, their contact with Christians.

As a consequence of these trends, the area of Germany where Jewish communities were located was substantially reduced, during the middle decades of the sixteenth century. Jewish life was also subjected to a new wave of oppressive restrictions. The sea change that led to the relaxation of the Christian–Jewish confrontation, partial disengagement, and the primacy

---

4 J. Friedrich Battenberg, "Des Kaisers Kammerknecht. Gedanken zur rechtlich-sozialen Situation der Juden in Spätmittelalter und früher Neuzeit," *Historische Zeitschrift* 245 (1987): 579.

5 Jonathan I. Israel, *European Jewry in the Age of Mercantilism, 1550–1750* (Oxford, 1985), 12–13.

of economic motives in determining policies of the German principalities toward the Jewish population came about only in the last third of the sixteenth century, when the early impact of the Reformation had played itself out. What caused the easing of tensions was not the Reformation but the religious deadlock that could not be broken because of the political and military stalemate in the Low Countries, France, Switzerland, and within Germany itself. The great powers of the age had exhausted themselves without resolving the Catholic–Protestant confrontation. However impossible on theological grounds such a result seemed to contemporaries, the undeniable outcome of decades of strife was that neither side had been able to defeat the other completely. The German lands, like the Low Countries, Switzerland, and much of the rest of Europe, were hopelessly split along religious lines.

For contemporaries, the religious stalemate was deeply demoralizing. This circumstance was especially troubling in Germany, since – in contrast to most of the other countries affected by religious division – the religious division became increasingly threefold. In a sense it amounted to a triangular theological war: the Catholic revival of the late sixteenth century was matched by the spread of a well-organized Calvinist Reformed movement, especially in the Palatinate, Hesse, the Lower Rhine, and East Friesland. Reformed Calvinism scarcely proved less antagonistic to the Lutheran Reformation than reviving Catholicism did. As a result of this unbreakable impasse, all three of the major churches in Germany were permanently weakened, politically as well as intellectually. They were also weakened in terms of popular prestige, which prepared the ground for eventual secularization and the Enlightenment. Thus, the situation in which German Jewry found itself, from the last third of the sixteenth century onward, was profoundly different from the situation prevailing during the previous century. Not only was Jewish life more secure and relatively free from active persecution, but also, and perhaps especially, religion ceased to dictate the terms and form of Jewish settlement, economic activity, and, indeed, religious activity.[6]

A number of essays in this volume suggest en passant that the significance of the *Hofjuden* (court Jews) has traditionally been somewhat overestimated. In contrast, I would like to argue rather strongly the opposite. Far from being overstated, the full significance of the *Hofjuden* for the overall development of German Jewry has still not been sufficiently brought out.

6 Israel, *European Jewry*, 36–44. See also R. Po-chia Hsia, "Die Juden im Alten Reich. Forschungsaufgaben zur Geschichte der Juden im späten Mittelalter und in der frühen Neuzeit," in Georg Schmidt, ed., *Stände und Gesellschaft im Alten Reich* (Stuttgart, 1989), 217–19.

During the seventeenth and early eighteenth centuries, the entire profile of German life was transformed. The shaping force was neither the Reformation nor the rural context within which the mass of small German-Jewish communities of central-southern Germany lived. What transformed German-Jewish life was the restless, insistent desire of the German princes to raise their revenues, sustain larger standing armies, gain access to new forms of credit and sources of military supply, and expand their domestic economies. The court Jews provided much that was useful to the German princes and their generals: cash, credit, military supplies, horses, and contacts with Europe's chief commercial centers, such as Amsterdam and Hamburg. They were also a useful channel through which to obtain certain luxuries and exotic goods that had to be shipped from distant parts of the globe to the great entrepôts of Amsterdam and Hamburg. These items included spices, jewelry, oriental porcelain, and many other goods in demand at German princely courts after 1650. Consequently, a great many German courts – northern and southern, Lutheran, Calvinist, and Catholic – sooner or later sought the services of and were prepared to grant residence and privileges to certain Jews.

But the court Jews were not detachable from their relatives, associates, and assistants or their religious entourages. They could not have functioned as they did, and they could not have operated at all, had it not been for the rapidly expanding economic roles of the several strata of the Jewish population beneath them. In terms of their secular functions, they could be compared to the apex of a pyramid, the base of which was formed by the mass of poor peddlers, hawkers, and small-time money changers and dealers. Indispensable to their operations were the moderately affluent Jewish merchants, factors, and money changers to be found in major commercial and financial centers such as Frankfurt am Main, Hamburg, Berlin, Breslau, Emden, and Hanover. But also indispensable were the countless small dealers and itinerant buyers who roamed the countryside, particularly in the central and southern regions of the country. These were the men who at the local level bought grain, horses, and other supplies needed by the military garrisons and standing armies located all around.

The slow growth in the number and size of the scattered rural Jewish communities in the central-southern zone, moreover, cannot be separated from the more rapid growth of the urban Jewish communities. Neither can they be separated from communities located in small towns near large cities, such as Fürth or Hanau, that were active in long-distance trade and finance. Dynamic urban centers were located throughout Germany, not just in the north. Before 1570, none of them, not even Frankfurt am Main, had amounted to more than a small fraction of its subsequent size. The large, thriving communities of the central-southern zone drew their vitality in part from and interacted with the numerous tiny nearby rural Jewish congregations.

The great northern centers that arose in the seventeenth century – Hamburg, Berlin, and Emden – and many smaller towns were not the only places intimately involved in commerce with neighboring countries. One of the most characteristic features of the large Jewish communities of the central-southern zone from the late sixteenth century was that they too were in close contact with communities to the west (in Alsace-Lorraine), to the northwest (in the Netherlands), or, in the case of Fürth, to the east (with Bohemia). A large part of the usefulness of the southern as well as of the northern court Jews was precisely their close involvement and interaction with Jewish communities in neighboring and more distant lands.

Stefi Jersch-Wenzel has shown how the mercantilist attitude of the Brandenburg electors, especially the Great Elector (1640–88), led not only to the reintroduction of Jewish life to major states from which the Jews had been expelled during the Reformation era but also to the rise of economically highly dynamic communities.[7] This development took place not only in Berlin but also in the smaller towns of Brandenburg. Beyond Brandenburg-Prussia, Jews were also readmitted at the end of the sixteenth century to several places in northern Germany from which the Jews had been expelled following the Reformation. The urban centers that reopened their doors to the Jews included maritime cities such as Hamburg and Emden and several princely towns such as Hanover and Wolfenbüttel, from which, as Rotraud Ries shows, the Jews had been expelled (1557) in the wake of the Reformation. But the phenomenon of princes establishing commercially active Jewish communities to encourage trade, centered on groups of privileged rich Jews, either in their capital towns or in towns selected to play a special role in interregional or long-distance trade, was no less prevalent in the zone of long-established, small and scattered rural Jewish communities in central and southern Germany.[8]

The rapid buildup of Jewish population in the new centers of southern Germany was made possible precisely by the proximity of numerous tiny and heavily restricted rural communities where the younger men, in par-

---

7 Stefi Jersch-Wenzel, *Juden und "Franzosen" in der Wirtschaft des Raumes Berlin-Brandenburg zur Zeit des Merkantilismus* (Berlin, 1978).
8 Selma Stern, *Jud Süss. Ein Beitrag zur deutschen und zur jüdischen Geschichte* (Munich, 1973), 6.

ticular, found few opportunities. Two prominent examples of the great impact of mercantilism in southern Germany in the seventeenth and early eighteenth centuries illustrate this emerging pattern. The Jewish community in the new city of Mannheim enjoyed especially favorable privileges accorded to it by the elector of the Palatinate and subsequently grew from fifteen families, in 1663, to seventy-eight by 1680. When Margrave Karl Wilhelm of Baden-Durlach established his capital in Karlsruhe in 1715, he accorded at the same time favorable terms to the Jews, setting in train a rapid increase in the Jewish population in the new courtly city. The immigrants arrived from numerous small places in the Palatinate, from the bishopric of Speyer, as well as from Baden-Baden.[9]

The transformation, then, was a pan-German phenomenon and showed many common features in the various parts of Germany. The network of tiny rural communities continued to subsist, decade after decade, and century after century, on largely the same heavily restricted basis as at the end of the Middle Ages.[10] But even here the general changes taking place throughout the Holy Roman Empire and adjoining parts of Europe manifested themselves, during and after the Thirty Years' War, in the loosening of some of the restrictions and conferring of more religious freedom. In part, these reforms were undoubtedly intended to counteract the increasing pull of big cities and distant opportunities on the small Jewish congregations of these regions. In Hesse-Darmstadt, for instance, Landgrave Ernst Ludwig (1688–1739) extended the religious rights of his Jewish subjects with the *Toleranzpatent* of 1695. Moreover, he also took steps to attract Jewish entrepreneurs through, for example, the award of the state tobacco monopoly to the *Hoffaktor* (court Jew) Löw Isaak in 1718.[11]

The established rural framework of small communities in southern-central Germany became demographically and economically somewhat more flexible without losing much of its traditional character. In the new mercantilist context, especially in the commercial cities of Berlin and Hamburg, the scope for Jewish economic activity and communal growth was greater. But here too the privileges and opportunities offered by the princes and city governments were aimed primarily at the rich and moderately affluent; they kept in place much of the restrictive legislation designed to suppress the greater number of poor Jews. The new Jewish silk and tobacco

---

9 B. Rosenthal, "Aus den Jugendjahren der jüdischen Gemeinde Karlsruhe," *Monatsschrift für Geschichte und Wissenschaft des Judentums* 71 (1927): 207–8.

10 In addition to Michael Toch's essay in this volume (Chapter 5), see his "Siedlungsstruktur der Juden Mitteleuropas im Wandel vom Mittelalter zur Neuzeit," *Zeitschrift für historische Forschung* (forthcoming).

11 J. Friedrich Battenberg, *Judenverordnungen in Hessen-Darmstadt* (Wiesbaden, 1987), 12.

manufacturers of Berlin, Hanover, and Mannheim, for example, were obliged to employ primarily Christian rather than Jewish laborers; the exclusion of Jews from the craft guilds also continued largely unchanged.

The inevitable result was that during the eighteenth century German Jewry faced a steadily worsening economic and social crisis. In the conditions prevailing in ancien régime Germany, there was only one solution: emigration. The high levels of German-Jewish emigration in the eighteenth century, especially to the Dutch Republic, England, and America, were therefore symptomatic of the deteriorating situation. Another symptom was the rise of organized criminality, especially house-burglary rings and rings for disposing of stolen goods, which became prevalent not only in Germany but also in the United Provinces and among German Jews in England. Reflecting the situation in Germany itself, the available data indicate that among the German Jews who had gone to the Netherlands the number of indigent Jews receiving communal charity escalated after 1720.[12]

All considered, the far-reaching transformation of German Jewry that took place in the late Middle Ages and the early modern period consists of two clearly distinguishable long phases. This periodization applies equally well in all regions of Germany and neighboring countries. The first phase is marked by progressive decline, contraction, and marginalization, from the Black Death down to the 1570s. The second phase is characterized by revival, expansion, and a broadening of the scope of Jewish activity, from the 1570s onward. It cannot be said that southern-central Germany followed a path different from the north with respect to the fundamental trends, even though the structure and distribution of Jewish society in the Palatinate, Hesse, Franconia, and scattered areas farther to the south were profoundly different from those in most of northern Germany. The turning point, occurring in the last third of the sixteenth century, resulted not from Luther's theology and the Reformation but rather from the deadlock among the churches and the rise of mercantilism.

By the eighteenth century, German Jewry presented an entirely different profile from that of only a century and a half before. Nevertheless, the improvement in material circumstances and the extension of religious freedom went hand in hand with an alarming growth in the number of Jewish poor. It has been estimated that around 1750 about 60 percent of the approximately 70,000 Jews living in Germany – excluding Austria – lived a marginal existence of poverty, peddling, begging, and thieving.[13] In the main,

---

12 B. W. de Vries, *From Peddlars to Textile Barons: The Economic Development of a Jewish Minority Group in the Netherlands* (Amsterdam, 1989), 29–35.

13 David Sorkin, *The Transformation of German Jewry, 1780–1840* (Oxford, 1987), 43.

German Jewry still presented to the world a picture of economic and cultural destitution. The great process of *embourgeoisement,* which transformed German Jewry into one of the most affluent, predominantly middle-class, and cultured segments of the Jewish people (a result of the first two-thirds of the nineteenth century), was yet to come.

20

The Jewish Minority and the Christian
Majority in Early Modern Central Europe

HARTMUT LEHMANN

In statistical terms, Jews were but a small minority within the predominately Christian society of early modern Germany. Of course, from the fourteenth to the eighteenth century the figures changed; of course, there were villages and towns with a somewhat larger proportion of Jewish citizens; and of course, early modern German society was not uniform but divided up in numerous ways – legally, culturally, economically, and politically. In relation to the *ständische Gesellschaft* (society of estates) of early modern Germany, the Jews have to be seen not as a *innerständische* (intra-estate) group but as a *nebenständische* (group existing alongside the estates) minority with a special legal status and with its own cultural and social hierarchy. The essays in this volume analyze some aspects of the life of this minority and some aspects of Christian–Jewish relations. In my brief comment, I want to focus on the changes that took place in the history of the Christian majority from the fifteenth through the eighteenth century, with particular reference to the effect that these changes may have had on the relationship between the Christian majority and the Jewish minority.[1]

In somewhat simplified terms, one can say that by the High Middle Ages the Christianization of central Europe was complete. Notwithstanding the rivalry for leadership between emperors and popes, both secular and ecclesiastical rulers were determined to promote the hegemony of Christianity. Whatever non-Christian or pre-Christian beliefs still existed were suppressed and lived on, at best, only on the local level if at all.

In the late Middle Ages, however, this Christian society underwent a deep, severe crisis. The Black Death had decimated the population; also as the power and the glory of the emperors faded, regionalism triumphed, and

---

1 Essentially, I am arguing that we have to analyze the problems and development of the Christian majority if we want to come to a better understanding of the various stages in the history of the Jewish minority. This is not just a matter of overall terminology and/or of periodization; rather, I think, only in this way can we address crucial questions concerning the social and cultural setting as well as the political and economic conditions that shaped the life of the Jews in early modern central Europe.

local authorities took charge of public as well as spiritual affairs. In the form of a dramatically higher mortality rate, the crisis could be felt in almost every town and village. In attempting to explain the causes of the crisis, the local authorities, both secular and ecclesiastical, pointed to the Jewish minority as the scapegoat. This strategy was equally convenient because the Jews were almost defenseless and slandering them was highly popular. The results are well known. In the course of the late fourteenth and fifteenth centuries, many of the cities and territories of the empire persecuted and expelled the members of the Jewish communities.

In the early sixteenth century, the urge to redress some of the grievances against papal financial exploitation of central Europe, coupled with religious fervor and the new learning provided by humanism, led to a split within Christianity. The schism started in Saxony but rapidly spread to other territories and to many imperial cities by the 1520s and 1530s. Since the 1530s, the wish to reform the church, broadly defined, also grew stronger within the ranks of those who remained loyal to the pope. Both the rivalry for leadership of a renewed Christianity and the concentration on reform measures and means resulted in what may perhaps be called a relative disregard, or neglect, of the Jewish minority.

As we know, Protestants made a few attempts to convince prominent Jews of the validity of their cause. At the same time, on a much broader scale, Christian anti-Semitism persisted. Nevertheless, we should not be blinded by the anti-Semitic tracts of Luther and others. Sixteenth-century Christian infighting relieved some of the pressure that had fallen on the Jewish minority. The new minority that had to suffer most was the so-called left wing of the Reformation, the Anabaptists. On some of the estates and in some of the cities of eastern-central Europe, the persecuted, nonconformist Christian minority found places of refuge. It was in this region, and in the countryside, that some sixteenth-century Jewish communities that had survived the late medieval pogroms were able to consolidate.

How Christian–Jewish relations changed in the period between the Reformation and the Enlightenment is difficult to understand.[2] There are three developments within central European Christendom that should be distinguished. First, we should see that as a result of a series of bad harvests, living conditions in central Europe deteriorated rapidly after the 1580s. Again,

---

2 Hartmut Lehmann, *Das Zeitalter des Absolutismus,* pt. 3: *Not, Angst, Hoffnung. Die Krise des Glaubens im 17. Jahrhundert* (Stuttgart, 1980), 105–69; Hartmut Lehmann, "Hexenglaube und Hexenprozesse in Europa um 1600," in Christian Degn, Hartmut Lehmann, and Dagmar Unverhau, eds., *Hexenprozesse. Deutsche und skandinavische Beiträge* (Neumüster, 1983), 14–27; Hartmut Lehmann, "Frömmigkeitsgeschichtliche Auswirkungen der 'Kleinen Eiszeit,'" in Wolfgang Schieder, ed., *Volksreligiosität in der modernen Sozialgeschichte* (Göttingen, 1986), 31–50.

scapegoats were sought, found, and persecuted. I am speaking, of course, of the culmination of witch trials in the decades before and after 1600. Witches were considered to be the agents of the devil, who had set out to ruin the crops in order to undermine God's rule. At the same time, within some Protestant circles the conviction grew rapidly that the end of the world was approaching, either in the form of the Last Judgment or in the form of a glorious reign of a thousand years of God's faithful children before the final verdict. Some of those espousing eschatological theology and explaining the Apocalypse believed that God's first people, the Jews, and God's last people, namely themselves, would go through this most dramatic period of transition together. Many of the theological arguments, and some of the attitudes that were derived from them, can still be found in late seventeenth- and early eighteenth-century Pietism among the followers of Spener, Francke, and Zinzendorf. In the seventeenth century and beyond, the wish of pious Protestants to prepare themselves for Christ's return may help to explain why scapegoating, renewed after 1580, was directed less against Jewish communities than against those believed to be conspiring with the devil, namely witches.

The second development that we should be aware of resulted from the triumph of Renaissance values and Renaissance life-style north of the Alps in the second half of the sixteenth century. In medicine and in alchemy, in the art of building fortresses and manufacturing arms, in philosophy and law, a new awareness of the rational capacity and the inner-worldly capability of men can be found. Stimulated by the example of Italy, this new consciousness was inspired by the reception of pre-Christian, Greek, and Roman theories, such as stoicism, and seemed to correspond perfectly well to the new splendor at the courts and the new assertiveness of most of the rulers. In relation to Christian tradition, the Renaissance has to be seen as a first effective push toward secularization.

After the outbreak of the Thirty Years' War, the economic and military necessities of the struggle for survival further undermined Christian values among the ruling class, much as the war caused many simple folk to look for consolation in prayer. Within the realm of Renaissance science and culture, hostility to Jewish contributions was declining; within the realm of Renaissance politics and the financing of the big war, Jewish contributions were sought for and welcomed. This is the historical place for the rise of the *Hofjudentum* (court Jews).

The third development we should take into account resulted from the fears caused by Renaissance culture and from the opposition to the progress of secularization. The mass production of edifying literature: the hundreds and thousands of hymns and funeral sermons, the piles of pious treatises and pamphlets – all of this has to be seen as a huge effort by the learned middle class to counter secularization and to re-Christianize central Europe. Johann Arndt, the most popular seventeenth-century German author, attempted to stem the tide of "atheism," as he called it. His efforts, as well as those of many others, including Johann Philipp Spener and the early Pietists, have to be called the first campaign of re-Christianization in central Europe.[3] With regard to Jews, the attitude of this new breed of Christians was quite clear: they invited Jews to join their effort; if they refused to be converted to Christianity, however, they were considered as part of the atheists' camp, which was doomed to God's wrath in due course.

Let me sketch what followed with a few brief remarks. The Enlightenment, including enlightened despotism, marked the second wave of secularization in central Europe. In the same measure as Jews attempted to win emancipation with the help of enlightened allies, they distanced themselves from the camp of staunch Christian traditionalists.

By contrast, the *Erweckungsbewegung,* the great central European awakening of the early nineteenth century, formed the second wave of re-Christianization, joined the battle against enlightenment, liberalism, and all those who supported the ideas of the French Revolution. With regard to Jews, the approach was *Judenmission* (mission to the Jews) as an integral part of domestic mission.

Finally, through nationalism and Darwinism, Christian anti-Semitism was transformed in the late nineteenth century into modern racist anti-Semitism, gaining influence as part of another wave of secularization. There were also renewed efforts to save Christianity and re-Christianize what seemed to have been lost to atheism. By 1933, to be sure, in relation to the role of the Jewish minority in Germany, Christians in Germany were profoundly confused. With very few exceptions, they were not prepared to stand up against the Nazi policy of destruction.

In conclusion, I should like to add three remarks referring to special aspects in the life of the Jewish minority in the Holy Roman Empire from the fourteenth through the eighteenth century:

1. As Carlo Ginzburg (Chapter 14) has pointed out, the Christian population in early modern Europe associated Jews with heresy, with disbelief, and with the devil. Other groups fell under the same verdict – for example,

---

3 On the problem of "re-Christianization" in seventeenth-century central Europe, see Hartmut Lehmann, "Zur Erforschung der Religiosität im 17. Jahrhundert," in Monika Hagenmaier and Sabine Holtz, eds., *Krisenbewusstsein und Krisenbewältigung in der Frühen Neuzeit. Festschrift für Hans-Christoph Rublack* (Frankfurt/Main, 1992), 3–11.

the Anabaptists and those singled out, labeled, and persecuted as witches. The aggressive potential of the Christian majority could be directed against Jews, Anabaptists, and against those called witches in a similar manner, and the destruction of these various nonconforming groups served to strengthen the self-definition of the Christian majority as good Christians in a similar way. If I am not mistaken, however, discrimination and persecution were never exercised against all those who could be victims of Christian hegemony at the same time. Rather, we should distinguish very carefully between different forms and waves of xenophobia, of fighting heresy, and of opposing demonic power. On the one hand, Würzburg and Bamberg were centers of the persecution of witches in the decades before and after 1600, but as Friedrich Battenberg has pointed out (Chapter 16), Jews were nevertheless safer and better off in ecclesiastical principalities than under secular princes in the same epoch. On the other hand, although the Frankfurt ghetto was pillaged in the early seventeenth century, no witches were put to death in this city in the course of that century. Future research should look into this matter more closely. In order to understand the ordeal of Jews in early modern Germany, their destiny has to be compared to, and be seen in relation with, the destiny of other minorities and other groups considered outsiders by the Christian majority.

2. In the early modern period, in central Europe as elsewhere, contacts between members of the Christian majority and members of the Jewish minority varied according to social rank and status. This is true for vagrant Jews and Christians meeting "on the road" and in taverns; this is true for Jewish physicians looking after their middle-class Christian patients; and the same holds true for the *Hofjuden* who procured supplies for Christian courts. At the same time, contacts between Christian and Jewish deviants and outcasts, just like contacts between the members of the Jewish *nebenständische* groups and members of the Christian *Stände,* were characterized by specific, indistinguishable traits. Christian beggars very often took away from Jewish beggars the little these possessed, for example, some dice; Christian patients could delay paying or refuse to pay the bills of Jewish physicians, if they considered the treatment they had received unsatisfactory; *Hofjuden,* as is well known, depended completely on the goodwill of the princes who demanded their services. A considerable degree of arbitrariness on the Christian side, however, is only one aspect of Jewish–Christian relations. There is yet another side to observe.

In order to do business with Christians, Jews had to offer Christians especially advantageous conditions. Doing business outside of their own groups was, therefore, a high-risk affair, which in turn implied the possibility of failure. And if failure occurred, Christian arbitrariness was reinforced. Terms such as "exclusion" and "engagement," accordingly, seem to be too neutral if one wants to characterize Christian–Jewish relations. Rather, we should be aware of a vicious cycle of discrimination on the part of Christians, high-risk ventures on the part of the Jews, and discrimination renewed and reinforced if the Jewish partner failed to deliver what the Christian partner expected to receive. In early modern Germany, Christian anti-Semitism persisted, therefore, not exclusively on an ideological, a religious, or an intellectual level. Rather, Christian prejudices were deeply rooted in what Christians believed to be experiences of their daily life.

3. In exploring the background of Jewish emancipation, we should be cautious not to overestimate the influence of the Enlightenment when analyzing the causes for the improvement in the treatment of Jews in the eighteenth century. As I have pointed out, two seventeenth-century movements called for a revision of traditional Christian anti-Semitism. One of these relied on what can be called *Nützlichkeitserwägungen,* that is, arguments from utility, reflecting Renaissance values; the other employed what can be called *Endzeiterwägungen,* that is, latter-day arguments, stressing the urgent need for seeking salvation before the imminent Last Judgment. These *Endzeiterwägungen* were sometimes based on highly specialized theologies such as chiliasm and millenarianism, sometimes just on a new appreciation of the Apocalypse. Some members of the pious middle class were affected by these considerations, just as were members of some of the German courts. Each in its own way, these attitudes formed traditions that supported Enlightenment concepts regarding an improvement in the treatment of Jews.

21

The Jews of the Netherlands in the Early Modern Period

RICHARD H. POPKIN

The other essays in this volume describe the tragic history of the Jews in German lands from the Middle Ages to the Enlightenment. In this chapter, I focus on a quite different world that existed in the Netherlands, just across Germany's western border. (A somewhat similar story could be told about the condition of Jews living across the eastern border of Germany, in Lithuania and Poland, in the first half of the seventeenth century.) In the Middle Ages, Jews lived in various Dutch cities without the accompanying purges that occurred in German towns. After the success of the Dutch in the rebellion against Spain and the emergence of a new polity, in the Dutch Republic, however, a different kind of Jewish life emerged, different from what existed anywhere else in Europe.

What happened in the Netherlands suggests that there may not necessarily be any connection between the medieval persecutions of Jews in Germany, the repressions associated with the Reformation and the Counter-Reformation, the decimation of Jewish communities during the Thirty Years' War, and the Nazi era. What happened in the Netherlands was an alternative scenario, in which the Jewish community was accepted and flourished, until the German army under Hitler conquered the country. There had been no ghettos in the Netherlands until 1940. Although seventeenth-century Dutch Jews lived mainly near the synagogues, as a matter of law they could live where they pleased. Christians too lived in the heart of the Jewish community. Let us remember that Rembrandt lived and painted in his house at 1 Joodenbreestraat, a block from the Spanish and Portuguese synagogue and just behind the house where Spinoza was born. Moreover, Rembrandt's house belonged to Baron Francis Boreel, the Dutch ambassador to France.

Some of the richest homes in the country belonged to important Jewish merchants. Jewish intellectuals could and did argue about the merits and demerits of Christianity and defended their religious views without fear of im-

311

prisonment or death. Isaac Orobio de Castro circulated his polemic against Christianity to the Jesuits in Brussels (who liked it very much) and was under no pressure to convert. No one suggested, as Lavater did to Mendelssohn, that if Orobio was so bright and rational he had no choice but to be a Christian. And Rabbi Menasseh ben Israel, who taught Hebrew to so many Christian scholars and told them about Judaism, was subjected to conversionist activity only when he was in England, not in Holland. In fact, at the end of the seventeenth century the Protestant historian of Judaism, Jacques Basnage, ended his mammoth *Histoire des Juifs* with the suggestion that Christians should give up trying to convert Jews and leave the job to God. The Christians had botched the job in Spain and had created fake Christians; likewise, they had failed in the Netherlands, because the Jews were better versed in the texts and were better arguers.

Another factor in the Dutch situation was the fervent philo-Semitism issuing from the millenarian convictions of various Protestant groups. The Jews, it was believed, would play a most important role in ushering in the reign of Christ, and it was the Jewish messianic expectation, a political messiah, that was about to be fulfilled.

An indication that people realized at the time that there was a radical difference between the Dutch and German worlds with regard to Jews appears in an unpublished paper of John Dury. Trained in Leiden, Dury was a Scottish millenarian who had been a preacher in Germany, an important agent of the Cromwell government, and the official English emissary sent to Europe with the mission of reuniting all of the Protestant churches. In that last capacity, he spent a good deal of time in German territory, finally settling down in Kassel. He once received a query from Germany asking if one could be a faithful follower of the Law of Moses and a true and believing Christian. Dury's answer after much discussion, was yes, but that if one wanted to do it, the place to do it was Amsterdam, not Germany. Earlier Dury had been asked, while a guest of the Landgrave of Hesse, whether Jews should be readmitted to England and whether Jews could be members of a Christian commonwealth. A close friend of Menasseh ben Israel, Dury had dedicated the English edition of Menasseh's *Hope of Israel* to the English Parliament. In this dedication he asserted that Jews could indeed be admitted to a Christian commonwealth, but then he explained that controls were needed and described the strict way Jews in Kassel were pressed weekly to convert and were made to hear sermons on which they were later examined.

Two years later, in 1658, Dury headed up a Christian fund-raising campaign for the Jews of Jerusalem, after he had been informed of what

Rabbi Nathan Shapira had said to the millenarians of Amsterdam. In examining Dury's various positions, one can see the basic focus of his views on the role of the Jews in modern society in his conviction that the Jews had a most positive role to play in the final drama of world history that was about to take place. Two great events will precede the Second Coming: the conversion of the Jews and the reunion of all Christians.

The philo-Semitism of Dury and of his Dutch friends made them desire, first, the existence of free Jewish communities, then Jewish interaction with Protestant Christianity, followed finally by voluntary conversion. In 1640, Dury proposed establishing the first college of Jewish studies in the modern world, which would make Christianity less offensive to the Jews and Judaism better understood by Christians. His proposed school was to have had a staff of rabbis and ministers. Perhaps the result was supposed to be the fusion of Judaism and Christianity as proposed by the Quakers: to be Jews internally, rather than externally, and thereby become Jewish Christians or Christian Jews, playing an anticipatory role in the emergence of the climax of the Divine Drama.

An aspect of this comes out in the reaction of Dury and his friends to the appearance of Sabbatai Zevi, the Jewish messianic pretender from Smyrna. Dury received a letter from Peter Serrarius in Amsterdam telling him that the king of the Jews had arrived. Serrarius became a Christian follower of Sabbatai Zevi, defended him after his conversion to Islam, and died on the way to meet him. The great preacher Jean de Labadie told a thousand people that the king of the Jews had arrived and sought to show that God was telling the Christians to reform by giving the Jews their messiah. Dury himself tried to figure out where Sabbatai fitted into the millenarian scenario. Dury's son-in-law, Henry Oldenburg, secretary of England's Royal Society, became a follower, as did some of the Puritan preachers in distant New England. In England, Dury was called by some a Jewish Quaker; in Germany, in contrast, there was an enormous outpouring of literature denouncing him as a fraud and a fake, indicating not only how gullible the Jews were but also how bad they were.

Dutch and associated English and American millenarians viewed Jewish developments positively and saw them as integral parts of the millenarian drama unfolding before their very eyes. This outlook led to a fusion of Jewish and Christian religious as well as commercial interests and behavior. The commercial miracle of seventeenth-century Holland was seen by its Jewish and Christian participants as obviously part of God's action on their history. Hence there were no demands to exclude or restrict Jewish business interests but rather efforts to encourage them.

In this Dutch world next door to Germany, one began to find Jewish Christians and Christian Jews. Some of the same phenomena occurred in England, in the American colonies, and among the upper class in Transylvania. Some important Christian religious leaders adopted or accepted some Jewish practices. Extremist Protestants who were not tolerated in England moved to the Netherlands, and some, including Quakers, even lived in the Jewish community of Amsterdam. With this situation it was hard to maintain separateness between Jews and Christians. Some Jews, such as Rabbi Nathan Shapira, Baruch de Spinoza, and Moses Germanus, were Jews who accepted some aspects of Christianity. Moses Germanus, originally a German Catholic, later a follower of Jakob Spener, and finally a convert to Judaism who became a rabbi in Amsterdam, tried to see Christianity as the best expression of Jewish ethics and Jesus as a great rabbi. This sort of view, instead of being stomped upon as heresy, was adopted by radical thinkers of the early Enlightenment and became a part of the beginning of higher criticism of the Bible.

This picture, of course, exaggerates the philo-Semitism and the conjoining of Judaism and Christianity in the Netherlands. There was also some opposition. Leiden University, for example, had a chair of anti-Jewish argumentation. Demands were also made by various groups to control and restrict Jewish behavior. Moreover, Jews were not citizens, and could not become citizens, until the Napoleonic conquest of the Netherlands. Yet Jewish merchants were considered equal to their Dutch neighbors as stockholders in the India Company, and Jewish intellectuals were regarded almost as equal to their Dutch counterparts.

The Jewish community of Amsterdam emerged in the early seventeenth century. Hugo Grotius proposed recognizing its independence but restricting its activities. Instead, a more casual relationship developed. The community could function freely as long as it did not cause scandal, took care of its indigent members, and preserved a social order harmonious with the larger society. Its early members were mainly people who had been raised as Christians in Spain, Portugal, Belgium, France, and Italy. In the Netherlands they shook off their enforced Christianity and publicly became Jews. This would have been considered a most serious crime elsewhere in Christian Europe. Many had received advanced intellectual training in Christian universities. In their free situation they could defend their religious views and openly oppose those of others without fear of arrest. They could also print the Jewish classics. Amsterdam quickly became the western center of Hebrew publishing. The publication of the text of the *Mishna* with vocalization and its translation into Spanish and Latin became a great joint

Jewish–Christian project that went on for decades, with rabbis and Christian scholars working together first in Amsterdam and then later in England. Jews like Menasseh became the Hebrew teachers for the Christian world and a source of information and explanation of the mysteries of Judaism for Christian scholars. The Portuguese synagogue in Amsterdam became one of the great tourist sites, which even the queen of England visited when she was there.

In this world in which so much intellectual and cultural exchange was occurring, Jews also debated with Christians. One of the great debates took place in 1687 between Isaac Orobio de Castro and Philip van Limborch, a debate that John Locke attended. Orobio and others wrote, but did not publish, their defenses of Judaism and polemics against Christianity. Publishing would have constituted "scandal" and hence violated the tacit agreement with the Dutch authorities. In 1715, many manuscripts of these anti-Christian writings were sold for the first time in an auction in The Hague. They quickly became part of the debating material used by English deists and French philosophes. Judaism was placed intellectually on the same level as Christianity and could provide reasons for rejecting the latter.

In 1715, Jacques Basnage described some of the anti-Christian polemics in extremely neutral terms in his *Histoire des Juifs*. But he made no effort to refute them. Although he said that he expected the Second Coming in 1716, he made clear that he felt it was not his job to try to convert the Jews. Only God could do that. As far as I know, nobody suggested then that this anti-Christian material be burned, destroyed, or locked up. Some of it made its way to the American colonies, where it undermined the confidence of some Christians. It is an indication of how things changed that these manuscripts were not published then or in the succeeding years. A toned-down version of one of them was printed in England in the 1840s, with the title page stating that it was "printed," not published, and that it was only for the use of Jewish students. The first actual publication of a full text of one of the main manuscripts took place only a few years ago.

The free intellectual atmosphere of the Netherlands allowed the leader of the Amsterdam synagogue, the economist and banker Isaac de Pinto, to challenge Voltaire's anti-Semitic views in print. The acceptance of Jews as part of the social milieu in Holland prepared the stage for emancipation, though it was a difficult process in the Netherlands, as well as in relatively tolerant England and even Revolutionary France. Only in the newly established United States of America was there no established church or traditional anti-Semitic baggage, and, as a result, Jews were able to become citizens there as soon as the Constitution had been ratified.

When one looks at the situation of Moses Mendelssohn reluctantly trying to avoid presenting his reasons for remaining a Jew and not becoming
a Christian, and the controversy this case produced in Germany, and contrasts this with the contemporary situation of articulate Jews in the Netherlands, England, France, and America, one can see that relations between
Jews and Christians were developing differently in Germany. Regarding
England, France, and America, one can say that there were relatively few
Jews in these societies, and that England had riots each time an attempt was
made to legalize their status. Thus, the situations in these countries were not
similar to the German one, except for the Jews of Alsace, who were part of
older German history. But the Netherlands acquired a large Jewish population without legalized inhibitions and prohibitions and without ghettos.

Of course many reasons can be offered for the differences. But as a comment on the sad history that the essays in this volume tell, a sad history heading towards a monumental disaster in the twentieth century, one has to ask
if what happened in Germany was necessary. Was it the necessary outcome
of previous historical circumstances? The Dutch counterexample suggests
that alternative historical developments were possible, at least from the early
seventeenth century onward. This should make us look more closely into
both the Dutch and the German situations to try to comprehend why such
different histories took place in such close geographical proximity.

22

Jewish Identity in a World of Corporations and Estates

MACK WALKER

We may begin the final commentary in this volume by returning to elementary levels. This happens to suit my own particular role and qualifications here, which is to know the least, among all the contributors, about the subject matter at hand. I have participated in order to learn, as a starting postulate, about the circumstances of a dispersed people – Diaspora – who nevertheless preserved a degree of identity and cultural integrity, despite their dispersion among a different, commonly hostile, politically dominant population or populations.

This beginning formulation has led me, as an everyday historian of central Europe in early modern times, to two further or subsidiary questions. One has to do with the external walls and internal webs of social entities – an issue broached at the very start of the discussion – and the relation between them; and the second, more particularly and contextually, has to do with the special sensibilities governing a society of estates and corporations, of legally and traditionally differentiated groups, which central European society surely was in early modern times, if ever there was one; and that is an issue that has come up especially in the later chapters of this volume.

Elaborating these two, briefly: the first question, having regard to the perennial social issues of group inclusion and exclusion, asks: What are the specific roles and connections between Christian *exclusion* of Jews as alien and Jewish internal coherence or *inclusion* over against a hostile environment? This is the question reified by the discussion of actual stone-and-mortar walls, and how they came to be built.

The second question, about the society of corporations and estates, asks with plain logic: In what respects were the Jews *like* other corporations and estates, in that time and space, all of which had their distinctive characteristics or at least their definitions and boundaries, rights and disabilities; and in what respects were the Jews *unlike* the other corporations and estates? But

317

then of course one can collapse these two into a redundancy by taking note that defined walls and webs are a fundamental feature of the society of corporations and estates.

Or one can pull out Occam's razor, in such a way as to produce a banality. Thus, to question 1: The sole necessary, and maybe sufficient, associative feature dividing Christians from Jews was religion; this association was the principle of inclusion, and also of exclusion. Question 2: In what respects are Jews different from the other corporations and estates of that time and place, of early modern Europe? One can answer: all the others (Ottoman territory aside), whatever their differences, were Christians; all Jews, whatever their differences, were not. Occam's razor also has a way of putting an end to things.

At this stage of the reasoning, a remark comes to mind that I have heard attributed to the late Dorothy Parker, who commented, a propos of somebody's sophistry, "That's profound on the surface. But at a deeper level, it's superficial." This is a remark that one might fairly address to any academic effort to cope with the awesome and appalling history of the Jewish experience of Europe; but we keep digging anyhow, as we must.

What have we learned about these questions from the contributors to this volume? Respecting the walls, we have been told several times that, Occam's razor notwithstanding, religious issues in a theological or doctrinal sense, albeit ubiquitous, were not their main supporting factor but that confessional or ecclesiastical issues might be, as, for example, in Jewish resistance to the conversion demanded by the society dominant in that space as price of admission. On the cultural side, we may note the anthropological function: atrocity stories, representations of desecrations of the host, of ritual murders and the like, served to erect Christian walls against the Jews living among them, even as they spun webs of Christian cohesion. Respecting the webs internal to Jewish society, we have learned rather less, it seems to me as a layman. The fascinating question of language, especially the origins, vocabulary, and grammar of Yiddish, and its relation to German, is a very technical one, which generated lively interest and considerable heat in the discussions but at this stage few conclusions. The apparent sensitivity of this matter, taken together with the current state of the art of linguistic analysis, suggest that it is a subject worth pursuing.

Returning to question 2: In what respects were the Jews like other groups, in this estate-ordered, corporate society of legally and traditionally endorsed walls and webs, and in what respects were they unlike the others? Christopher Friedrichs (Chapter 17) quite rightly observes that it is not enough to say that Jews were excluded from certain occupations; so were most, if not all, other groups. If Jews could not enter artisanal trades, neither could Christian peasants, or noblemen for that matter – prohibited by guild statute, municipal constitution, police ordinance, or indeed by the explicit provisions of the Prussian General Code of 1794. But one pervasive quality that this society did engender in the mentalities of all its inhabitants was an intense and externalized obsession with borders and boundaries, and conversely with preservation of internal purity and integrity – the repulsion or purging of contamination and corruption. Several participants have mentioned that Christian anti-Semitism was associated with the Christian Everyman's own social and moral uncertainty, anxiety, and guilt, in the Europe notably of the sixteenth century and again of the twentieth.

Professor Guggenheim's story of the *Schalantjude* and his likeness to the contemporary Gentile *Landstreicher* (Chapter 9) stimulates a final set of reflections on the theme I have adopted. Guggenheim remarks that when Jews began to be readmitted to central European civil life after the Black Death persecutions, they returned as individuals, not as corporations – not as guilds, or as congregations, or civic personalities but rather as individuals in this corporate society, and thus wanderers, comparable to non-Jewish vagabonds. This suggests the categorical question of whether or not the Jews of the time really are to be considered, as my formulation has done, as an element of that society of corporations and estates at all or, more pertinently, whether or not that society at large did or could consider Jews as part of it at all.

The Christian society of central Europe in early modern times did devise a category in which to place people who seemed not to fit into the corporate scheme of things: people like wholesale merchants or bankers with distant and dubious connections or professional intellectuals ill-located in the chain of production, or illicit craftsmen, or beggars, or other drifters away, in growing number, from the corporate society enshrined in the dominant mentality of that time and place. At the end of the eighteenth century, this category was itself codified in that same Prussian General Code, for example, as the *Stand der Eximirten,* the "estate" of persons "exempted" from the corporate scheme – a category reminiscent, by the way, of the imperial status and sponsorship of Jews under the Holy Roman Empire. This odd notion was theorized in Hegel's *Philosophy of Right* as the *Allgemeiner Stand,* the "general estate," a category in which to collectivize the socially and spatially mobile and indeterminate.

It seems questionable whether a society or mentality of estates, despite these legal and sociological devices, could consider the inhabitants of such categories, or manage them mentally or emotionally, as estates at all. How,

then, were they to think of them? As formal categories (rather like "prole-
tariat"), they lacked both the internal integrity and the external boundaries
of concrete social estates, which, in turn, they tended to infect and to break
down. What about Jews? Are they, were they, to be located in this estateless category, and their condition in Christian society to be explained in
this way?

But the Jews, however scattered in space and social location, were not
really estateless. What made them different from both categories, of closed
social corporation and of ranging individuality, may simply be that this was
a scattering, a Diaspora, but which nonetheless by definition did preserve a
cultural integrity and identity despite its dispersion among a different, commonly hostile, and politically dominant population.

Index

References to figures are indicated by italic page numbers.

321